GEGE AKUTAMI

The other day, I saw a video of myself
laughing hysterically. I was a little taken
aback by how demonic I looked...

I hope you enjoy that type of
person's first graphic novel.

GEGE AKUTAMI published a few short
works before starting *Jujutsu Kaisen*, which began
serialization in *Weekly Shonen Jump* in 2018.

JUJUTSU KAISEN

VOLUME 1
SHONEN JUMP MANGA EDITION

BY GEGE AKUTAMI

TRANSLATION Stefan Koza
TOUCH-UP ART & LETTERING Snir Aharon
DESIGN Shawn Carrico
EDITOR John Bae
CONSULTING EDITOR Erika Onabe

Printed in Italy

Published by VIZ Media, LLC
P.O. Box 77010
San Francisco, CA 94107

15
First printing, December 2019
Fifteenth printing, July 2022

VIZ MEDIA
viz.com

SHONEN JUMP

ratings.viz.com
RATED T+ OLDER TEEN

PARENTAL ADVISORY
JUJUTSU KAISEN is rated T+ for Older Teen and is recommended for ages 16 and up. This volume contains fantasy violence.

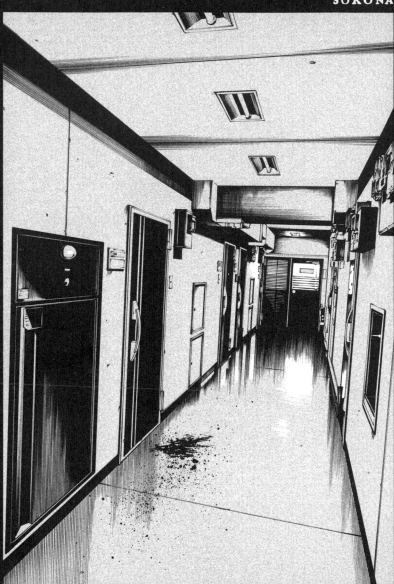

JUJUTSU KAISEN

1
RYOMEN SUKUNA

STORY AND ART BY GEGE AKUTAMI

JUJUTSU KAISEN

1

RYOMEN SUKUNA

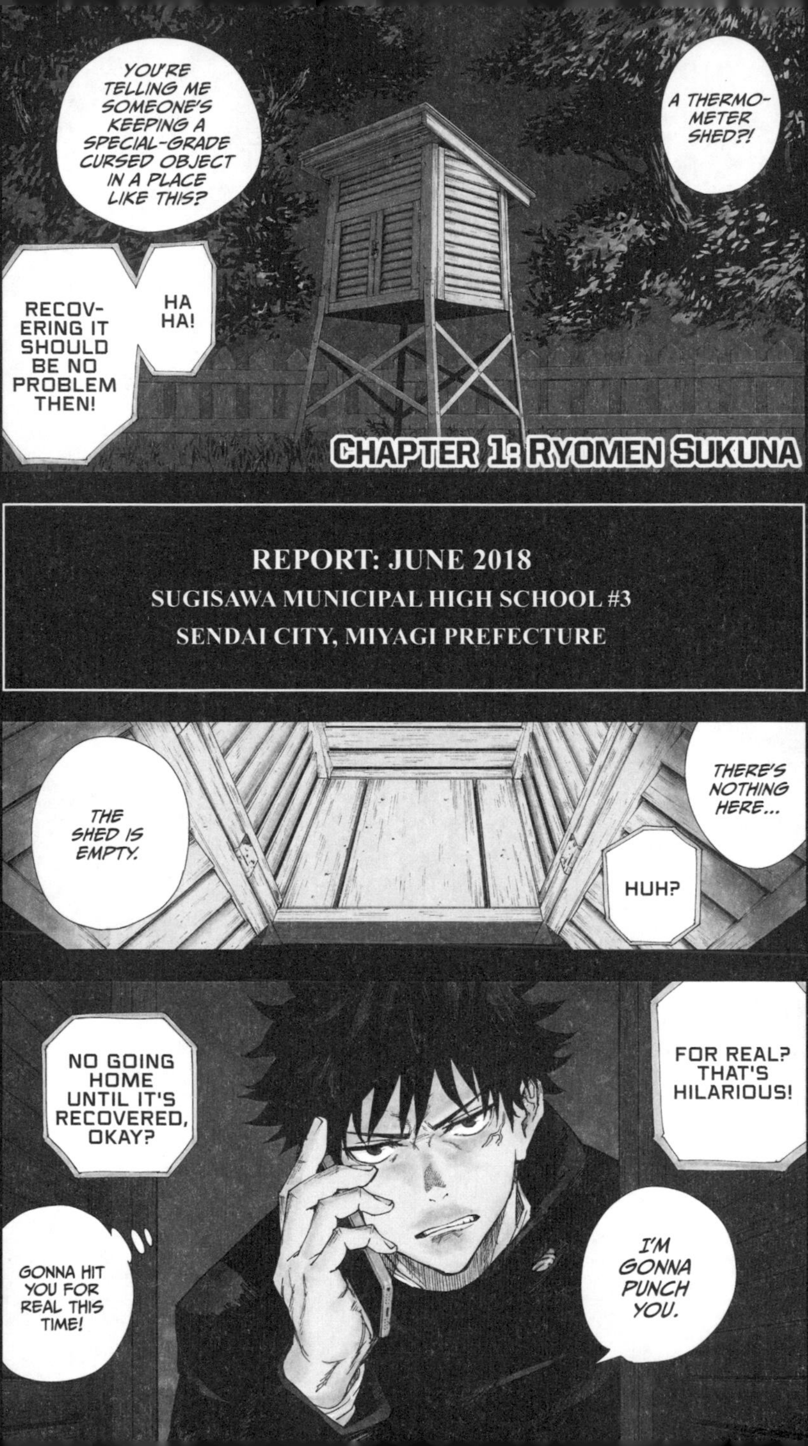
A THERMOMETER SHED?!
YOU'RE TELLING ME SOMEONE'S KEEPING A SPECIAL-GRADE CURSED OBJECT IN A PLACE LIKE THIS?
HA HA!
RECOVERING IT SHOULD BE NO PROBLEM THEN!
CHAPTER 1: RYOMEN SUKUNA
REPORT: JUNE 2018
SUGISAWA MUNICIPAL HIGH SCHOOL #3
SENDAI CITY, MIYAGI PREFECTURE
THERE'S NOTHING HERE...
HUH?
THE SHED IS EMPTY.
FOR REAL? THAT'S HILARIOUS!
NO GOING HOME UNTIL IT'S RECOVERED, OKAY?
I'M GONNA PUNCH YOU.
GONNA HIT YOU FOR REAL THIS TIME!

CHAPTER 1: RYOMEN SUKUNA

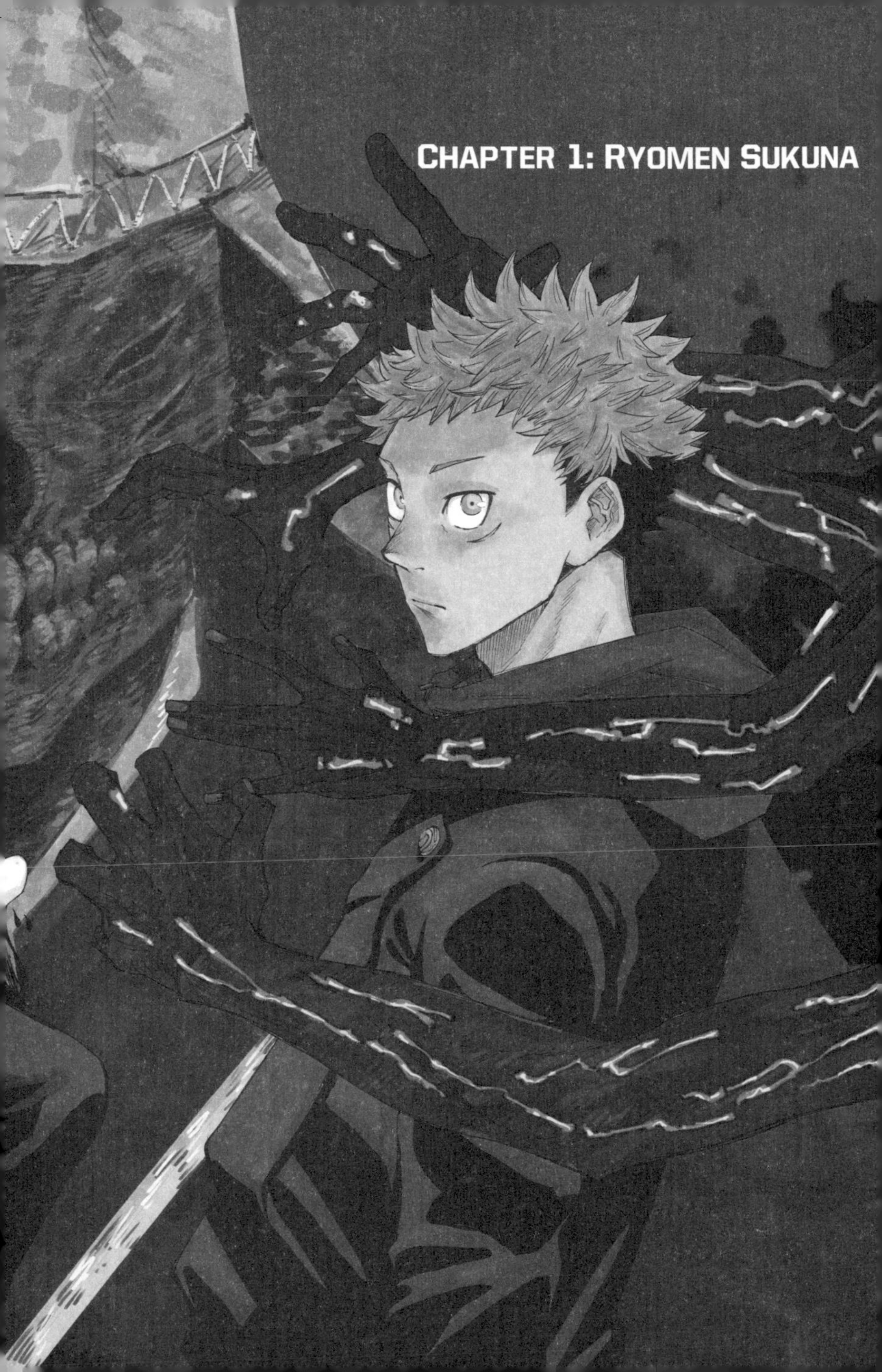

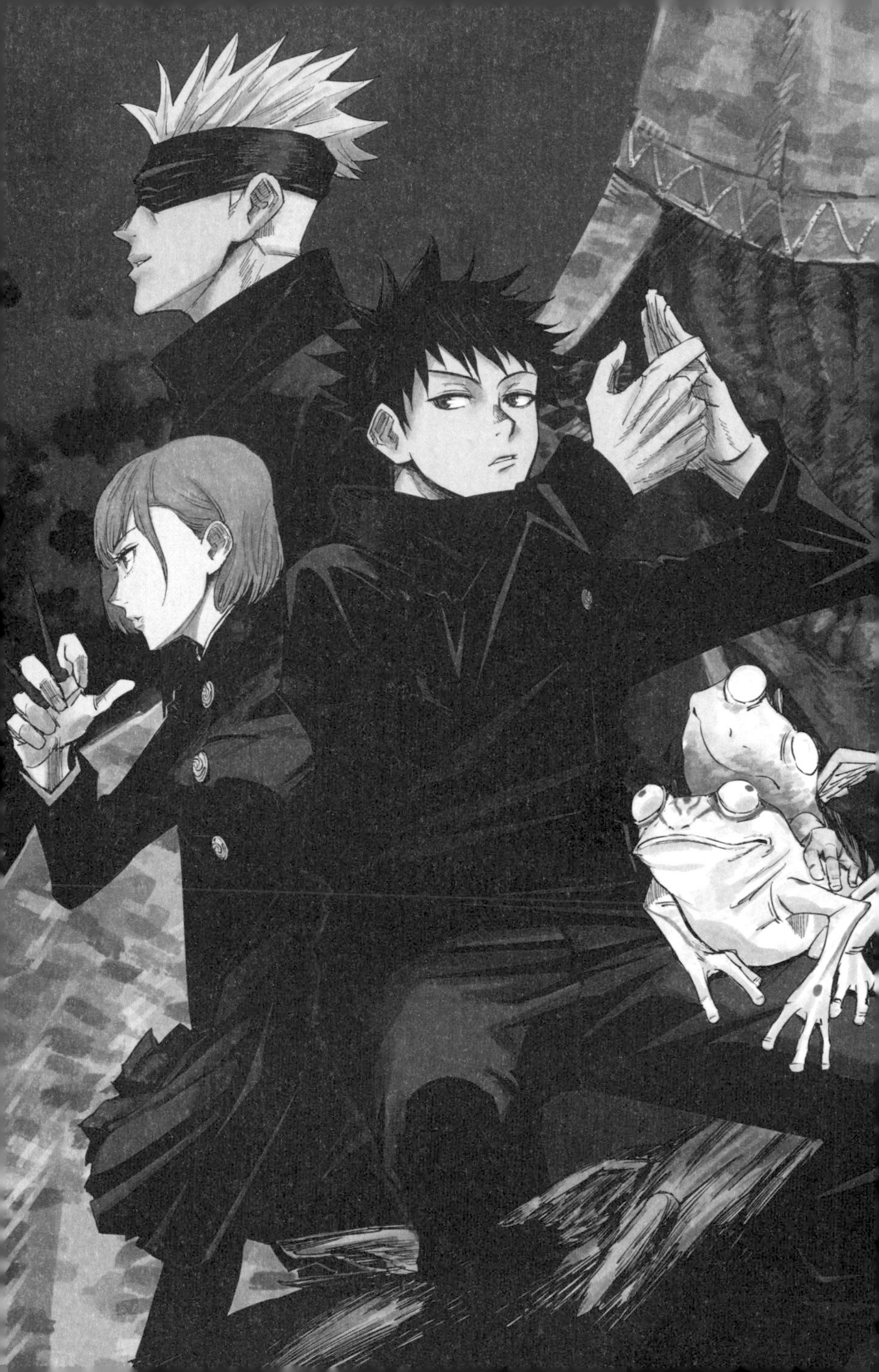

JUJUTSU KAISEN

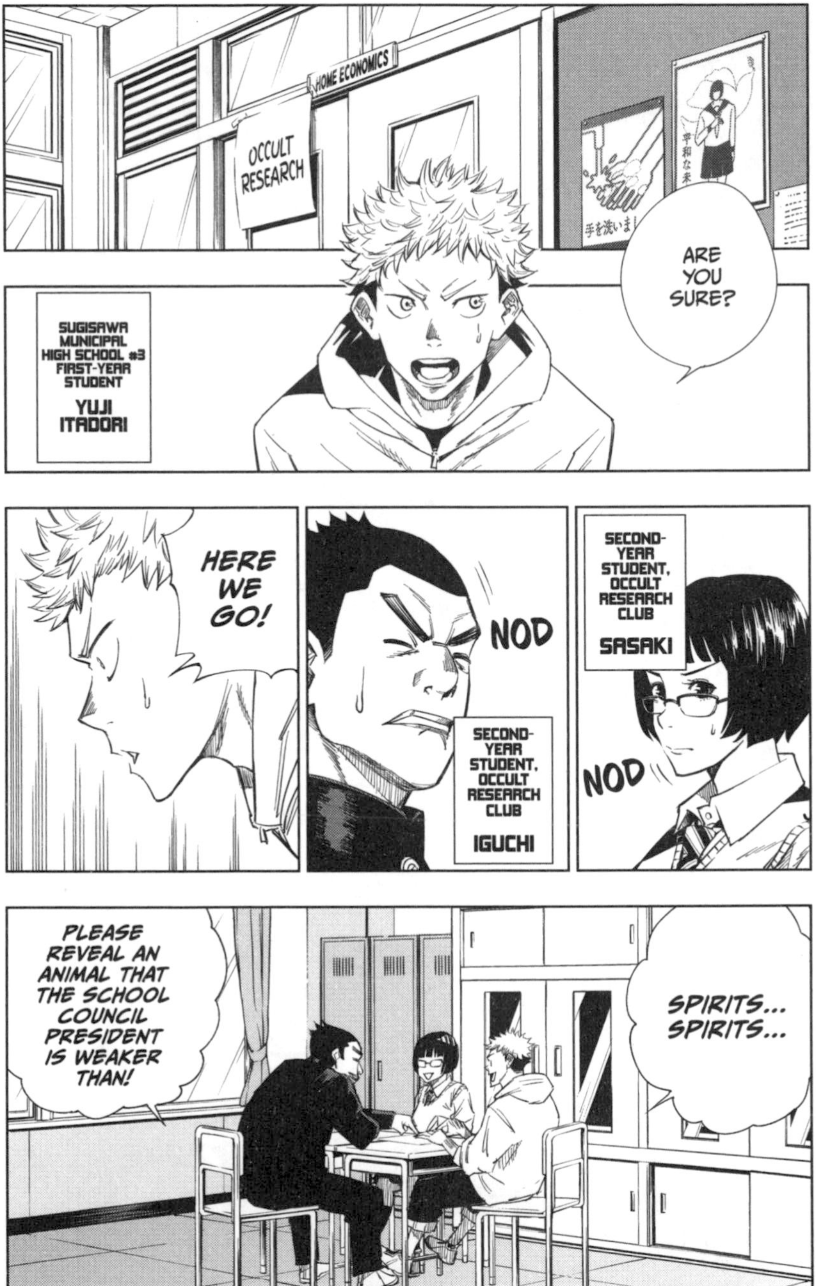
HOME ECONOMICS
OCCULT RESEARCH
平和な未
手を洗いまし
ARE YOU SURE?
SUGISAWA MUNICIPAL HIGH SCHOOL #3 FIRST-YEAR STUDENT
YUJI ITADORI
SECOND-YEAR STUDENT, OCCULT RESEARCH CLUB
SASAKI
NOD
NOD
SECOND-YEAR STUDENT, OCCULT RESEARCH CLUB
IGUCHI
HERE WE GO!
SPIRITS... SPIRITS...
PLEASE REVEAL AN ANIMAL THAT THE SCHOOL COUNCIL PRESIDENT IS WEAKER THAN!

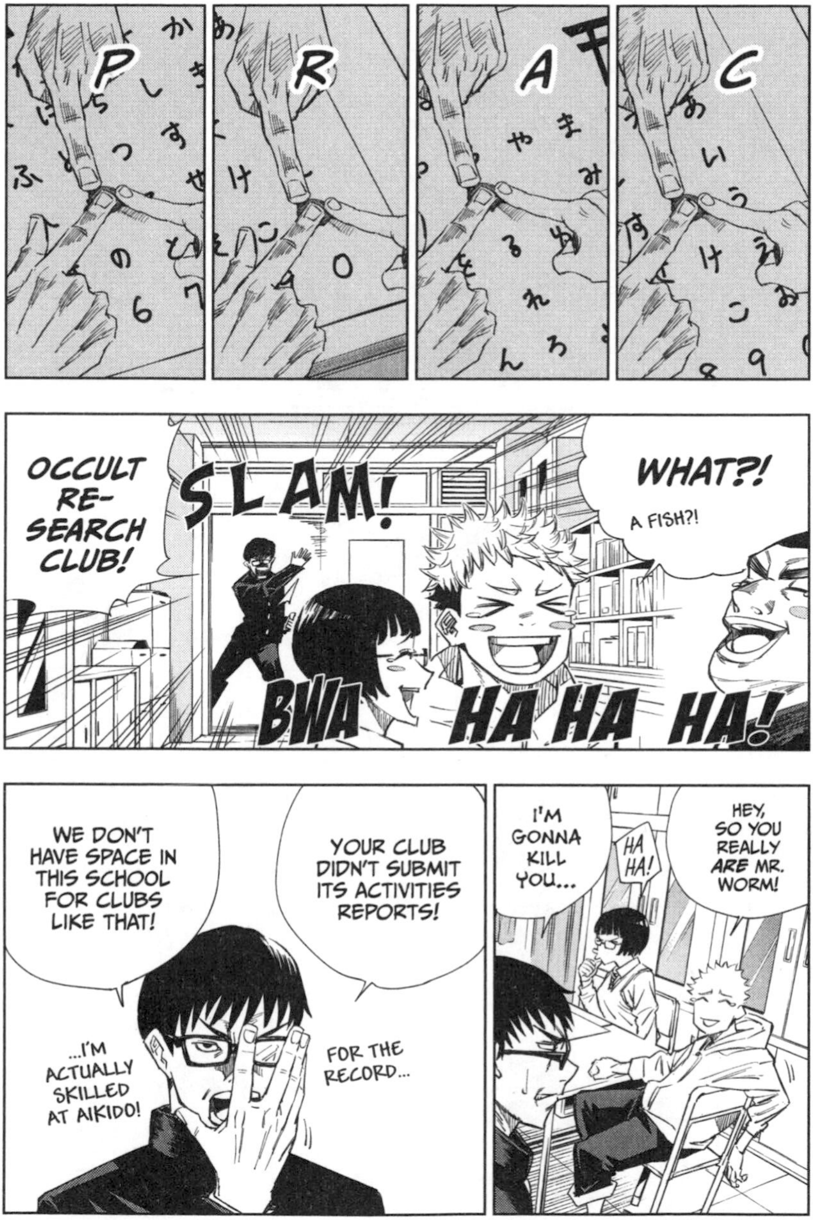

C
A
R
P
WHAT?!
A FISH?!
SLAM!
OCCULT RE-SEARCH CLUB!
BWA HA HA HA!
HEY, SO YOU REALLY ARE MR. WORM!
HA HA!
I'M GONNA KILL YOU...
YOUR CLUB DIDN'T SUBMIT ITS ACTIVITIES REPORTS!
WE DON'T HAVE SPACE IN THIS SCHOOL FOR CLUBS LIKE THAT!
FOR THE RECORD...
...I'M ACTUALLY SKILLED AT AIKIDO!

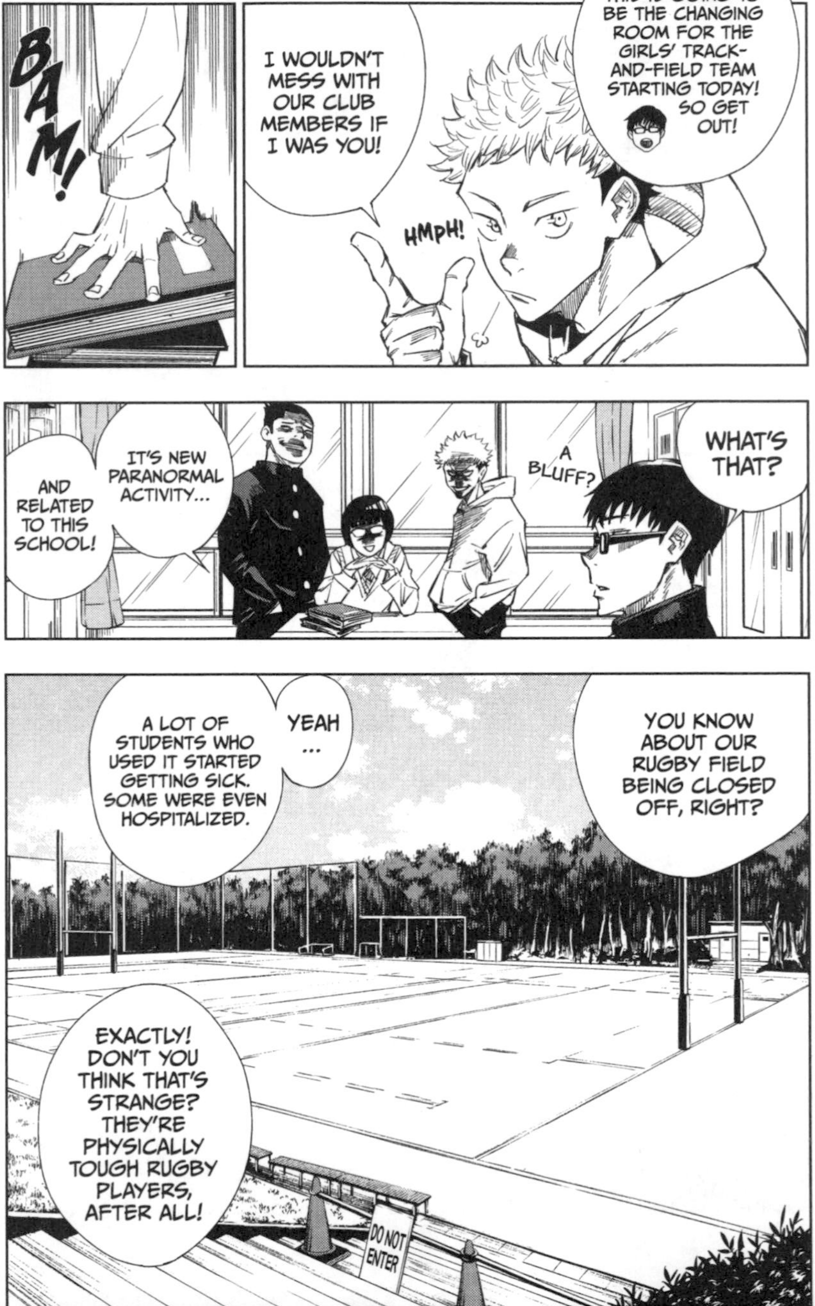
THIS IS GOING TO BE THE CHANGING ROOM FOR THE GIRLS' TRACK-AND-FIELD TEAM STARTING TODAY! SO GET OUT!
I WOULDN'T MESS WITH OUR CLUB MEMBERS IF I WAS YOU!
HMPH!
BAM!
WHAT'S THAT?
A BLUFF?
IT'S NEW PARANORMAL ACTIVITY...
AND RELATED TO THIS SCHOOL!
YOU KNOW ABOUT OUR RUGBY FIELD BEING CLOSED OFF, RIGHT?
YEAH ...
A LOT OF STUDENTS WHO USED IT STARTED GETTING SICK. SOME WERE EVEN HOSPITALIZED.
EXACTLY! DON'T YOU THINK THAT'S STRANGE? THEY'RE PHYSICALLY TOUGH RUGBY PLAYERS, AFTER ALL!
DO NOT ENTER

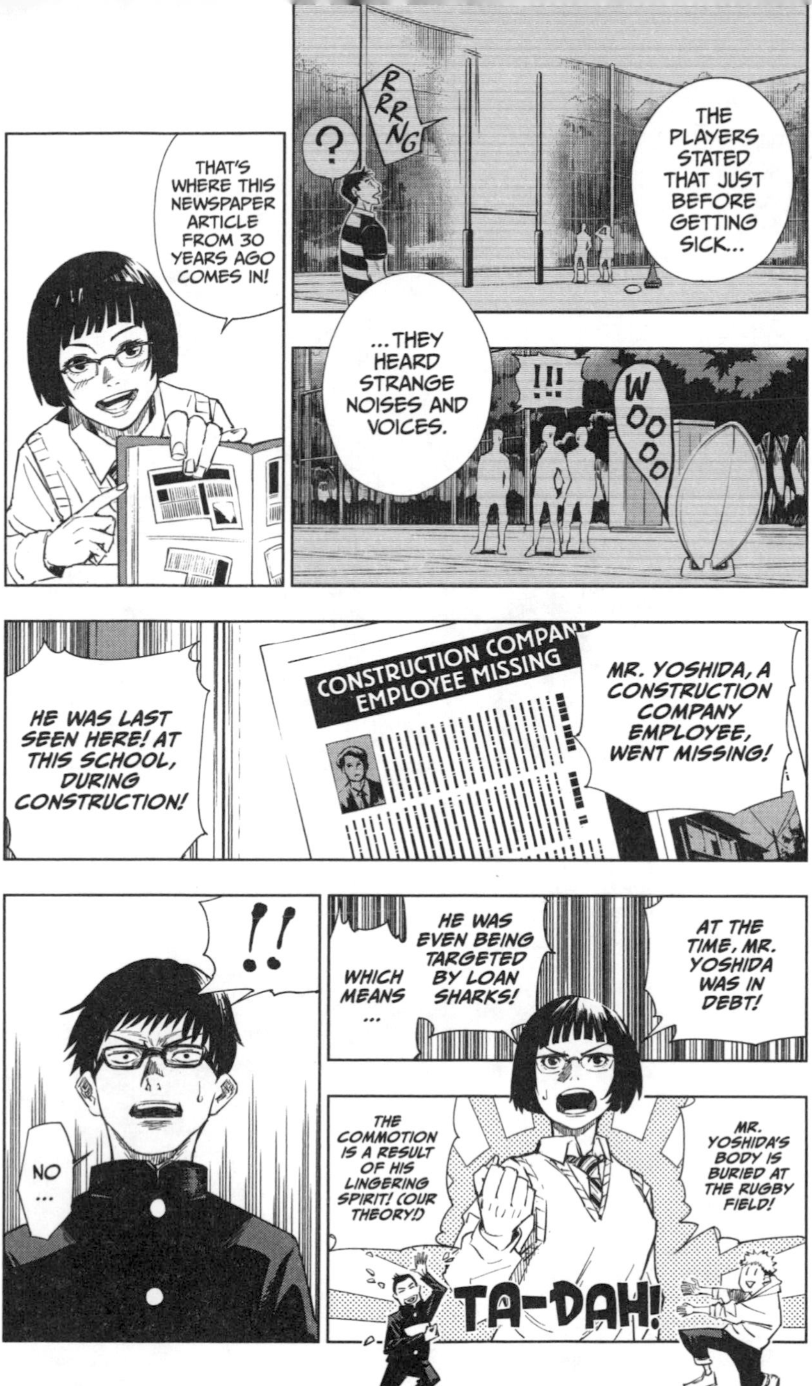
THE PLAYERS STATED THAT JUST BEFORE GETTING SICK...
RRRNG
?
...THEY HEARD STRANGE NOISES AND VOICES.
WOOOO
!!!
THAT'S WHERE THIS NEWSPAPER ARTICLE FROM 30 YEARS AGO COMES IN!
MR. YOSHIDA, A CONSTRUCTION COMPANY EMPLOYEE, WENT MISSING!
CONSTRUCTION COMPANY EMPLOYEE MISSING
HE WAS LAST SEEN HERE! AT THIS SCHOOL, DURING CONSTRUCTION!
AT THE TIME, MR. YOSHIDA WAS IN DEBT!
HE WAS EVEN BEING TARGETED BY LOAN SHARKS!
WHICH MEANS ...
MR. YOSHIDA'S BODY IS BURIED AT THE RUGBY FIELD!
THE COMMOTION IS A RESULT OF HIS LINGERING SPIRIT! (OUR THEORY!)
TA-DAH!
!!
NO ...

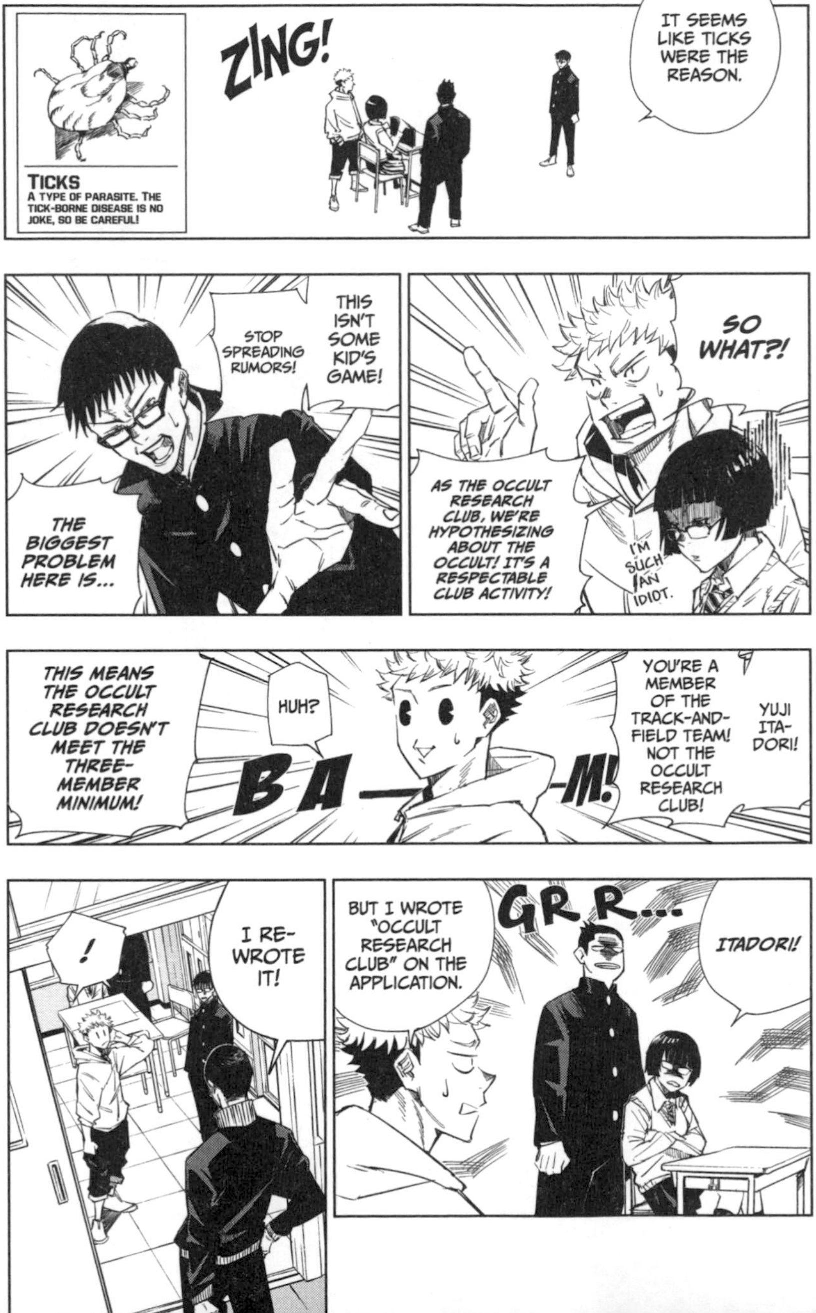
IT SEEMS LIKE TICKS WERE THE REASON.
ZING!
TICKS
A TYPE OF PARASITE. THE TICK-BORNE DISEASE IS NO JOKE, SO BE CAREFUL!
SO WHAT?!
AS THE OCCULT RESEARCH CLUB, WE'RE HYPOTHESIZING ABOUT THE OCCULT! IT'S A RESPECTABLE CLUB ACTIVITY!
I'M SUCH AN IDIOT.
THIS ISN'T SOME KID'S GAME!
STOP SPREADING RUMORS!
THE BIGGEST PROBLEM HERE IS...
YUJI ITADORI!
YOU'RE A MEMBER OF THE TRACK-AND-FIELD TEAM! NOT THE OCCULT RESEARCH CLUB!
BA——M!
HUH?
THIS MEANS THE OCCULT RESEARCH CLUB DOESN'T MEET THE THREE-MEMBER MINIMUM!
ITADORI!
GRR...
BUT I WROTE "OCCULT RESEARCH CLUB" ON THE APPLICATION.
I RE-WROTE IT!
!

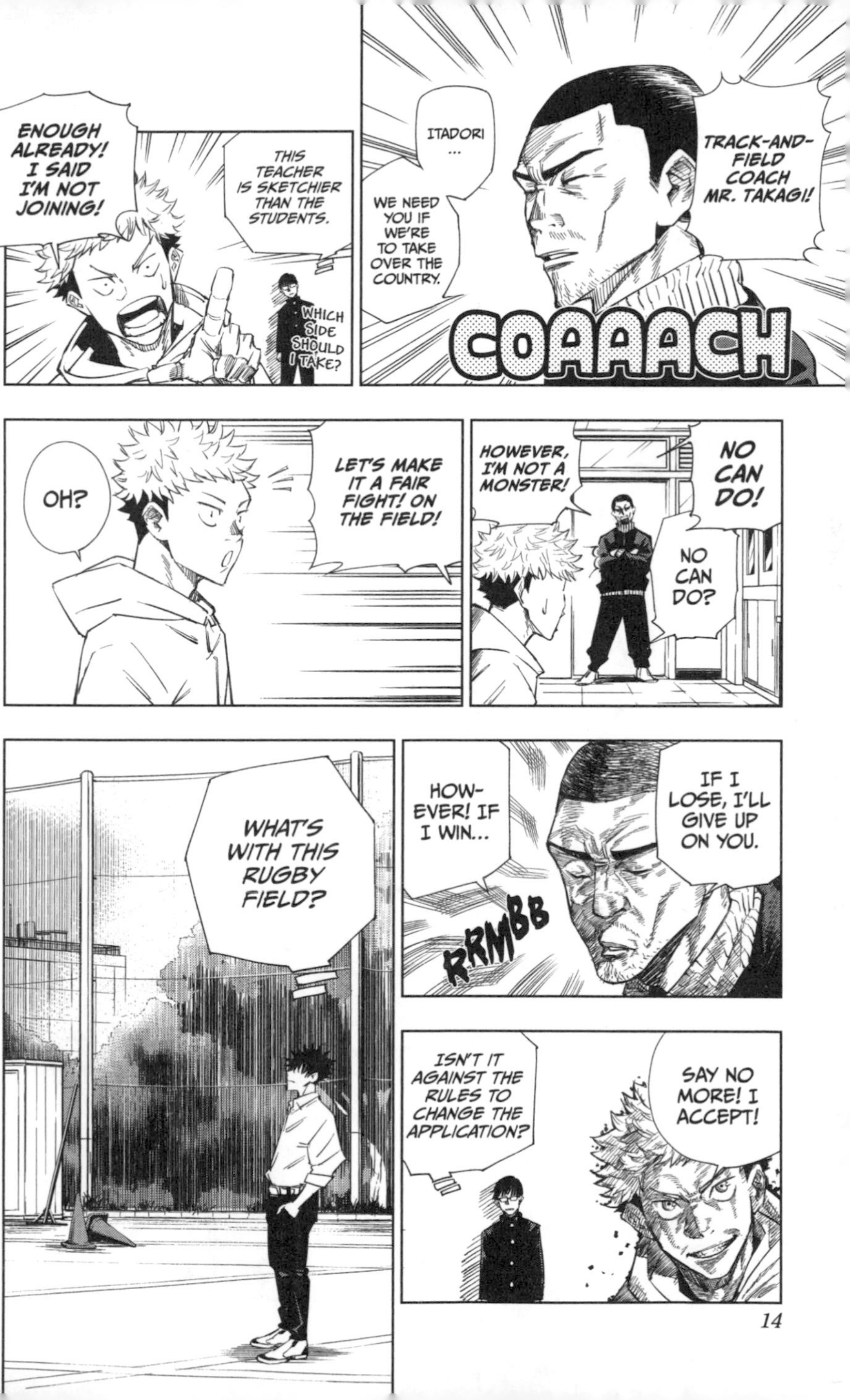
TRACK-AND-FIELD COACH MR. TAKAGI!
ITADORI ...
WE NEED YOU IF WE'RE TO TAKE OVER THE COUNTRY.
COAAACH
THIS TEACHER IS SKETCHIER THAN THE STUDENTS.
ENOUGH ALREADY! I SAID I'M NOT JOINING!
WHICH SIDE SHOULD I TAKE?
NO CAN DO!
HOWEVER, I'M NOT A MONSTER!
NO CAN DO?
LET'S MAKE IT A FAIR FIGHT! ON THE FIELD!
OH?
IF I LOSE, I'LL GIVE UP ON YOU.
HOW-EVER! IF I WIN...
RRMBB
SAY NO MORE! I ACCEPT!
ISN'T IT AGAINST THE RULES TO CHANGE THE APPLICATION?
WHAT'S WITH THIS RUGBY FIELD?

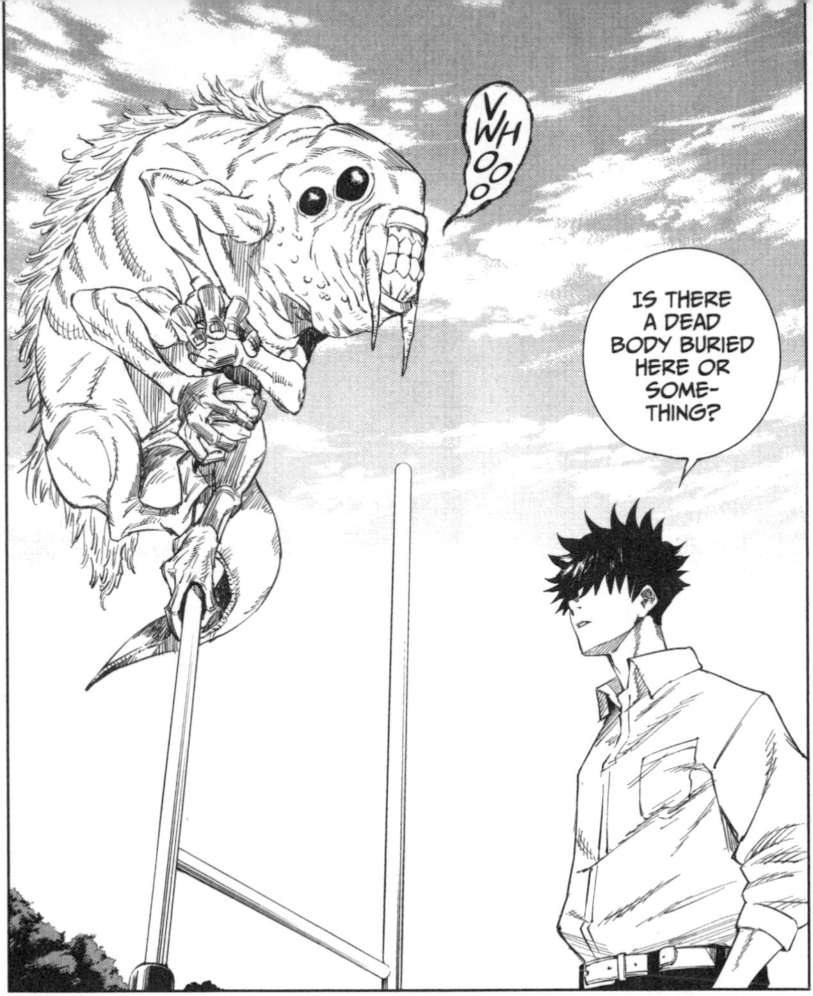
VWHOOO
IS THERE A DEAD BODY BURIED HERE OR SOME-THING?

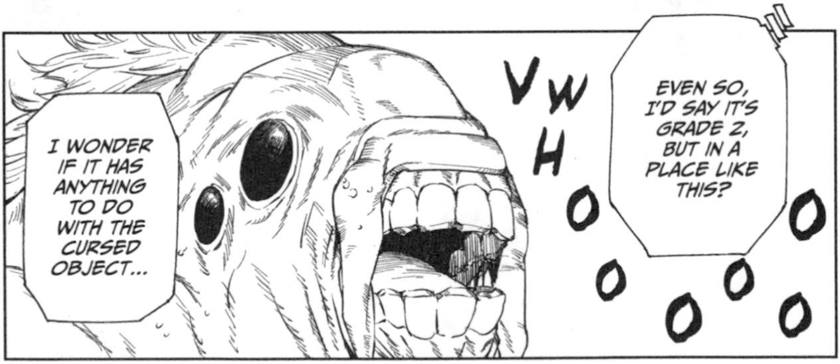
EVEN SO, I'D SAY IT'S GRADE 2, BUT IN A PLACE LIKE THIS?
VWHOOOOOO
I WONDER IF IT HAS ANYTHING TO DO WITH THE CURSED OBJECT...

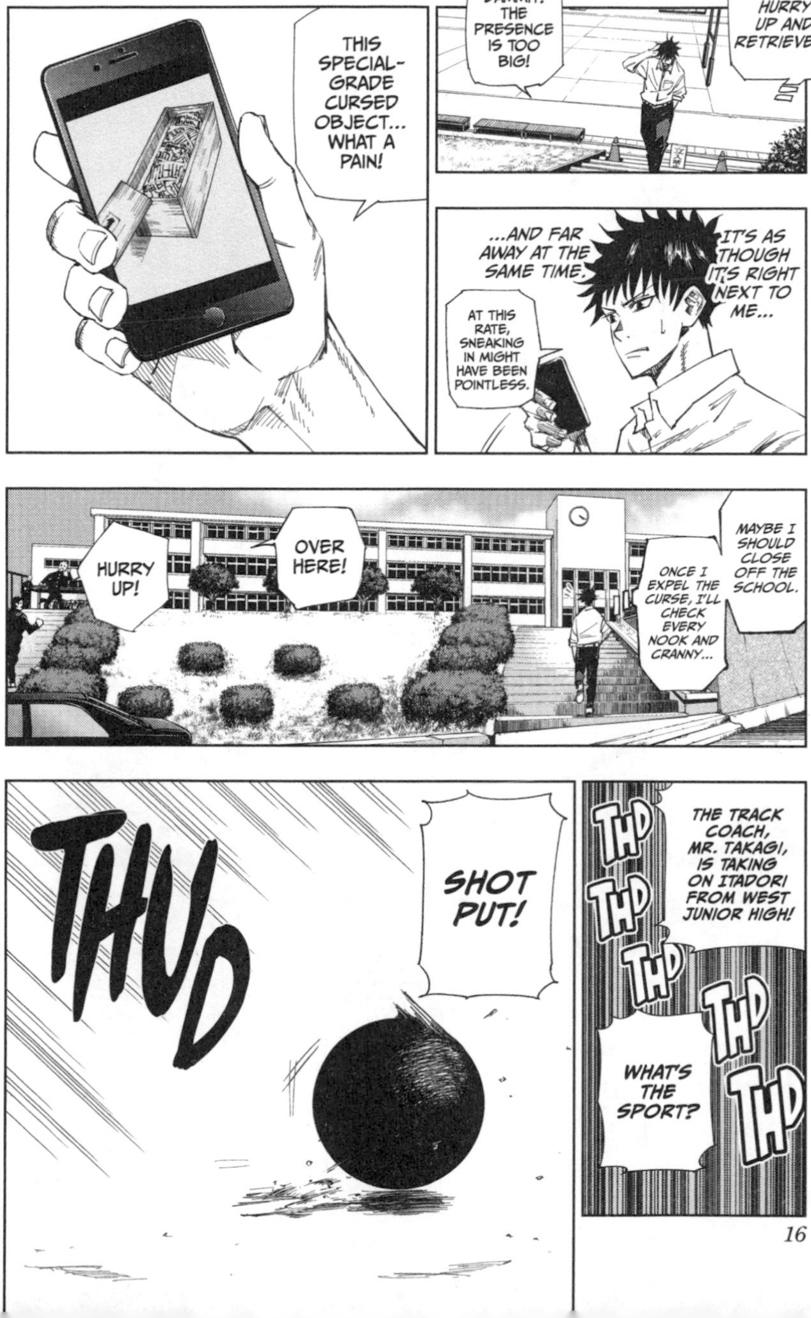
I'D BETTER HURRY UP AND RETRIEVE IT.
DAMMIT! THE PRESENCE IS TOO BIG!
IT'S AS THOUGH IT'S RIGHT NEXT TO ME...
...AND FAR AWAY AT THE SAME TIME.
AT THIS RATE, SNEAKING IN MIGHT HAVE BEEN POINTLESS.
THIS SPECIAL-GRADE CURSED OBJECT... WHAT A PAIN!
MAYBE I SHOULD CLOSE OFF THE SCHOOL.
ONCE I EXPEL THE CURSE, I'LL CHECK EVERY NOOK AND CRANNY...
OVER HERE!
HURRY UP!
THE TRACK COACH, MR. TAKAGI, IS TAKING ON ITADORI FROM WEST JUNIOR HIGH!
THD THD THD THD THD
WHAT'S THE SPORT?
SHOT PUT!
THUD

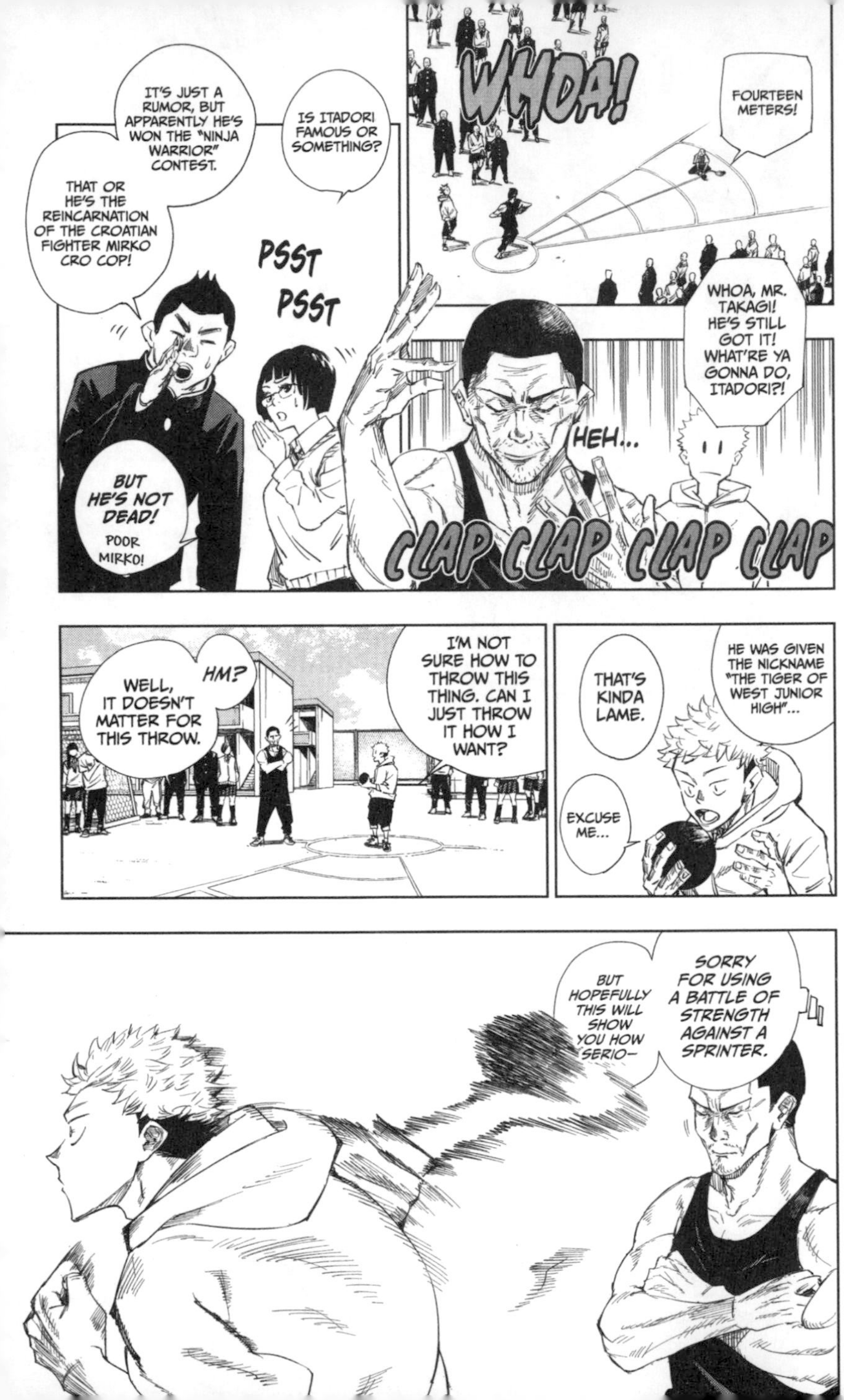
WHOA!
FOURTEEN METERS!
WHOA, MR. TAKAGI! HE'S STILL GOT IT! WHAT'RE YA GONNA DO, ITADORI?!
HEH...
CLAP CLAP CLAP CLAP
IS ITADORI FAMOUS OR SOMETHING?
IT'S JUST A RUMOR, BUT APPARENTLY HE'S WON THE "NINJA WARRIOR" CONTEST.
THAT OR HE'S THE REINCARNATION OF THE CROATIAN FIGHTER MIRKO CRO COP!
PSST PSST
BUT HE'S NOT DEAD! POOR MIRKO!
HE WAS GIVEN THE NICKNAME "THE TIGER OF WEST JUNIOR HIGH"...
THAT'S KINDA LAME.
EXCUSE ME...
I'M NOT SURE HOW TO THROW THIS THING. CAN I JUST THROW IT HOW I WANT?
HM?
WELL, IT DOESN'T MATTER FOR THIS THROW.
SORRY FOR USING A BATTLE OF STRENGTH AGAINST A SPRINTER.
BUT HOPEFULLY THIS WILL SHOW YOU HOW SERIO–

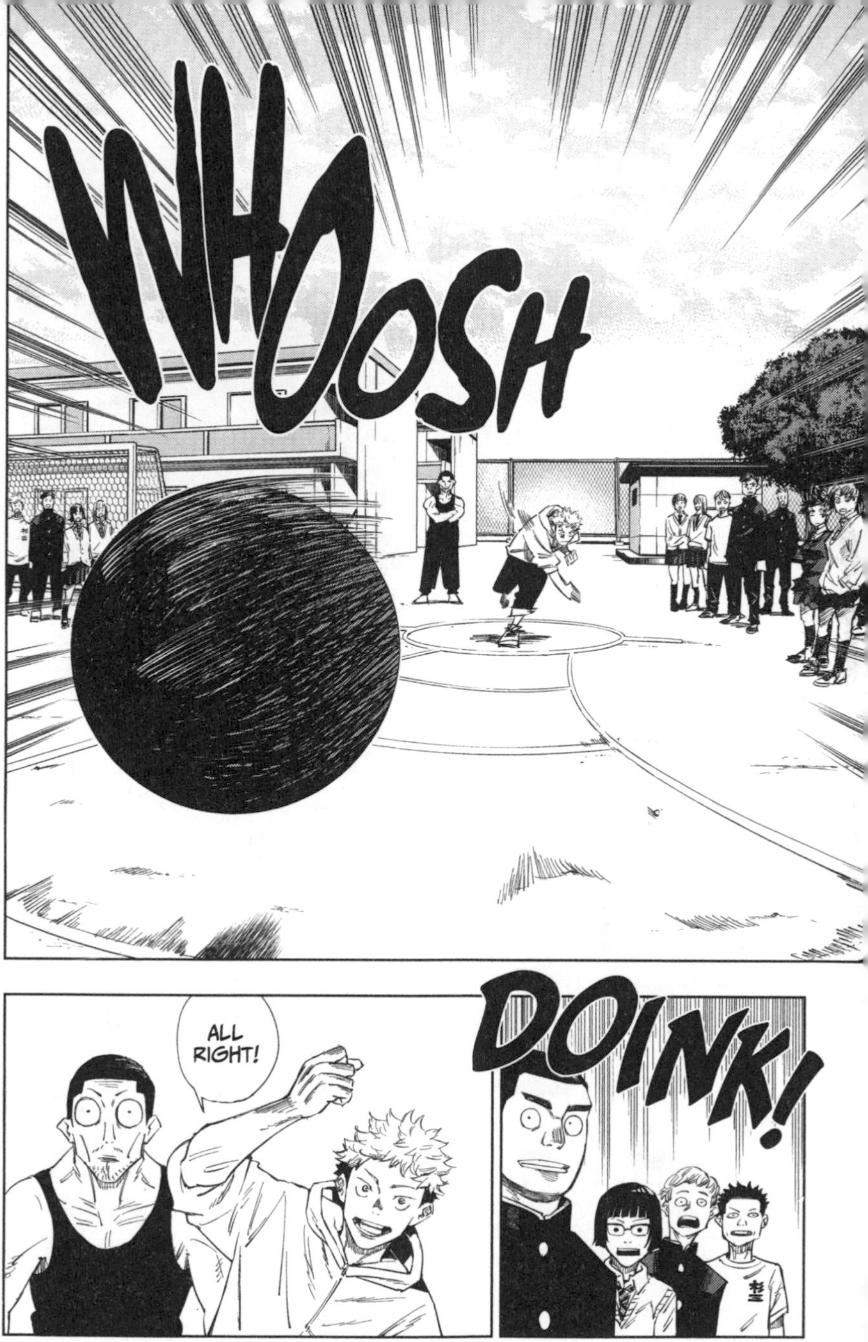
WHOOSH
DOINK!
ALL RIGHT!

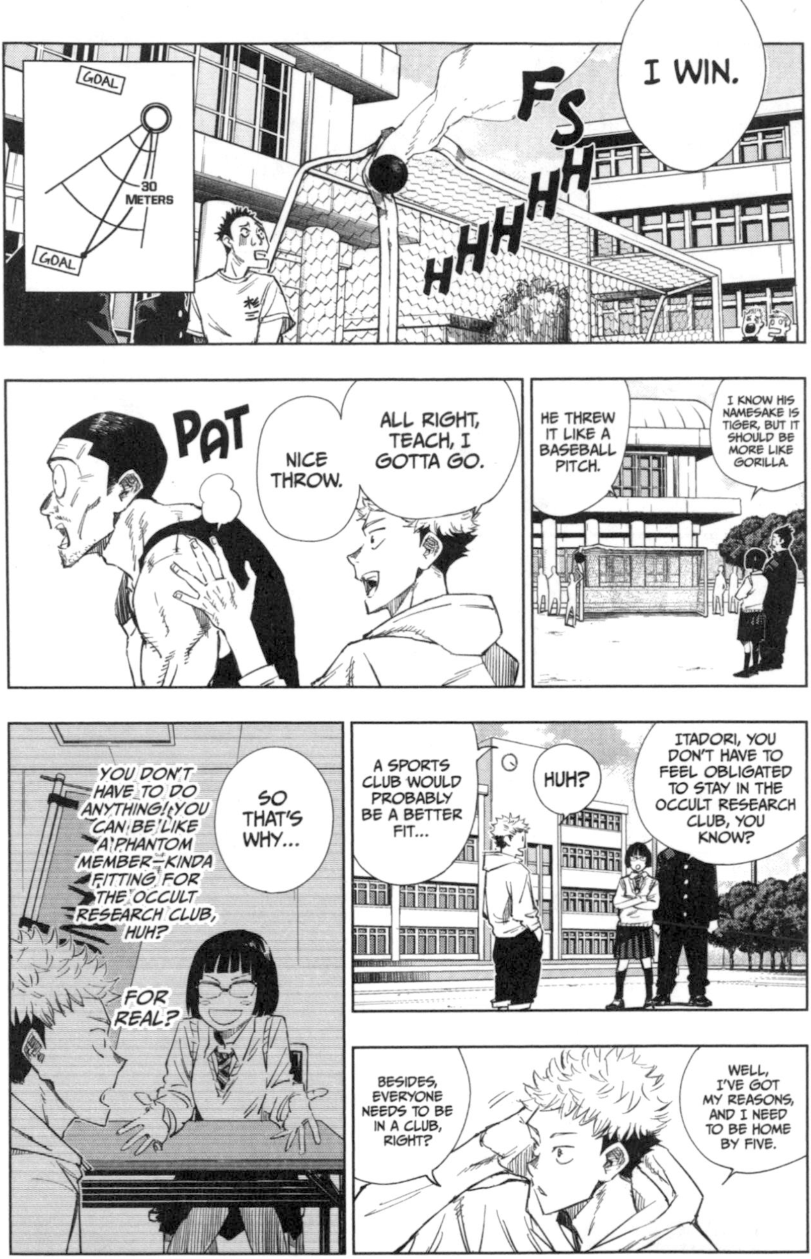
I WIN.
FSHHHHHHH
GOAL
30 METERS
GOAL
I KNOW HIS NAMESAKE IS TIGER, BUT IT SHOULD BE MORE LIKE GORILLA.
HE THREW IT LIKE A BASEBALL PITCH.
ALL RIGHT, TEACH, I GOTTA GO.
NICE THROW.
PAT
ITADORI, YOU DON'T HAVE TO FEEL OBLIGATED TO STAY IN THE OCCULT RESEARCH CLUB, YOU KNOW?
HUH?
A SPORTS CLUB WOULD PROBABLY BE A BETTER FIT...
WELL, I'VE GOT MY REASONS, AND I NEED TO BE HOME BY FIVE.
BESIDES, EVERYONE NEEDS TO BE IN A CLUB, RIGHT?
SO THAT'S WHY...
YOU DON'T HAVE TO DO ANYTHING! YOU CAN BE LIKE A PHANTOM MEMBER—KINDA FITTING FOR THE OCCULT RESEARCH CLUB, HUH?
FOR REAL?

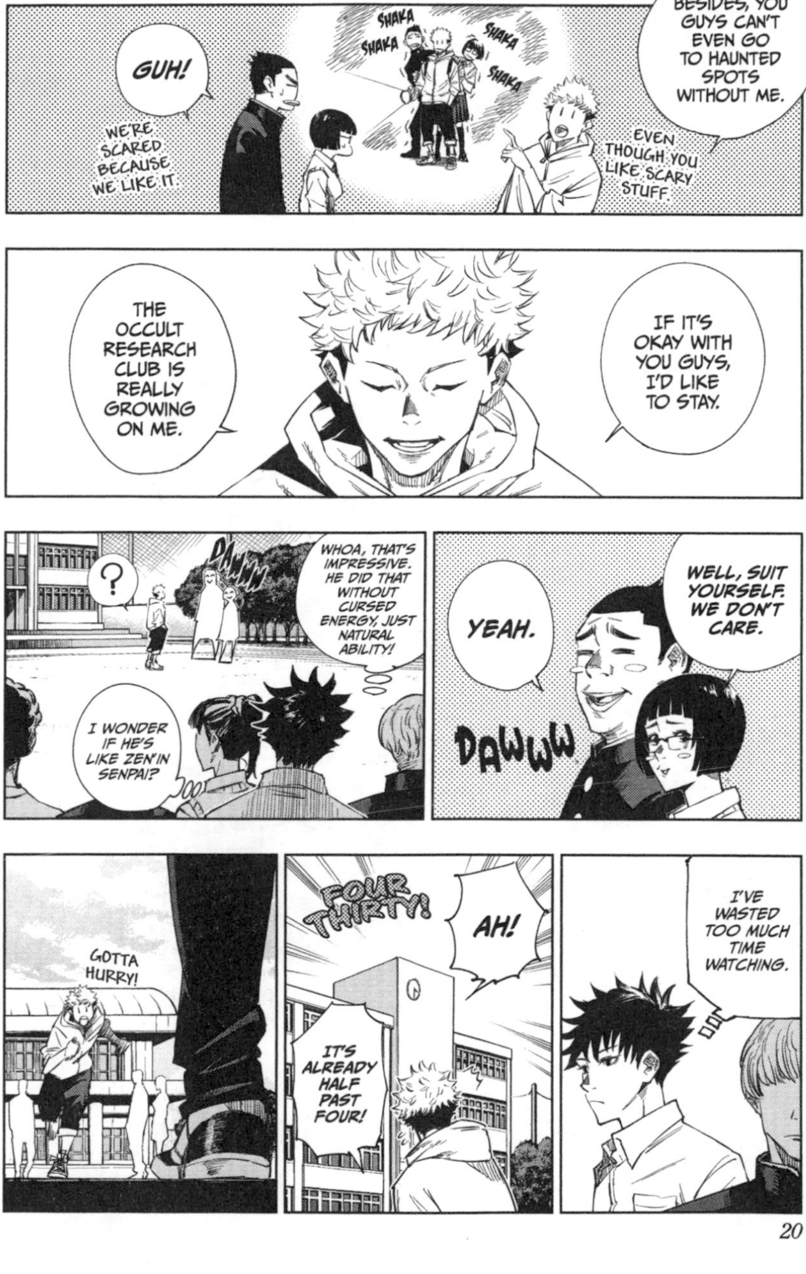
BESIDES, YOU GUYS CAN'T EVEN GO TO HAUNTED SPOTS WITHOUT ME.
EVEN THOUGH YOU LIKE SCARY STUFF.
SHAKA
SHAKA
SHAKA
SHAKA
GUH!
WE'RE SCARED BECAUSE WE LIKE IT.
IF IT'S OKAY WITH YOU GUYS, I'D LIKE TO STAY.
THE OCCULT RESEARCH CLUB IS REALLY GROWING ON ME.
WELL, SUIT YOURSELF. WE DON'T CARE.
YEAH.
DAWWW
WHOA, THAT'S IMPRESSIVE. HE DID THAT WITHOUT CURSED ENERGY, JUST NATURAL ABILITY!
?
I WONDER IF HE'S LIKE ZEN'IN SENPAI?
I'VE WASTED TOO MUCH TIME WATCHING.
FOUR THIRTY!
AH!
IT'S ALREADY HALF PAST FOUR!
GOTTA HURRY!

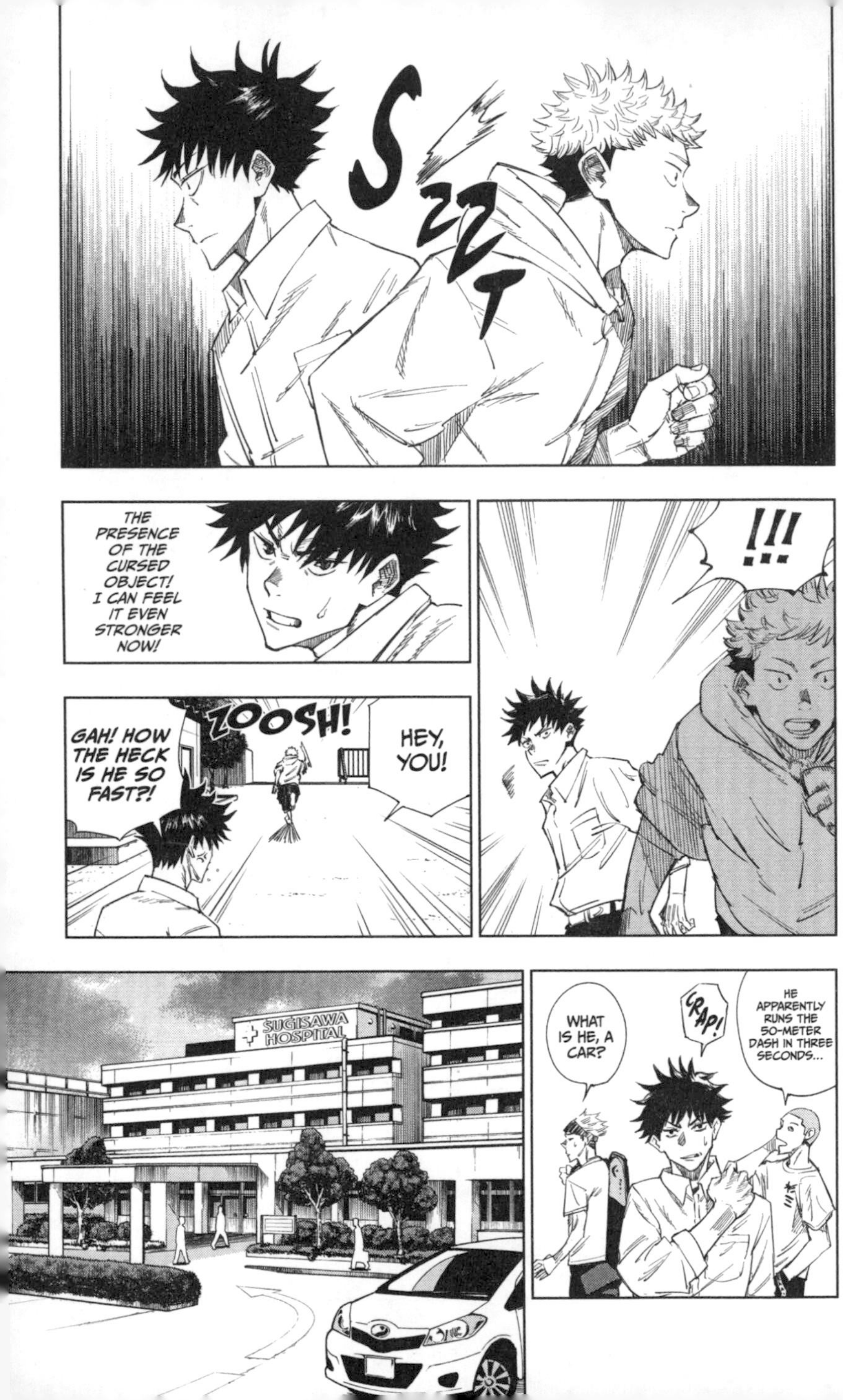
SZZZT
!!!
THE PRESENCE OF THE CURSED OBJECT! I CAN FEEL IT EVEN STRONGER NOW!
HEY, YOU!
ZOOSH!
GAH! HOW THE HECK IS HE SO FAST?!
HE APPARENTLY RUNS THE 50-METER DASH IN THREE SECONDS...
CRAP!
WHAT IS HE, A CAR?
SUGISAWA HOSPITAL

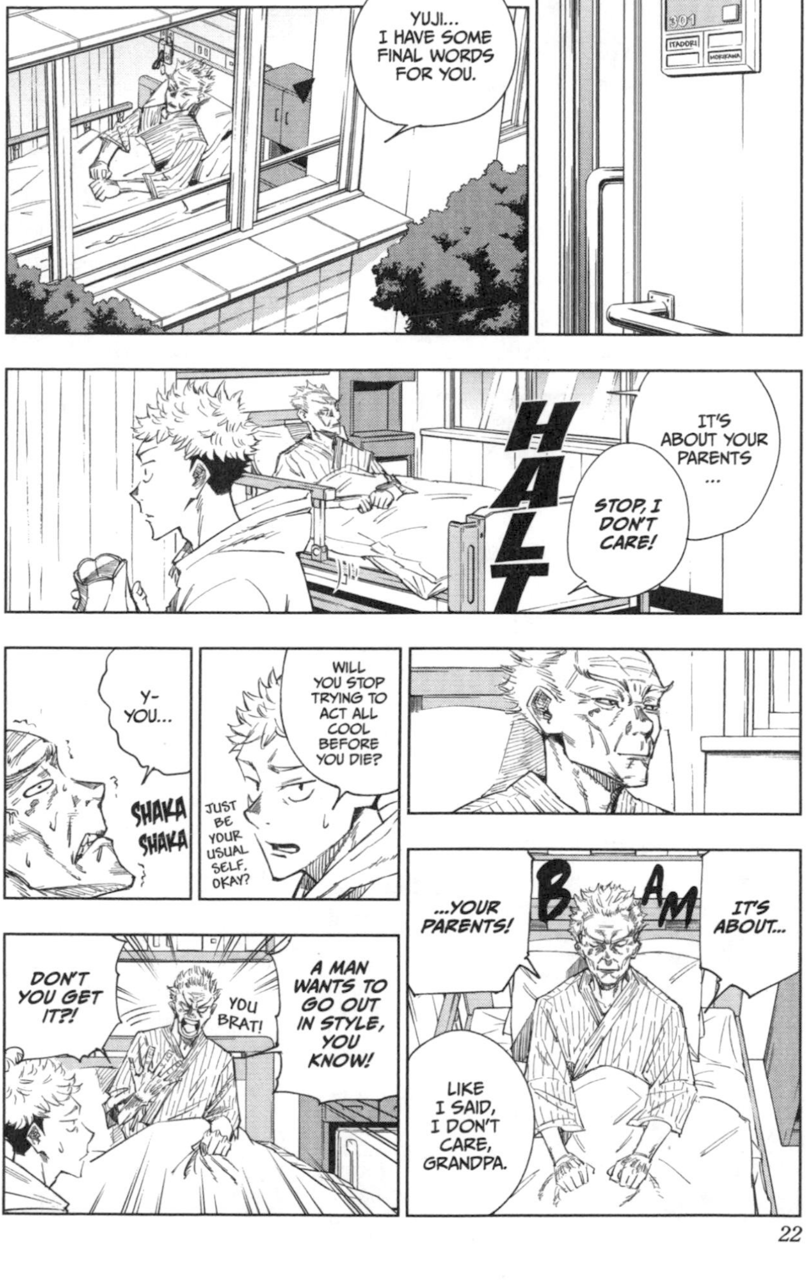
301
ITADORI
MORIKAWA
YUJI... I HAVE SOME FINAL WORDS FOR YOU.
IT'S ABOUT YOUR PARENTS ...
HALT
STOP, I DON'T CARE!
WILL YOU STOP TRYING TO ACT ALL COOL BEFORE YOU DIE?
JUST BE YOUR USUAL SELF, OKAY?
Y-YOU...
SHAKA SHAKA
IT'S ABOUT...
BAM
...YOUR PARENTS!
LIKE I SAID, I DON'T CARE, GRANDPA.
A MAN WANTS TO GO OUT IN STYLE, YOU KNOW!
YOU BRAT!
DON'T YOU GET IT?!

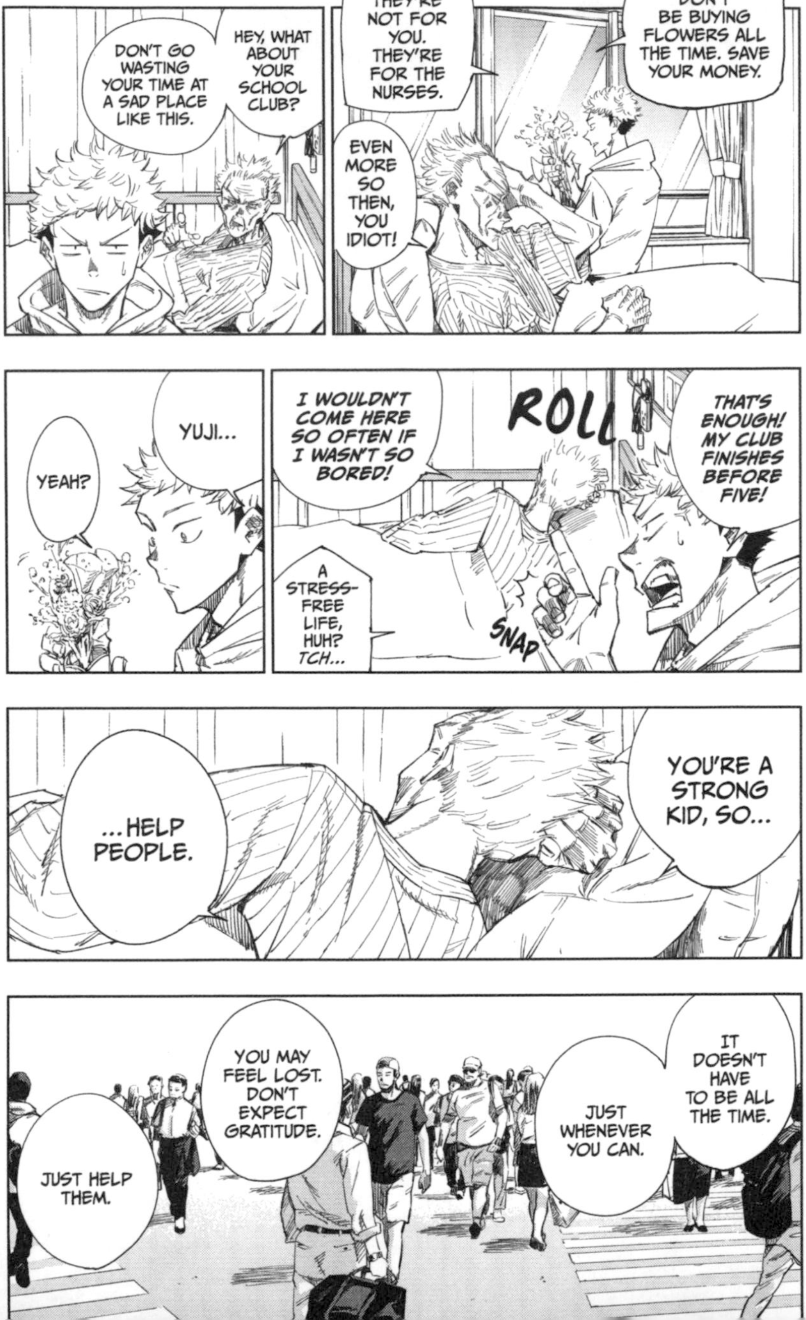
DON'T BE BUYING FLOWERS ALL THE TIME. SAVE YOUR MONEY.
THEY'RE NOT FOR YOU. THEY'RE FOR THE NURSES.
EVEN MORE SO THEN, YOU IDIOT!
HEY, WHAT ABOUT YOUR SCHOOL CLUB?
DON'T GO WASTING YOUR TIME AT A SAD PLACE LIKE THIS.
THAT'S ENOUGH! MY CLUB FINISHES BEFORE FIVE!
ROLL
I WOULDN'T COME HERE SO OFTEN IF I WASN'T SO BORED!
SNAP
A STRESS-FREE LIFE, HUH? TCH...
YUJI...
YEAH?
YOU'RE A STRONG KID, SO...
...HELP PEOPLE.
IT DOESN'T HAVE TO BE ALL THE TIME.
JUST WHENEVER YOU CAN.
YOU MAY FEEL LOST. DON'T EXPECT GRATITUDE.
JUST HELP THEM.

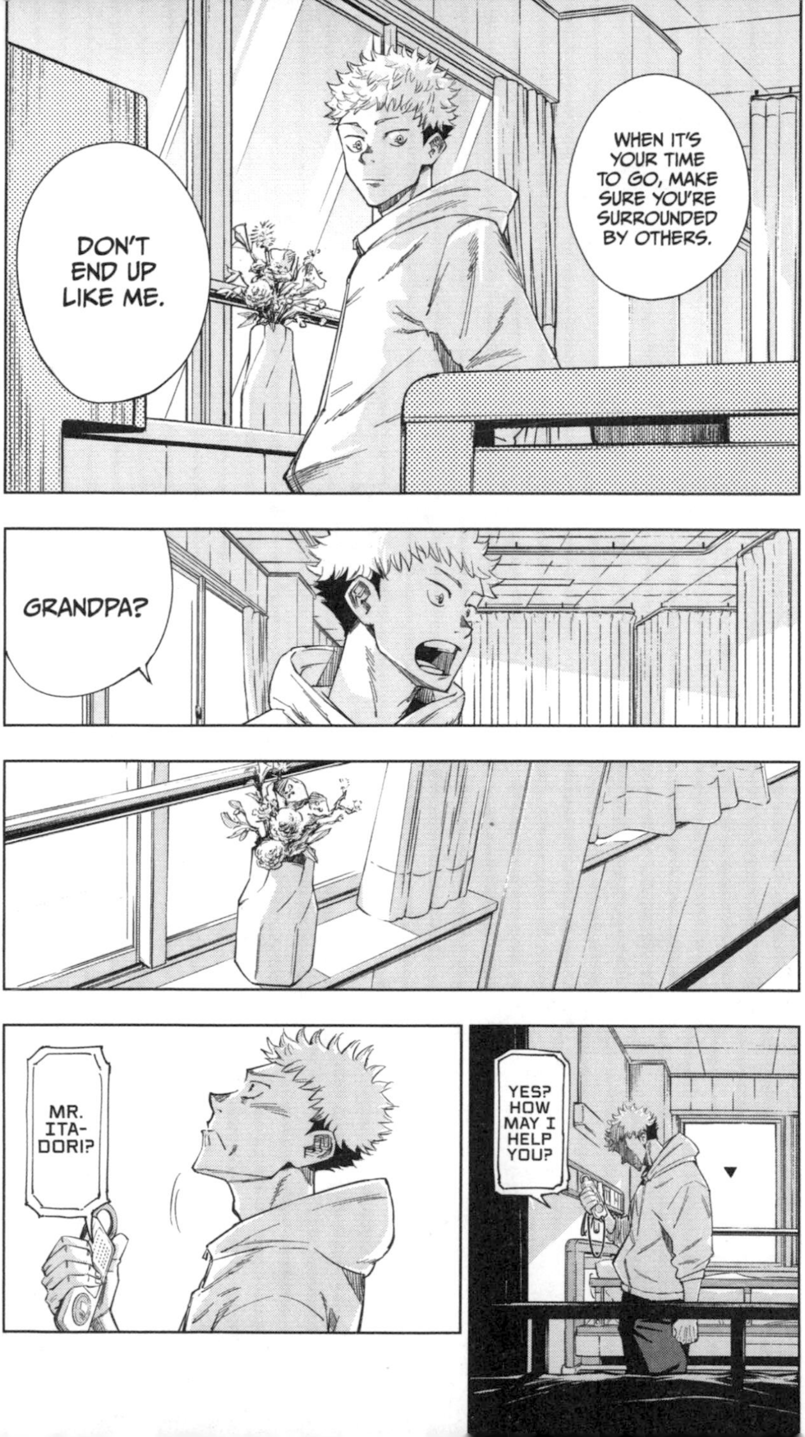
WHEN IT'S YOUR TIME TO GO, MAKE SURE YOU'RE SURROUNDED BY OTHERS.
DON'T END UP LIKE ME.
GRANDPA?
YES? HOW MAY I HELP YOU?
MR. ITA-DORI?

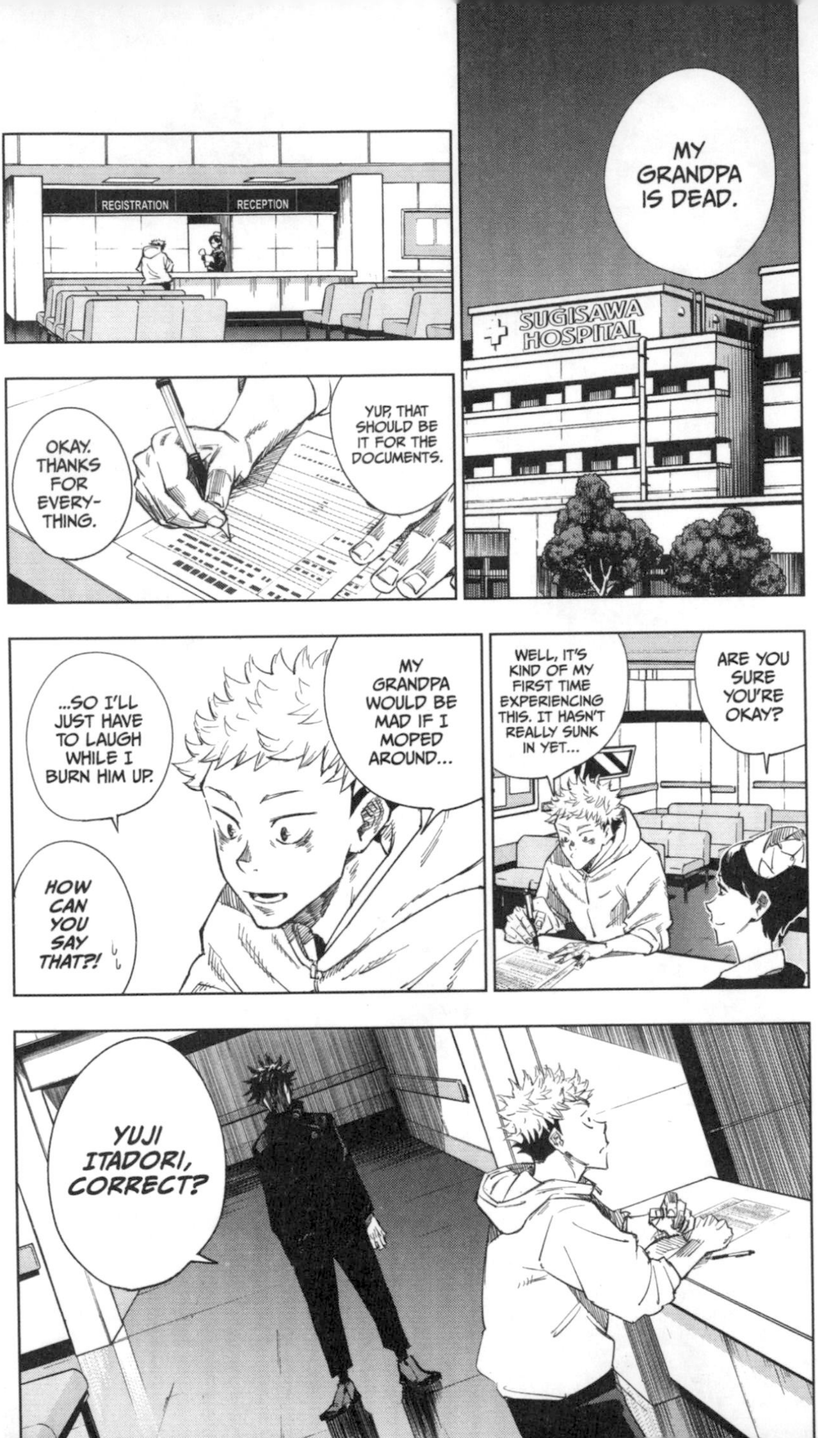
MY GRANDPA IS DEAD.
SUGISAWA HOSPITAL
REGISTRATION
RECEPTION
YUP, THAT SHOULD BE IT FOR THE DOCUMENTS.
OKAY. THANKS FOR EVERY-THING.
ARE YOU SURE YOU'RE OKAY?
WELL, IT'S KIND OF MY FIRST TIME EXPERIENCING THIS. IT HASN'T REALLY SUNK IN YET...
MY GRANDPA WOULD BE MAD IF I MOPED AROUND...
...SO I'LL JUST HAVE TO LAUGH WHILE I BURN HIM UP.
HOW CAN YOU SAY THAT?!
YUJI ITADORI, CORRECT?

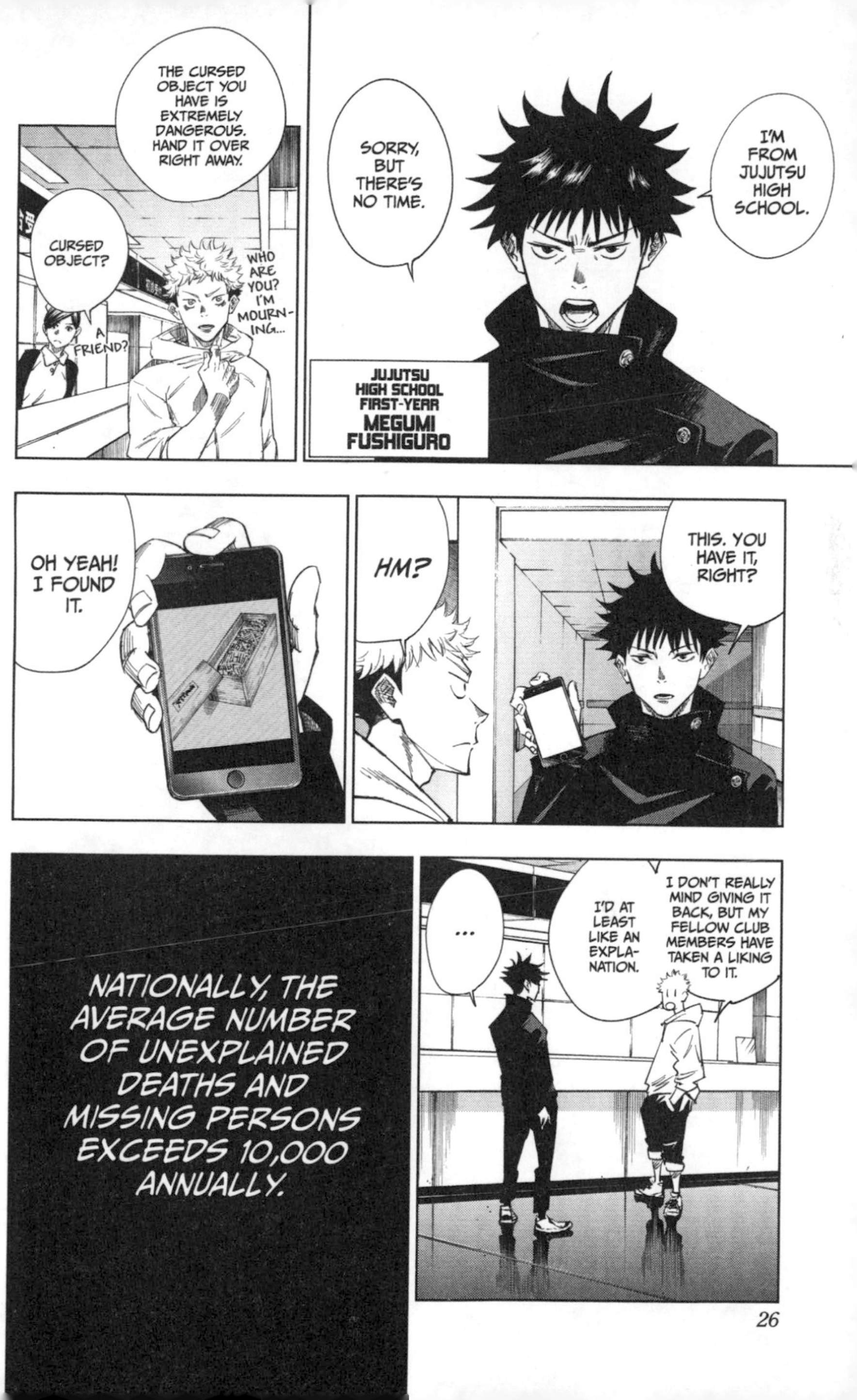
I'M FROM JUJUTSU HIGH SCHOOL.
SORRY, BUT THERE'S NO TIME.
JUJUTSU HIGH SCHOOL FIRST-YEAR MEGUMI FUSHIGURO
THE CURSED OBJECT YOU HAVE IS EXTREMELY DANGEROUS. HAND IT OVER RIGHT AWAY.
WHO ARE YOU? I'M MOURNING...
CURSED OBJECT?
A FRIEND?
THIS. YOU HAVE IT, RIGHT?
HM?
OH YEAH! I FOUND IT.
I DON'T REALLY MIND GIVING IT BACK, BUT MY FELLOW CLUB MEMBERS HAVE TAKEN A LIKING TO IT.
I'D AT LEAST LIKE AN EXPLANATION.
...
NATIONALLY, THE AVERAGE NUMBER OF UNEXPLAINED DEATHS AND MISSING PERSONS EXCEEDS 10,000 ANNUALLY.

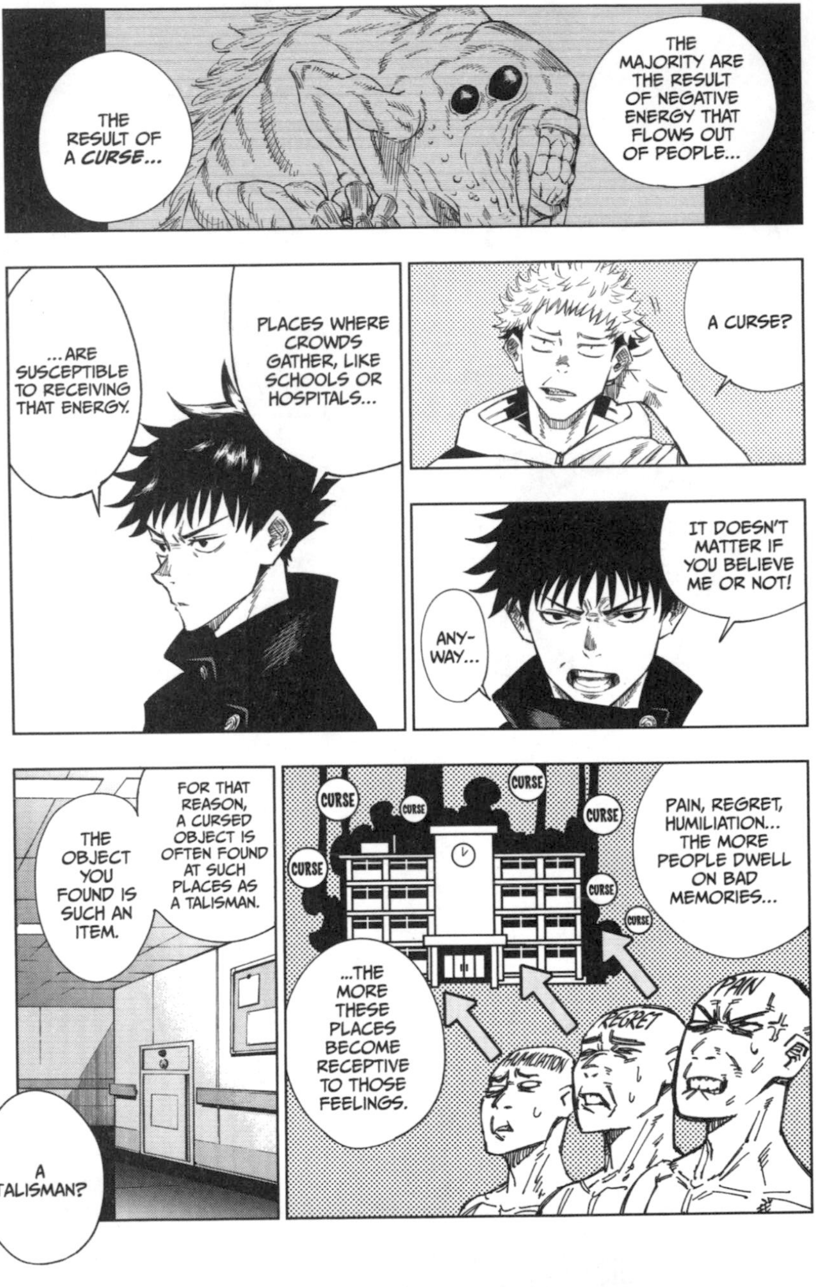
THE MAJORITY ARE THE RESULT OF NEGATIVE ENERGY THAT FLOWS OUT OF PEOPLE...
THE RESULT OF A *CURSE*...
A CURSE?
IT DOESN'T MATTER IF YOU BELIEVE ME OR NOT!
ANY-WAY...
PLACES WHERE CROWDS GATHER, LIKE SCHOOLS OR HOSPITALS...
...ARE SUSCEPTIBLE TO RECEIVING THAT ENERGY.
PAIN, REGRET, HUMILIATION... THE MORE PEOPLE DWELL ON BAD MEMORIES...
CURSE
CURSE
CURSE
CURSE
CURSE
CURSE
CURSE
...THE MORE THESE PLACES BECOME RECEPTIVE TO THOSE FEELINGS.
PAIN
REGRET
HUMILIATION
FOR THAT REASON, A CURSED OBJECT IS OFTEN FOUND AT SUCH PLACES AS A TALISMAN.
THE OBJECT YOU FOUND IS SUCH AN ITEM.
A TALISMAN?

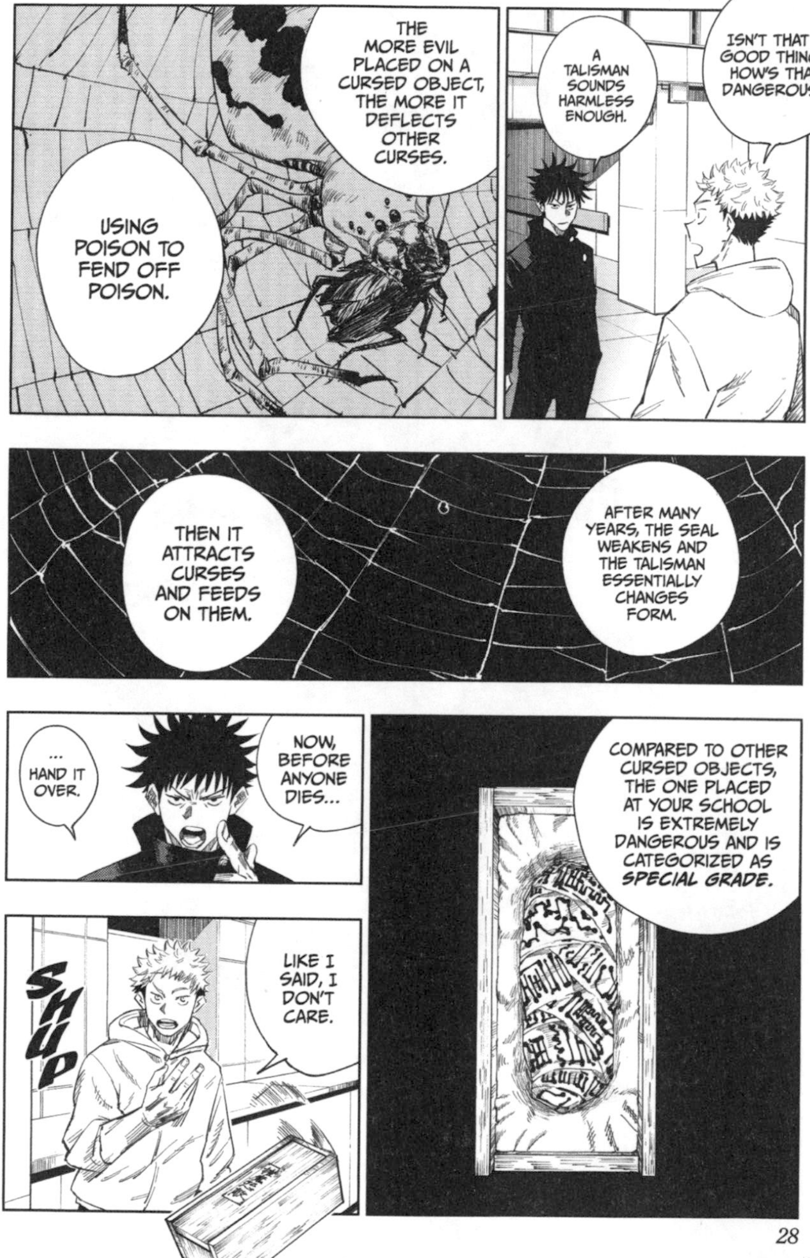
ISN'T THAT A GOOD THING? HOW'S THAT DANGEROUS?
A TALISMAN SOUNDS HARMLESS ENOUGH.
THE MORE EVIL PLACED ON A CURSED OBJECT, THE MORE IT DEFLECTS OTHER CURSES.
USING POISON TO FEND OFF POISON.
AFTER MANY YEARS, THE SEAL WEAKENS AND THE TALISMAN ESSENTIALLY CHANGES FORM.
THEN IT ATTRACTS CURSES AND FEEDS ON THEM.
COMPARED TO OTHER CURSED OBJECTS, THE ONE PLACED AT YOUR SCHOOL IS EXTREMELY DANGEROUS AND IS CATEGORIZED AS *SPECIAL GRADE*.
NOW, BEFORE ANYONE DIES...
... HAND IT OVER.
LIKE I SAID, I DON'T CARE.
SHUP

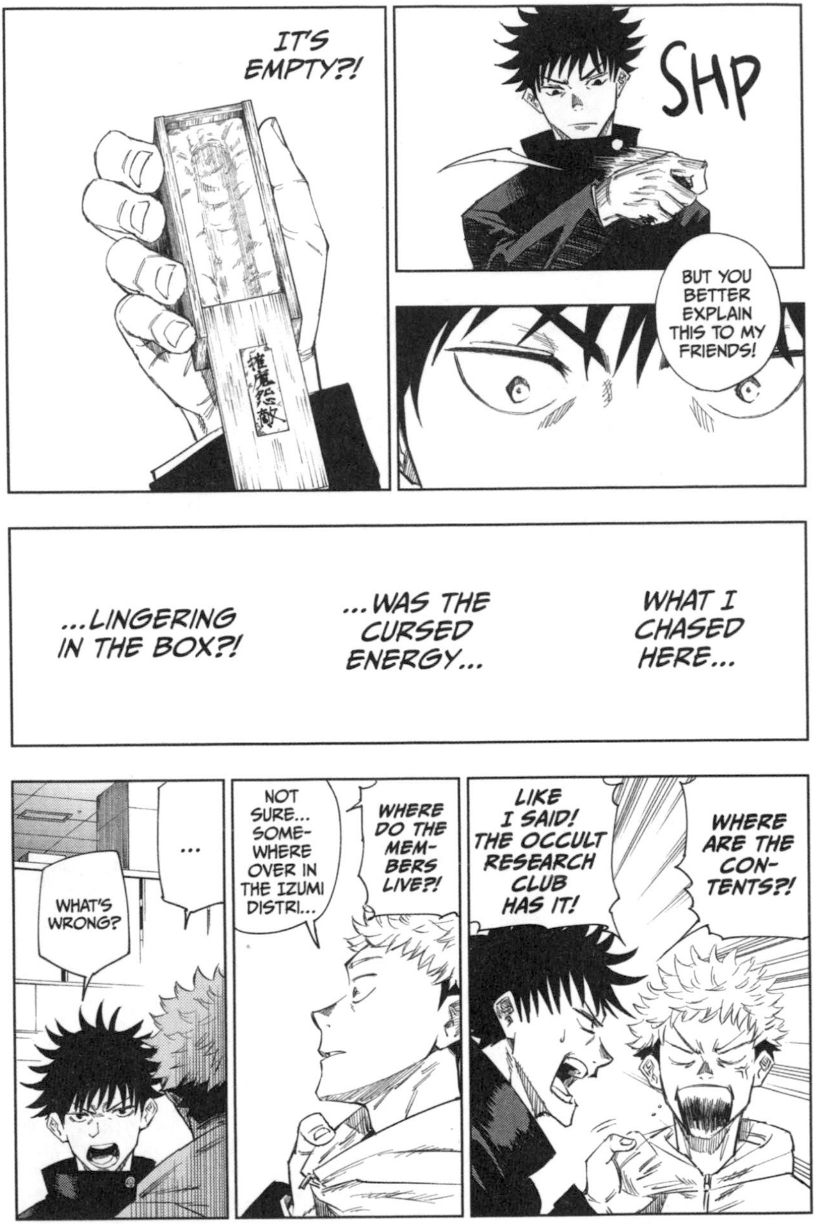
SHP
BUT YOU BETTER EXPLAIN THIS TO MY FRIENDS!
IT'S EMPTY?!
WHAT I CHASED HERE...
...WAS THE CURSED ENERGY...
...LINGERING IN THE BOX?!
WHERE ARE THE CON-TENTS?!
LIKE I SAID! THE OCCULT RESEARCH CLUB HAS IT!
WHERE DO THE MEM-BERS LIVE?!
NOT SURE... SOME-WHERE OVER IN THE IZUMI DISTRI...
...
WHAT'S WRONG?

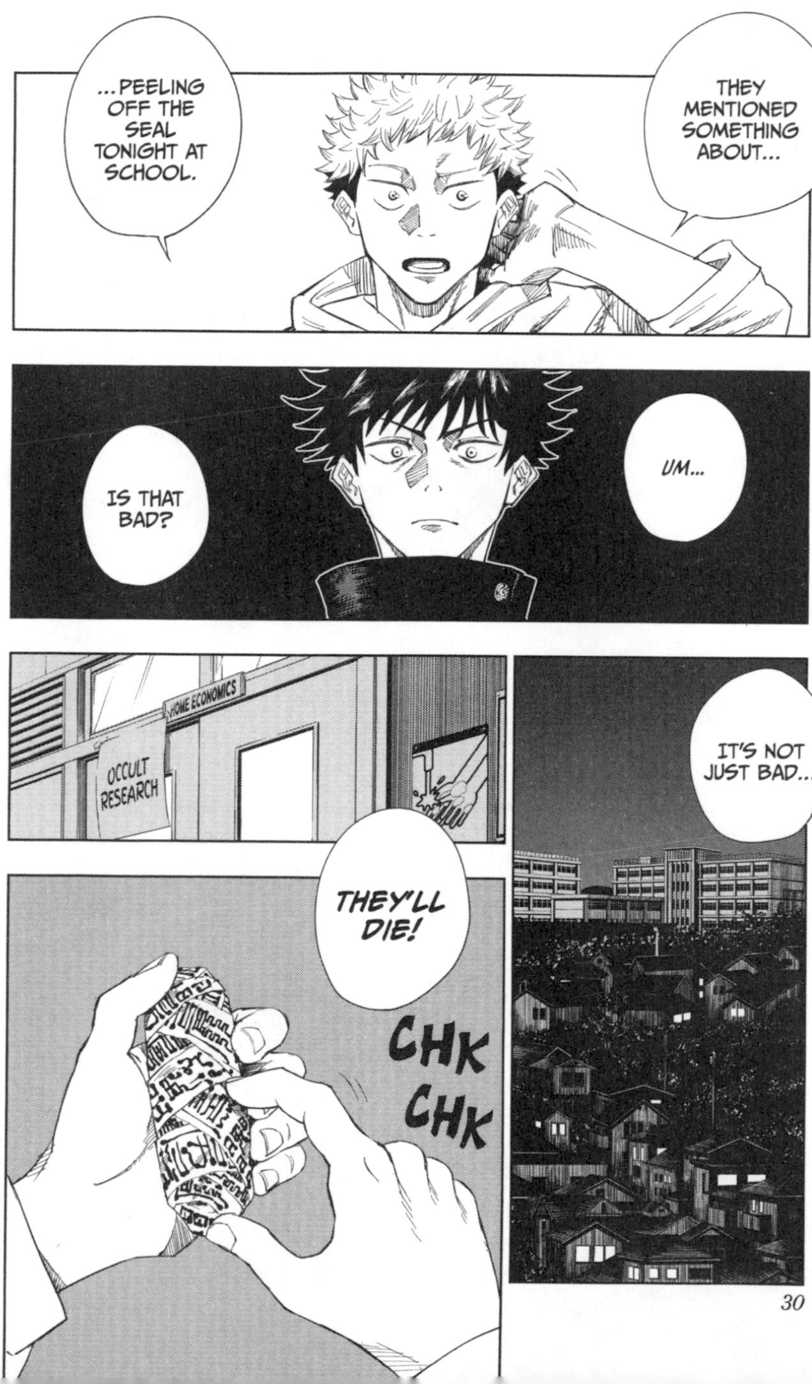
THEY MENTIONED SOMETHING ABOUT...
...PEELING OFF THE SEAL TONIGHT AT SCHOOL.
UM...
IS THAT BAD?
IT'S NOT JUST BAD...
HOME ECONOMICS
OCCULT RESEARCH
THEY'LL DIE!
CHK CHK

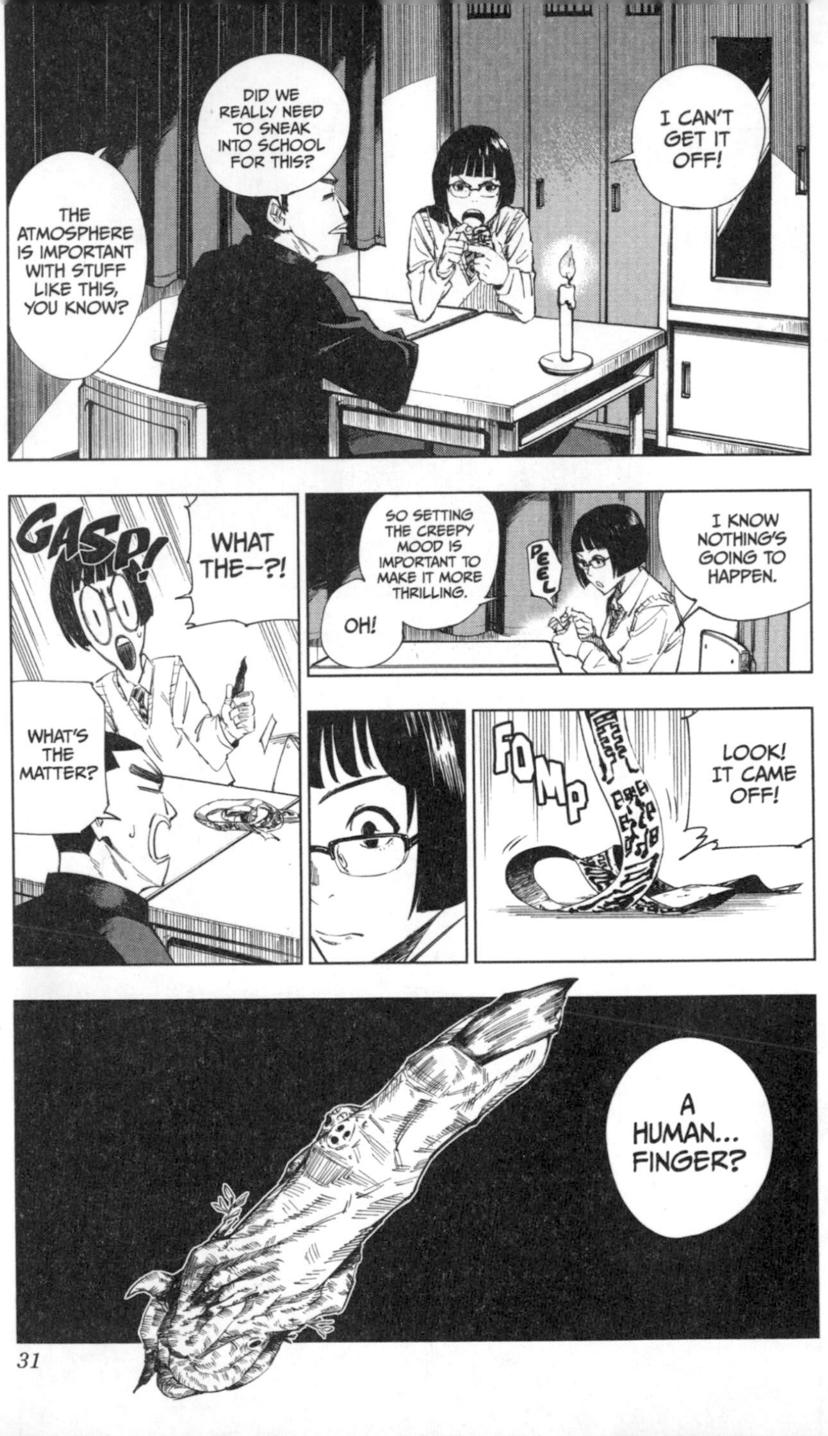
I CAN'T GET IT OFF!
DID WE REALLY NEED TO SNEAK INTO SCHOOL FOR THIS?
THE ATMOSPHERE IS IMPORTANT WITH STUFF LIKE THIS, YOU KNOW?
I KNOW NOTHING'S GOING TO HAPPEN.
PEEL
SO SETTING THE CREEPY MOOD IS IMPORTANT TO MAKE IT MORE THRILLING.
OH!
LOOK! IT CAME OFF!
FOMP
WHAT THE--?!
GASP!
WHAT'S THE MATTER?
A HUMAN... FINGER?

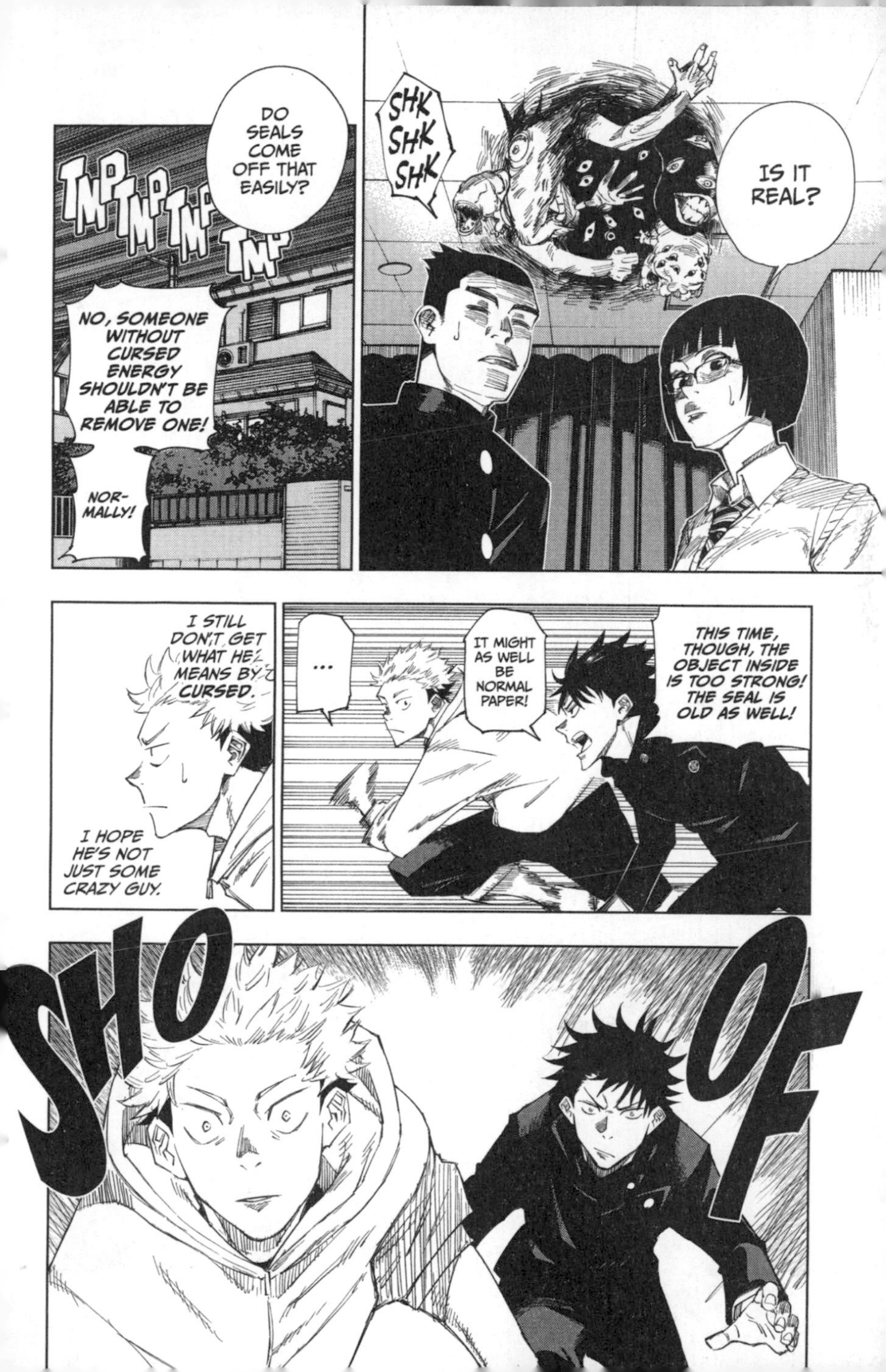
SHK SHK SHK
IS IT REAL?
DO SEALS COME OFF THAT EASILY?
TMP TMP TMP TMP
NO, SOMEONE WITHOUT CURSED ENERGY SHOULDN'T BE ABLE TO REMOVE ONE!
NOR-MALLY!
THIS TIME, THOUGH, THE OBJECT INSIDE IS TOO STRONG! THE SEAL IS OLD AS WELL!
IT MIGHT AS WELL BE NORMAL PAPER!
...
I STILL DON'T GET WHAT HE MEANS BY CURSED.
I HOPE HE'S NOT JUST SOME CRAZY GUY.
SHOOF

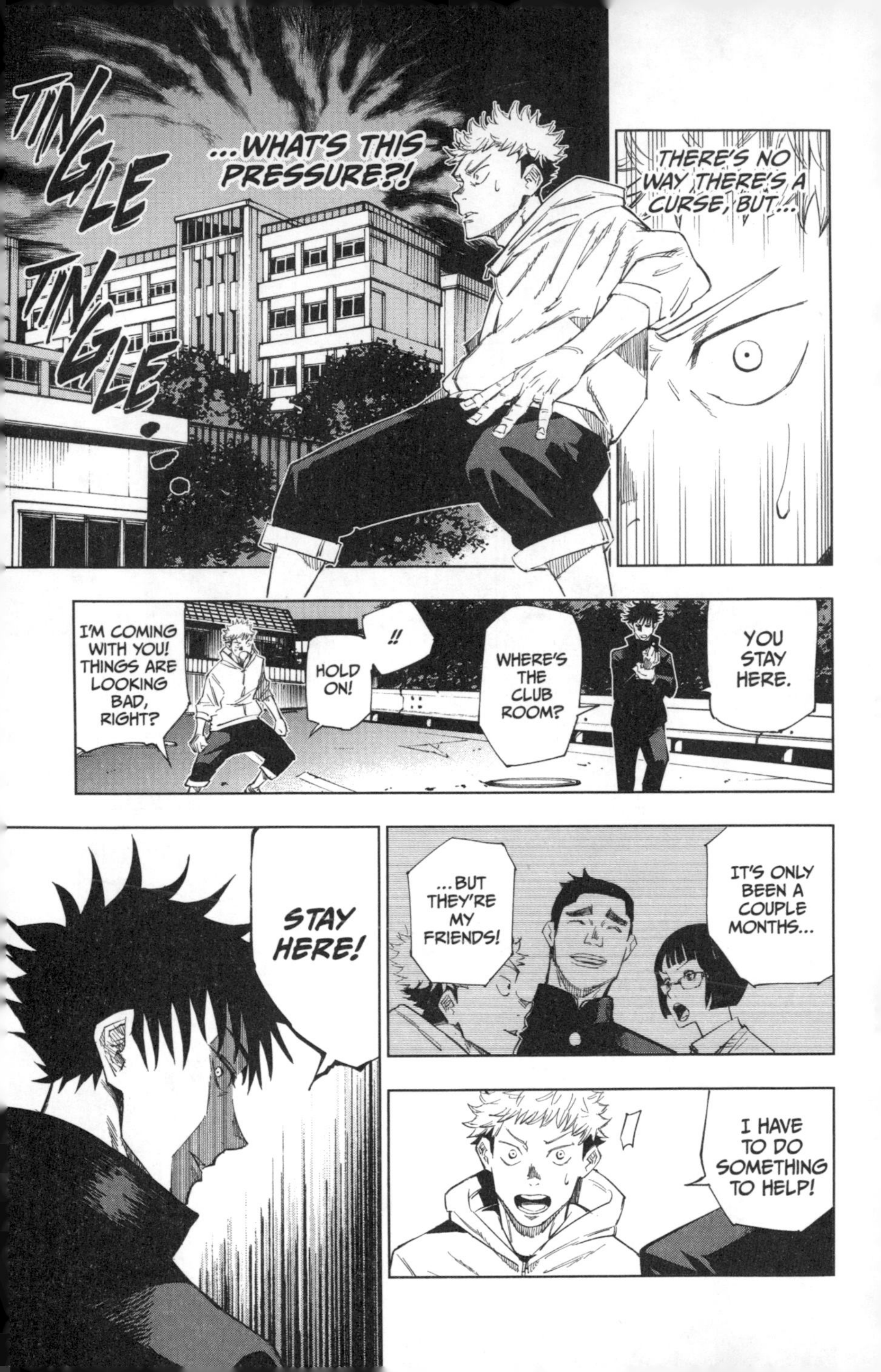
THERE'S NO WAY THERE'S A CURSE, BUT...
...WHAT'S THIS PRESSURE?!
TINGLE
TINGLE
YOU STAY HERE.
WHERE'S THE CLUB ROOM?
!!
HOLD ON!
I'M COMING WITH YOU! THINGS ARE LOOKING BAD, RIGHT?
IT'S ONLY BEEN A COUPLE MONTHS...
...BUT THEY'RE MY FRIENDS!
I HAVE TO DO SOMETHING TO HELP!
STAY HERE!

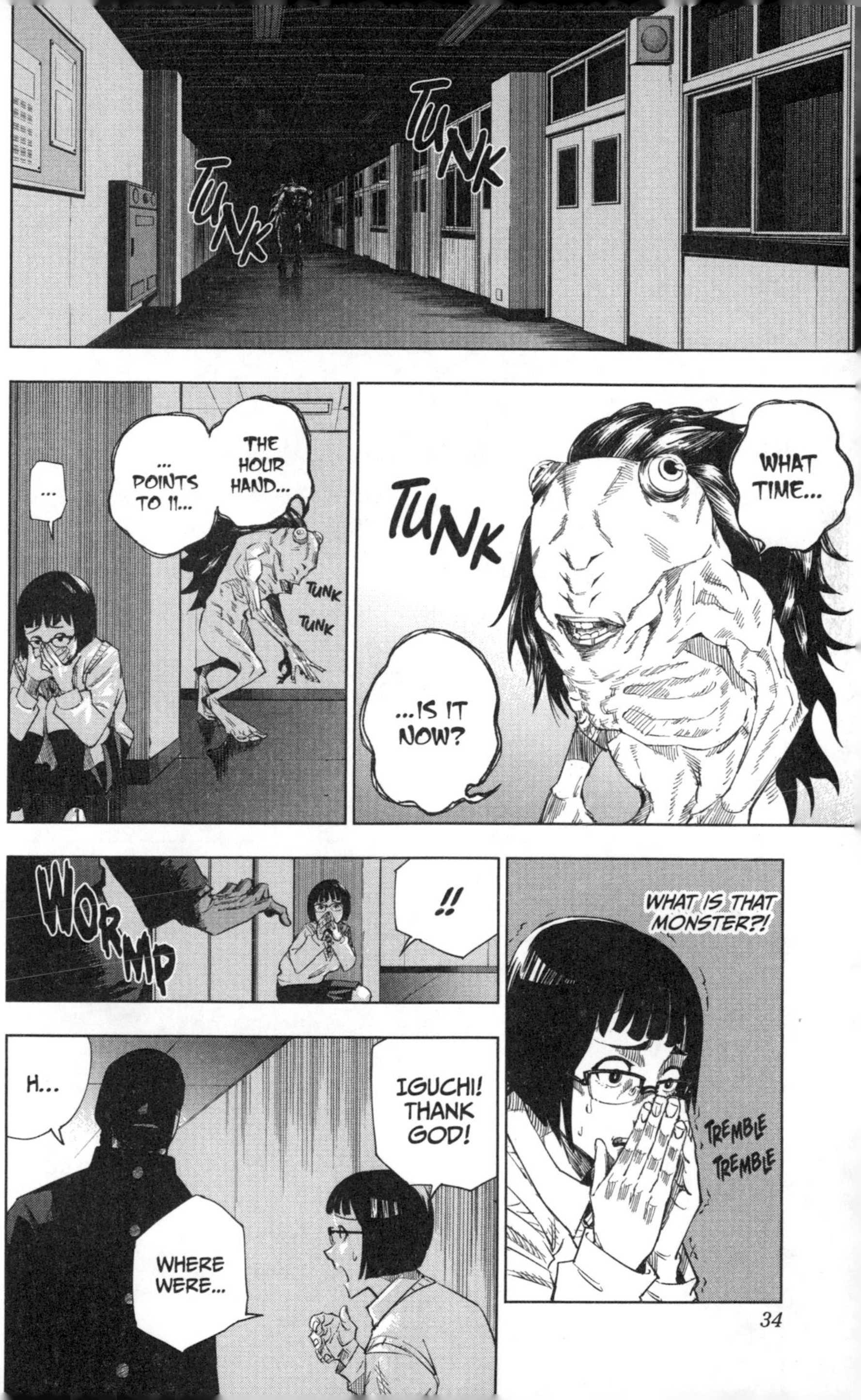
TUNK
TUNK
WHAT TIME...
TUNK
...IS IT NOW?
THE HOUR HAND...
...POINTS TO 11...
...
TUNK
TUNK
WHAT IS THAT MONSTER?!
TREMBLE
TREMBLE
!!
WORMP
IGUCHI! THANK GOD!
H...
WHERE WERE...

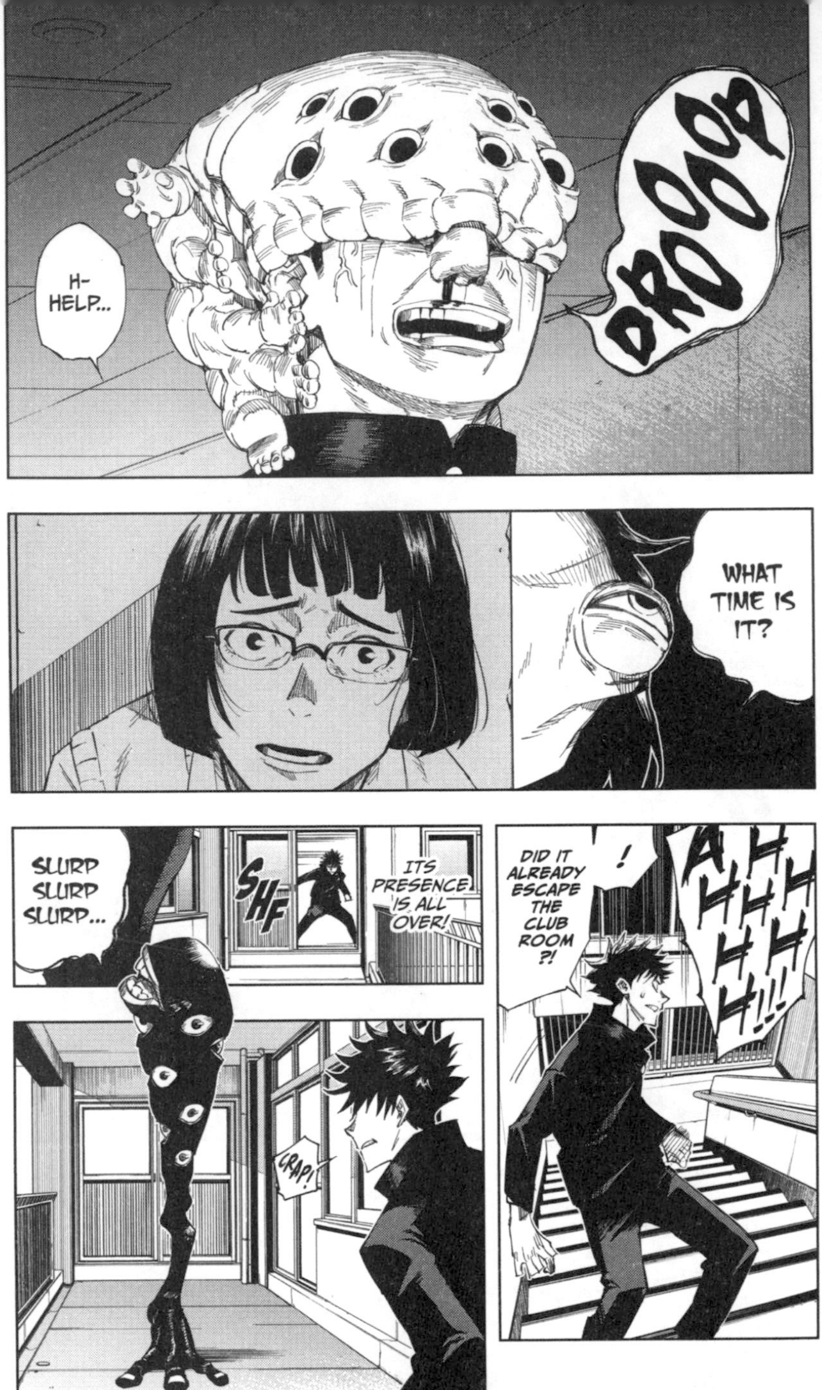
DROOOOP
H-HELP...
WHAT TIME IS IT?
AHHHHHHHHH!!!
!
DID IT ALREADY ESCAPE THE CLUB ROOM?!
ITS PRESENCE IS ALL OVER!
SHF
SLURP SLURP SLURP...
CRAP!

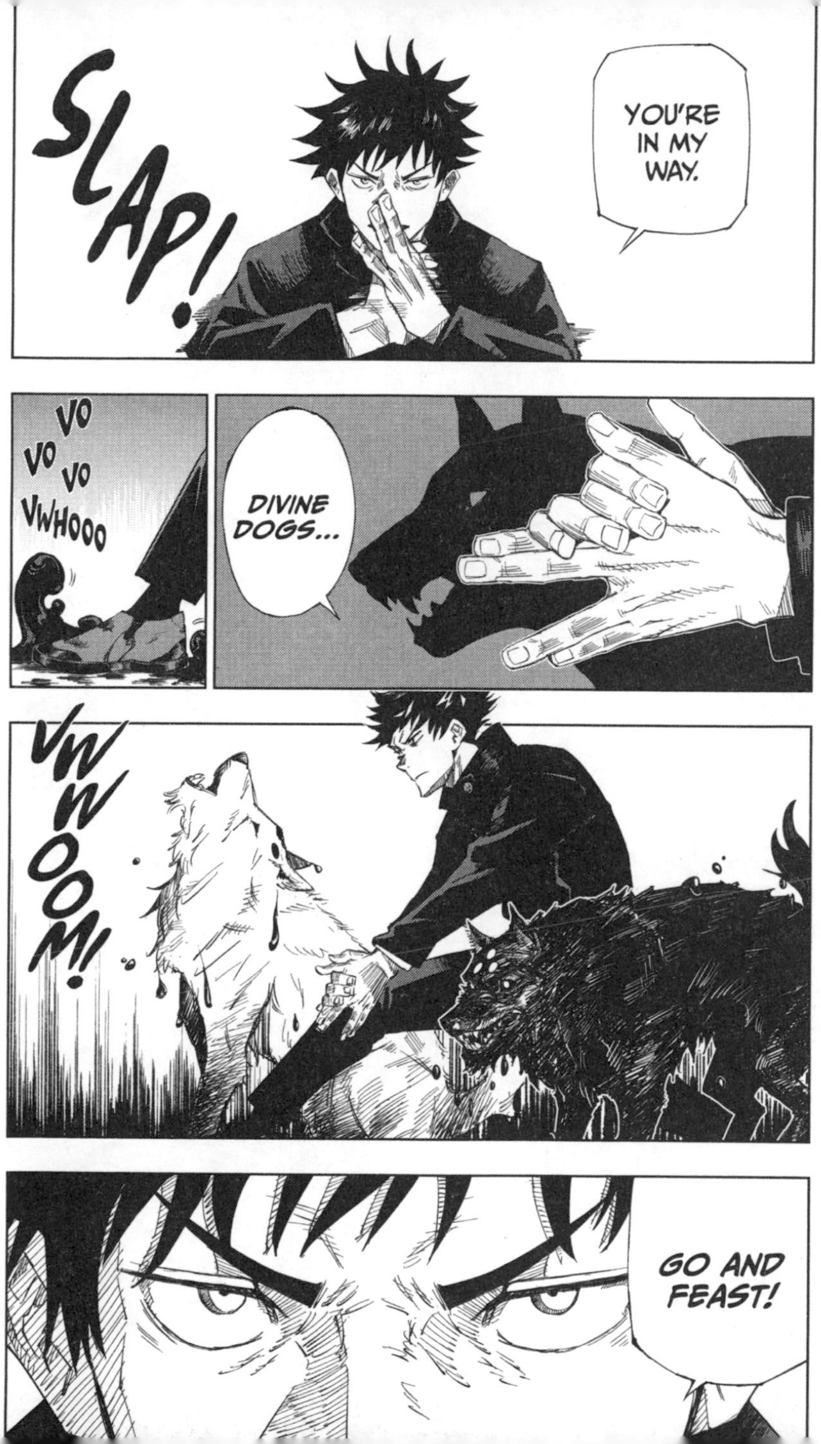
YOU'RE IN MY WAY.
SLAP!
DIVINE DOGS...
VO VO VO VWHOOO
VWWOOM!
GO AND FEAST!

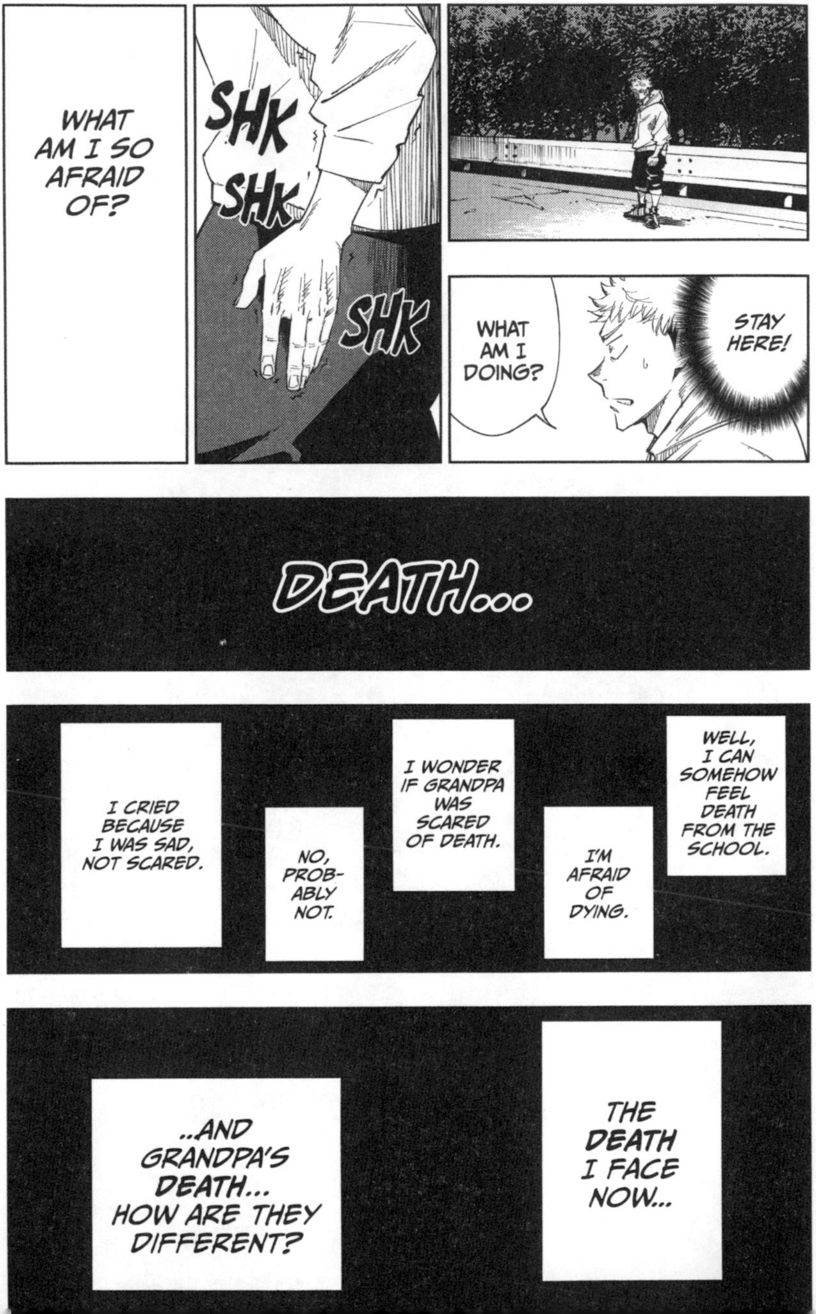
STAY HERE!
WHAT AM I DOING?
SHK
SHK
SHK
WHAT AM I SO AFRAID OF?
DEATH...
WELL, I CAN SOMEHOW FEEL DEATH FROM THE SCHOOL.
I'M AFRAID OF DYING.
I WONDER IF GRANDPA WAS SCARED OF DEATH.
NO, PROB-ABLY NOT.
I CRIED BECAUSE I WAS SAD, NOT SCARED.
THE DEATH I FACE NOW...
..AND GRANDPA'S DEATH... HOW ARE THEY DIFFERENT?

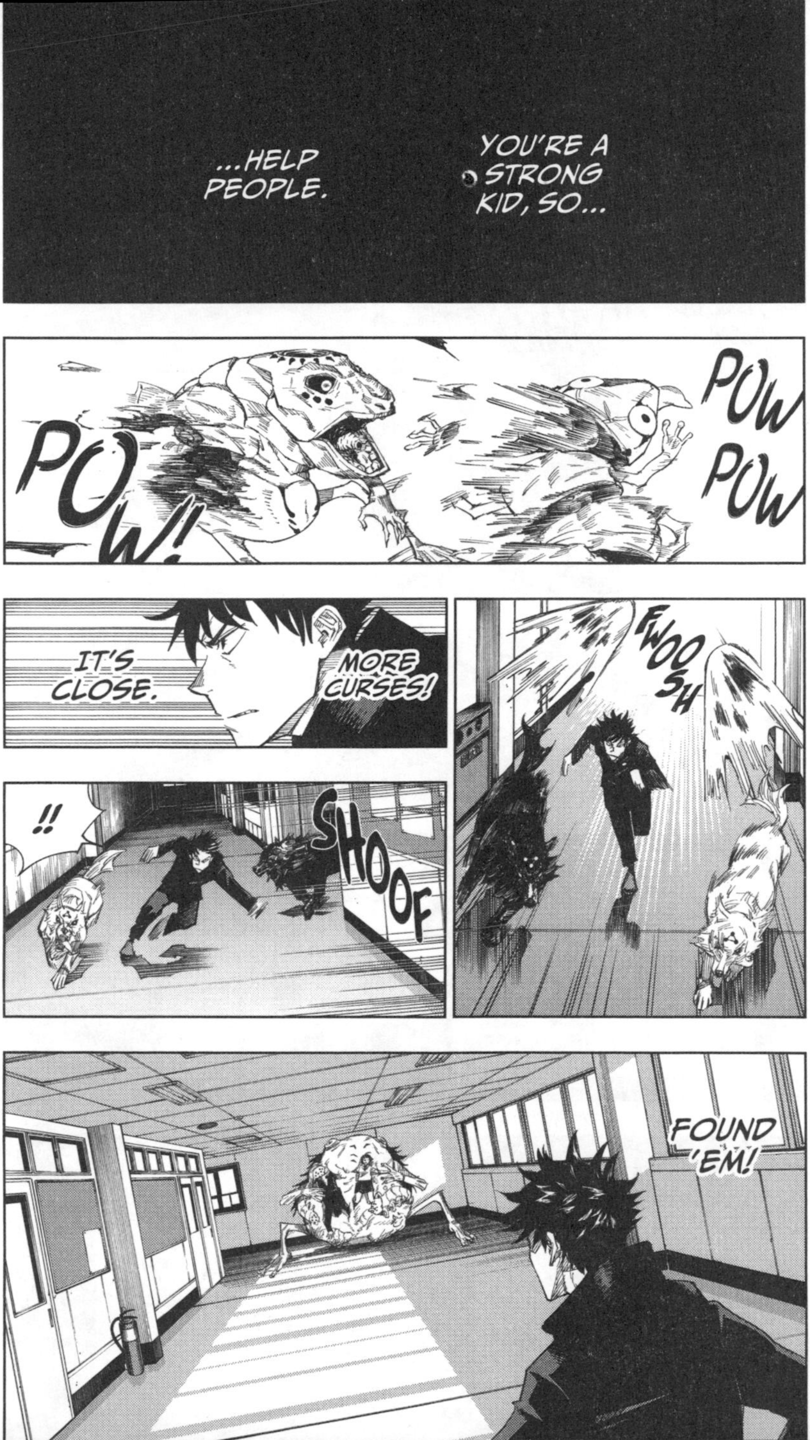
YOU'RE A STRONG KID, SO...
...HELP PEOPLE.
POW POW
POW!
FWOOSH
MORE CURSES!
IT'S CLOSE.
SHOOF
!!
FOUND 'EM!

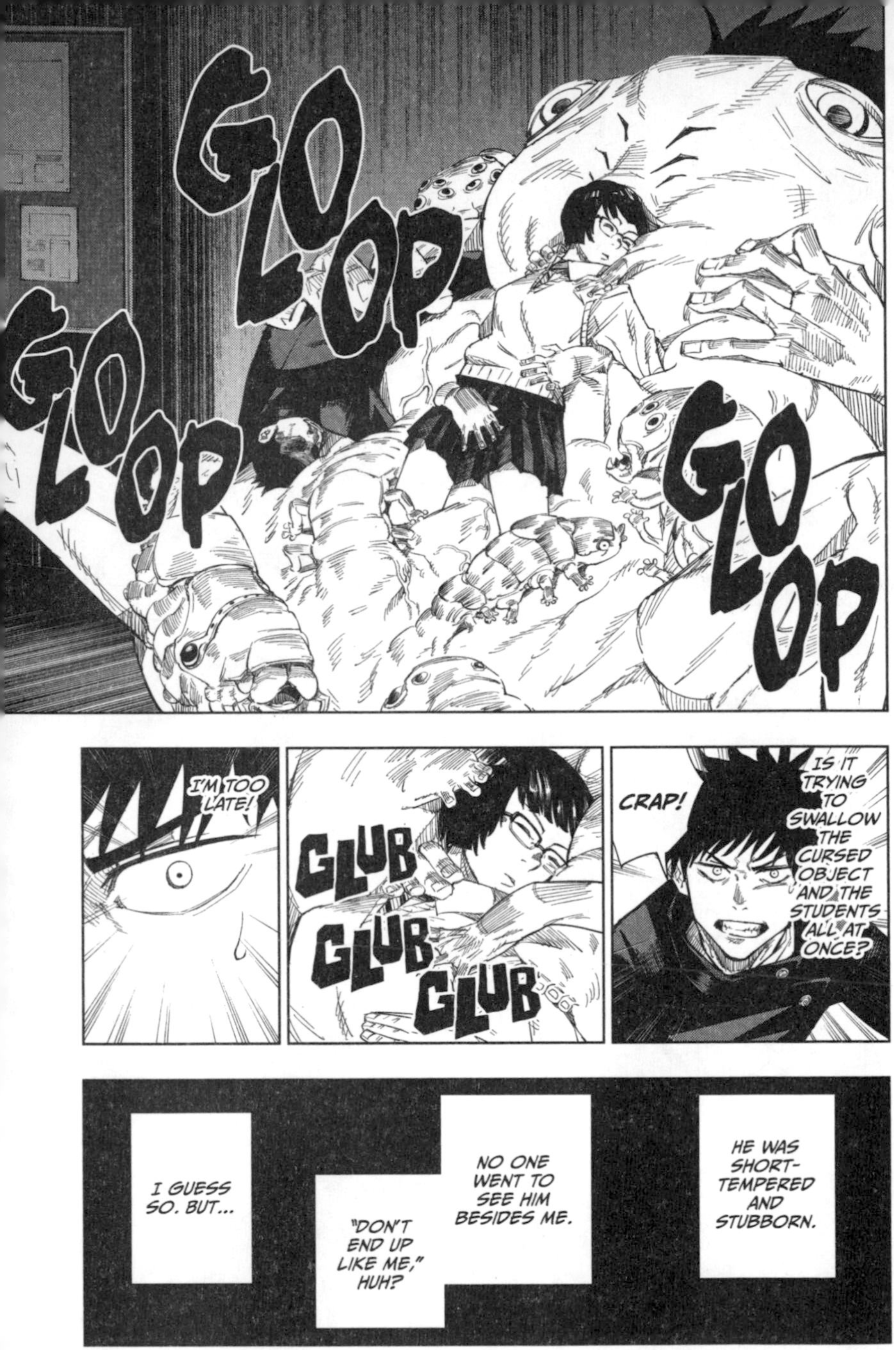
GLOOP
GLOOP
GLOOP
IS IT TRYING TO SWALLOW THE CURSED OBJECT AND THE STUDENTS ALL AT ONCE?
CRAP!
GLUB GLUB GLUB
I'M TOO LATE!
HE WAS SHORT-TEMPERED AND STUBBORN.
NO ONE WENT TO SEE HIM BESIDES ME.
"DON'T END UP LIKE ME," HUH?
I GUESS SO. BUT...

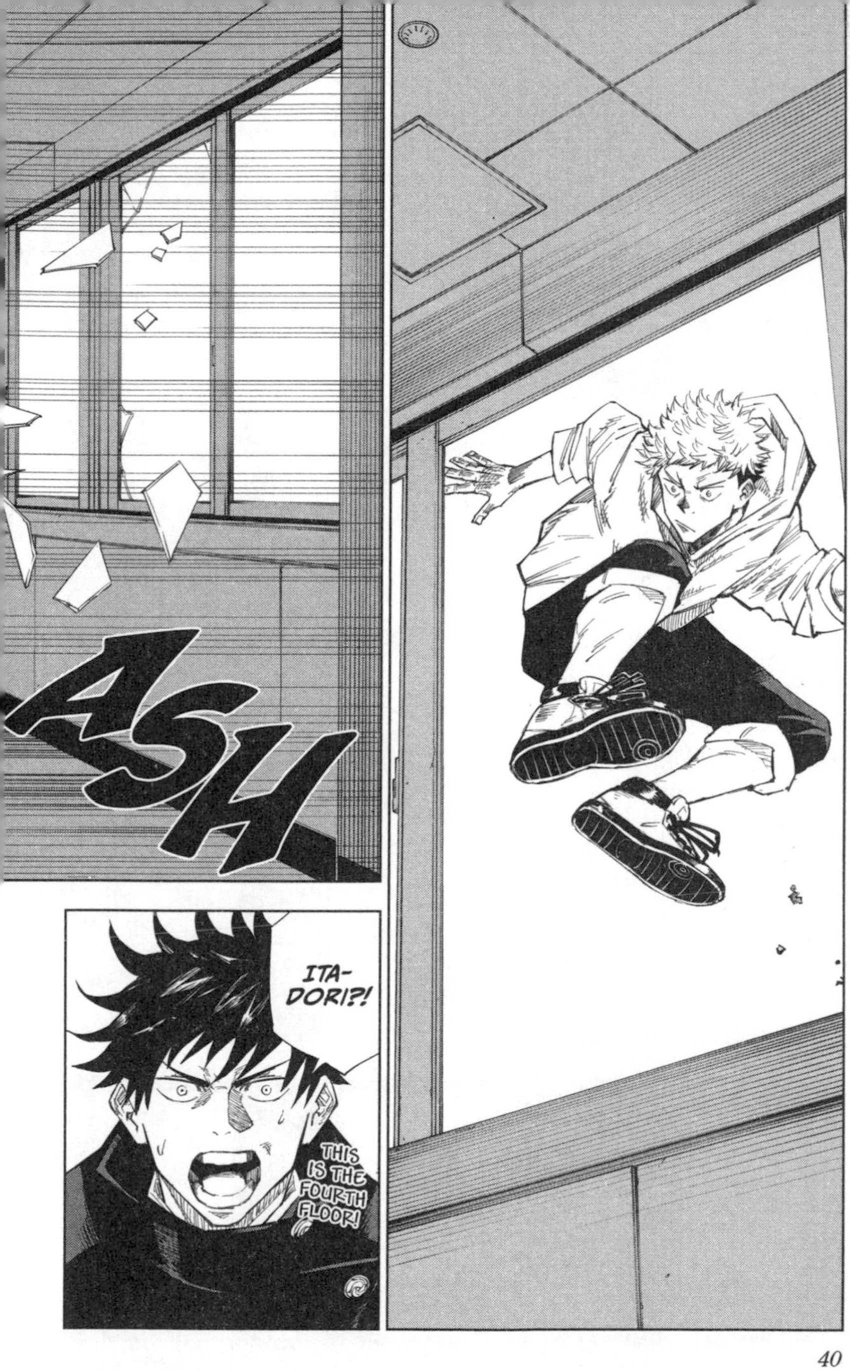
ASH
ITA-DORI?!
THIS IS THE FOURTH FLOOR!

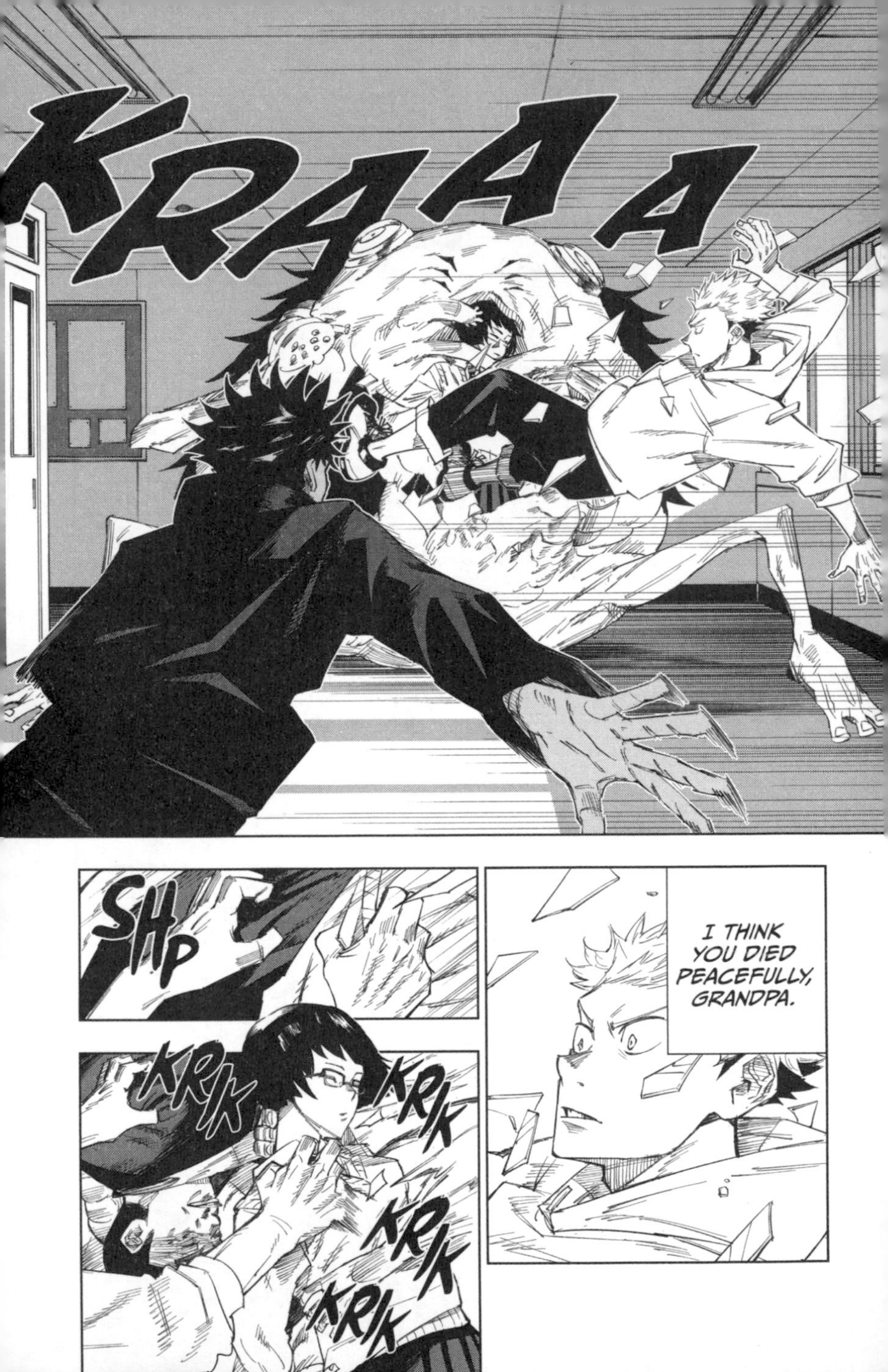
KRAAAA
I THINK YOU DIED PEACEFULLY, GRANDPA.
SHP
KRIK
KRIK
KRIK
KRIK

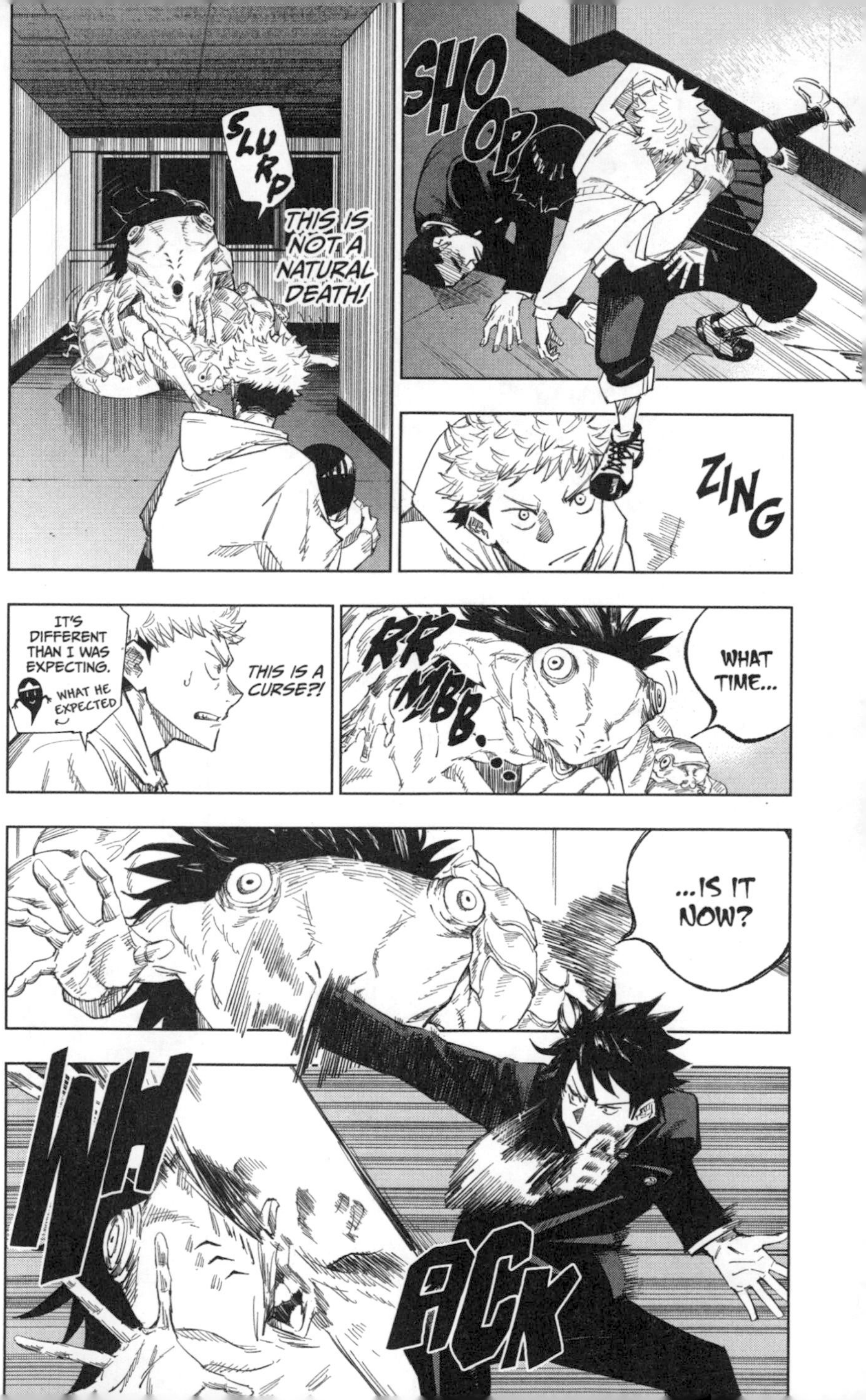
SHOOP
ZING
SLURP
THIS IS NOT A NATURAL DEATH!
WHAT TIME...
RRMBB...
THIS IS A CURSE?!
IT'S DIFFERENT THAN I WAS EXPECTING.
WHAT HE EXPECTED
...IS IT NOW?
WHACK

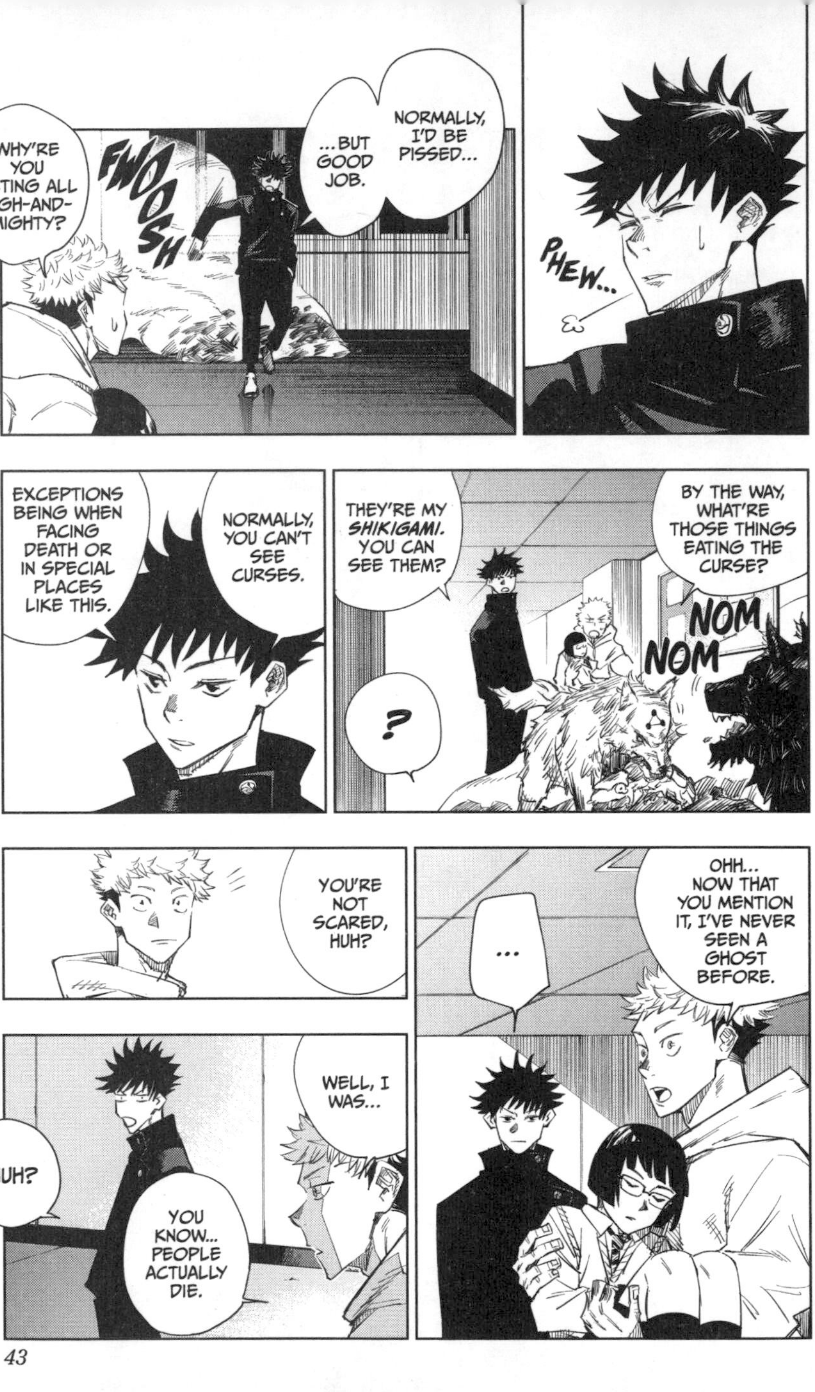
PHEW...
NORMALLY, I'D BE PISSED...
...BUT GOOD JOB.
FWOOSH
WHY'RE YOU ACTING ALL HIGH-AND-MIGHTY?
BY THE WAY, WHAT'RE THOSE THINGS EATING THE CURSE?
NOM NOM
THEY'RE MY *SHIKIGAMI.* YOU CAN SEE THEM?
?
NORMALLY, YOU CAN'T SEE CURSES.
EXCEPTIONS BEING WHEN FACING DEATH OR IN SPECIAL PLACES LIKE THIS.
OHH... NOW THAT YOU MENTION IT, I'VE NEVER SEEN A GHOST BEFORE.
...
YOU'RE NOT SCARED, HUH?
WELL, I WAS...
YOU KNOW... PEOPLE ACTUALLY DIE.
HUH?

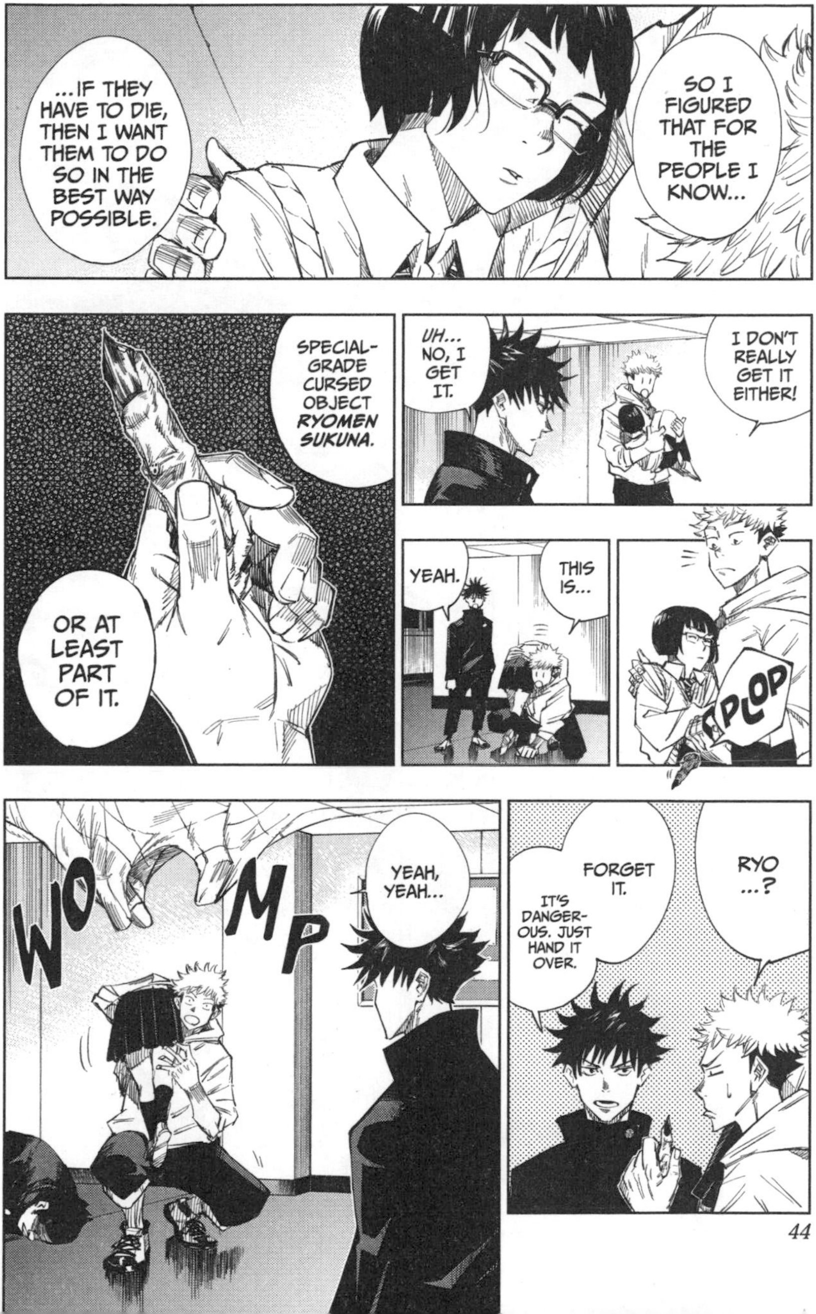
SO I FIGURED THAT FOR THE PEOPLE I KNOW...
...IF THEY HAVE TO DIE, THEN I WANT THEM TO DO SO IN THE BEST WAY POSSIBLE.
I DON'T REALLY GET IT EITHER!
UH... NO, I GET IT.
PLOP
THIS IS...
YEAH.
SPECIAL-GRADE CURSED OBJECT *RYOMEN SUKUNA.*
OR AT LEAST PART OF IT.
RYO...?
FORGET IT.
IT'S DANGER-OUS. JUST HAND IT OVER.
YEAH, YEAH...
WOMP

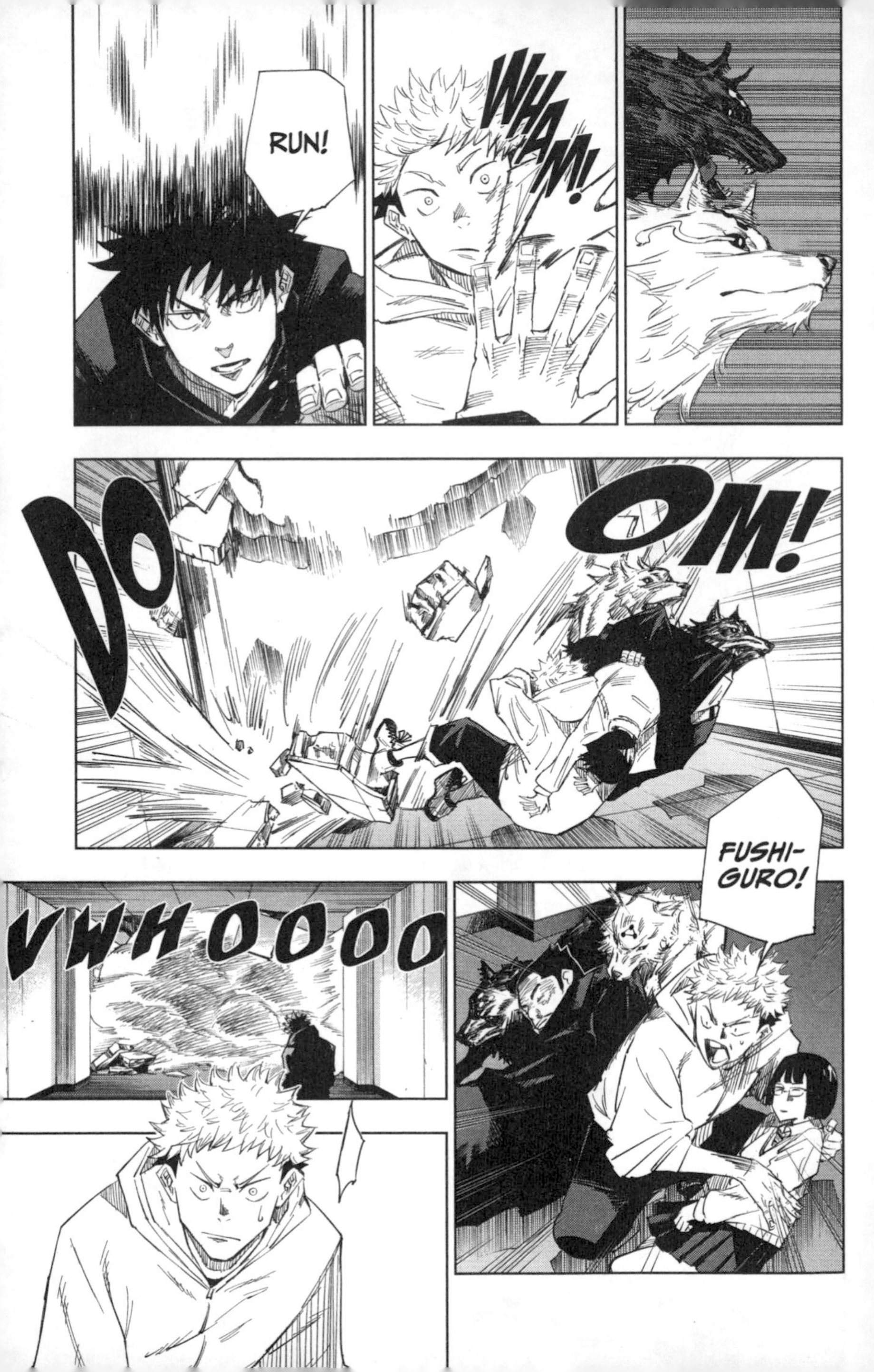
WHAM!
RUN!
DOOM!
FUSHI-
GURO!
VWHOOOO
!

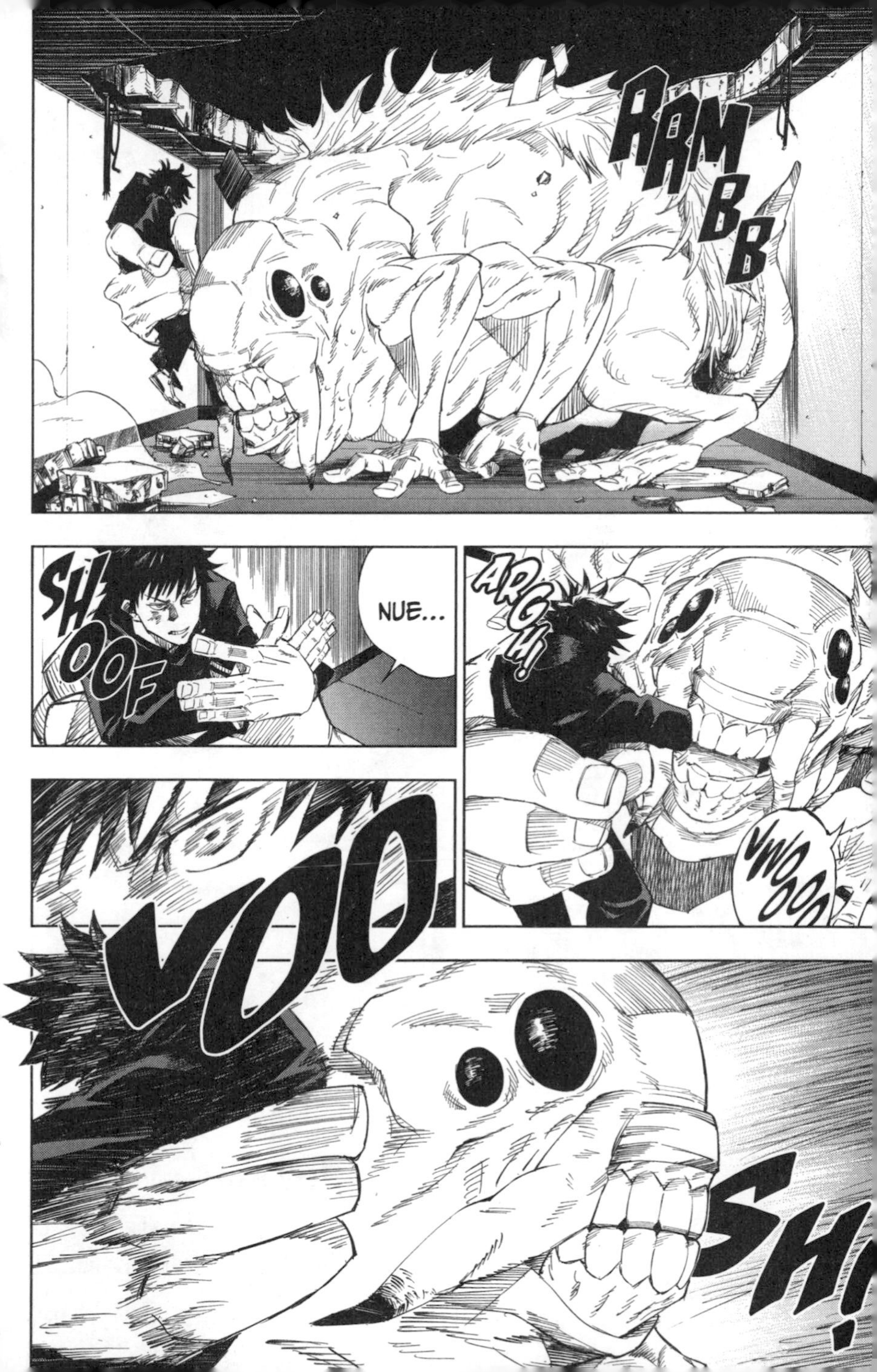
RAMBBB
NUE...
SHOOF
ARGH!
VWOOOO
VOO
SH!

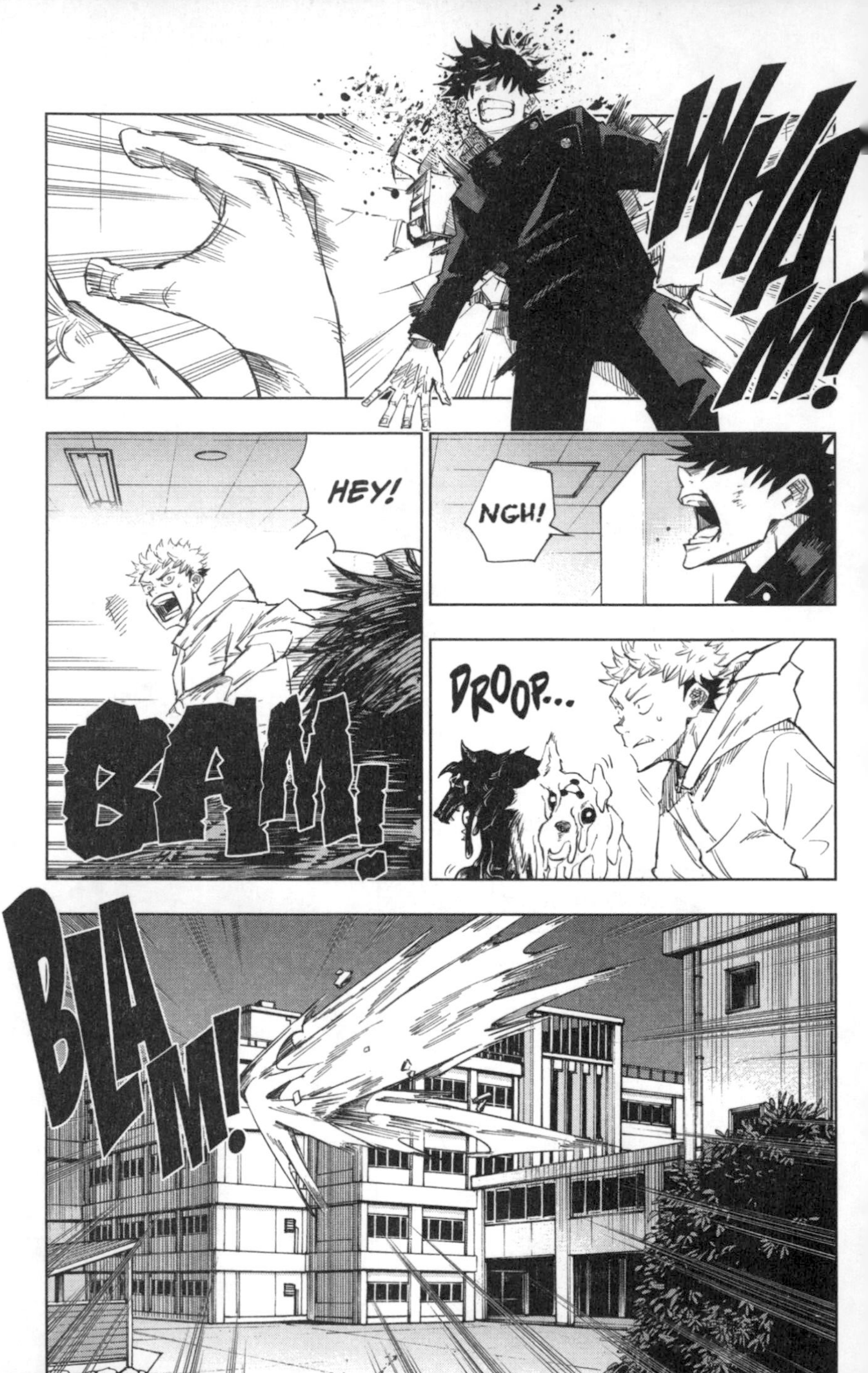
WHAM!
NGH!
DROOP...
HEY!
BAM!
BLAM!

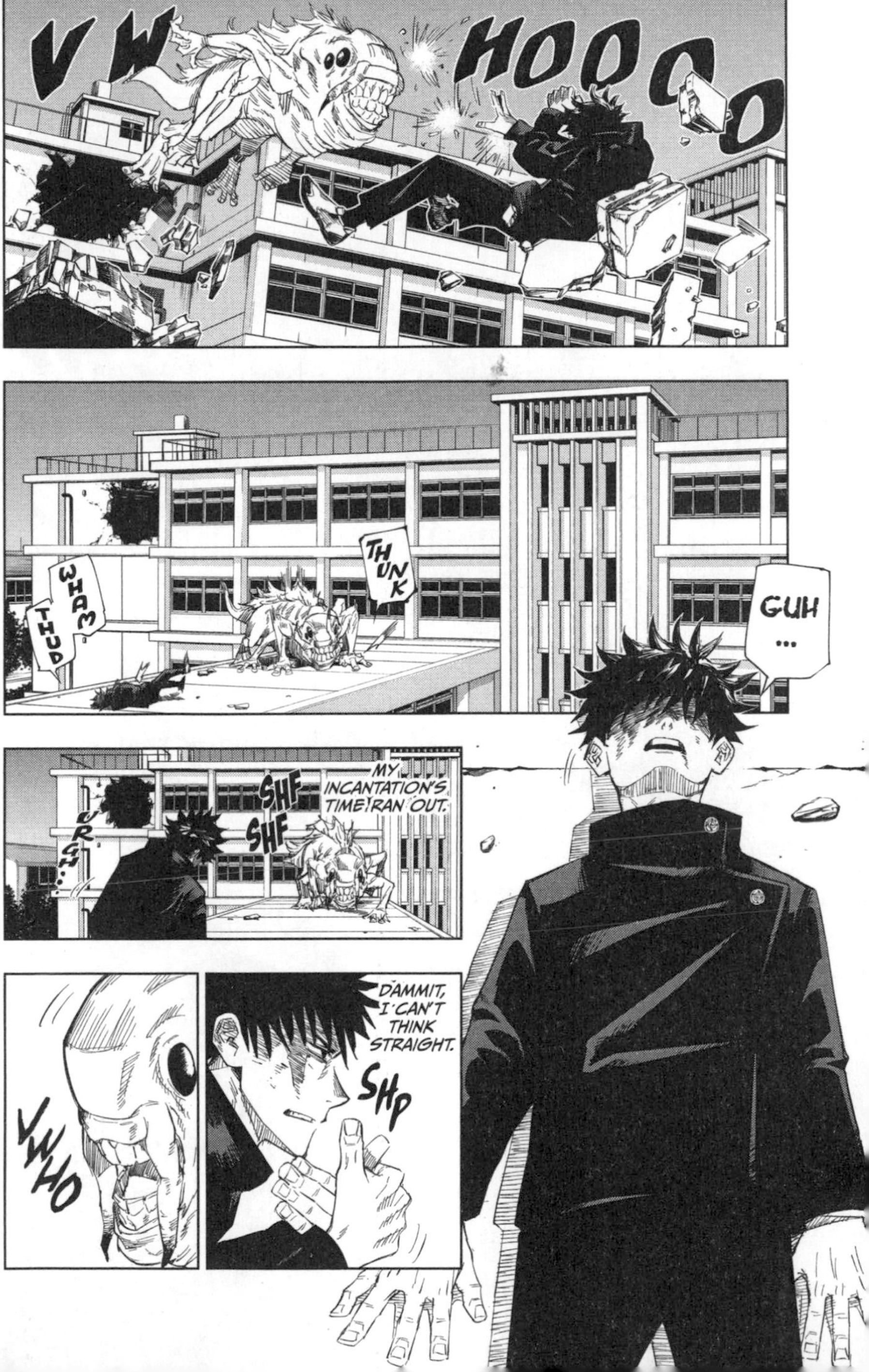
VWHOOOOO
GUH...
THUNK
WHAM
THUD
MY INCANTATION'S TIME RAN OUT.
SHF SHF
URGH...
DAMMIT, I CAN'T THINK STRAIGHT.
SHP
VWHO

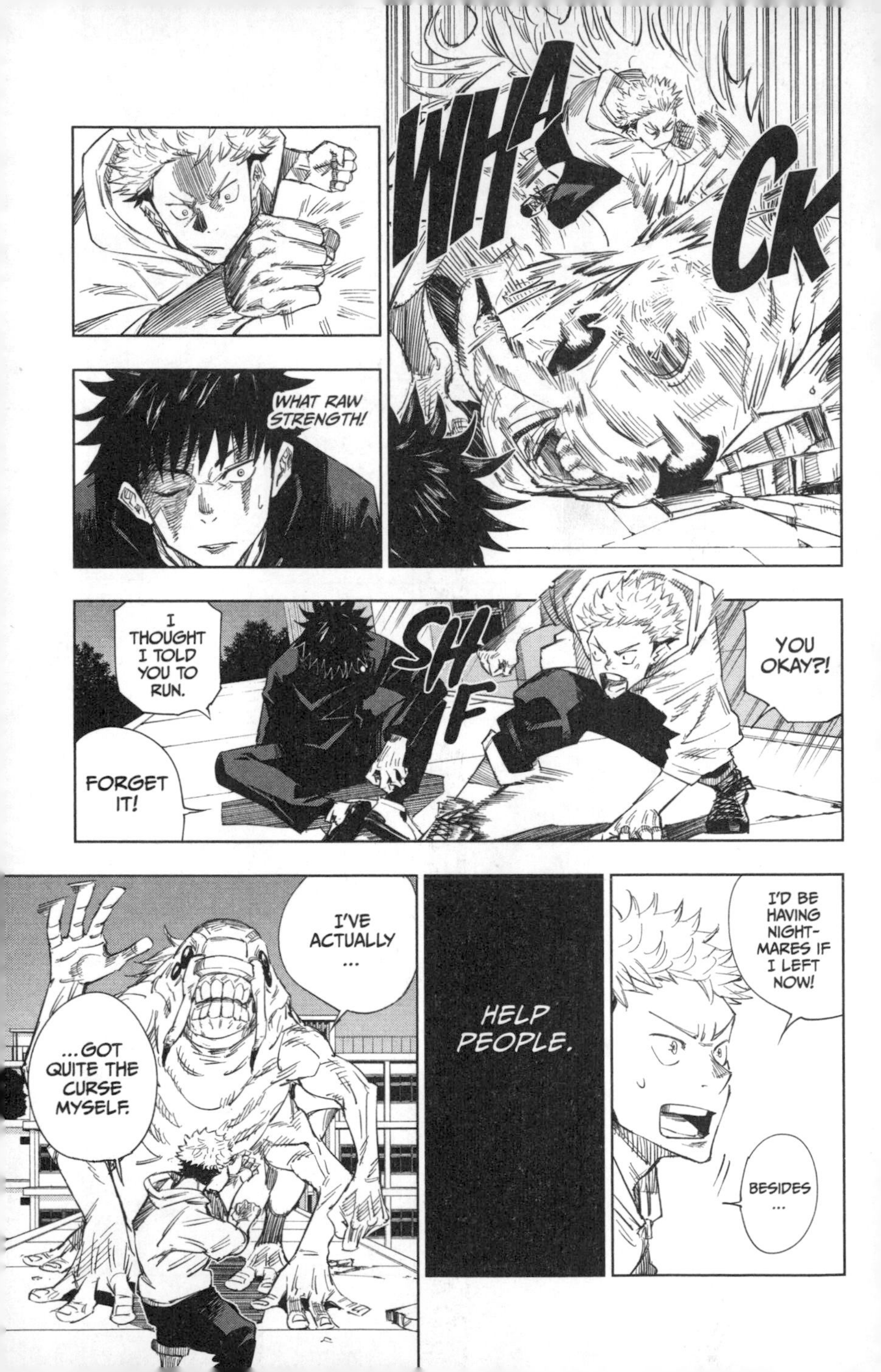
WHACK
WHAT RAW STRENGTH!
YOU OKAY?!
SHF
I THOUGHT I TOLD YOU TO RUN.
FORGET IT!
I'D BE HAVING NIGHT-MARES IF I LEFT NOW!
BESIDES ...
HELP PEOPLE.
I'VE ACTUALLY ...
...GOT QUITE THE CURSE MYSELF.

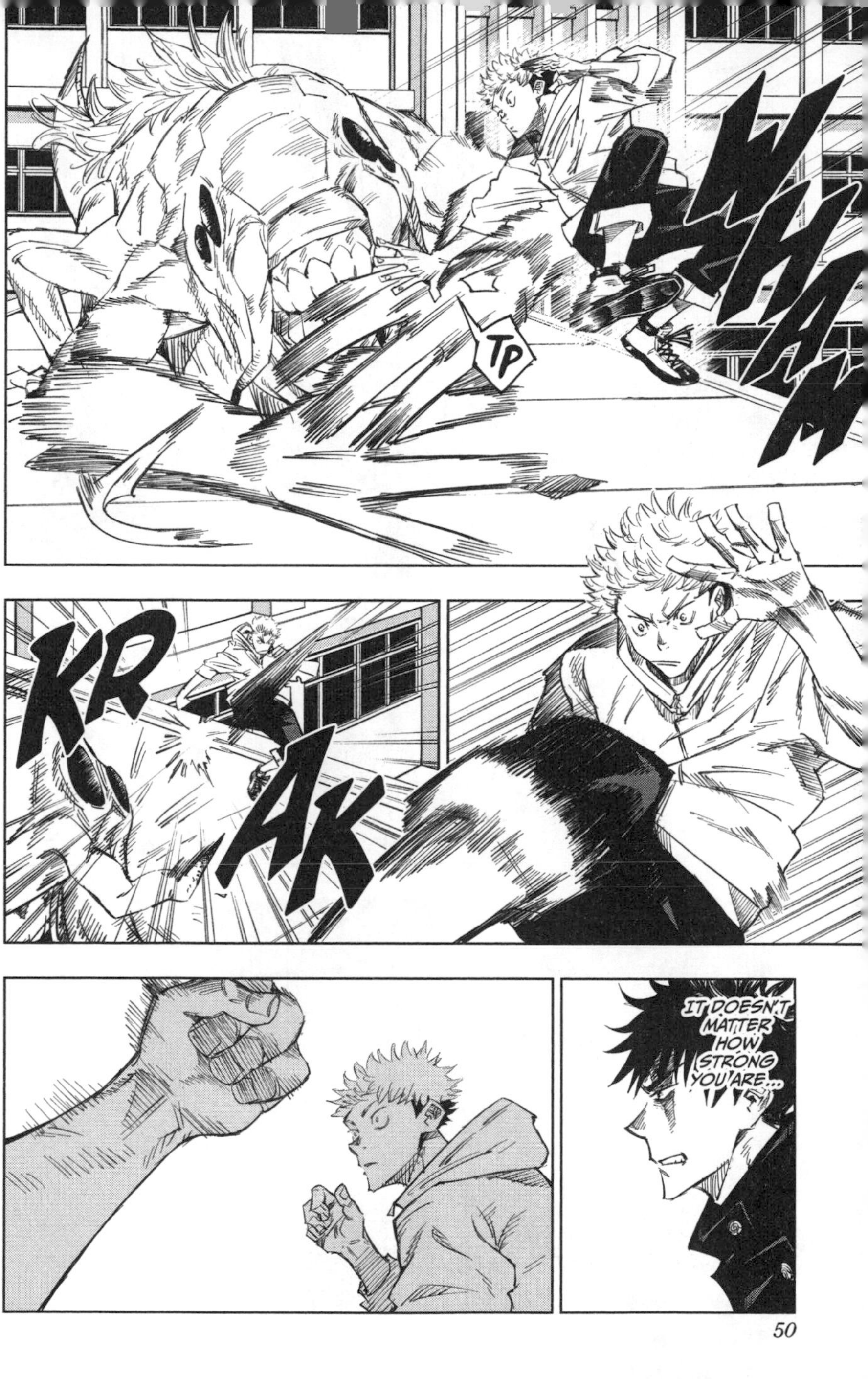
WHAM
TP
KRAK
IT DOESN'T MATTER HOW STRONG YOU ARE...

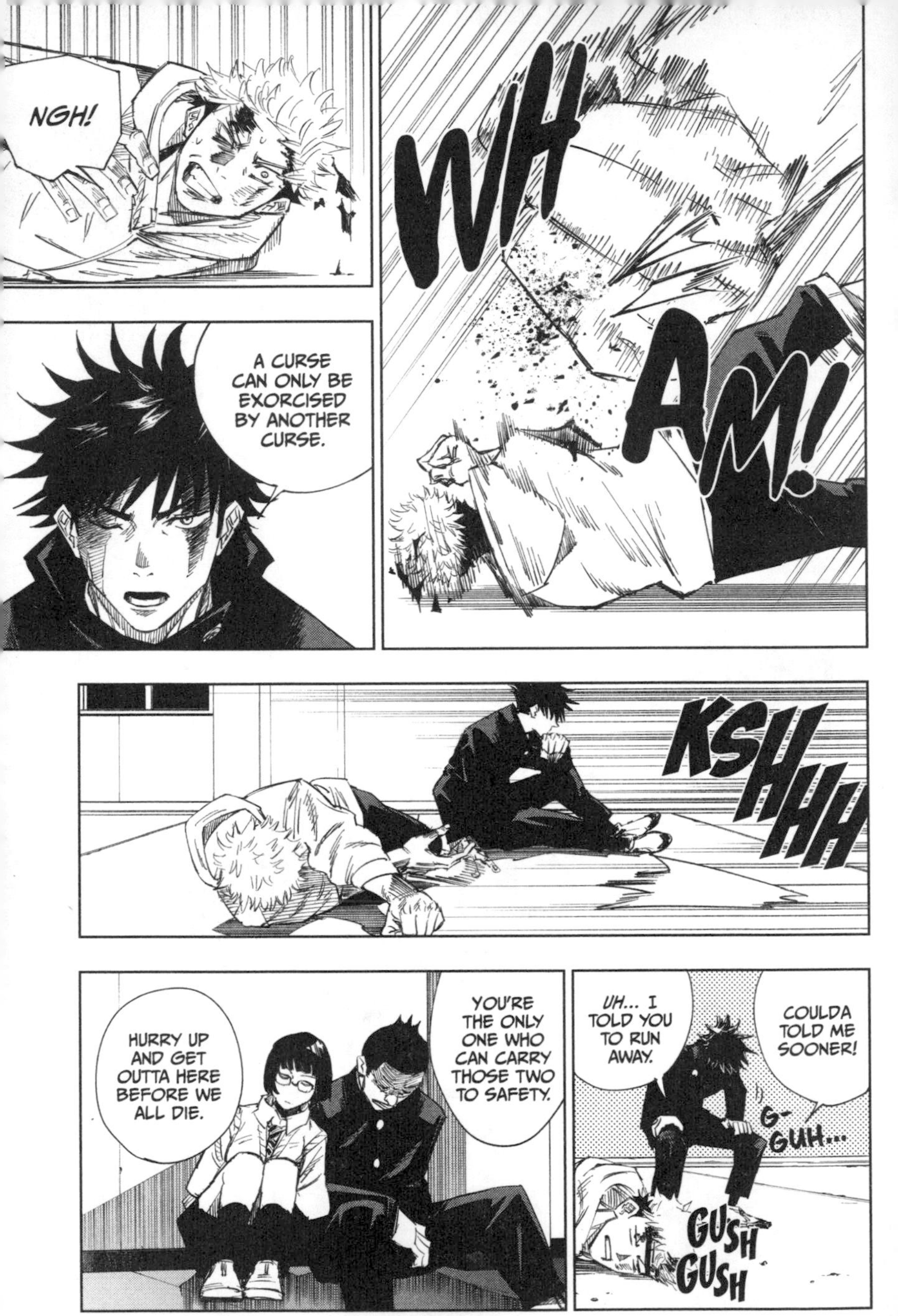
WHAM!
NGH!
A CURSE CAN ONLY BE EXORCISED BY ANOTHER CURSE.
KSHHHH
COULDA TOLD ME SOONER!
UH... I TOLD YOU TO RUN AWAY.
G-GUH...
GUSH GUSH
YOU'RE THE ONLY ONE WHO CAN CARRY THOSE TWO TO SAFETY.
HURRY UP AND GET OUTTA HERE BEFORE WE ALL DIE.

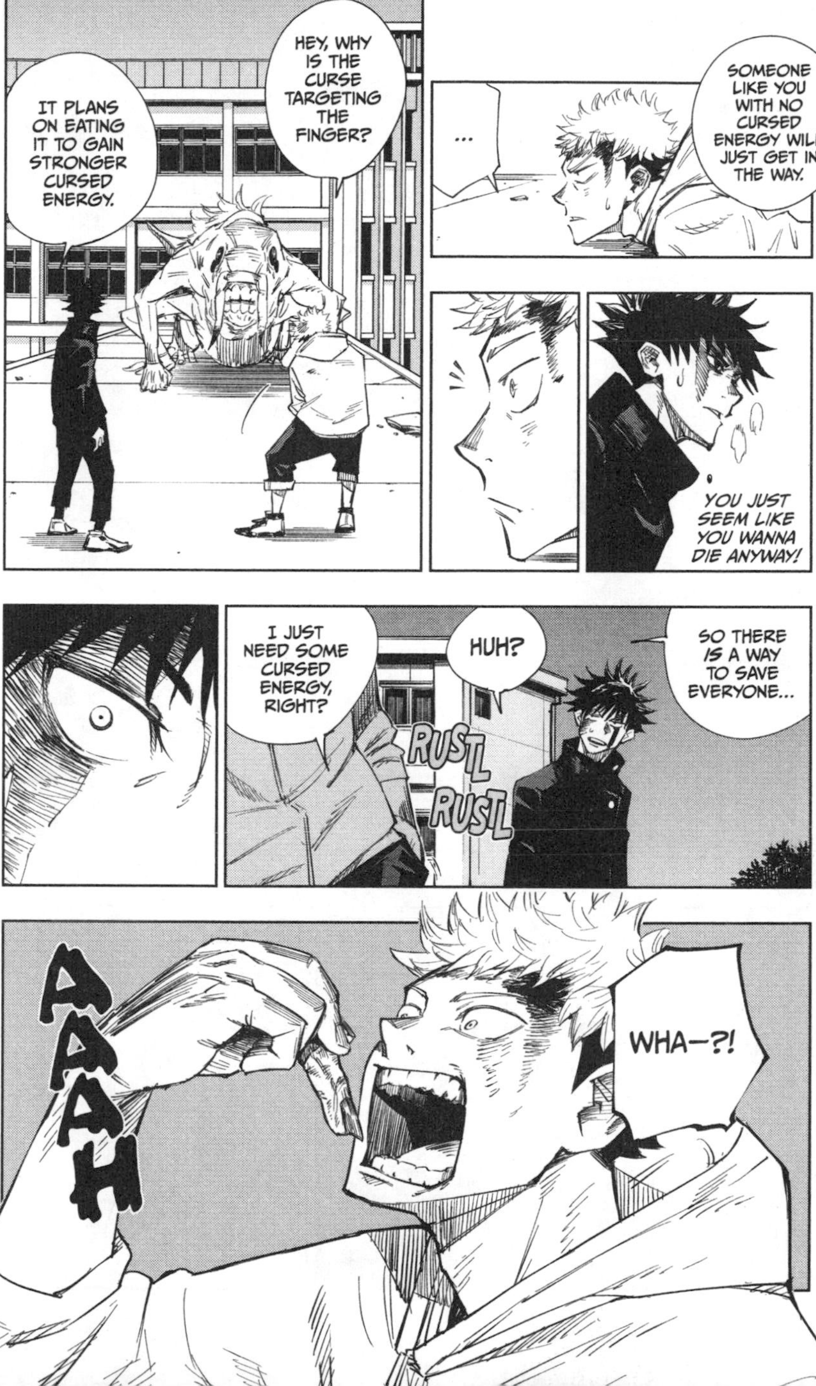
SOMEONE LIKE YOU WITH NO CURSED ENERGY WILL JUST GET IN THE WAY.
...
YOU JUST SEEM LIKE YOU WANNA DIE ANYWAY!
HEY, WHY IS THE CURSE TARGETING THE FINGER?
IT PLANS ON EATING IT TO GAIN STRONGER CURSED ENERGY.
SO THERE *IS* A WAY TO SAVE EVERYONE...
HUH?
I JUST NEED SOME CURSED ENERGY, RIGHT?
RUSTL
RUSTL
WHA-?!
AAAH

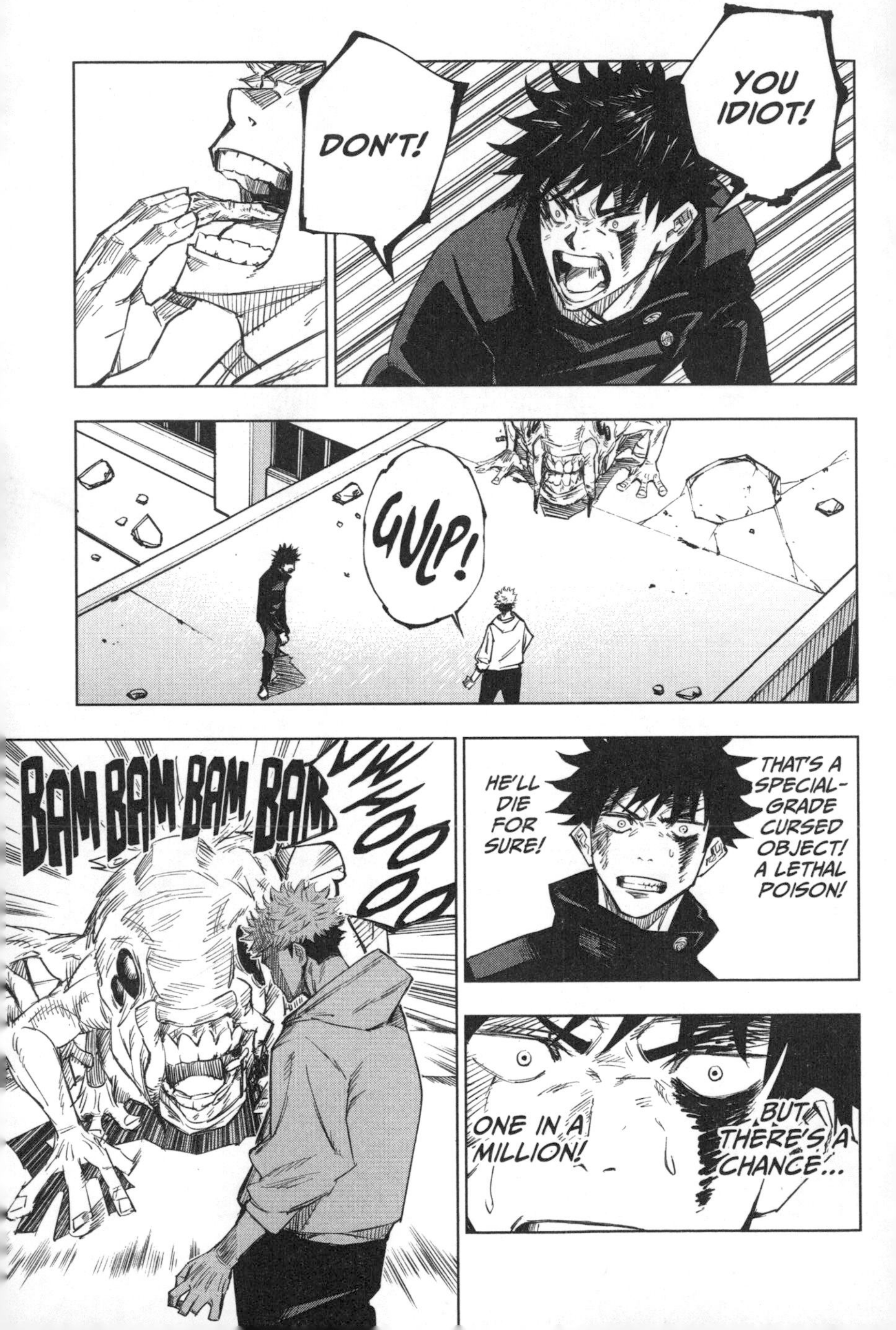
YOU IDIOT!
DON'T!
GULP!
THAT'S A SPECIAL-GRADE CURSED OBJECT! A LETHAL POISON!
HE'LL DIE FOR SURE!
BUT THERE'S A CHANCE...
ONE IN A MILLION!
BAM BAM BAM BAM
WHOOOOO

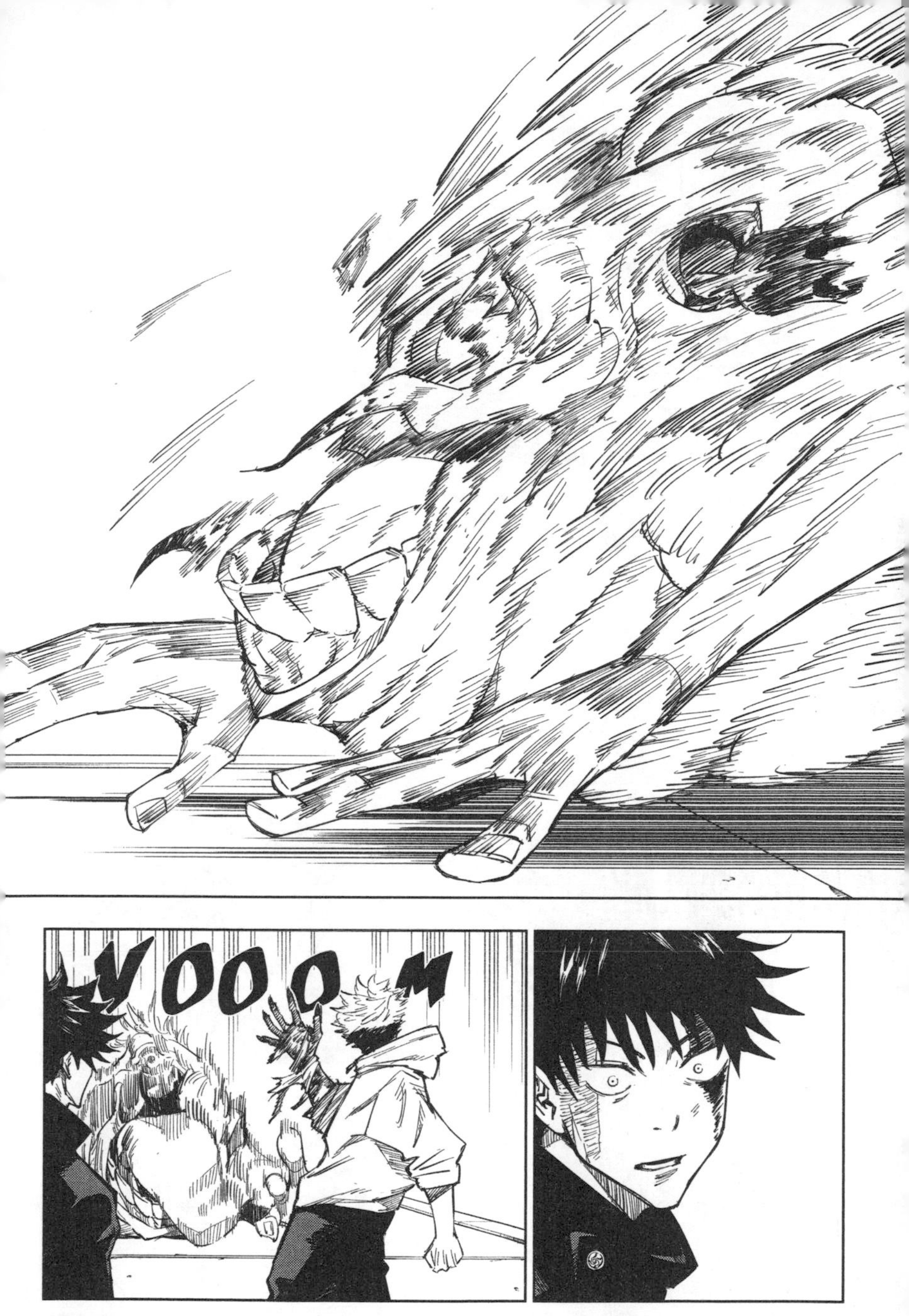
VOOOM

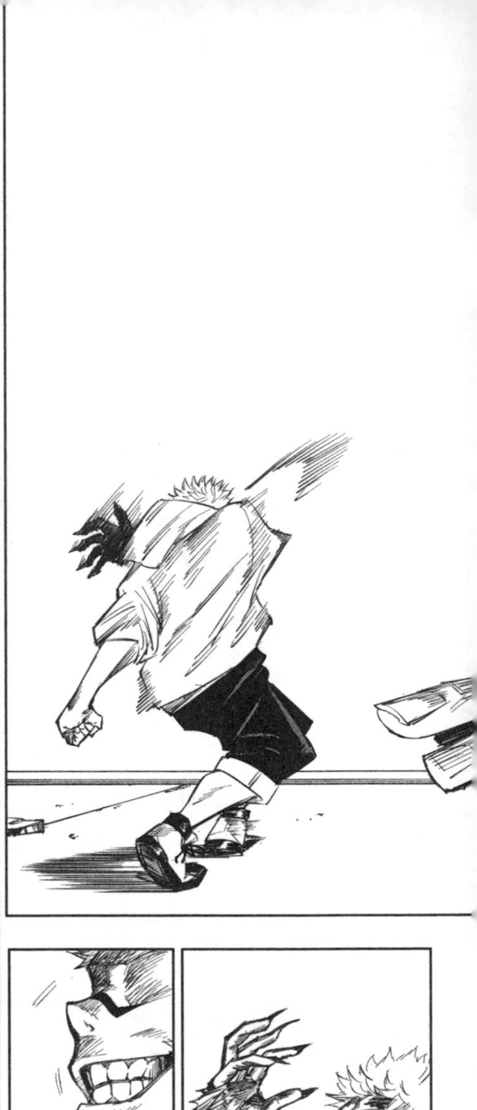
HEH ...
HEE HEE ...
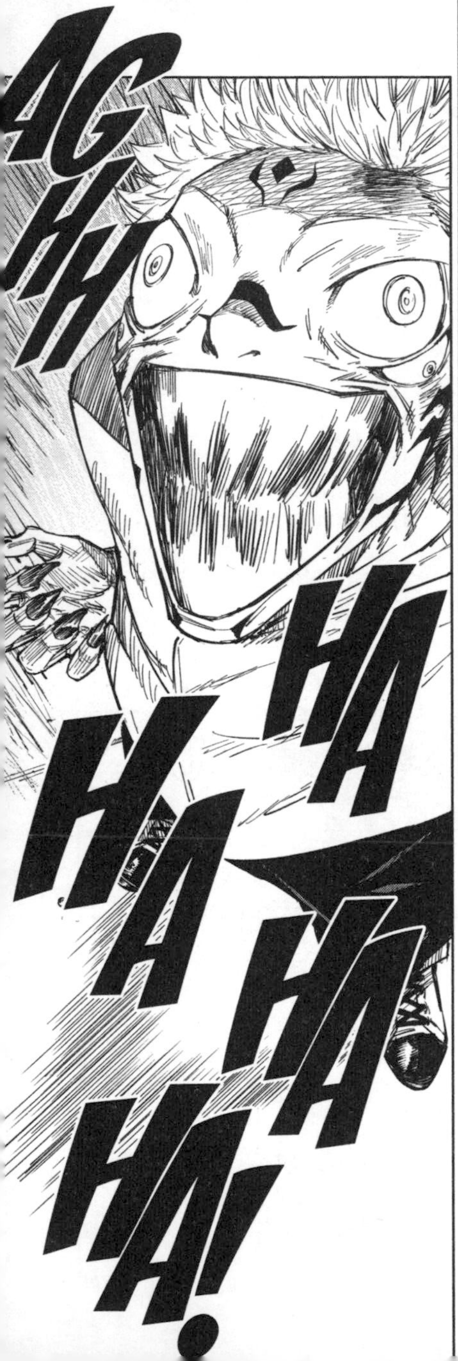
AGHH
HA HA HA HA HA!

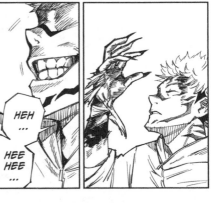

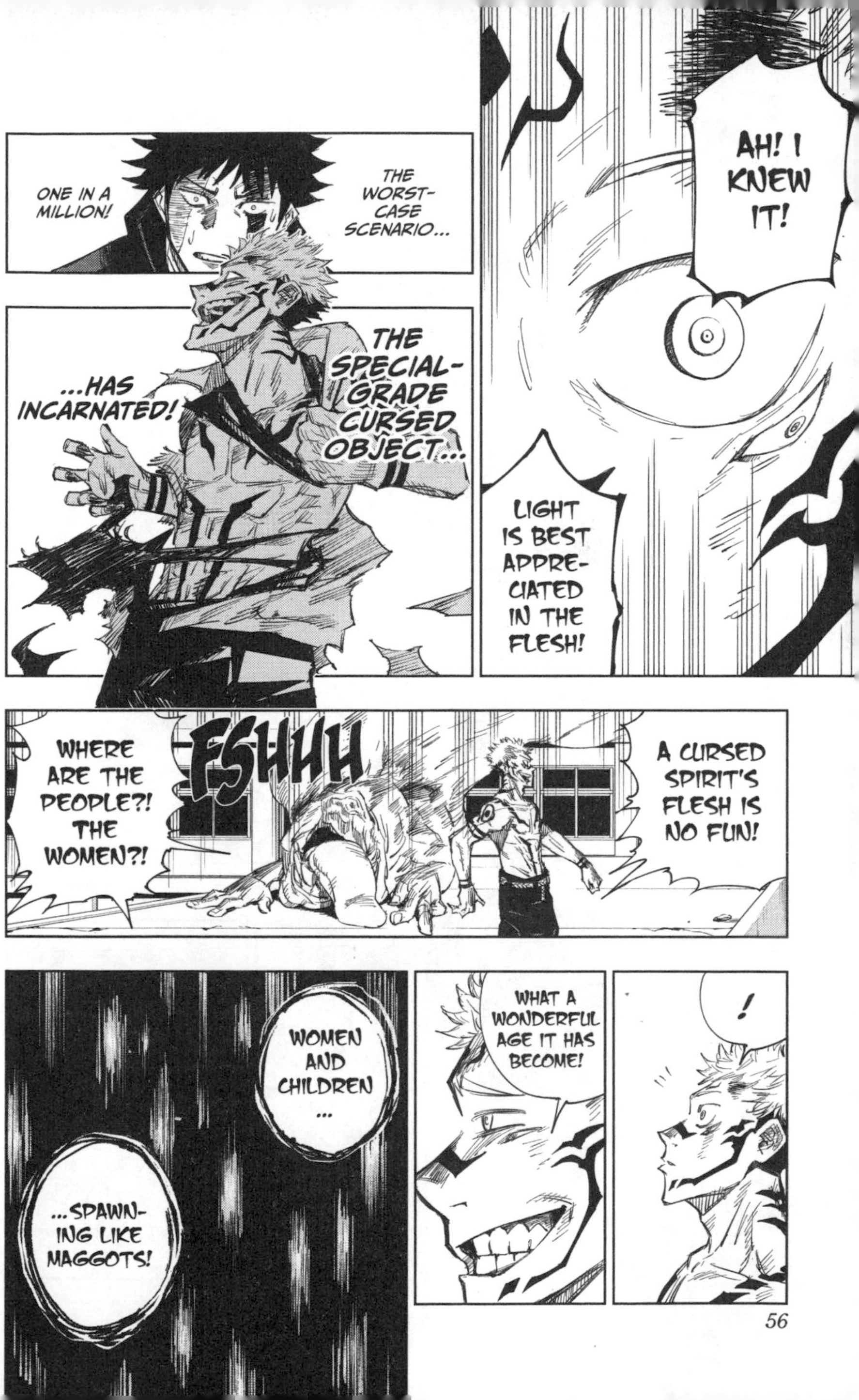
AH! I KNEW IT!
LIGHT IS BEST APPRE-CIATED IN THE FLESH!
THE WORST-CASE SCENARIO...
ONE IN A MILLION!
THE SPECIAL-GRADE CURSED OBJECT...
...HAS INCARNATED!
A CURSED SPIRIT'S FLESH IS NO FUN!
FSHHH
WHERE ARE THE PEOPLE?! THE WOMEN?!
!
WHAT A WONDERFUL AGE IT HAS BECOME!
WOMEN AND CHILDREN ...
...SPAWN-ING LIKE MAGGOTS!

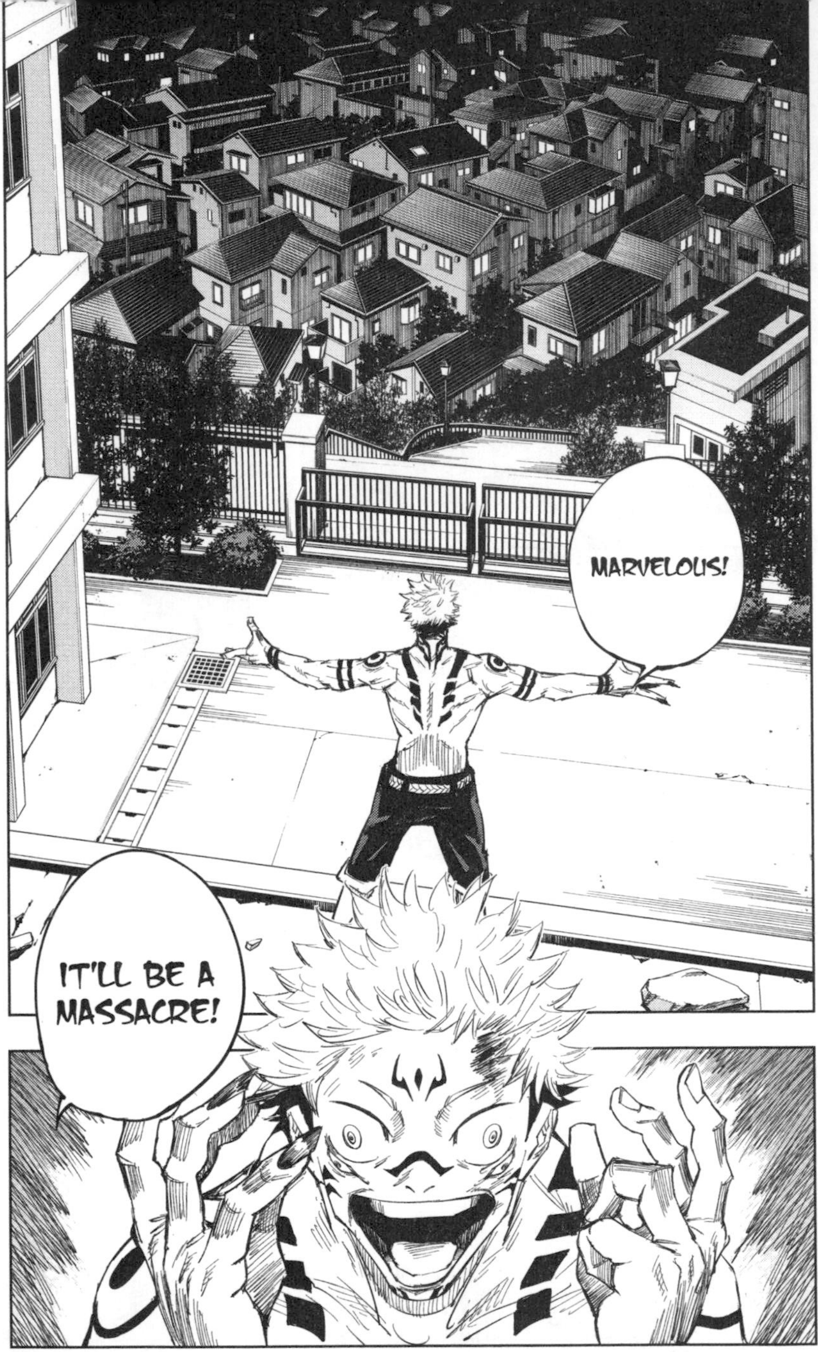
MARVELOUS!
IT'LL BE A MASSACRE!

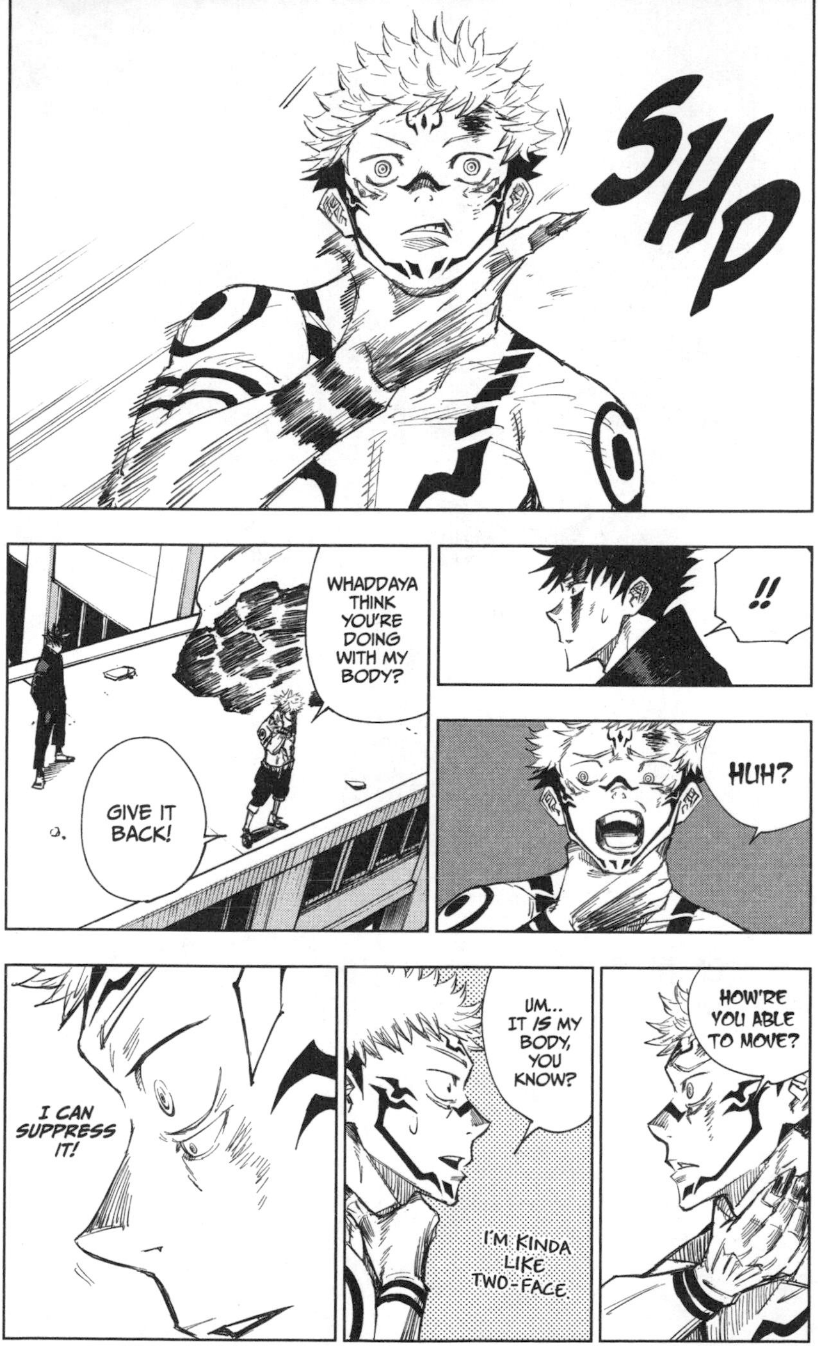
SHP
!!
HUH?
WHADDAYA THINK YOU'RE DOING WITH MY BODY?
GIVE IT BACK!
HOW'RE YOU ABLE TO MOVE?
UM... IT IS MY BODY, YOU KNOW?
I'M KINDA LIKE TWO-FACE.
I CAN SUPPRESS IT!

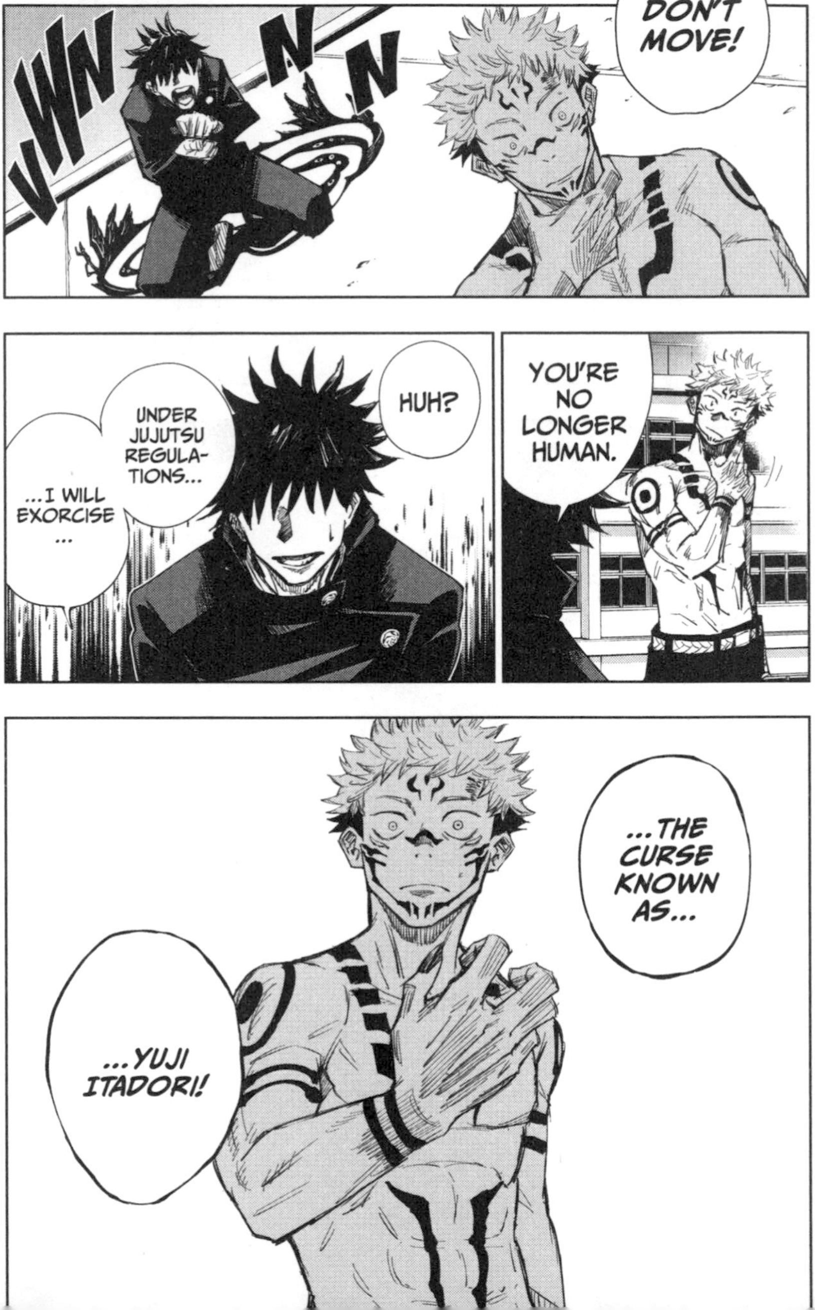
DON'T MOVE!
VWNNN
YOU'RE NO LONGER HUMAN.
HUH?
UNDER JUJUTSU REGULATIONS...
...I WILL EXORCISE ...
...THE CURSE KNOWN AS...
...YUJI ITADORI!

YUJI ITADORI

• He's 173 centimeters tall and will probably keep growing.

• He's actually heavy and weighs about 80 kilograms, but his body fat percentage is in the single digits.

• He loves TV.

• He has a huge repertoire of half-cocked impersonations.

• He isn't picky with food. (After all, he ate a finger!)

• He's not really a hoodie guy. He just wears it because he can be indecisive.

Chapter 2: Secret Execution

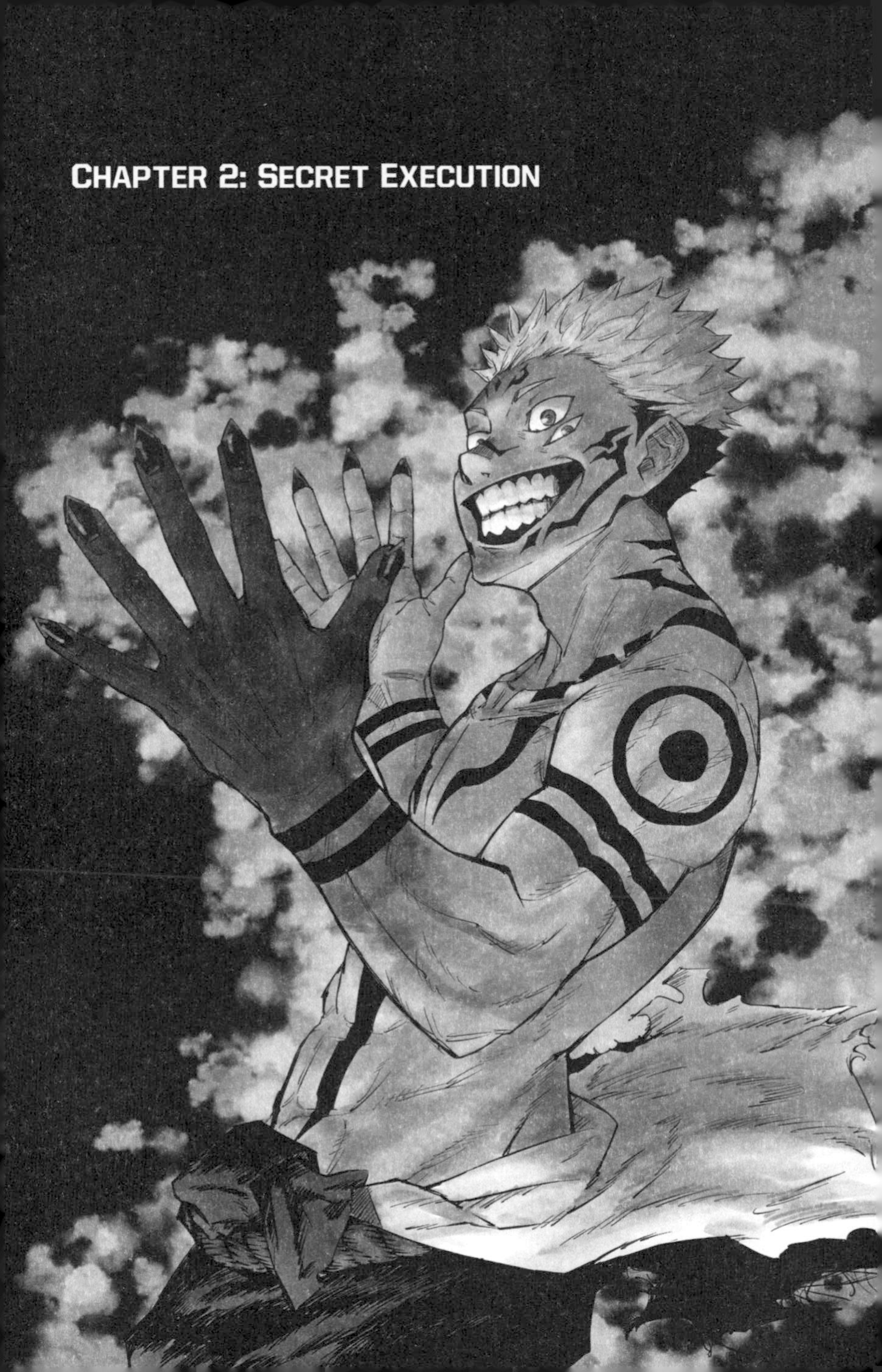

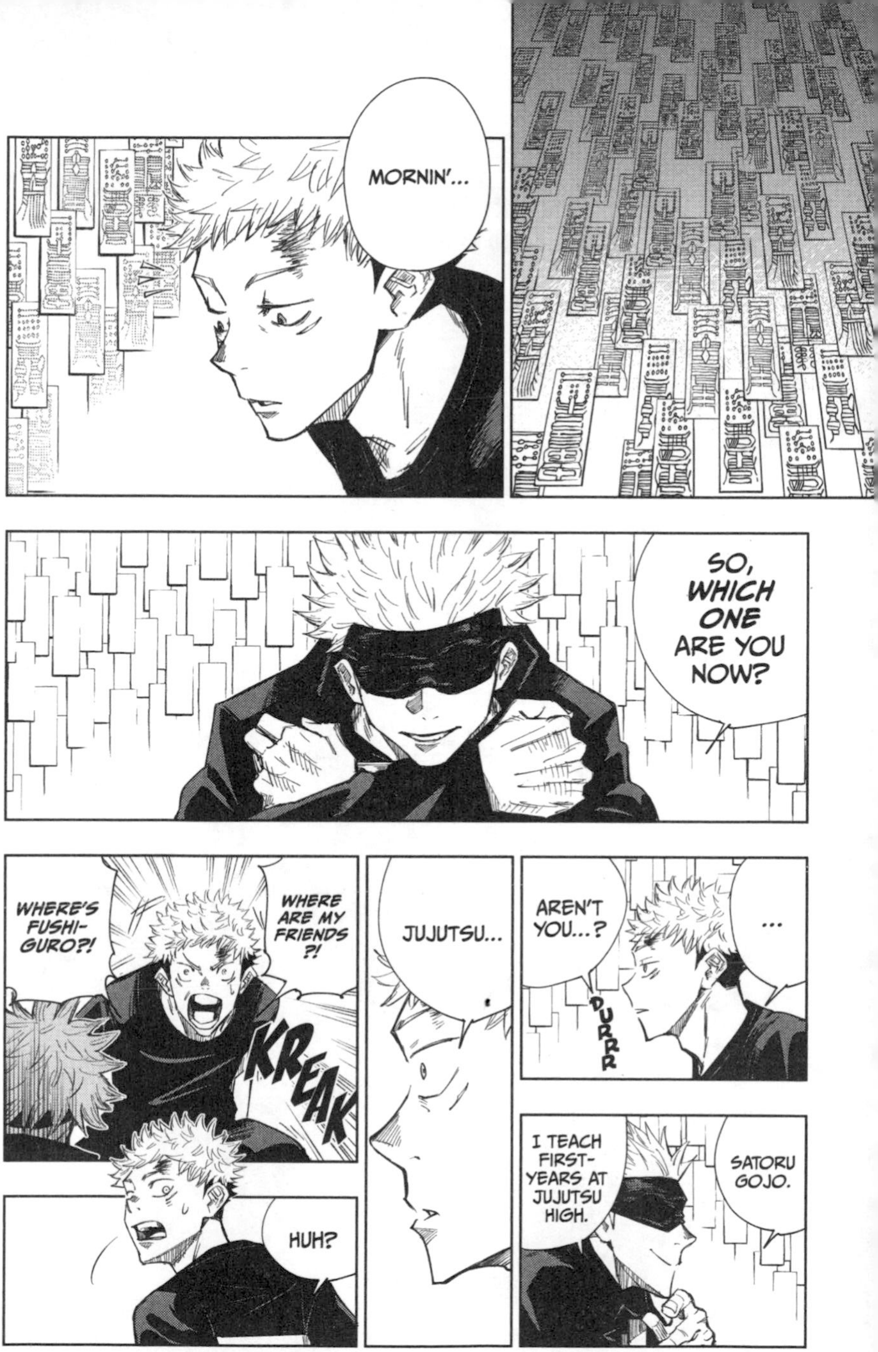
MORNIN'...
SO, WHICH ONE ARE YOU NOW?
...
AREN'T YOU...?
DURRR
SATORU GOJO.
I TEACH FIRST-YEARS AT JUJUTSU HIGH.
JUJUTSU...
WHERE ARE MY FRIENDS?!
WHERE'S FUSHIGURO?!
KREAK
HUH?

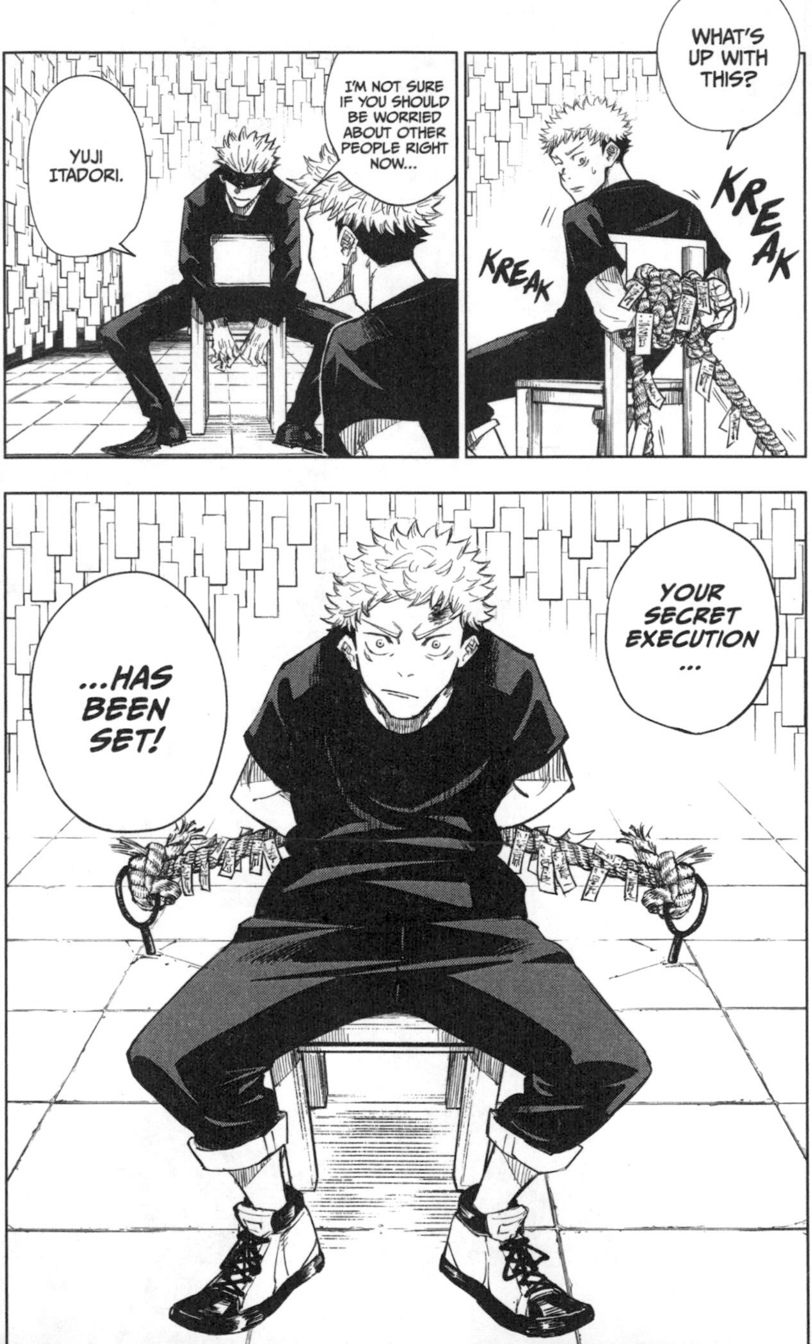
WHAT'S UP WITH THIS?
KREAK
KREAK
I'M NOT SURE IF YOU SHOULD BE WORRIED ABOUT OTHER PEOPLE RIGHT NOW...
YUJI ITADORI.
YOUR SECRET EXECUTION ...
...HAS BEEN SET!

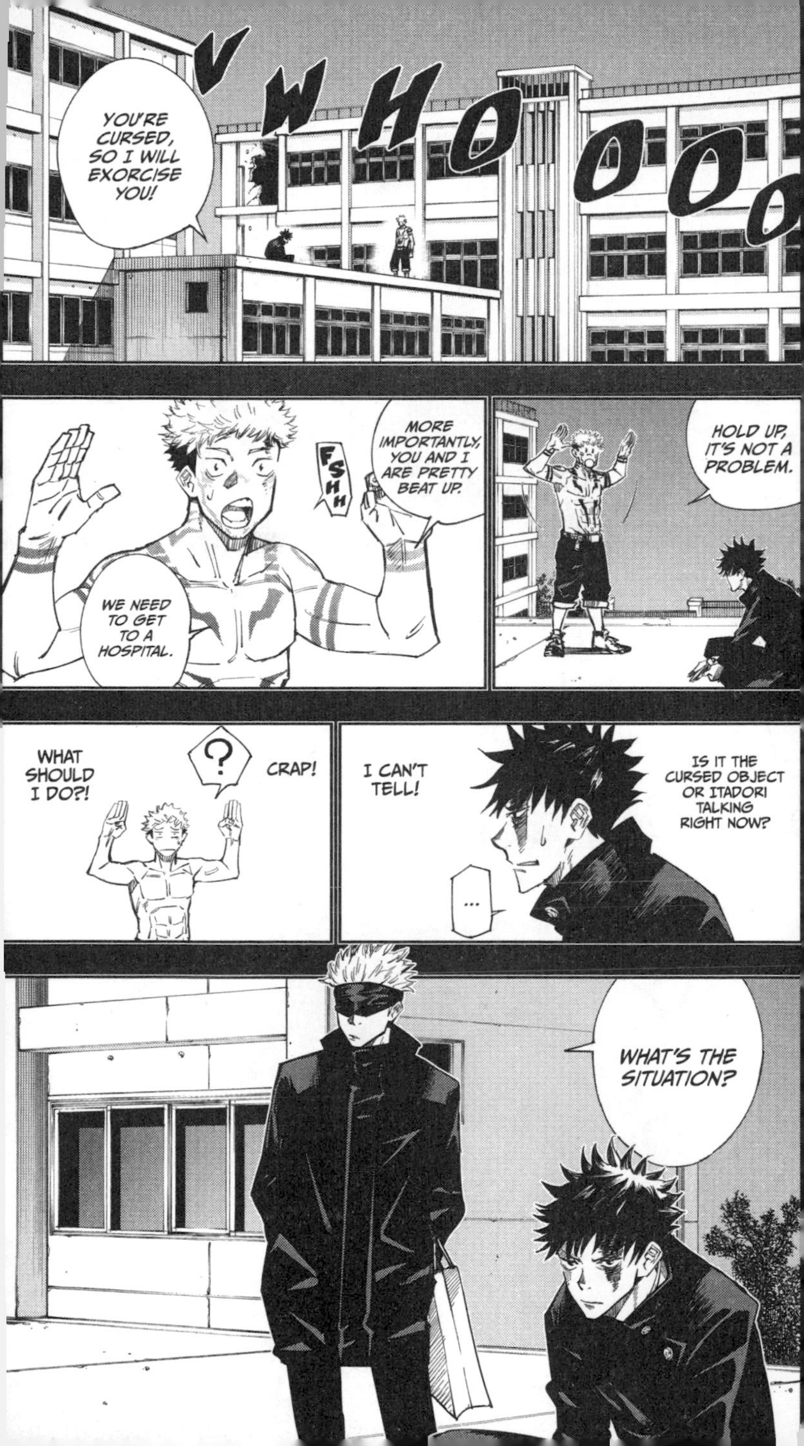
VWHOOOO
YOU'RE CURSED, SO I WILL EXORCISE YOU!
HOLD UP, IT'S NOT A PROBLEM.
MORE IMPORTANTLY, YOU AND I ARE PRETTY BEAT UP.
FSHH
WE NEED TO GET TO A HOSPITAL.
IS IT THE CURSED OBJECT OR ITADORI TALKING RIGHT NOW?
I CAN'T TELL!
...
CRAP!
?
WHAT SHOULD I DO?!
WHAT'S THE SITUATION?

WHAT'RE YOU DOING HERE?!

GOJO SENSEI!

WHA—?!

YO!

...BUT THE HIGHER-UPS GOT INVOLVED AFTER HEARING THAT A SPECIAL-GRADE CURSED OBJECT WENT MISSING.

I AGREED TO COME AS LONG AS THEY ALSO GAVE ME TIME TO SEE THE SIGHTS.

MAN, YOU'RE REALLY MESSED UP.

I WASN'T GONNA COME AT FIRST...

I SHOULD SHOW ALL THE SECOND-YEARS...

KLIK

GRR...

SORRY...

I ATE IT.

DID YOU FIND IT?

SO...

...

UM...

Snf

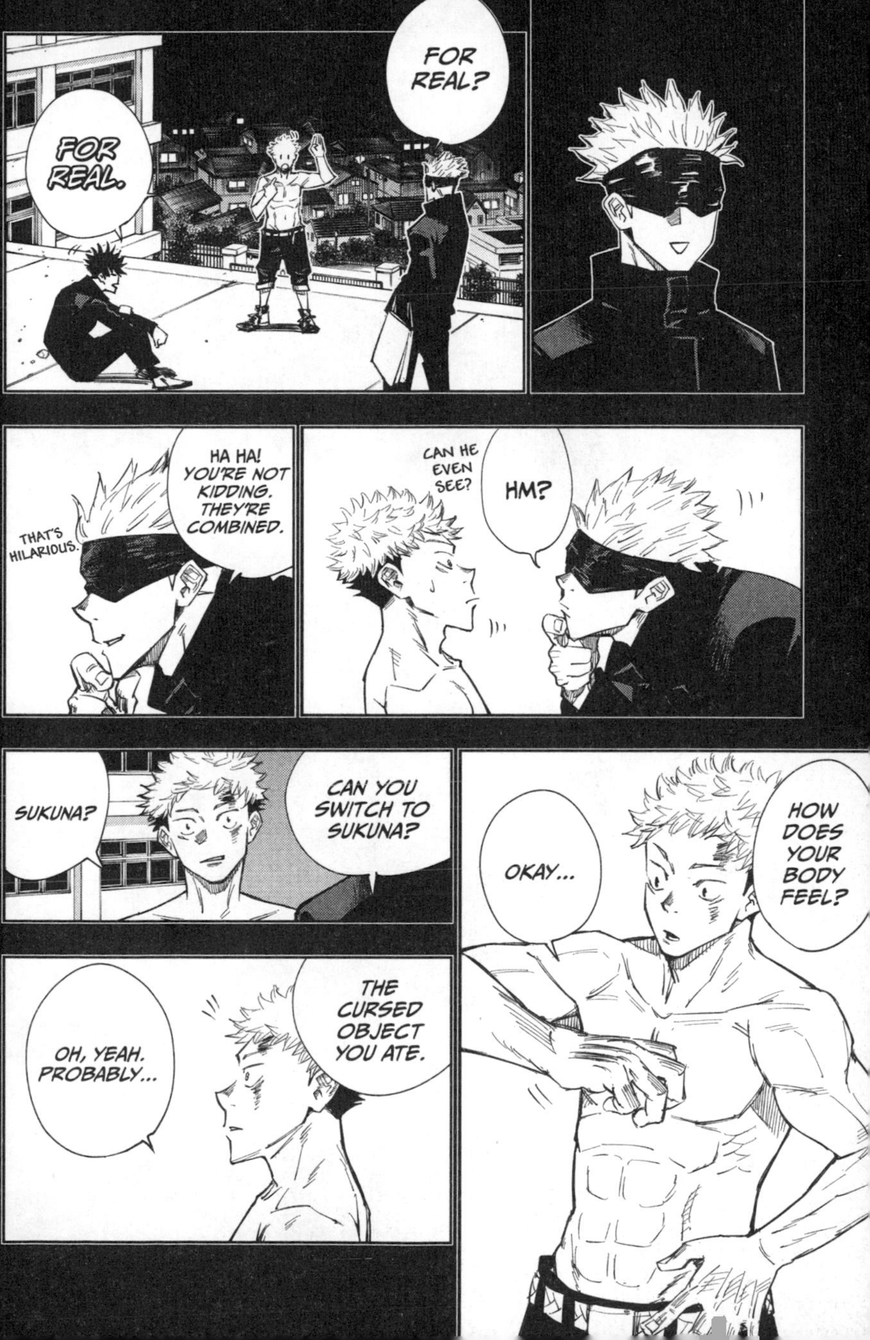
FOR REAL?
FOR REAL.
CAN HE EVEN SEE?
HM?
HA HA! YOU'RE NOT KIDDING. THEY'RE COMBINED.
THAT'S HILARIOUS.
HOW DOES YOUR BODY FEEL?
OKAY...
CAN YOU SWITCH TO SUKUNA?
SUKUNA?
THE CURSED OBJECT YOU ATE.
OH, YEAH. PROBABLY...

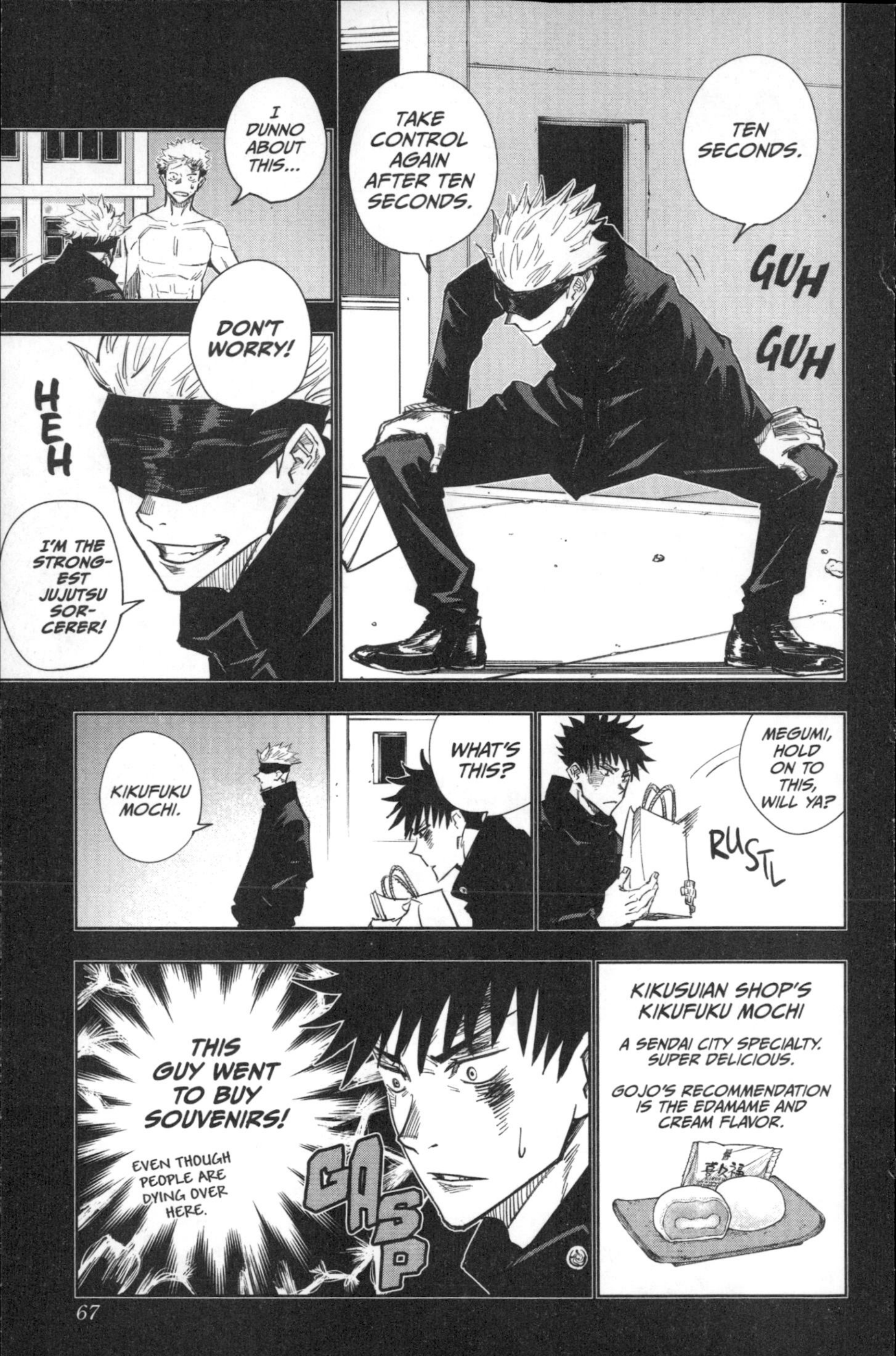
TEN SECONDS.
TAKE CONTROL AGAIN AFTER TEN SECONDS.
GUH GUH
I DUNNO ABOUT THIS...
DON'T WORRY!
HEH
I'M THE STRONG-EST JUJUTSU SOR-CERER!
MEGUMI, HOLD ON TO THIS, WILL YA?
RUSTL
WHAT'S THIS?
KIKUFUKU MOCHI.
KIKUSUIAN SHOP'S KIKUFUKU MOCHI
A SENDAI CITY SPECIALTY. SUPER DELICIOUS.
GOJO'S RECOMMENDATION IS THE EDAMAME AND CREAM FLAVOR.
THIS GUY WENT TO BUY SOUVENIRS!
EVEN THOUGH PEOPLE ARE DYING OVER HERE.
GASP

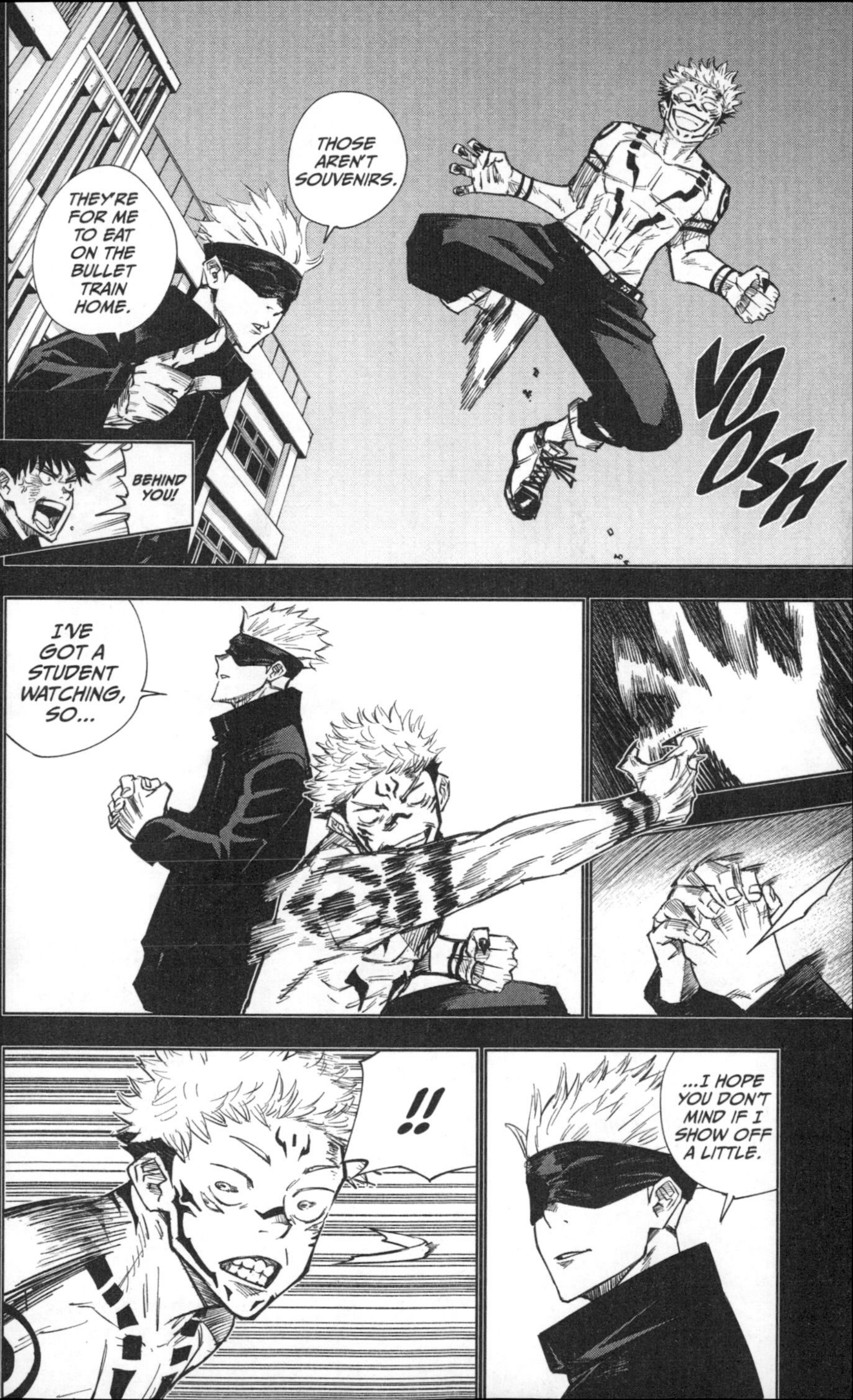
THOSE AREN'T SOUVENIRS.
THEY'RE FOR ME TO EAT ON THE BULLET TRAIN HOME.
VOOSH
BEHIND YOU!
I'VE GOT A STUDENT WATCHING, SO...
...I HOPE YOU DON'T MIND IF I SHOW OFF A LITTLE.
!!

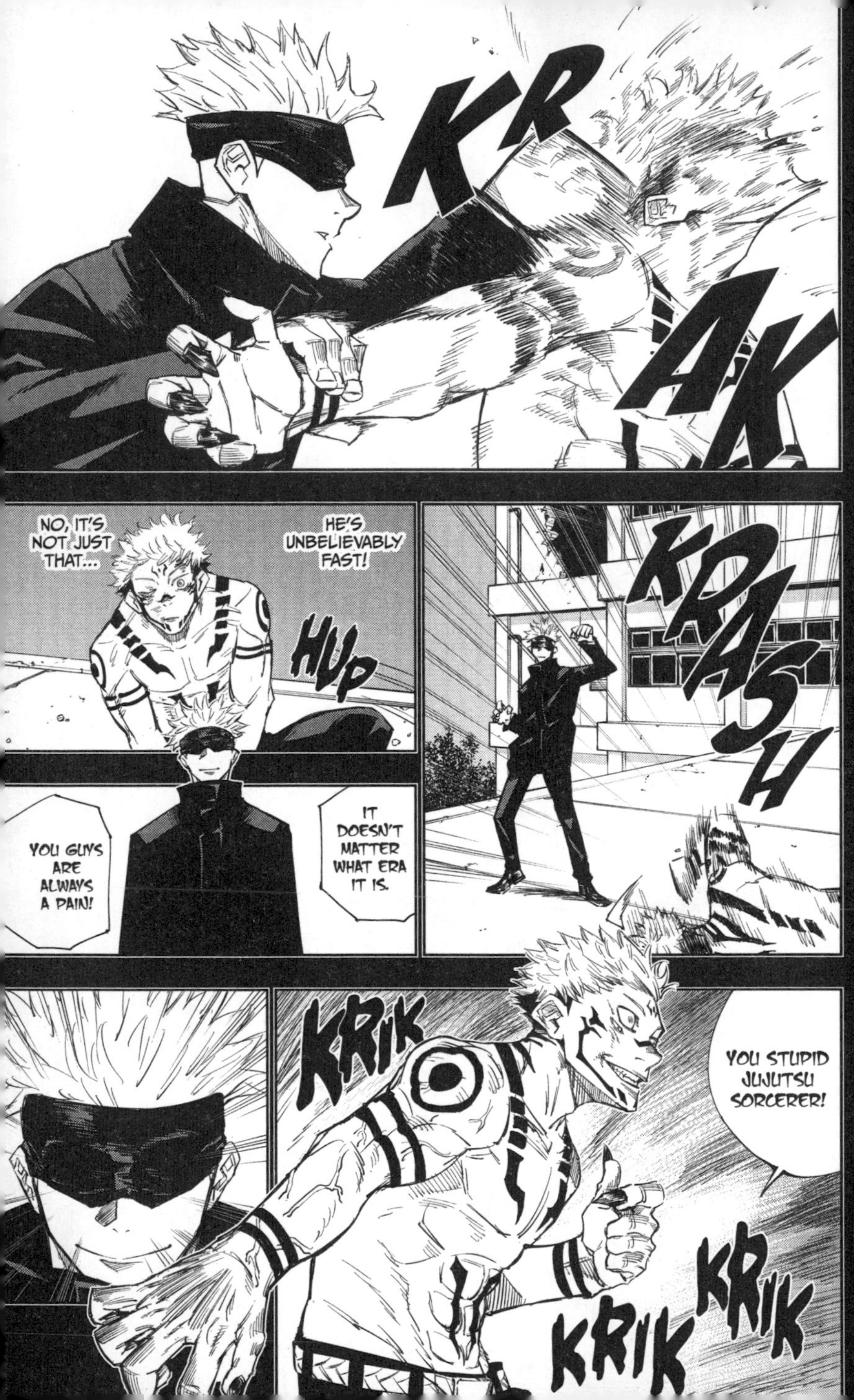
KR
AK
KRASH
HE'S UNBELIEVABLY FAST!
NO, IT'S NOT JUST THAT...
HUP
IT DOESN'T MATTER WHAT ERA IT IS.
YOU GUYS ARE ALWAYS A PAIN!
YOU STUPID JUJUTSU SORCERER!
KRIK
KRIK
KRIK

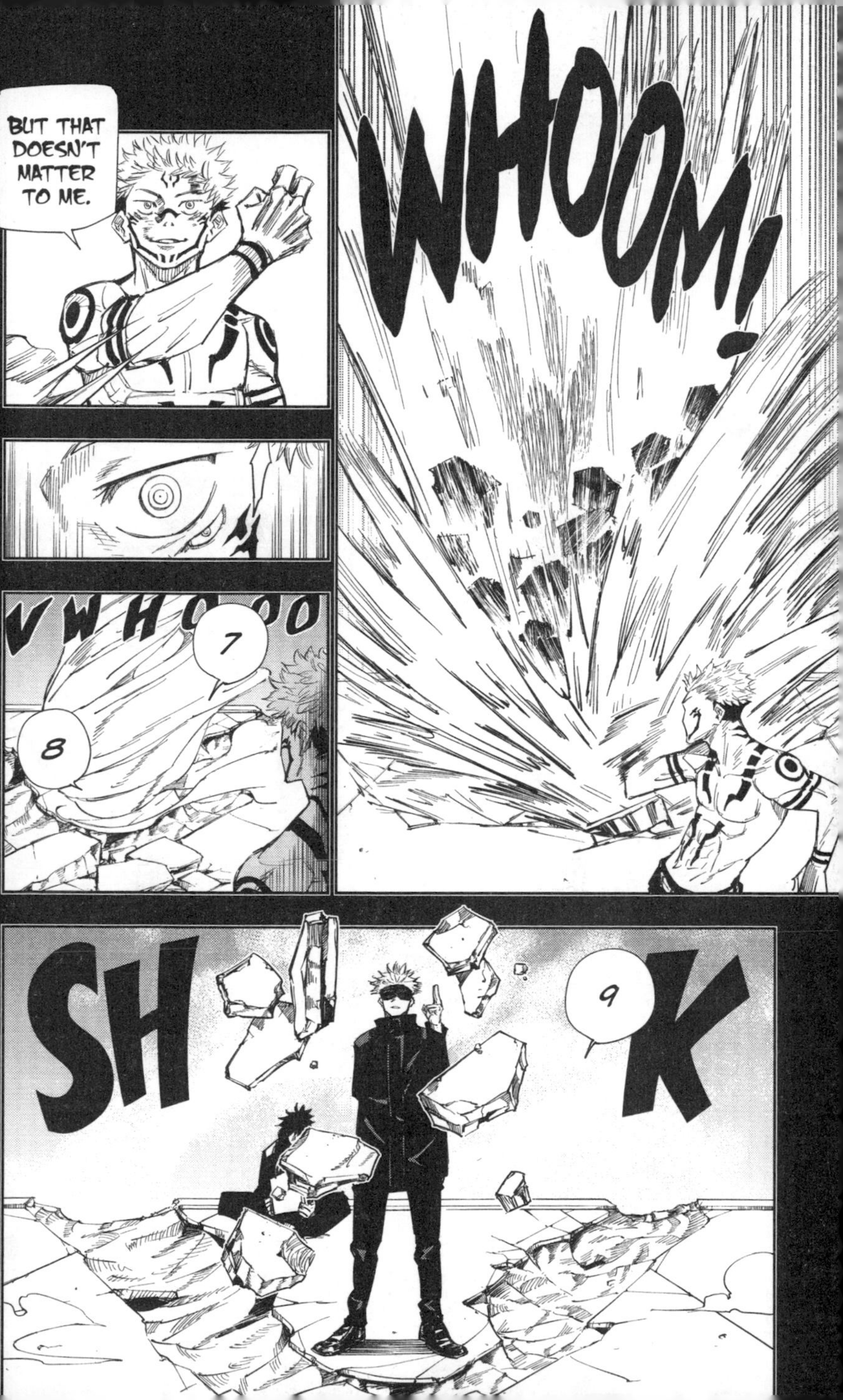
WHOOM!
BUT THAT DOESN'T MATTER TO ME.
VWHOOO
7
8
SH
K
9

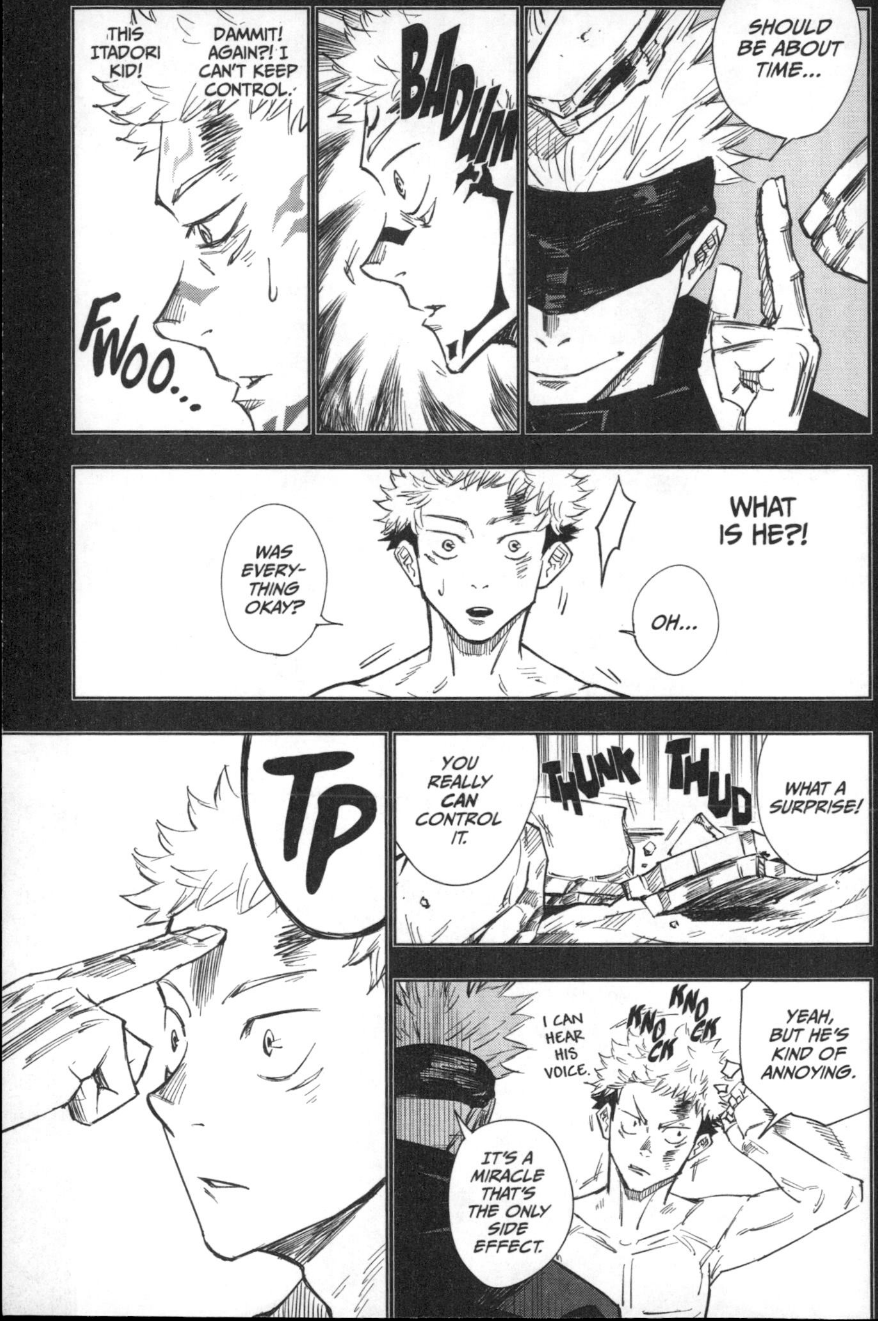
SHOULD BE ABOUT TIME...
BADUM
DAMMIT! AGAIN?! I CAN'T KEEP CONTROL.
THIS ITADORI KID!
FWOO...
WHAT IS HE?!
OH...
WAS EVERYTHING OKAY?
WHAT A SURPRISE!
THUD
THUNK
YOU REALLY CAN CONTROL IT.
YEAH, BUT HE'S KIND OF ANNOYING.
KNOCK KNOCK
I CAN HEAR HIS VOICE.
IT'S A MIRACLE THAT'S THE ONLY SIDE EFFECT.
TP

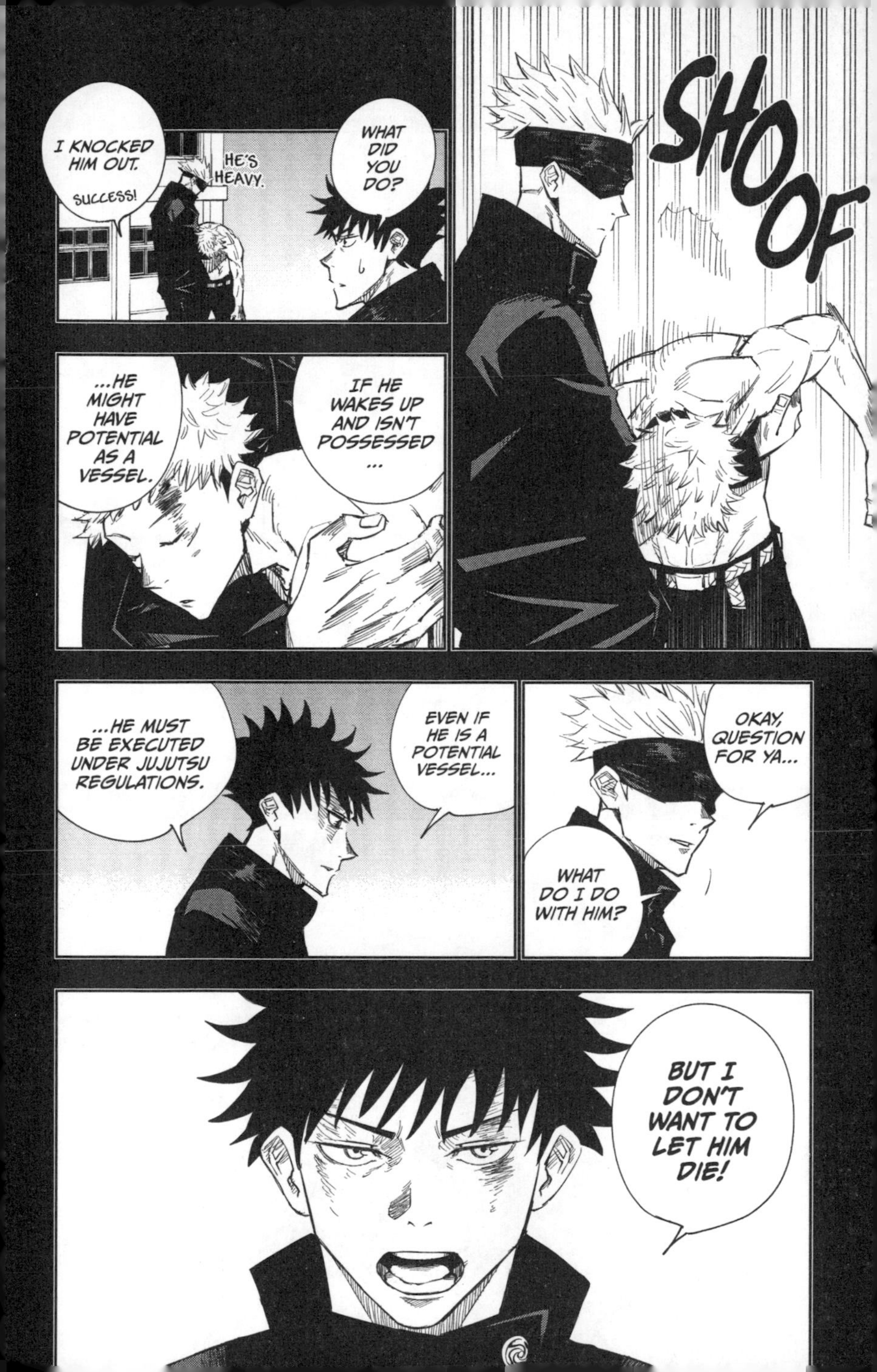
SHOOF
WHAT DID YOU DO?
I KNOCKED HIM OUT.
SUCCESS!
HE'S HEAVY.
IF HE WAKES UP AND ISN'T POSSESSED...
...HE MIGHT HAVE POTENTIAL AS A VESSEL.
OKAY, QUESTION FOR YA...
WHAT DO I DO WITH HIM?
EVEN IF HE IS A POTENTIAL VESSEL...
...HE MUST BE EXECUTED UNDER JUJUTSU REGULATIONS.
BUT I DON'T WANT TO LET HIM DIE!

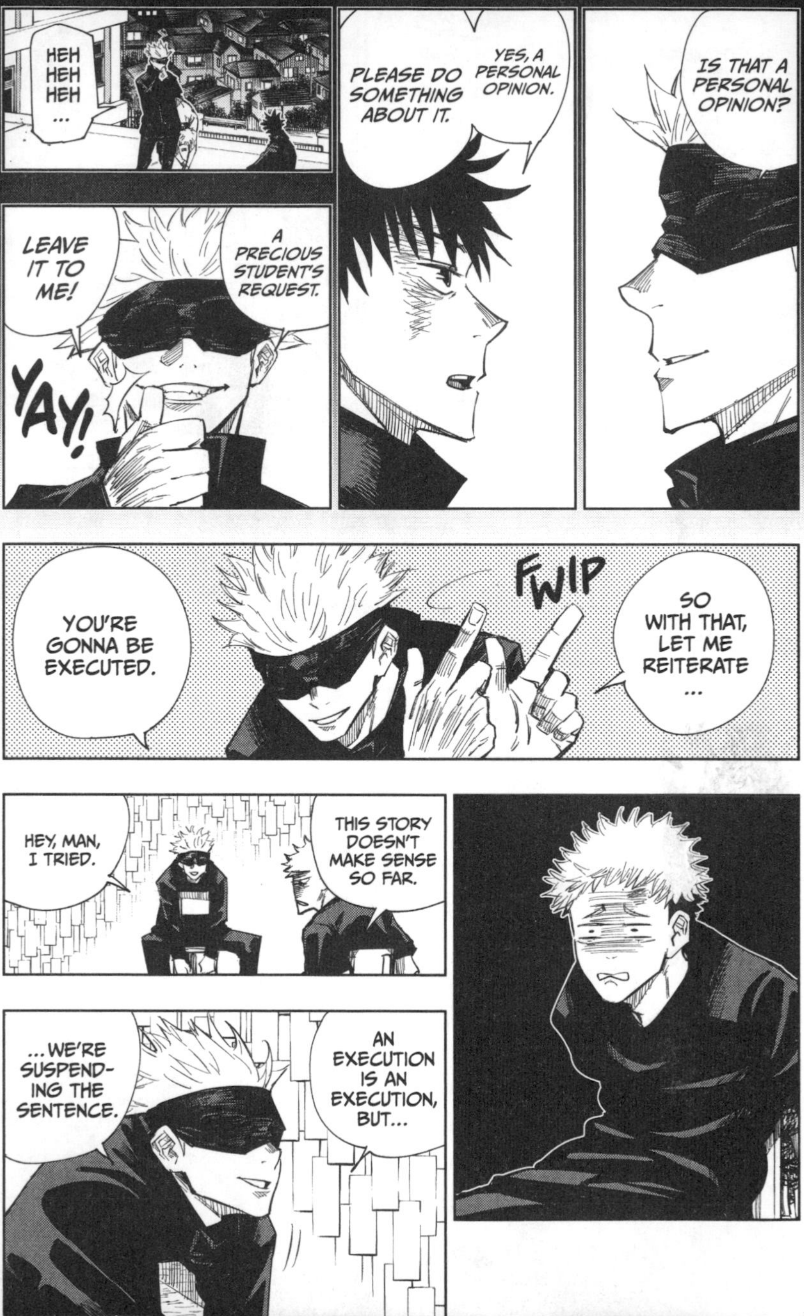
IS THAT A PERSONAL OPINION?
YES, A PERSONAL OPINION.
PLEASE DO SOMETHING ABOUT IT.
HEH HEH HEH ...
A PRECIOUS STUDENT'S REQUEST.
LEAVE IT TO ME!
YAY!
FWIP
SO WITH THAT, LET ME REITERATE ...
YOU'RE GONNA BE EXECUTED.
THIS STORY DOESN'T MAKE SENSE SO FAR.
HEY, MAN, I TRIED.
AN EXECUTION IS AN EXECUTION, BUT...
...WE'RE SUSPEND-ING THE SENTENCE.

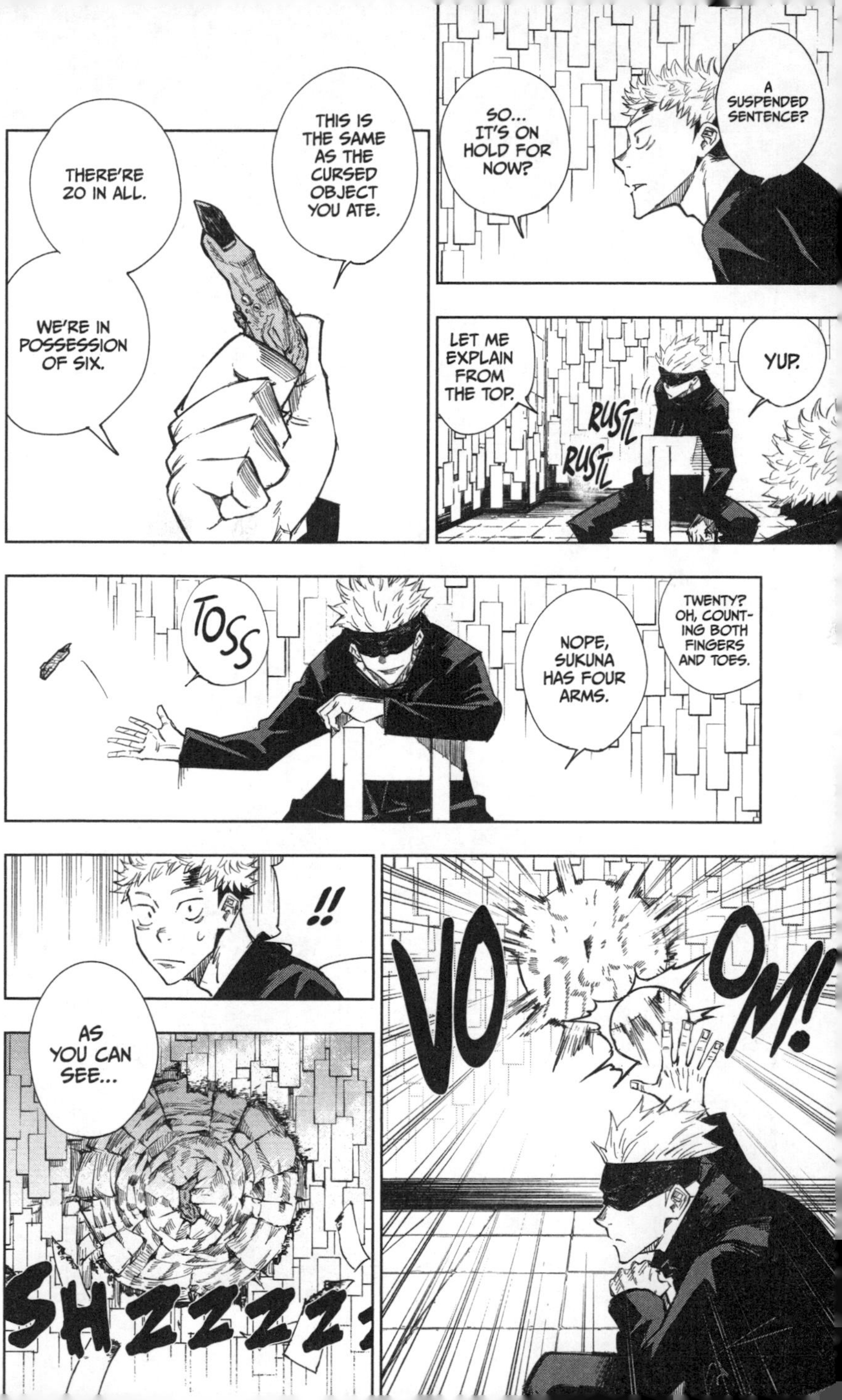
A SUSPENDED SENTENCE?
SO... IT'S ON HOLD FOR NOW?
YUP.
LET ME EXPLAIN FROM THE TOP.
RUSTL
RUSTL
THIS IS THE SAME AS THE CURSED OBJECT YOU ATE.
THERE'RE 20 IN ALL.
WE'RE IN POSSESSION OF SIX.
TWENTY? OH, COUNTING BOTH FINGERS AND TOES.
NOPE, SUKUNA HAS FOUR ARMS.
TOSS
VOOM!
!!
AS YOU CAN SEE...
SHZZZZZ

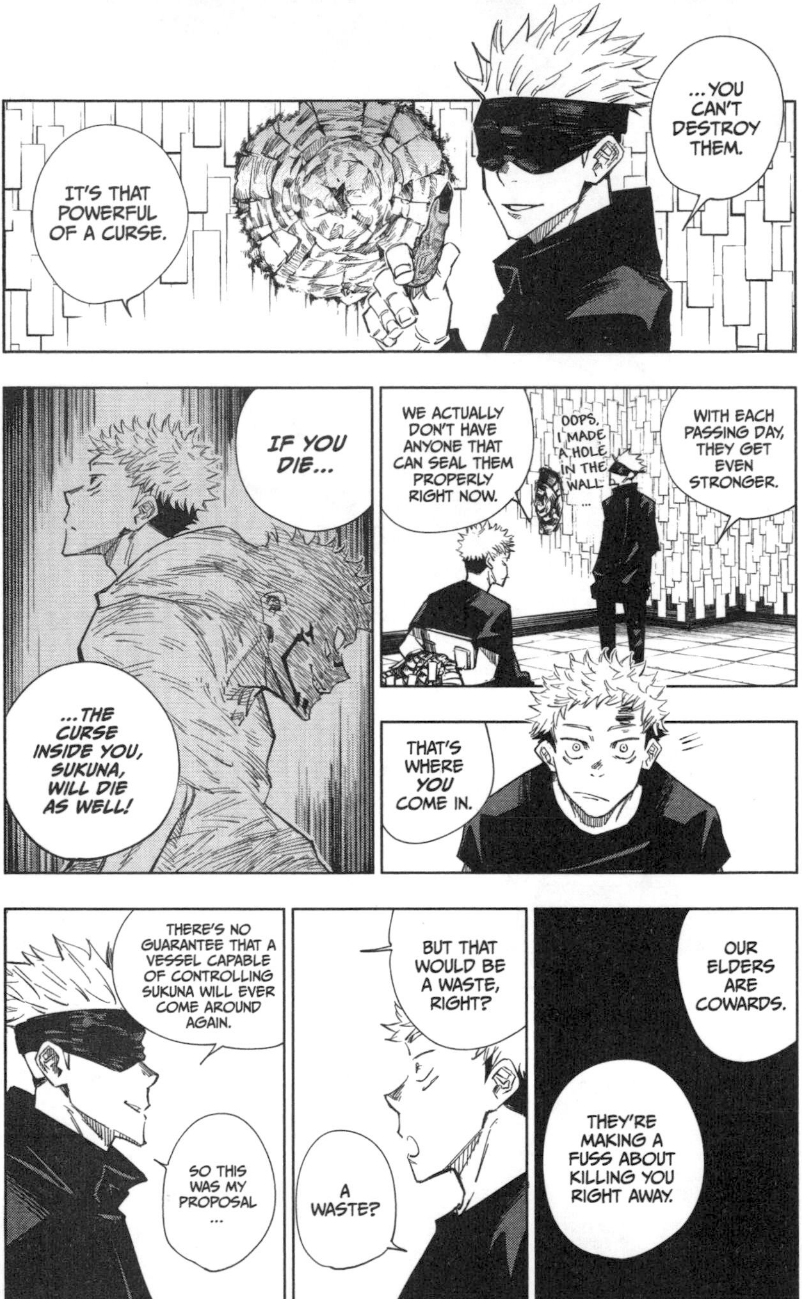
...YOU CAN'T DESTROY THEM.
IT'S THAT POWERFUL OF A CURSE.
WITH EACH PASSING DAY, THEY GET EVEN STRONGER.
OOPS, I MADE A HOLE IN THE WALL ...
WE ACTUALLY DON'T HAVE ANYONE THAT CAN SEAL THEM PROPERLY RIGHT NOW.
THAT'S WHERE YOU COME IN.
IF YOU DIE...
...THE CURSE INSIDE YOU, SUKUNA, WILL DIE AS WELL!
OUR ELDERS ARE COWARDS.
THEY'RE MAKING A FUSS ABOUT KILLING YOU RIGHT AWAY.
BUT THAT WOULD BE A WASTE, RIGHT?
A WASTE?
THERE'S NO GUARANTEE THAT A VESSEL CAPABLE OF CONTROLLING SUKUNA WILL EVER COME AROUND AGAIN.
SO THIS WAS MY PROPOSAL ...

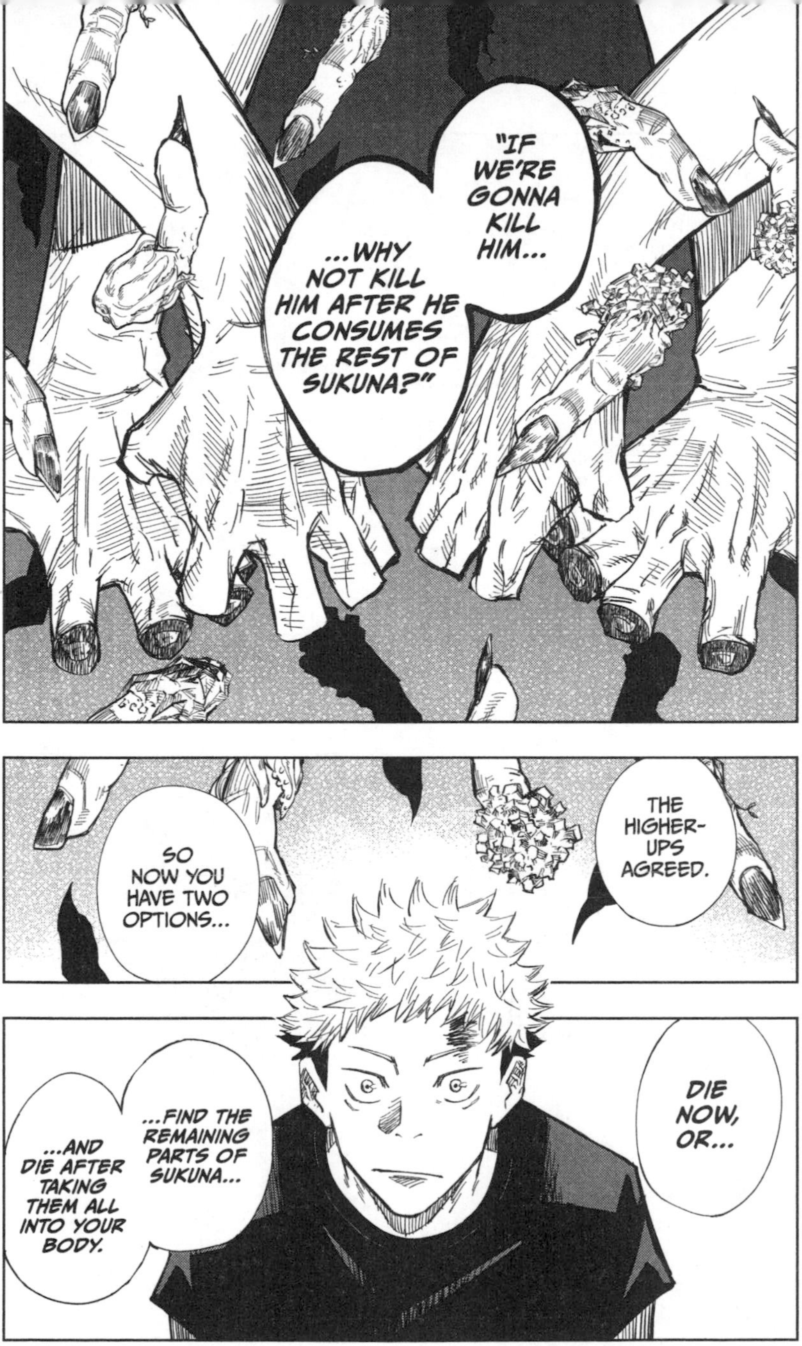
"IF WE'RE GONNA KILL HIM...
...WHY NOT KILL HIM AFTER HE CONSUMES THE REST OF SUKUNA?"
THE HIGHER-UPS AGREED.
SO NOW YOU HAVE TWO OPTIONS...
DIE NOW, OR...
...FIND THE REMAINING PARTS OF SUKUNA...
...AND DIE AFTER TAKING THEM ALL INTO YOUR BODY.

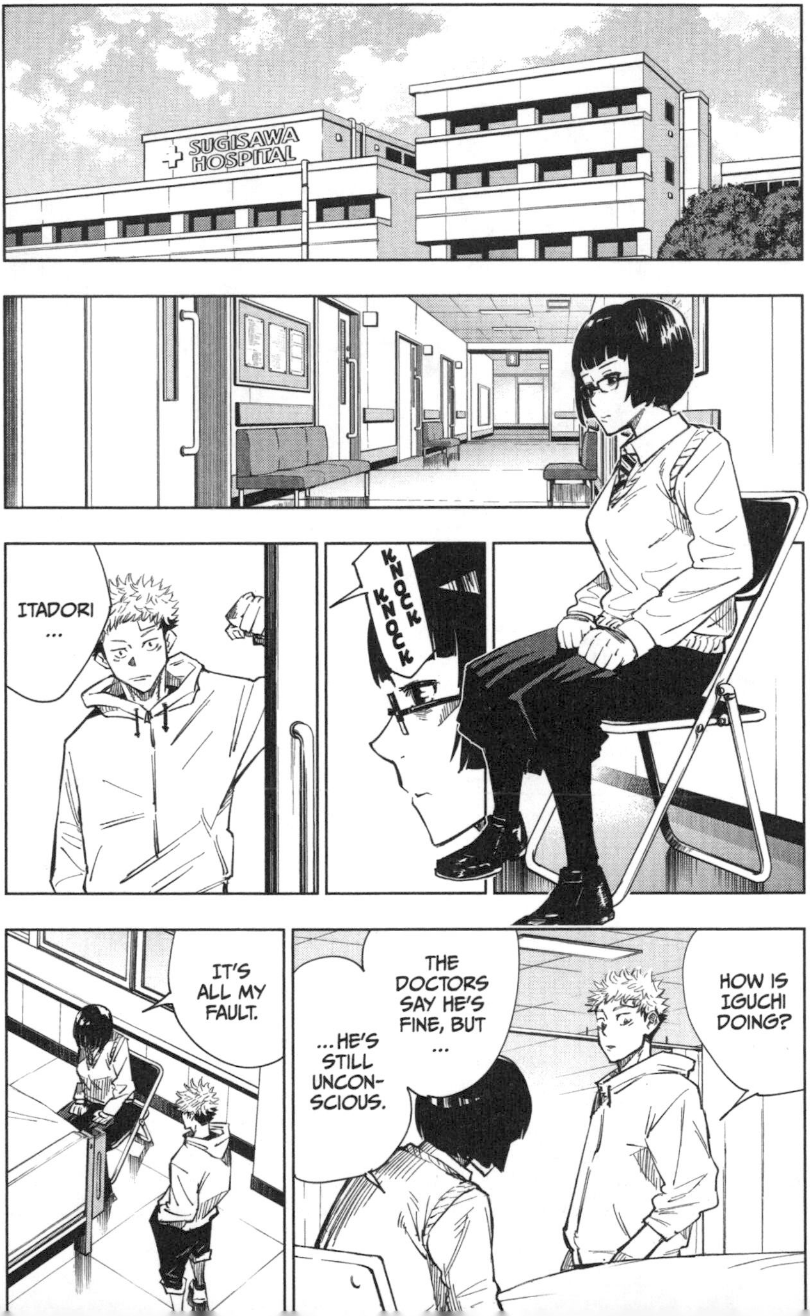
SUGISAWA HOSPITAL
KNOCK KNOCK
ITADORI ...
HOW IS IGUCHI DOING?
THE DOCTORS SAY HE'S FINE, BUT ...
...HE'S STILL UNCON-SCIOUS.
IT'S ALL MY FAULT.

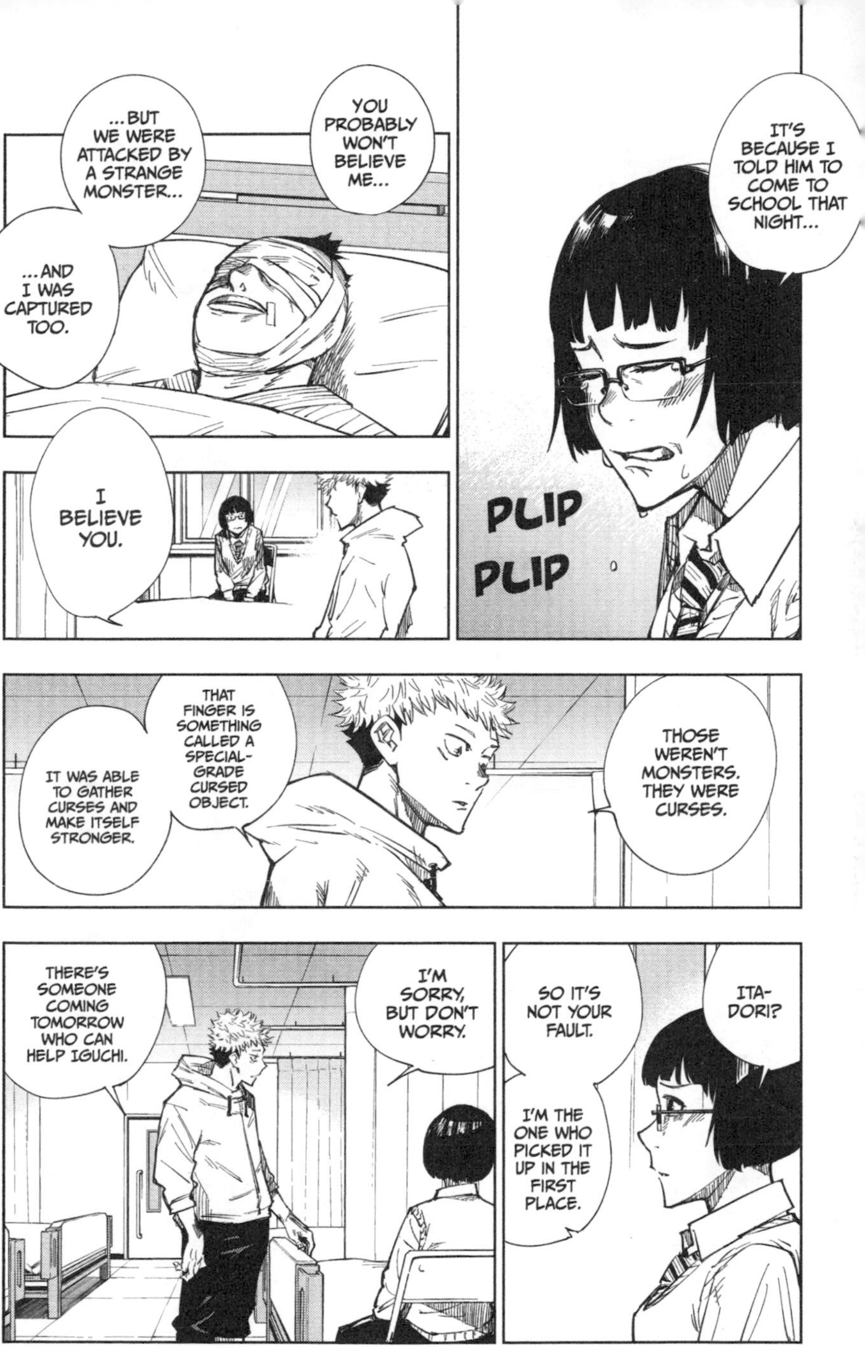
IT'S BECAUSE I TOLD HIM TO COME TO SCHOOL THAT NIGHT...
PLIP
PLIP
YOU PROBABLY WON'T BELIEVE ME...
...BUT WE WERE ATTACKED BY A STRANGE MONSTER...
...AND I WAS CAPTURED TOO.
I BELIEVE YOU.
THOSE WEREN'T MONSTERS. THEY WERE CURSES.
THAT FINGER IS SOMETHING CALLED A SPECIAL-GRADE CURSED OBJECT.
IT WAS ABLE TO GATHER CURSES AND MAKE ITSELF STRONGER.
ITA-DORI?
SO IT'S NOT YOUR FAULT.
I'M THE ONE WHO PICKED IT UP IN THE FIRST PLACE.
I'M SORRY, BUT DON'T WORRY.
THERE'S SOMEONE COMING TOMORROW WHO CAN HELP IGUCHI.

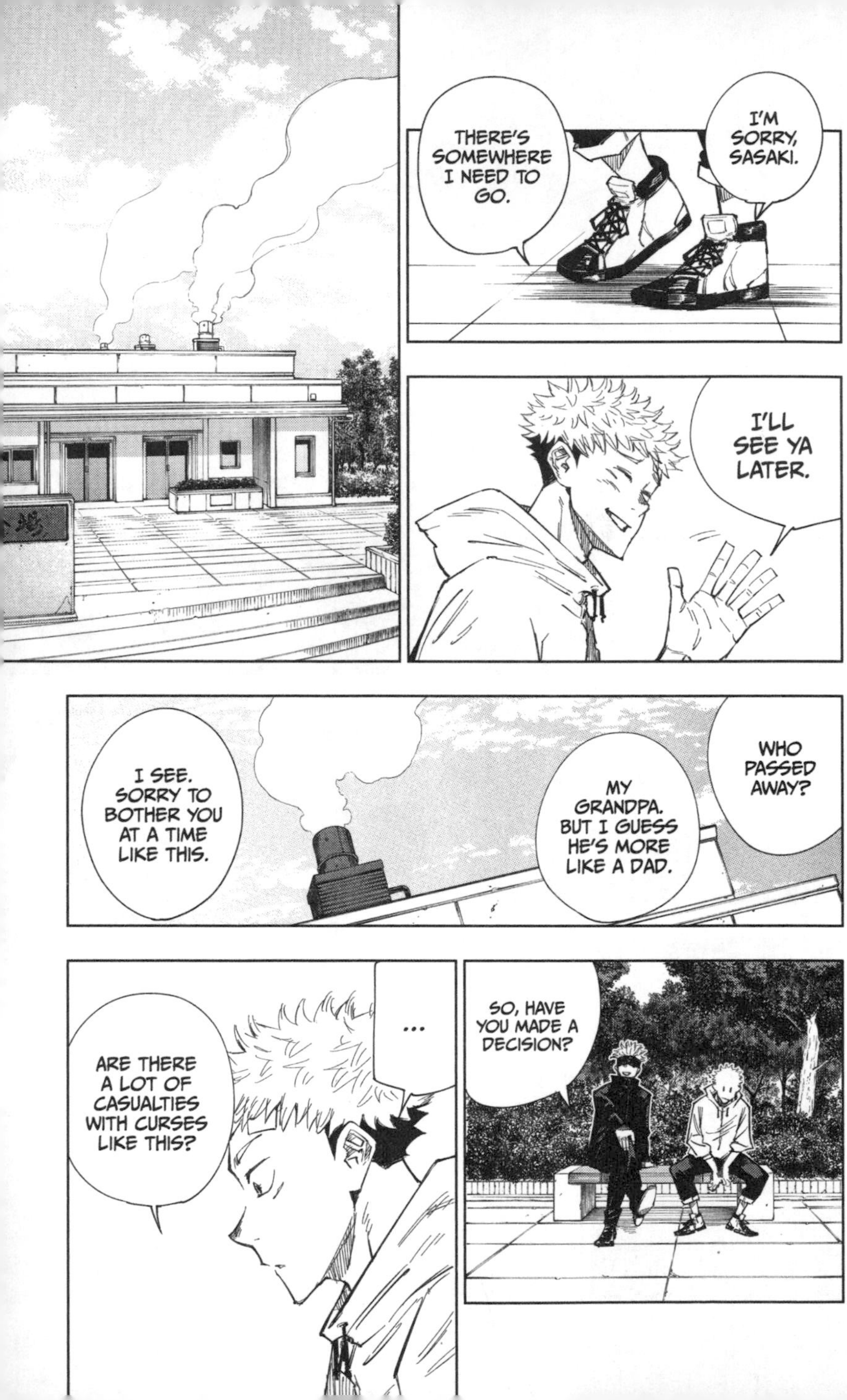
I'M SORRY, SASAKI.
THERE'S SOMEWHERE I NEED TO GO.
I'LL SEE YA LATER.
WHO PASSED AWAY?
MY GRANDPA. BUT I GUESS HE'S MORE LIKE A DAD.
I SEE. SORRY TO BOTHER YOU AT A TIME LIKE THIS.
SO, HAVE YOU MADE A DECISION?
...
ARE THERE A LOT OF CASUALTIES WITH CURSES LIKE THIS?

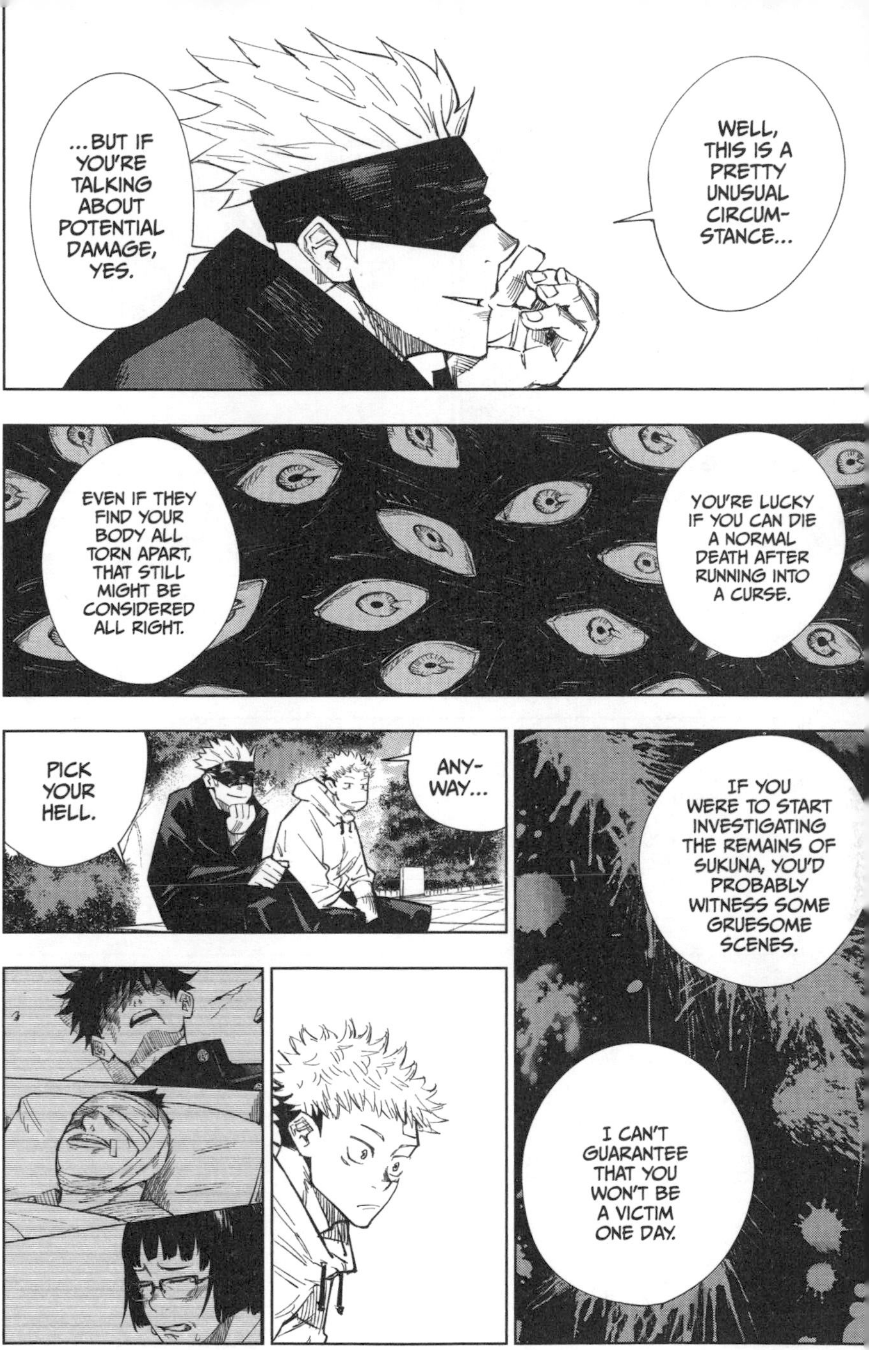
WELL, THIS IS A PRETTY UNUSUAL CIRCUM-STANCE...
...BUT IF YOU'RE TALKING ABOUT POTENTIAL DAMAGE, YES.
YOU'RE LUCKY IF YOU CAN DIE A NORMAL DEATH AFTER RUNNING INTO A CURSE.
EVEN IF THEY FIND YOUR BODY ALL TORN APART, THAT STILL MIGHT BE CONSIDERED ALL RIGHT.
IF YOU WERE TO START INVESTIGATING THE REMAINS OF SUKUNA, YOU'D PROBABLY WITNESS SOME GRUESOME SCENES.
I CAN'T GUARANTEE THAT YOU WON'T BE A VICTIM ONE DAY.
ANY-WAY...
PICK YOUR HELL.

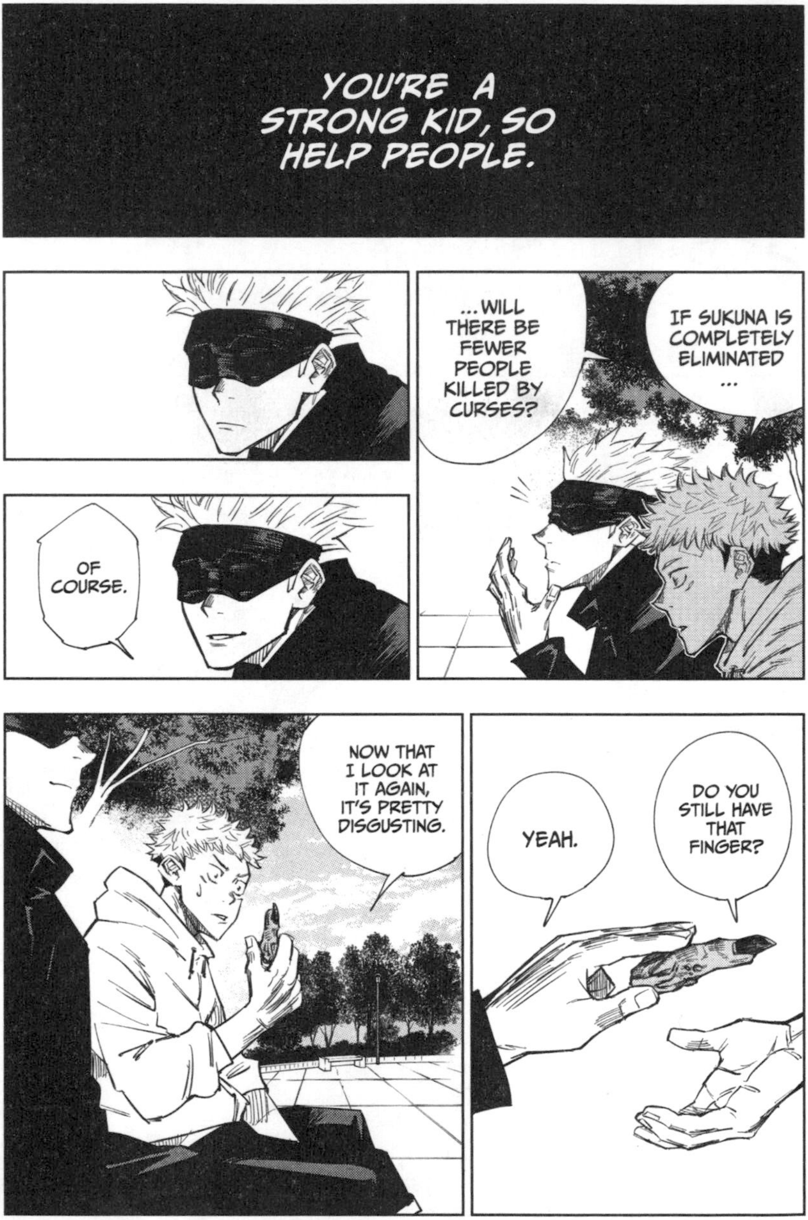
YOU'RE A STRONG KID, SO HELP PEOPLE.
IF SUKUNA IS COMPLETELY ELIMINATED ...
...WILL THERE BE FEWER PEOPLE KILLED BY CURSES?
OF COURSE.
DO YOU STILL HAVE THAT FINGER?
YEAH.
NOW THAT I LOOK AT IT AGAIN, IT'S PRETTY DISGUSTING.

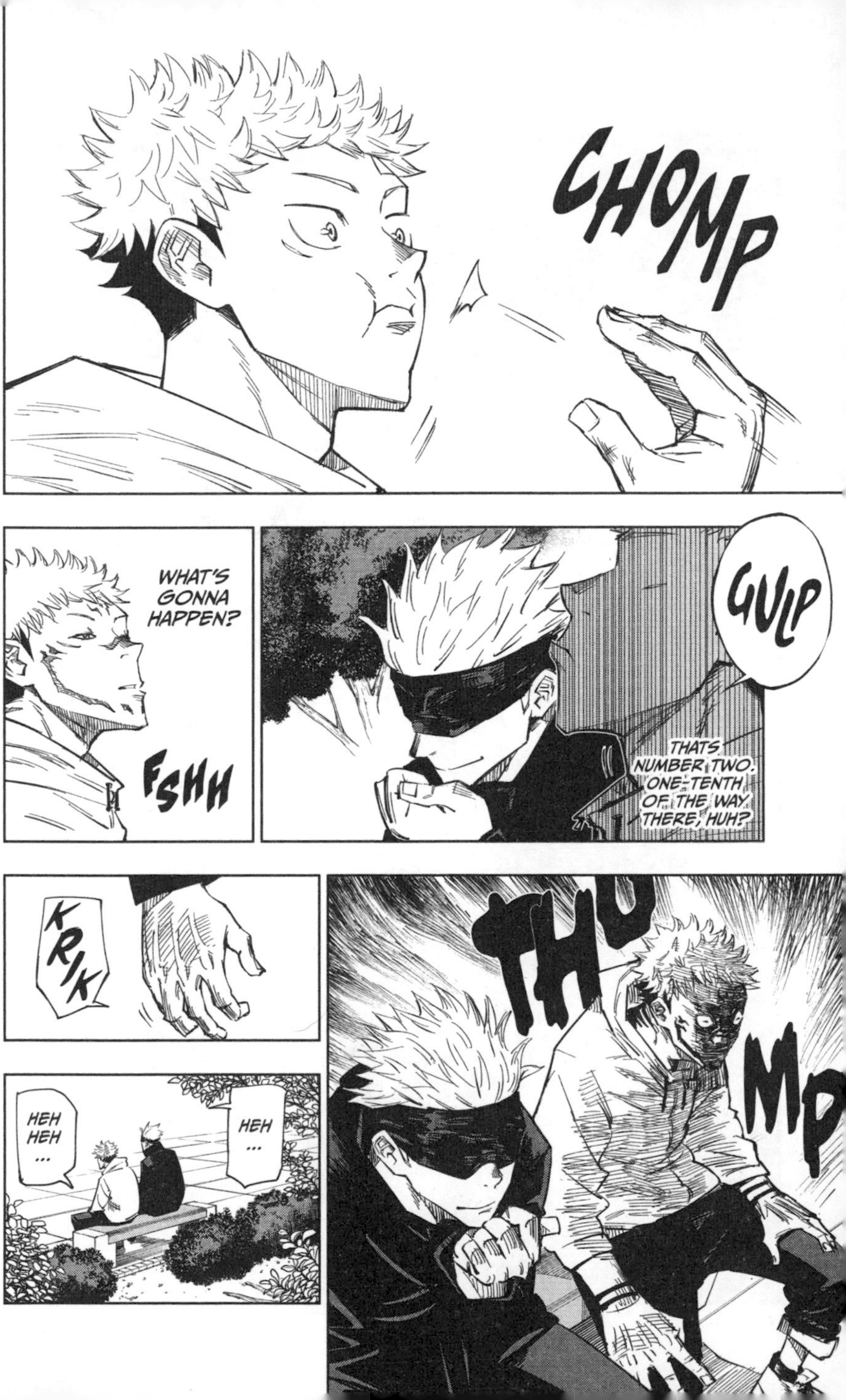
CHOMP
GULP
THATS NUMBER TWO. ONE-TENTH OF THE WAY THERE, HUH?
WHAT'S GONNA HAPPEN?
FSHH
THUMP
KRIK
HEH ...
HEH HEH ...

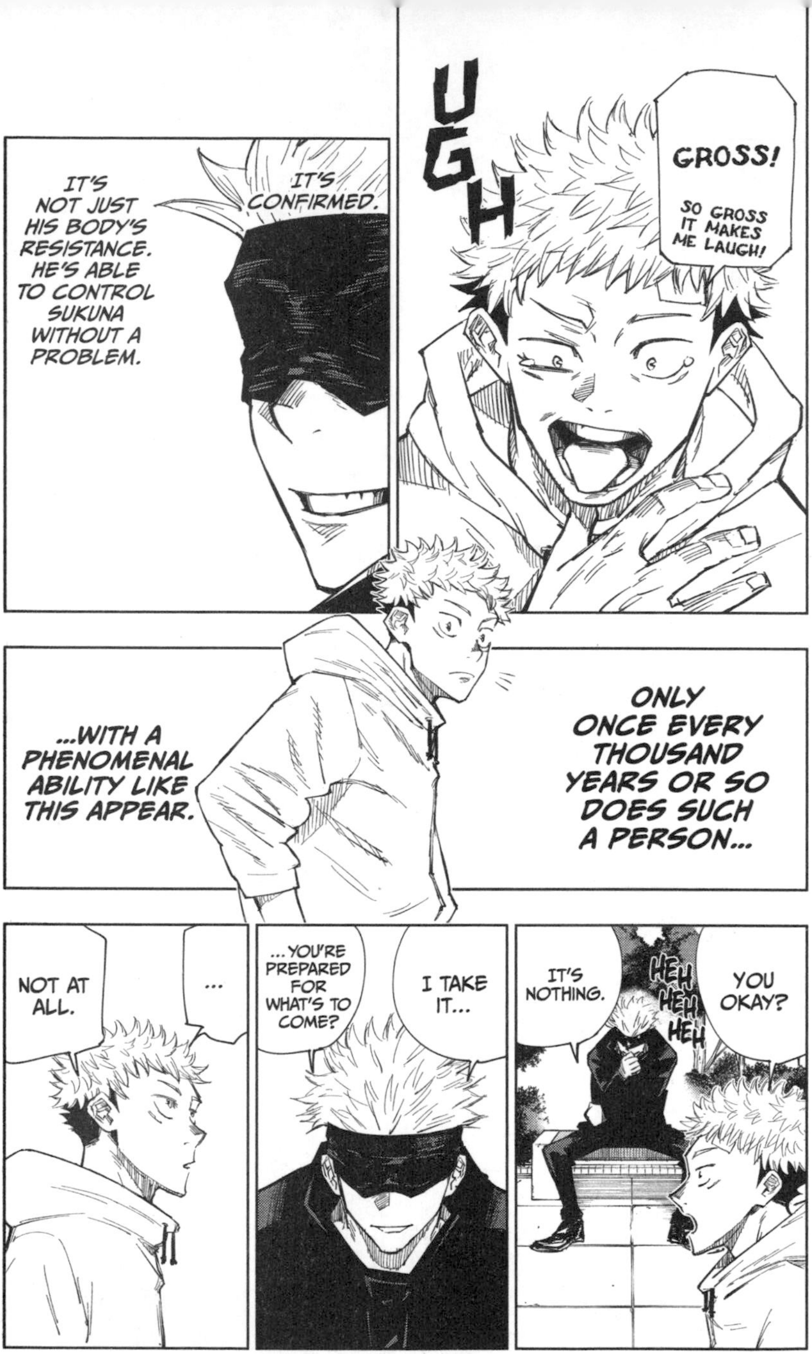
UGH
GROSS!
SO GROSS IT MAKES ME LAUGH!
IT'S CONFIRMED.
IT'S NOT JUST HIS BODY'S RESISTANCE. HE'S ABLE TO CONTROL SUKUNA WITHOUT A PROBLEM.
ONLY ONCE EVERY THOUSAND YEARS OR SO DOES SUCH A PERSON...
...WITH A PHENOMENAL ABILITY LIKE THIS APPEAR.
YOU OKAY?
HEH HEH HEH
IT'S NOTHING.
I TAKE IT...
...YOU'RE PREPARED FOR WHAT'S TO COME?
...
NOT AT ALL.

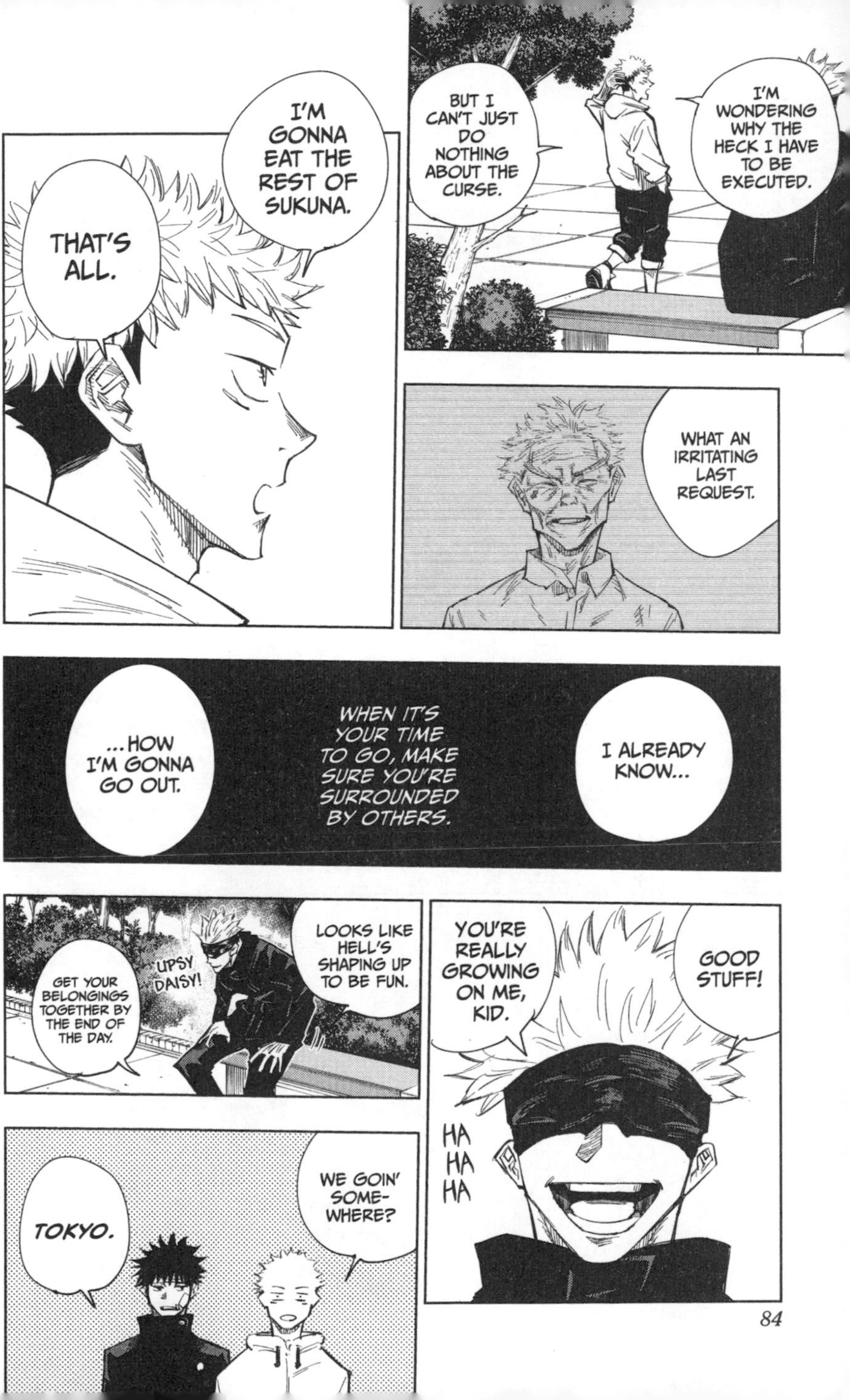
I'M WONDERING WHY THE HECK I HAVE TO BE EXECUTED.
BUT I CAN'T JUST DO NOTHING ABOUT THE CURSE.
WHAT AN IRRITATING LAST REQUEST.
I'M GONNA EAT THE REST OF SUKUNA.
THAT'S ALL.
I ALREADY KNOW...
WHEN IT'S YOUR TIME TO GO, MAKE SURE YOU'RE SURROUNDED BY OTHERS.
...HOW I'M GONNA GO OUT.
GOOD STUFF!
YOU'RE REALLY GROWING ON ME, KID.
HA HA HA
LOOKS LIKE HELL'S SHAPING UP TO BE FUN.
UPSY DAISY!
GET YOUR BELONGINGS TOGETHER BY THE END OF THE DAY.
WE GOIN' SOME-WHERE?
TOKYO.

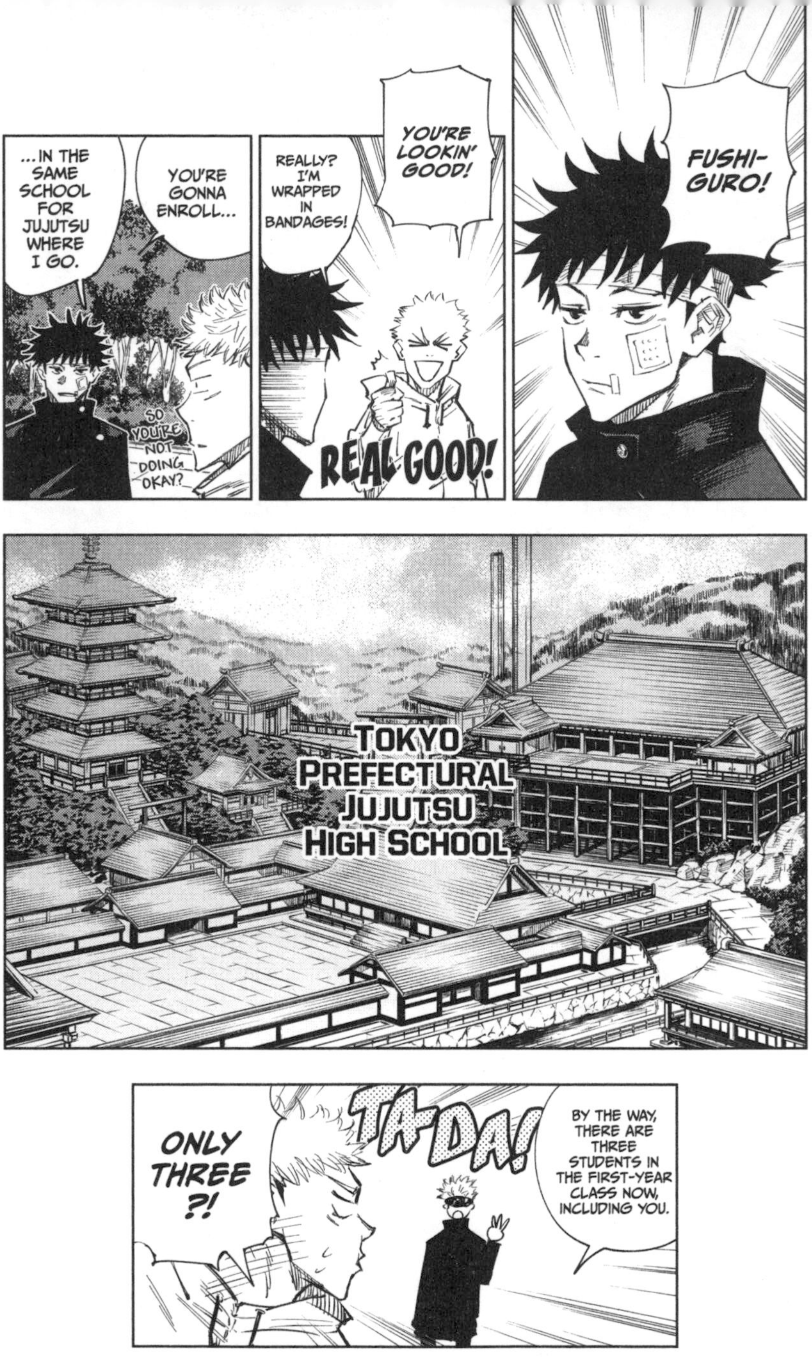
FUSHI-GURO!
YOU'RE LOOKIN' GOOD!
REALLY? I'M WRAPPED IN BANDAGES!
REAL GOOD!
YOU'RE GONNA ENROLL...
...IN THE SAME SCHOOL FOR JUJUTSU WHERE I GO.
SO YOU'RE NOT DOING OKAY?
TOKYO PREFECTURAL JUJUTSU HIGH SCHOOL
BY THE WAY, THERE ARE THREE STUDENTS IN THE FIRST-YEAR CLASS NOW, INCLUDING YOU.
TA-DA!
ONLY THREE?!

LET'S EAT KIKUFUKU

I get excited when I actually come across the regional products shown in travel shows. For example, the TV program *Doudesho* (How Do You Like Wednesday?) introduced me to Akafuku mochi.

So, I thought "I'm gonna do the same in my manga!" and introduced Kikufuku mochi.

And then you know what happened? Ikeda's Japanese Confectionary, the makers of Kikufuku mochi, sent me their product with a letter. Is it okay to be happy? Or should I feel a little embarrassed?

You can order products online and have them delivered, so those of you who are interested, please give their mochi a try! They're super delicious! I highly recommend the hoji-tea flavor! (I don't get any royalties by the way, so order away!)

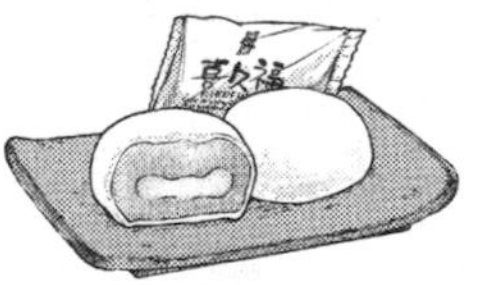

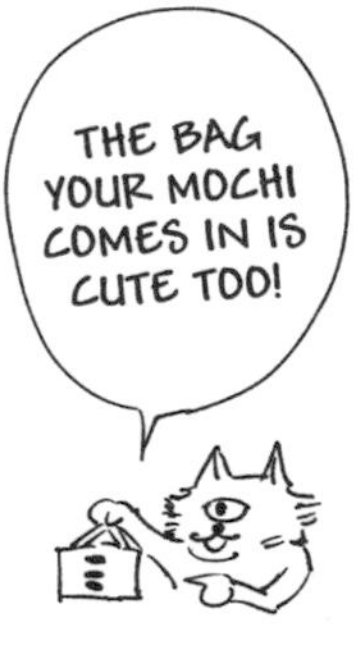
THE BAG YOUR MOCHI COMES IN IS CUTE TOO!

Chapter 3: For Myself

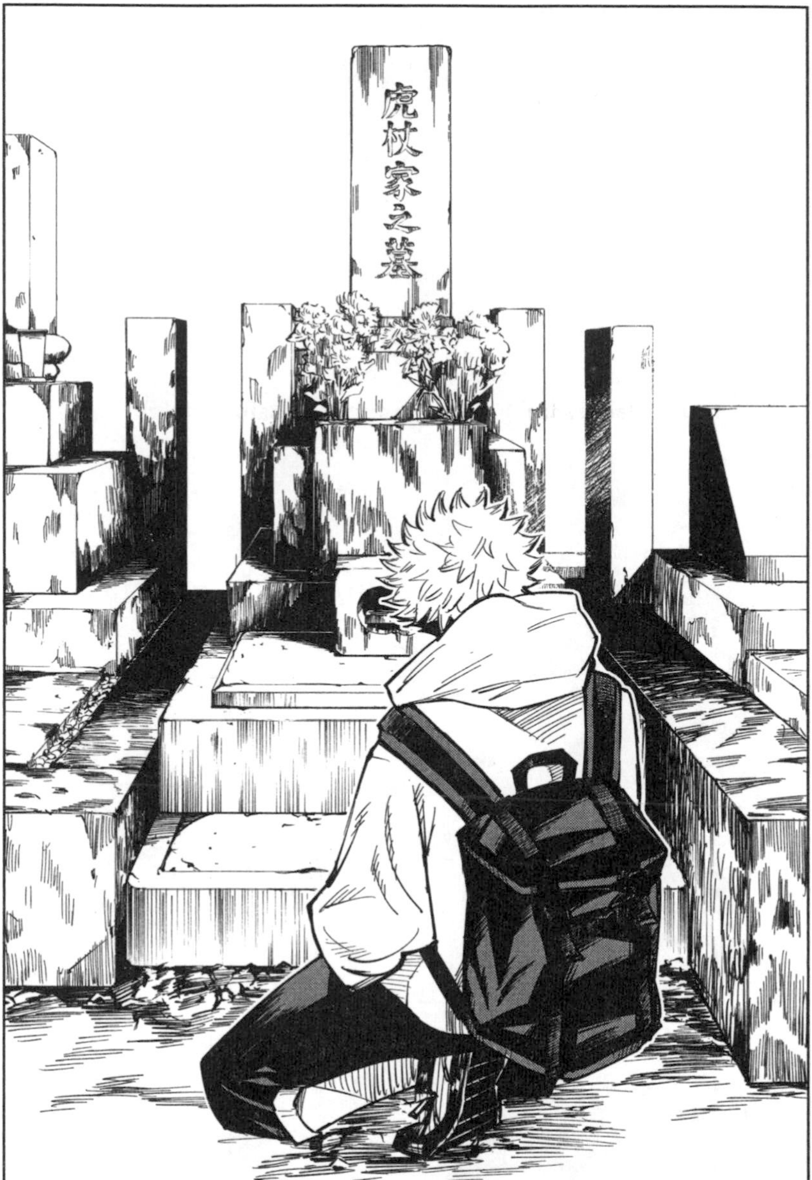
虎杖家之墓

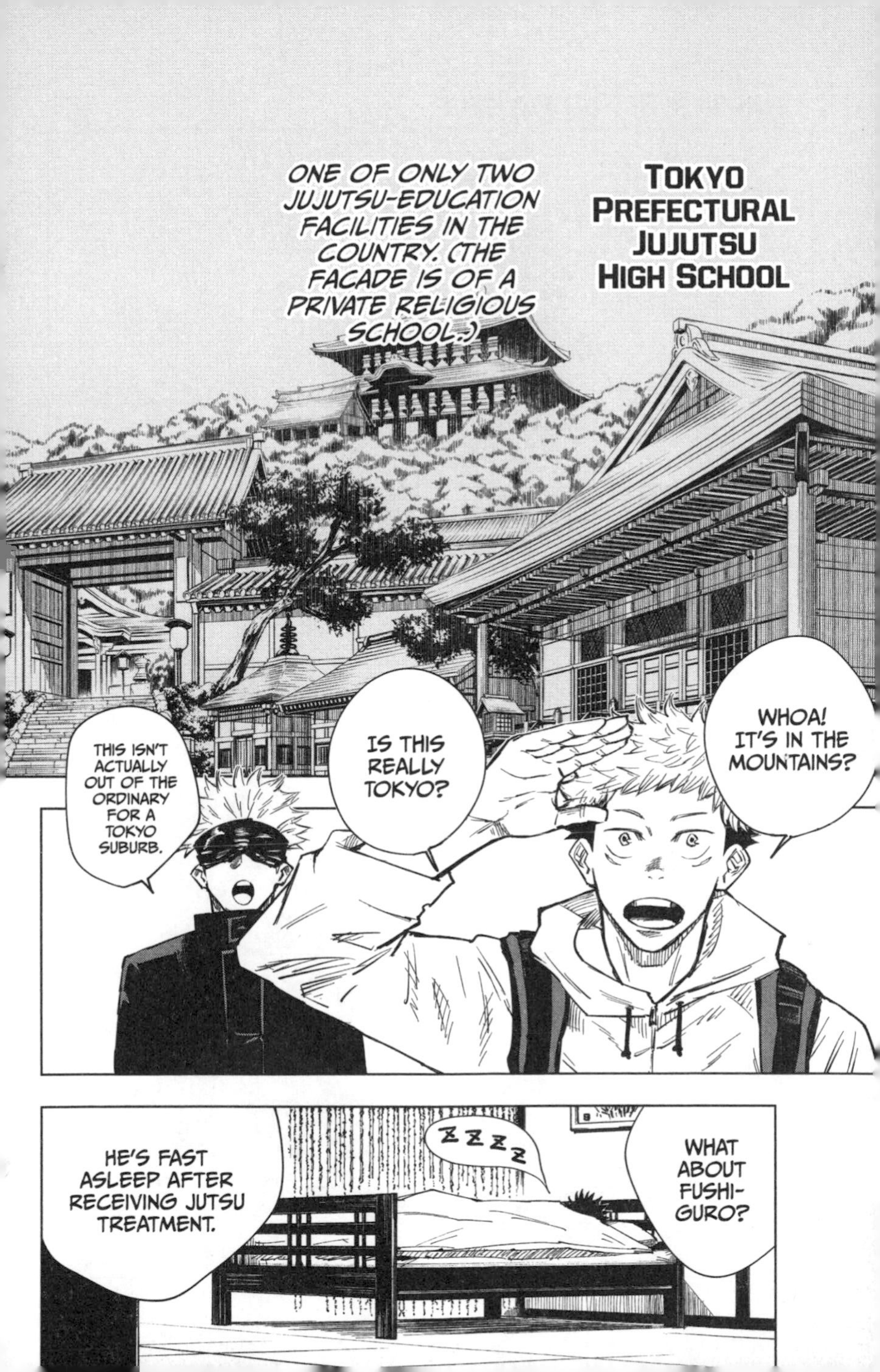
TOKYO PREFECTURAL JUJUTSU HIGH SCHOOL
ONE OF ONLY TWO JUJUTSU-EDUCATION FACILITIES IN THE COUNTRY. (THE FACADE IS OF A PRIVATE RELIGIOUS SCHOOL.)
WHOA! IT'S IN THE MOUNTAINS?
IS THIS REALLY TOKYO?
THIS ISN'T ACTUALLY OUT OF THE ORDINARY FOR A TOKYO SUBURB.
WHAT ABOUT FUSHI-GURO?
ZZZZ
HE'S FAST ASLEEP AFTER RECEIVING JUTSU TREATMENT.

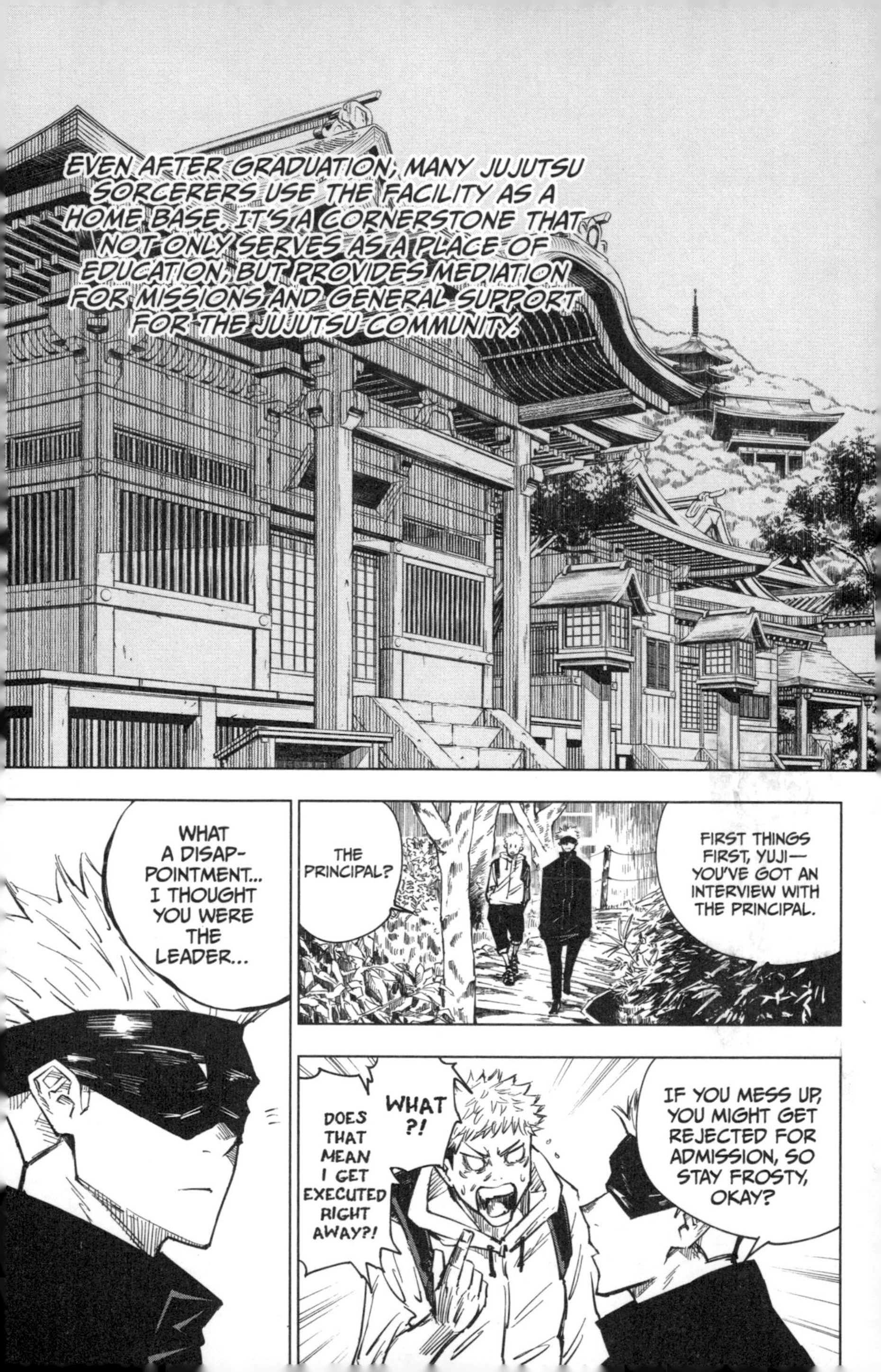
EVEN AFTER GRADUATION, MANY JUJUTSU SORCERERS USE THE FACILITY AS A HOME BASE. IT'S A CORNERSTONE THAT NOT ONLY SERVES AS A PLACE OF EDUCATION, BUT PROVIDES MEDIATION FOR MISSIONS AND GENERAL SUPPORT FOR THE JUJUTSU COMMUNITY.
FIRST THINGS FIRST, YUJI— YOU'VE GOT AN INTERVIEW WITH THE PRINCIPAL.
THE PRINCIPAL?
IF YOU MESS UP, YOU MIGHT GET REJECTED FOR ADMISSION, SO STAY FROSTY, OKAY?
WHAT?!
DOES THAT MEAN I GET EXECUTED RIGHT AWAY?!
WHAT A DISAPPOINTMENT... I THOUGHT YOU WERE THE LEADER...

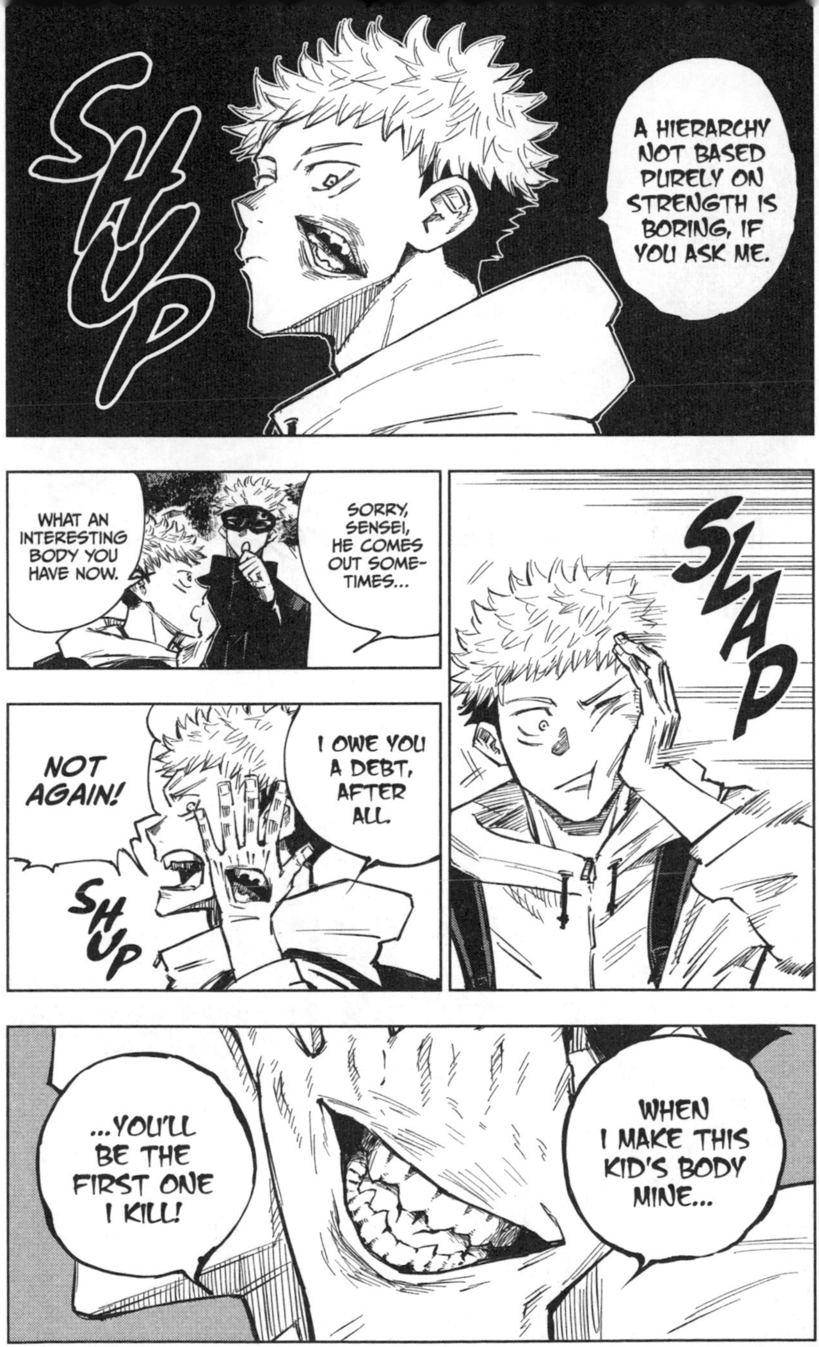
A HIERARCHY NOT BASED PURELY ON STRENGTH IS BORING, IF YOU ASK ME.
SHUP
SLAP
SORRY, SENSEI, HE COMES OUT SOME-TIMES...
WHAT AN INTERESTING BODY YOU HAVE NOW.
I OWE YOU A DEBT, AFTER ALL.
NOT AGAIN!
SHUP
WHEN I MAKE THIS KID'S BODY MINE...
...YOU'LL BE THE FIRST ONE I KILL!

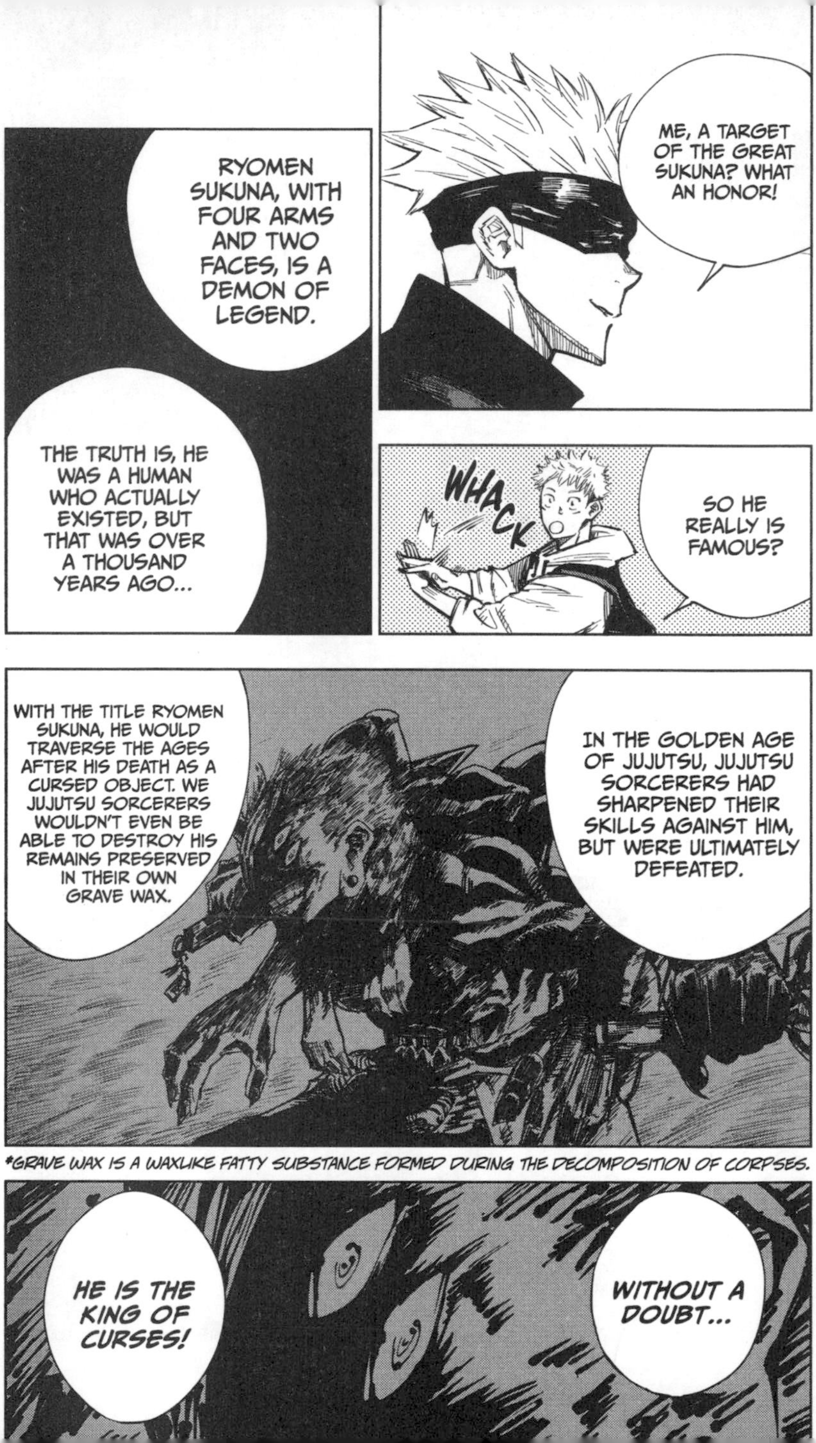
ME, A TARGET OF THE GREAT SUKUNA? WHAT AN HONOR!
WHACK
SO HE REALLY IS FAMOUS?
RYOMEN SUKUNA, WITH FOUR ARMS AND TWO FACES, IS A DEMON OF LEGEND.
THE TRUTH IS, HE WAS A HUMAN WHO ACTUALLY EXISTED, BUT THAT WAS OVER A THOUSAND YEARS AGO...
IN THE GOLDEN AGE OF JUJUTSU, JUJUTSU SORCERERS HAD SHARPENED THEIR SKILLS AGAINST HIM, BUT WERE ULTIMATELY DEFEATED.
WITH THE TITLE RYOMEN SUKUNA, HE WOULD TRAVERSE THE AGES AFTER HIS DEATH AS A CURSED OBJECT. WE JUJUTSU SORCERERS WOULDN'T EVEN BE ABLE TO DESTROY HIS REMAINS PRESERVED IN THEIR OWN GRAVE WAX.
WITHOUT A DOUBT...
HE IS THE KING OF CURSES!

*GRAVE WAX IS A WAXLIKE FATTY SUBSTANCE FORMED DURING THE DECOMPOSITION OF CORPSES.

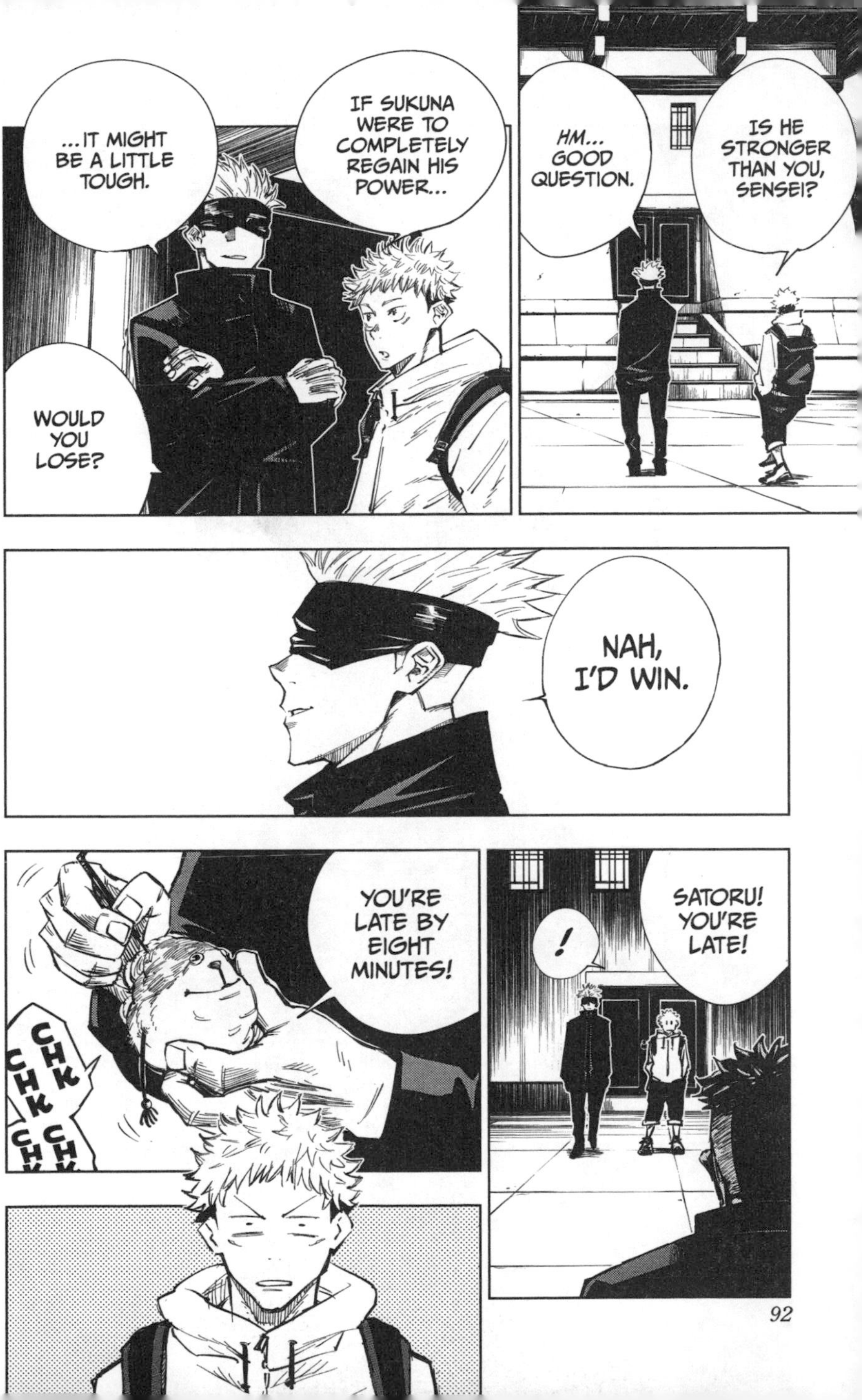
IS HE STRONGER THAN YOU, SENSEI?
HM... GOOD QUESTION.
IF SUKUNA WERE TO COMPLETELY REGAIN HIS POWER...
...IT MIGHT BE A LITTLE TOUGH.
WOULD YOU LOSE?
NAH, I'D WIN.
SATORU! YOU'RE LATE!
!
YOU'RE LATE BY EIGHT MINUTES!
CHK CHK CHK CHK

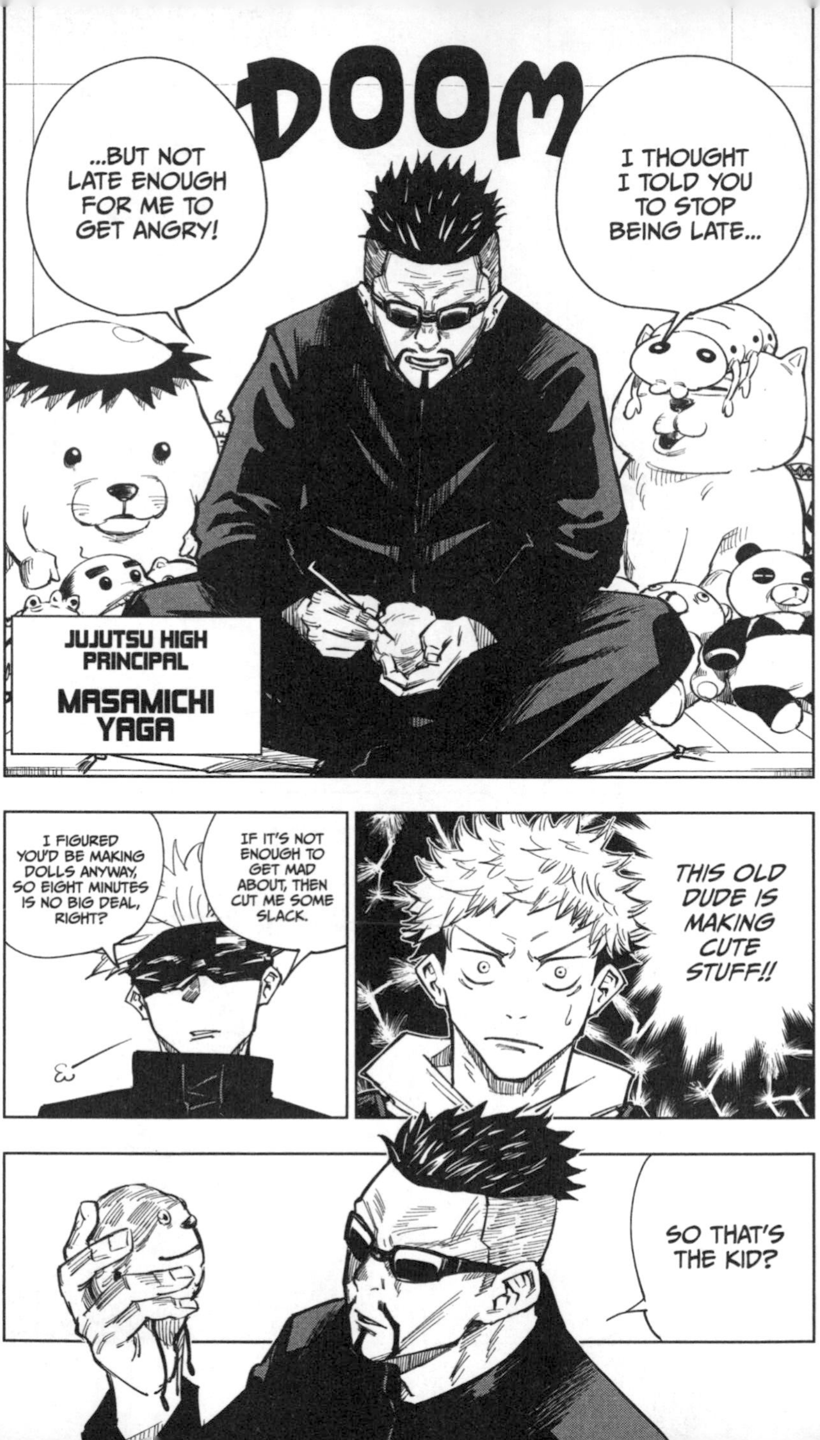
I THOUGHT I TOLD YOU TO STOP BEING LATE...
DOOM
...BUT NOT LATE ENOUGH FOR ME TO GET ANGRY!
JUJUTSU HIGH PRINCIPAL
MASAMICHI YAGA
THIS OLD DUDE IS MAKING CUTE STUFF!!
IF IT'S NOT ENOUGH TO GET MAD ABOUT, THEN CUT ME SOME SLACK.
I FIGURED YOU'D BE MAKING DOLLS ANYWAY, SO EIGHT MINUTES IS NO BIG DEAL, RIGHT?
SO THAT'S THE KID?

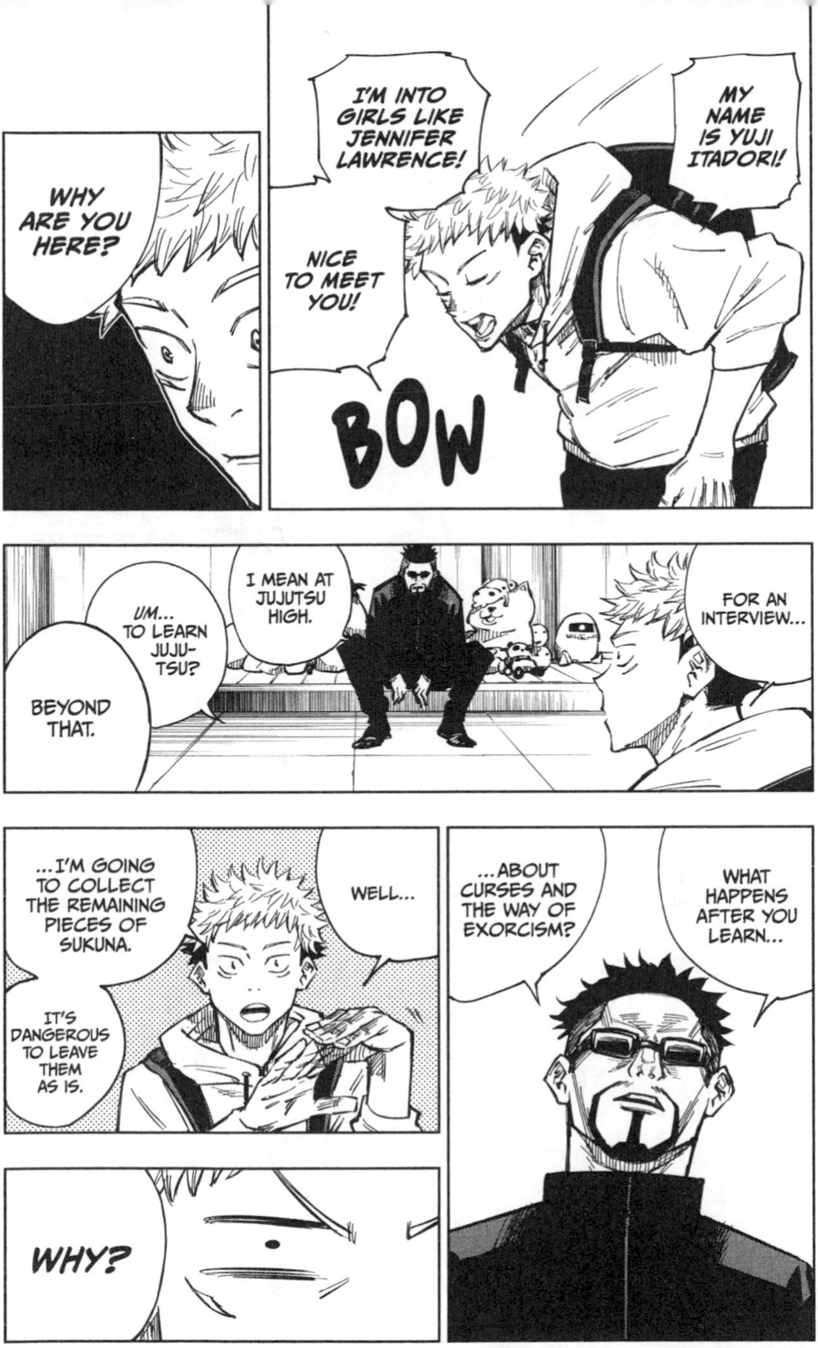
MY NAME IS YUJI ITADORI!
I'M INTO GIRLS LIKE JENNIFER LAWRENCE!
NICE TO MEET YOU!
BOW
WHY ARE YOU HERE?
FOR AN INTERVIEW...
I MEAN AT JUJUTSU HIGH.
UM... TO LEARN JUJU-TSU?
BEYOND THAT.
WHAT HAPPENS AFTER YOU LEARN...
...ABOUT CURSES AND THE WAY OF EXORCISM?
WELL...
...I'M GOING TO COLLECT THE REMAINING PIECES OF SUKUNA.
IT'S DANGEROUS TO LEAVE THEM AS IS.
WHY?

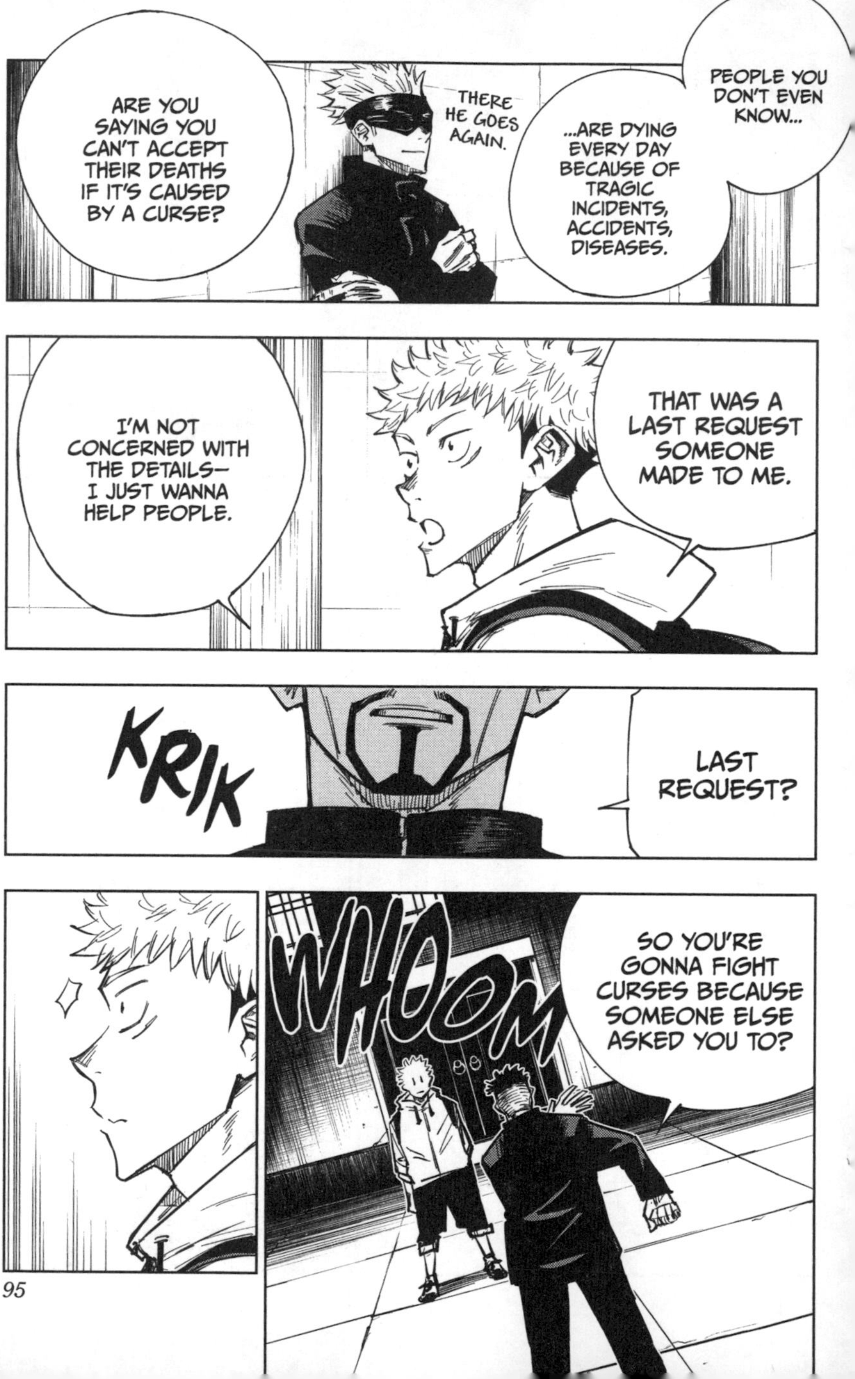
PEOPLE YOU DON'T EVEN KNOW...
...ARE DYING EVERY DAY BECAUSE OF TRAGIC INCIDENTS, ACCIDENTS, DISEASES.
THERE HE GOES AGAIN.
ARE YOU SAYING YOU CAN'T ACCEPT THEIR DEATHS IF IT'S CAUSED BY A CURSE?
THAT WAS A LAST REQUEST SOMEONE MADE TO ME.
I'M NOT CONCERNED WITH THE DETAILS— I JUST WANNA HELP PEOPLE.
LAST REQUEST?
KRIK
SO YOU'RE GONNA FIGHT CURSES BECAUSE SOMEONE ELSE ASKED YOU TO?
WHOOM

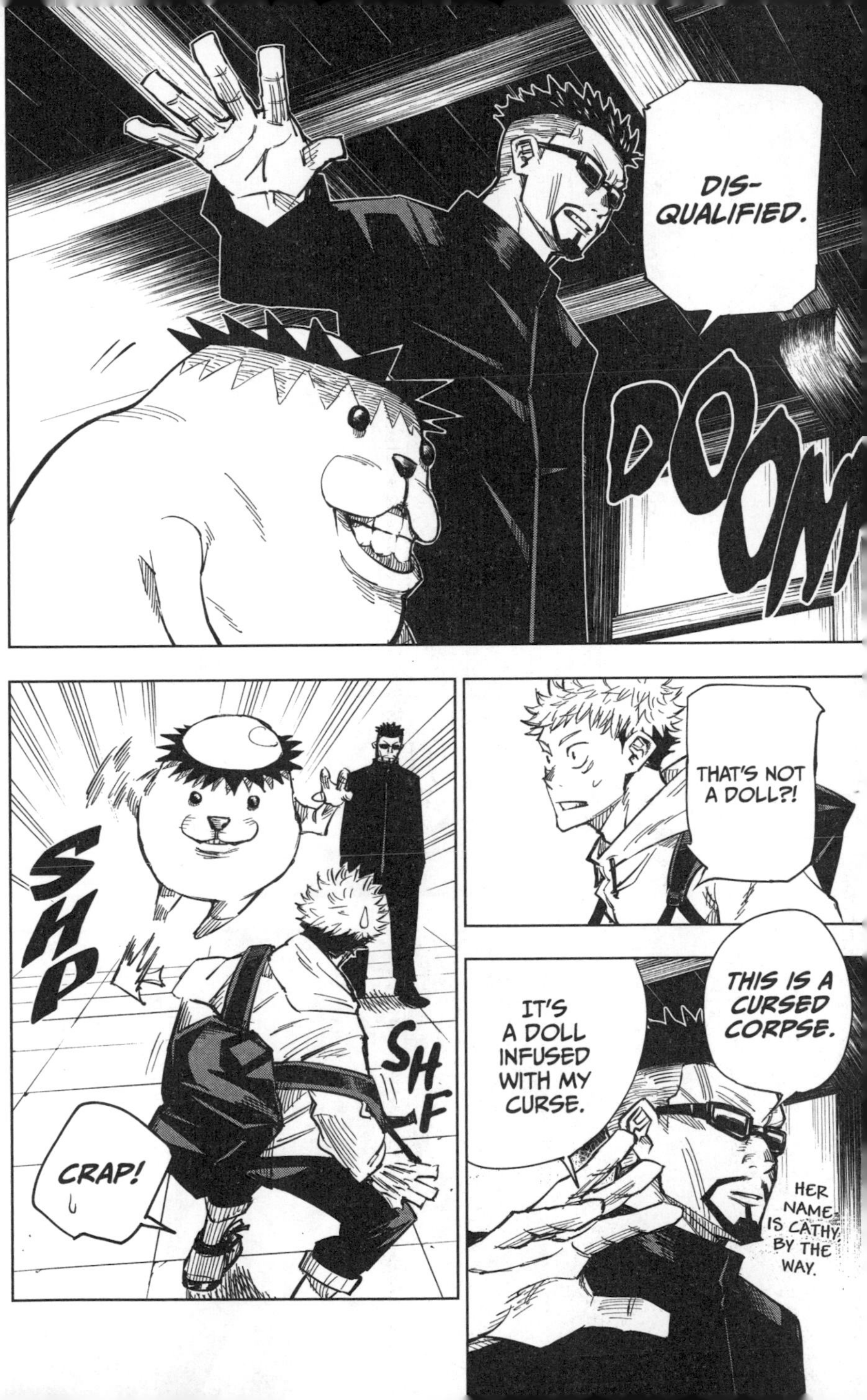
DIS-
QUALIFIED.
DOOM
THAT'S NOT A DOLL?!
THIS IS A CURSED CORPSE.
IT'S A DOLL INFUSED WITH MY CURSE.
HER NAME IS CATHY, BY THE WAY.
SHP
SHF
CRAP!

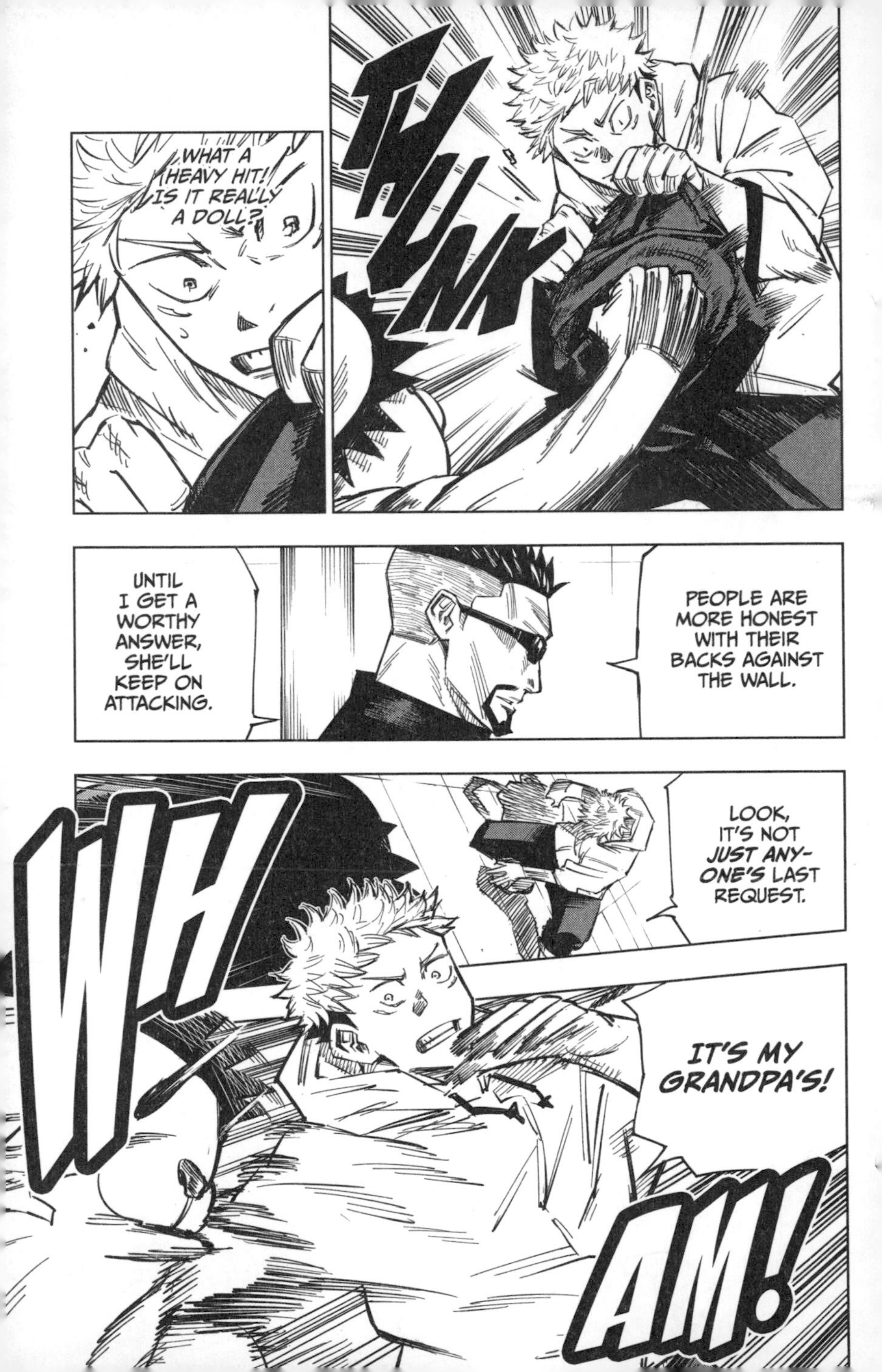
THUNK
WHAT A HEAVY HIT! IS IT REALLY A DOLL?
PEOPLE ARE MORE HONEST WITH THEIR BACKS AGAINST THE WALL.
UNTIL I GET A WORTHY ANSWER, SHE'LL KEEP ON ATTACKING.
LOOK, IT'S NOT JUST ANYONE'S LAST REQUEST.
IT'S MY GRANDPA'S!
WHAM!

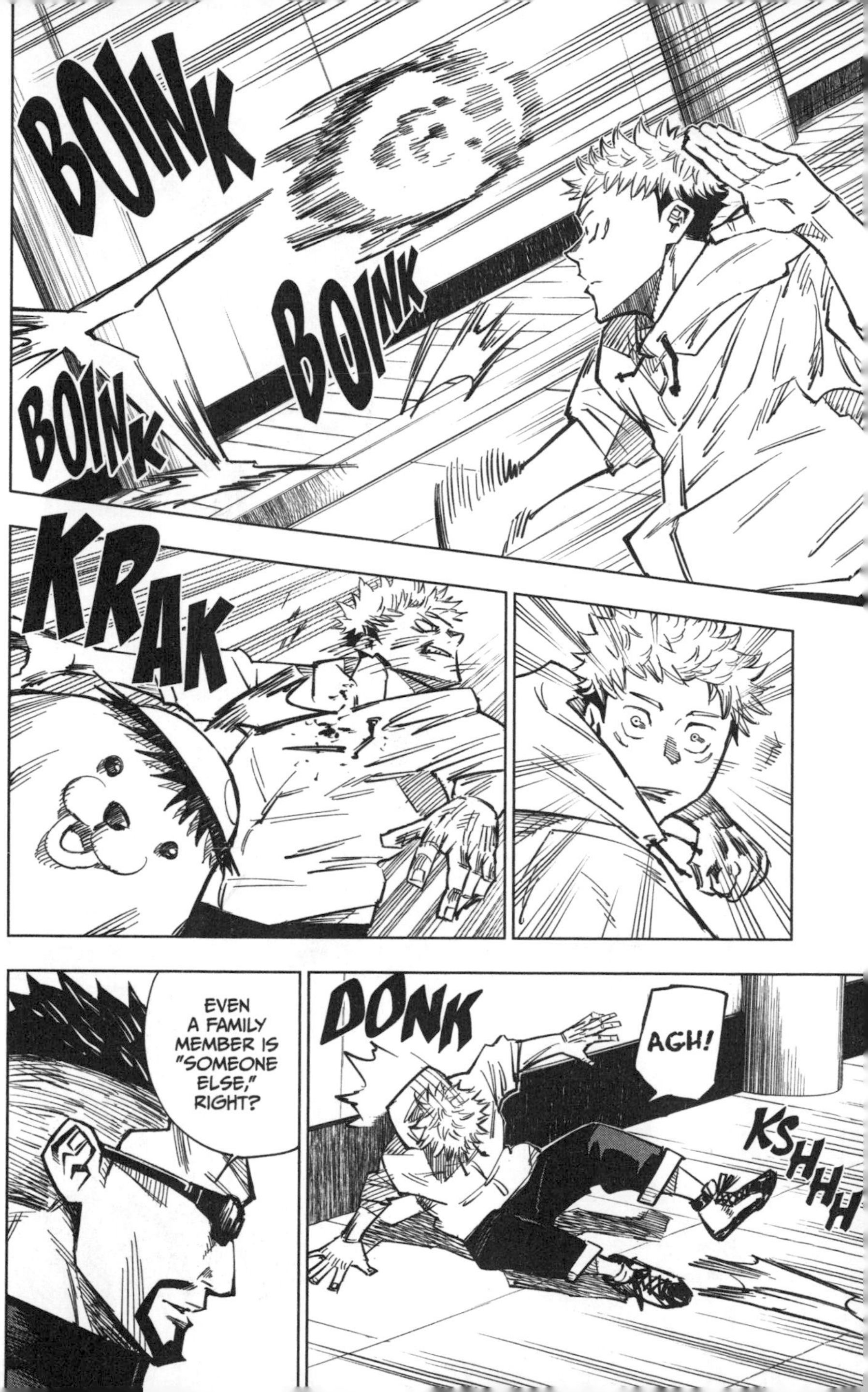
BOINK
BOINK
BOINK
KRAK
DONK
AGH!
KSHHH
EVEN A FAMILY MEMBER IS "SOMEONE ELSE," RIGHT?

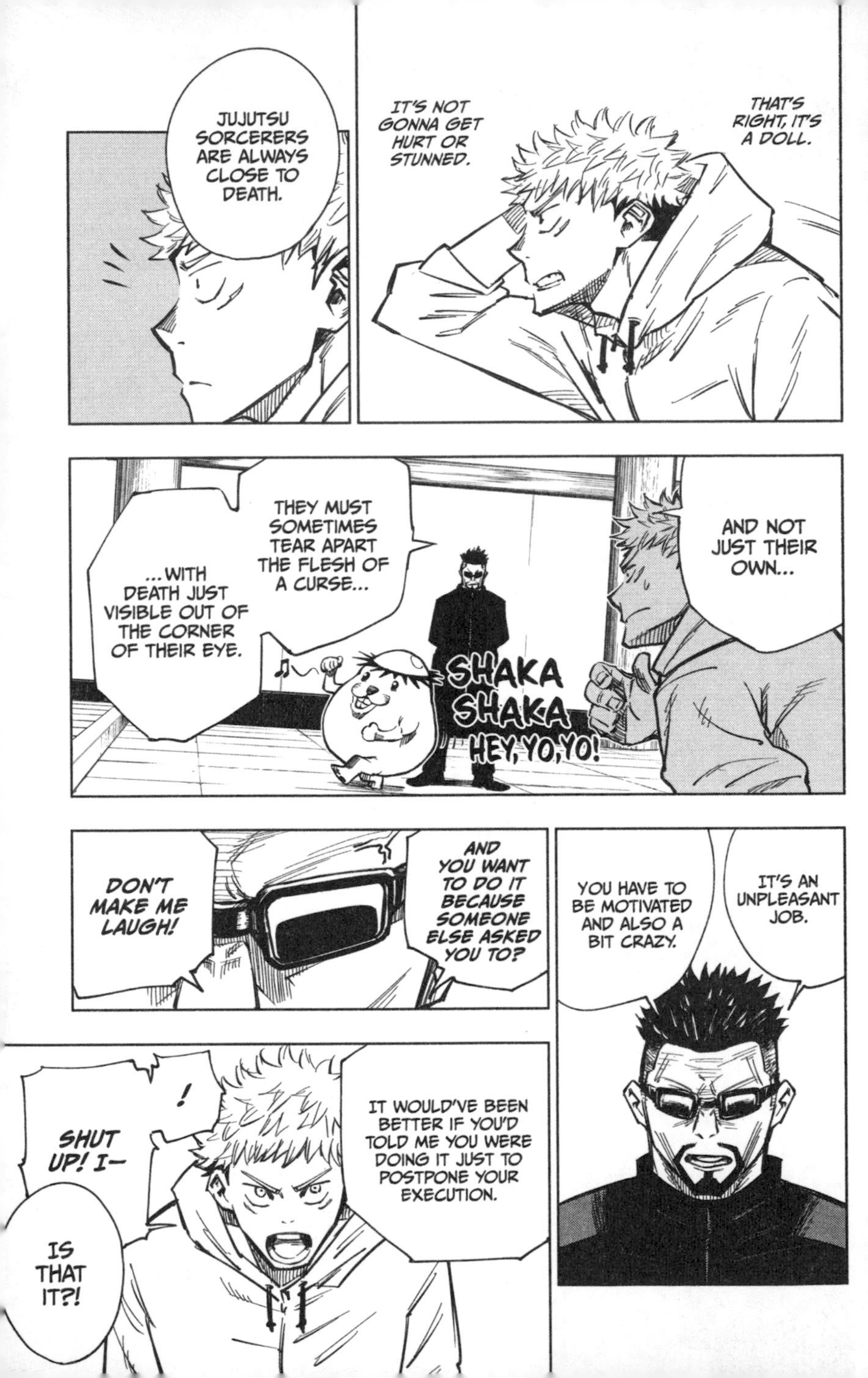
THAT'S RIGHT, IT'S A DOLL.
IT'S NOT GONNA GET HURT OR STUNNED.
JUJUTSU SORCERERS ARE ALWAYS CLOSE TO DEATH.
AND NOT JUST THEIR OWN...
THEY MUST SOMETIMES TEAR APART THE FLESH OF A CURSE...
...WITH DEATH JUST VISIBLE OUT OF THE CORNER OF THEIR EYE.
SHAKA SHAKA HEY, YO, YO!
IT'S AN UNPLEASANT JOB.
YOU HAVE TO BE MOTIVATED AND ALSO A BIT CRAZY.
AND YOU WANT TO DO IT BECAUSE SOMEONE ELSE ASKED YOU TO?
DON'T MAKE ME LAUGH!
IT WOULD'VE BEEN BETTER IF YOU'D TOLD ME YOU WERE DOING IT JUST TO POSTPONE YOUR EXECUTION.
!
SHUT UP! I—
IS THAT IT?!

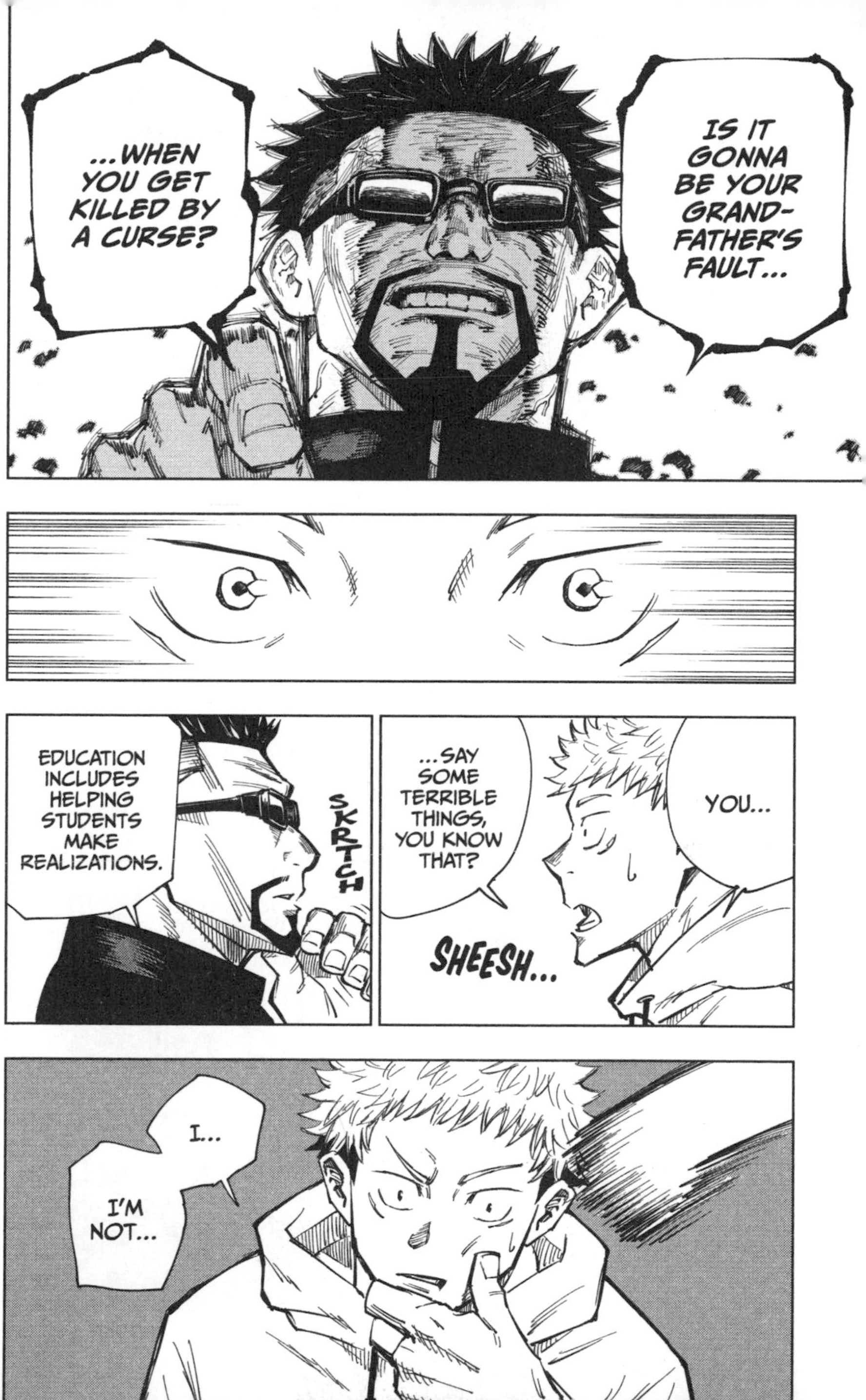
IS IT GONNA BE YOUR GRAND-FATHER'S FAULT...
...WHEN YOU GET KILLED BY A CURSE?
YOU...
...SAY SOME TERRIBLE THINGS, YOU KNOW THAT?
SHEESH...
EDUCATION INCLUDES HELPING STUDENTS MAKE REALIZATIONS.
SKRTCH
I...
I'M NOT...

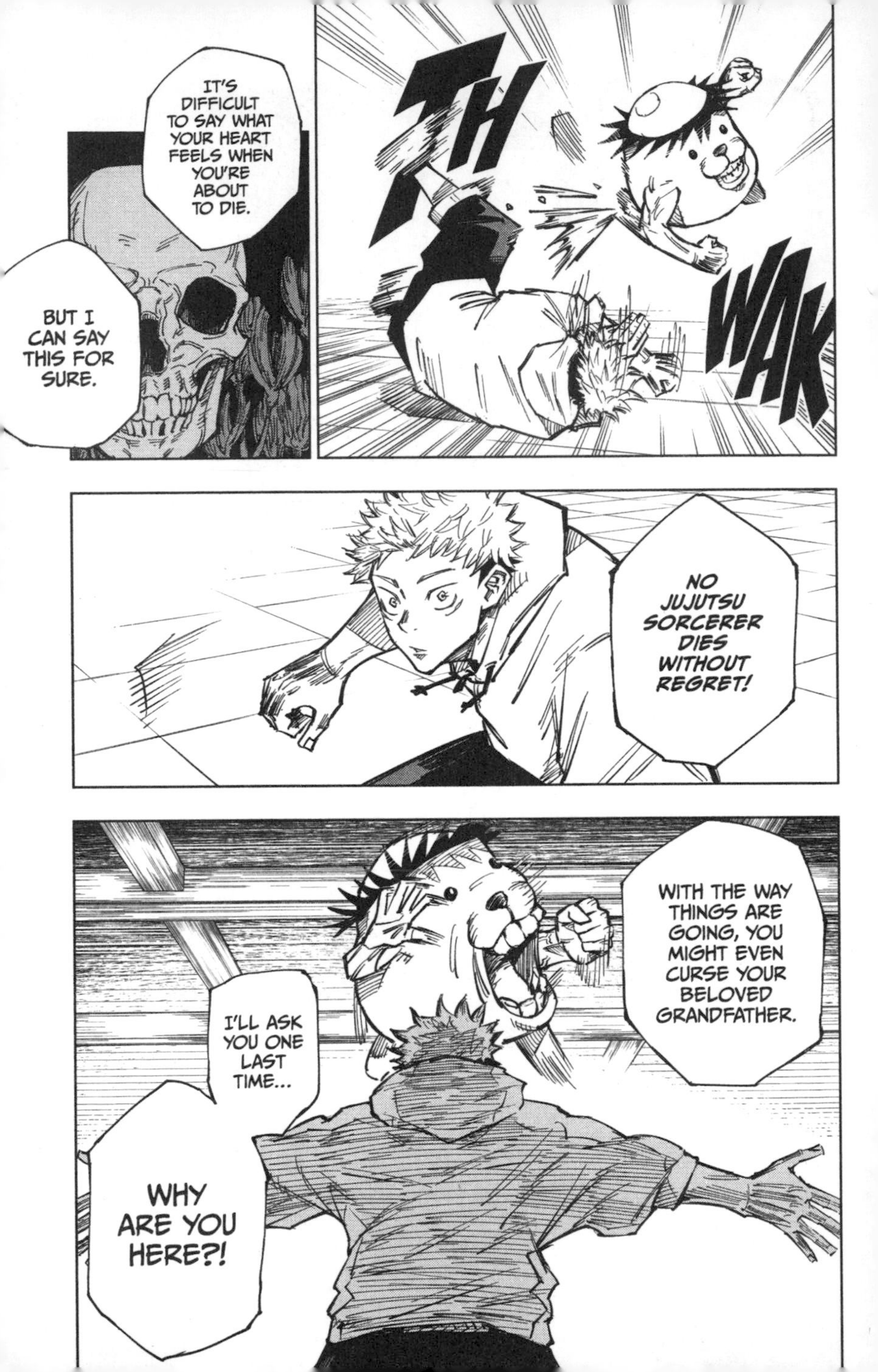

TH
WAK
IT'S DIFFICULT TO SAY WHAT YOUR HEART FEELS WHEN YOU'RE ABOUT TO DIE.
BUT I CAN SAY THIS FOR SURE.
NO JUJUTSU SORCERER DIES WITHOUT REGRET!
WITH THE WAY THINGS ARE GOING, YOU MIGHT EVEN CURSE YOUR BELOVED GRANDFATHER.
I'LL ASK YOU ONE LAST TIME...
WHY ARE YOU HERE?!

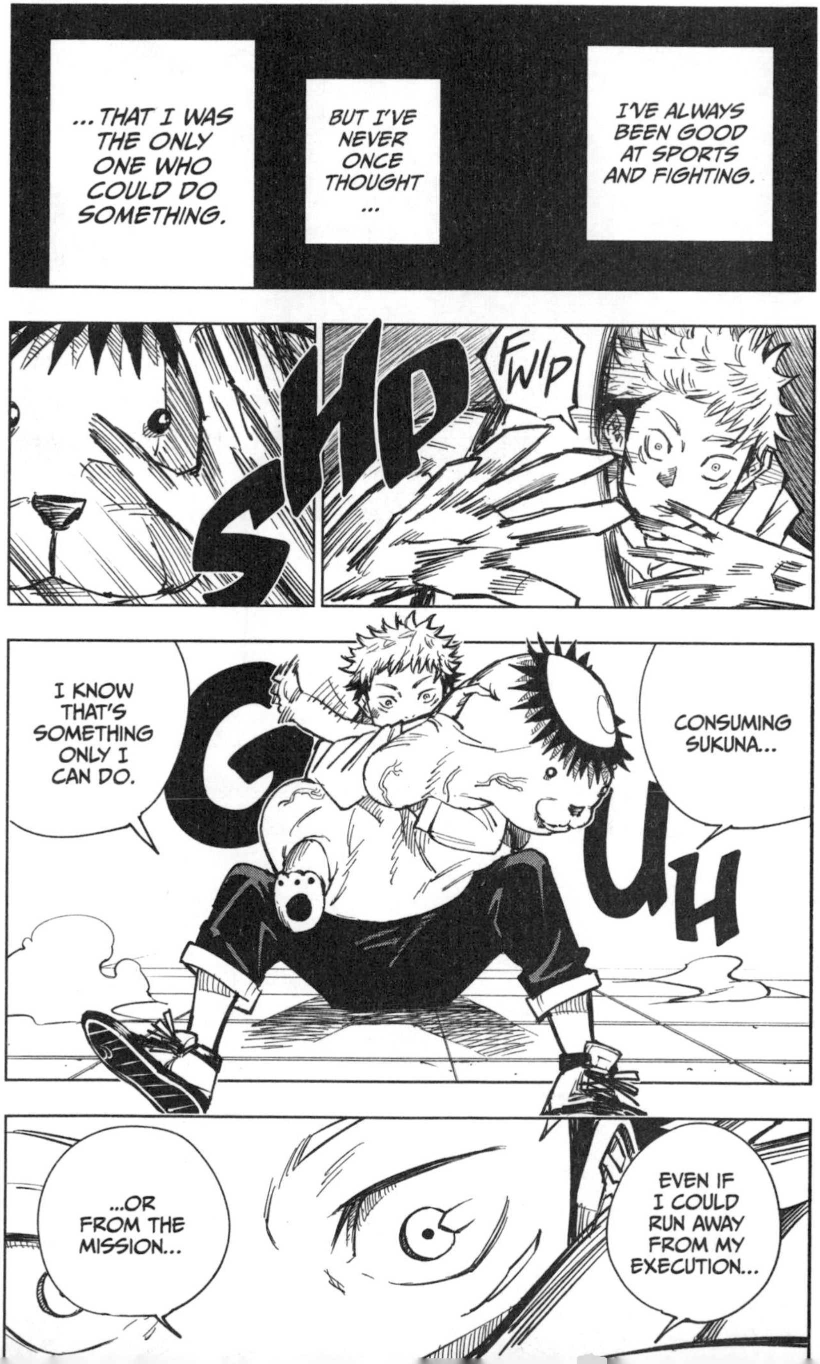
I'VE ALWAYS BEEN GOOD AT SPORTS AND FIGHTING.
BUT I'VE NEVER ONCE THOUGHT ...
...THAT I WAS THE ONLY ONE WHO COULD DO SOMETHING.
FWIP
SHP
CONSUMING SUKUNA...
GUH
I KNOW THAT'S SOMETHING ONLY I CAN DO.
EVEN IF I COULD RUN AWAY FROM MY EXECUTION...
...OR FROM THE MISSION...

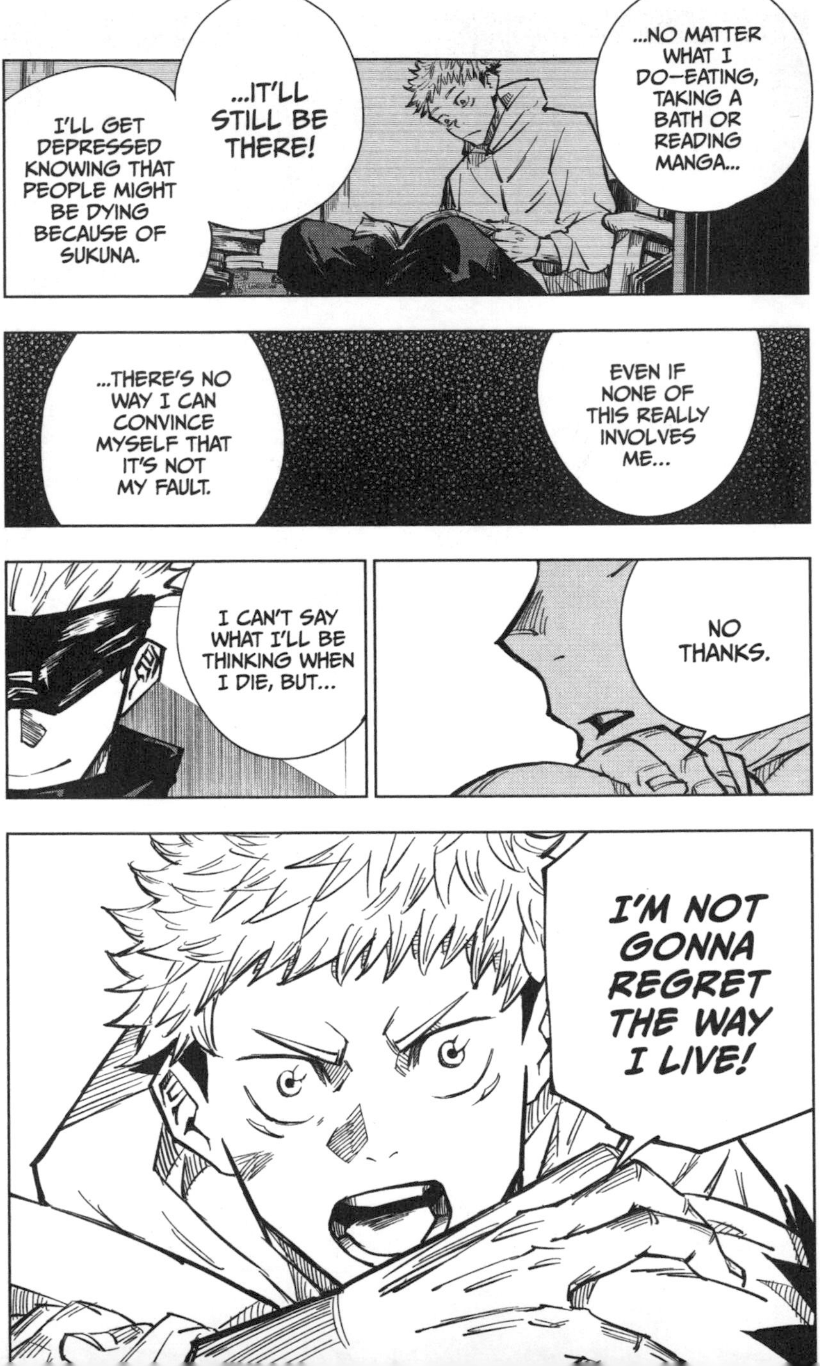
...NO MATTER WHAT I DO—EATING, TAKING A BATH OR READING MANGA...
...IT'LL STILL BE THERE!
I'LL GET DEPRESSED KNOWING THAT PEOPLE MIGHT BE DYING BECAUSE OF SUKUNA.
EVEN IF NONE OF THIS REALLY INVOLVES ME...
...THERE'S NO WAY I CAN CONVINCE MYSELF THAT IT'S NOT MY FAULT.
NO THANKS.
I CAN'T SAY WHAT I'LL BE THINKING WHEN I DIE, BUT...
I'M NOT GONNA REGRET THE WAY I LIVE!

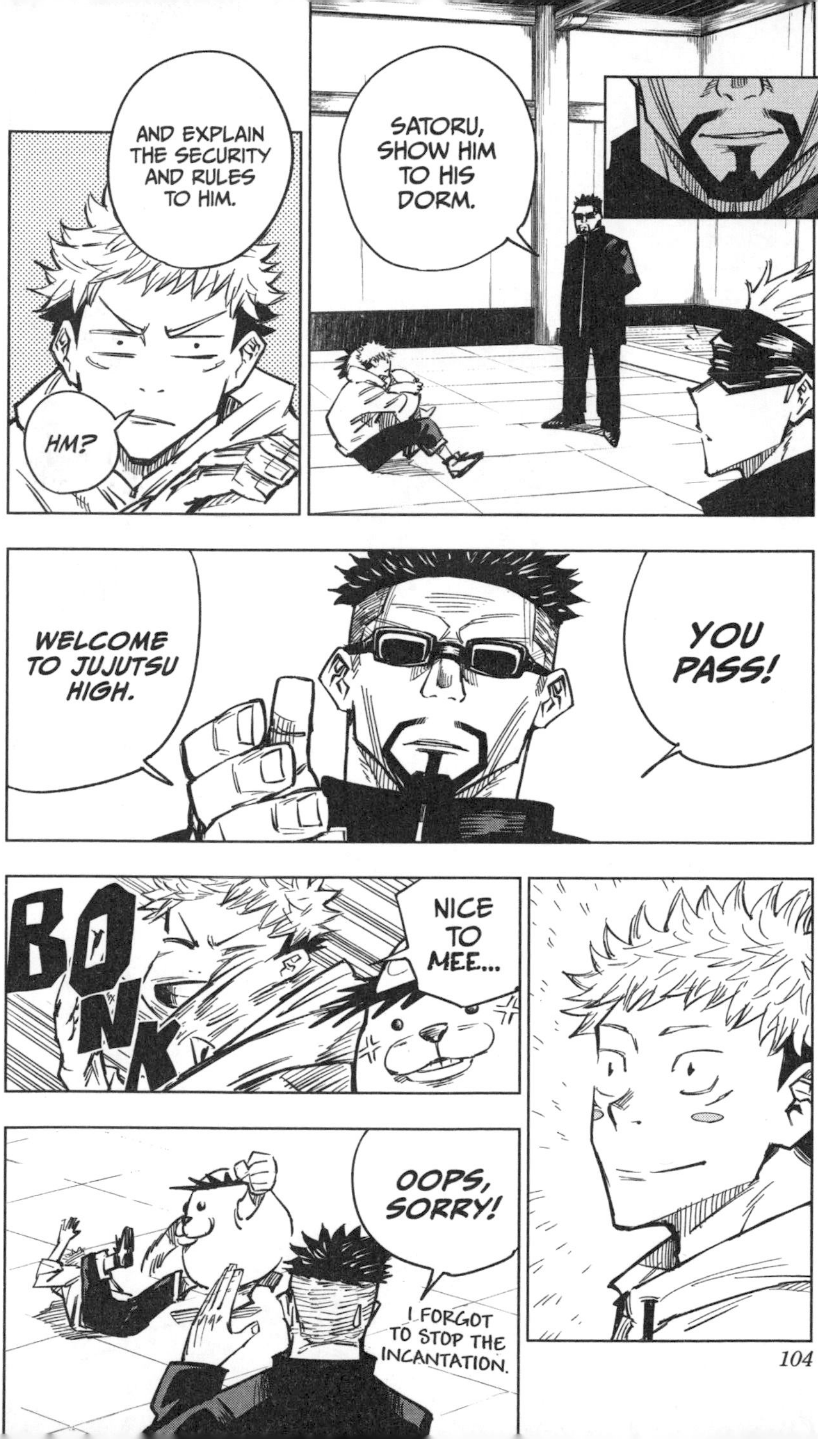
SATORU, SHOW HIM TO HIS DORM.
AND EXPLAIN THE SECURITY AND RULES TO HIM.
HM?
YOU PASS!
WELCOME TO JUJUTSU HIGH.
NICE TO MEE...
BONK
OOPS, SORRY!
I FORGOT TO STOP THE INCANTATION.

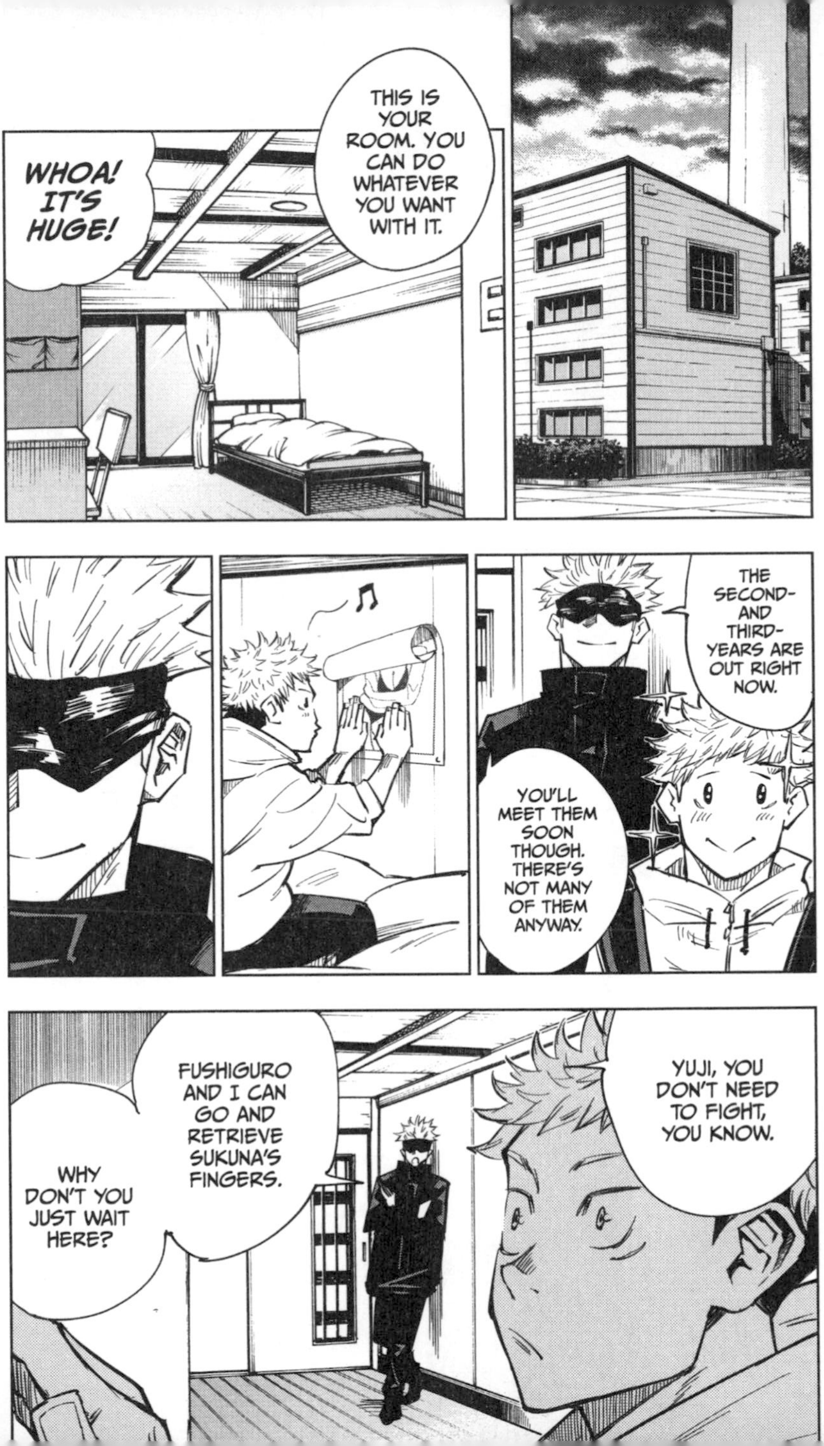
THIS IS YOUR ROOM. YOU CAN DO WHATEVER YOU WANT WITH IT.
WHOA! IT'S HUGE!
THE SECOND- AND THIRD-YEARS ARE OUT RIGHT NOW.
YOU'LL MEET THEM SOON THOUGH. THERE'S NOT MANY OF THEM ANYWAY.
YUJI, YOU DON'T NEED TO FIGHT, YOU KNOW.
FUSHIGURO AND I CAN GO AND RETRIEVE SUKUNA'S FINGERS.
WHY DON'T YOU JUST WAIT HERE?

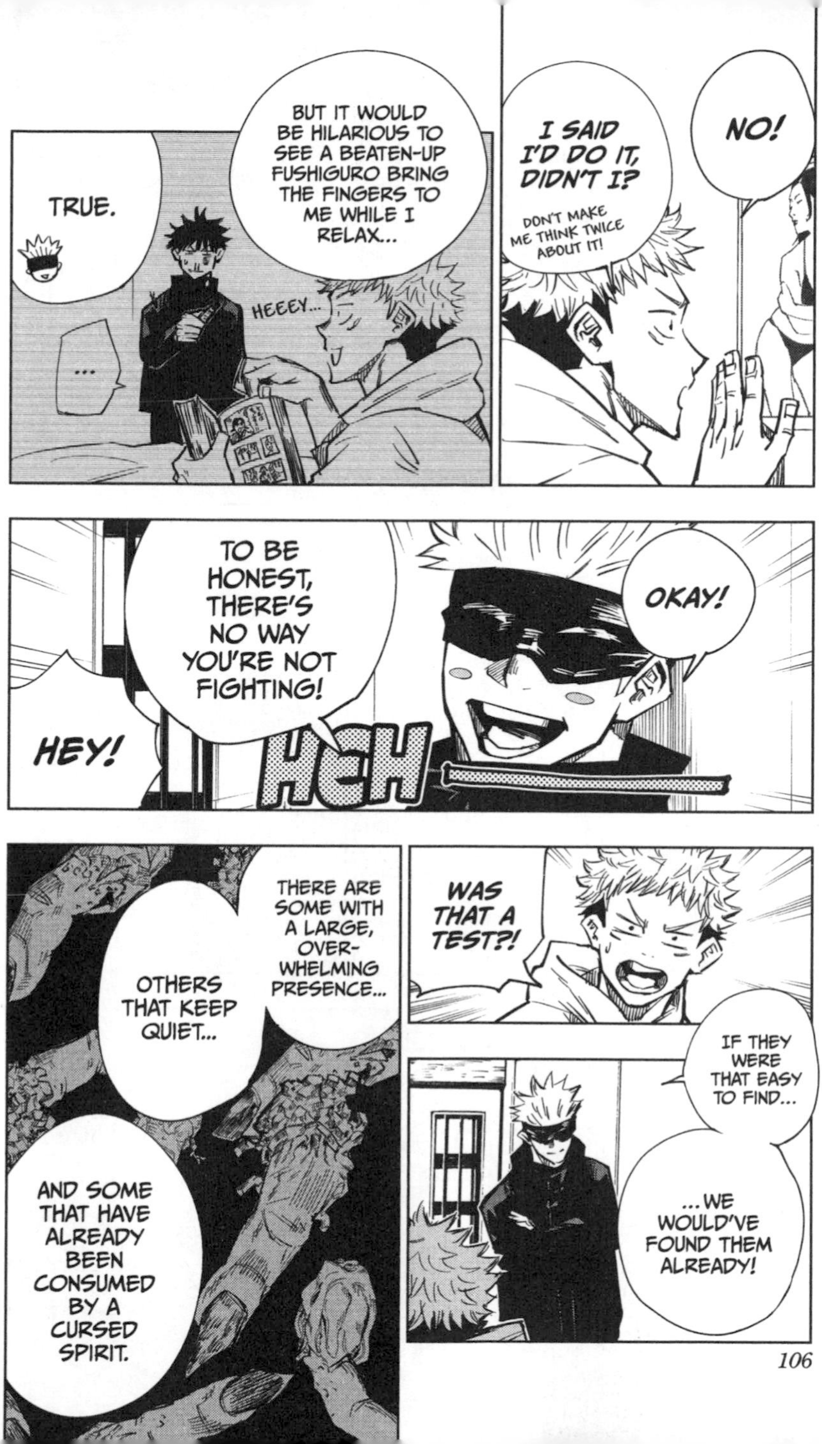
NO!
I SAID I'D DO IT, DIDN'T I?
DON'T MAKE ME THINK TWICE ABOUT IT!
BUT IT WOULD BE HILARIOUS TO SEE A BEATEN-UP FUSHIGURO BRING THE FINGERS TO ME WHILE I RELAX...
TRUE.
HEEEY...
...
OKAY!
TO BE HONEST, THERE'S NO WAY YOU'RE NOT FIGHTING!
HCH
HEY!
WAS THAT A TEST?!
IF THEY WERE THAT EASY TO FIND...
...WE WOULD'VE FOUND THEM ALREADY!
THERE ARE SOME WITH A LARGE, OVER-WHELMING PRESENCE...
OTHERS THAT KEEP QUIET...
AND SOME THAT HAVE ALREADY BEEN CONSUMED BY A CURSED SPIRIT.

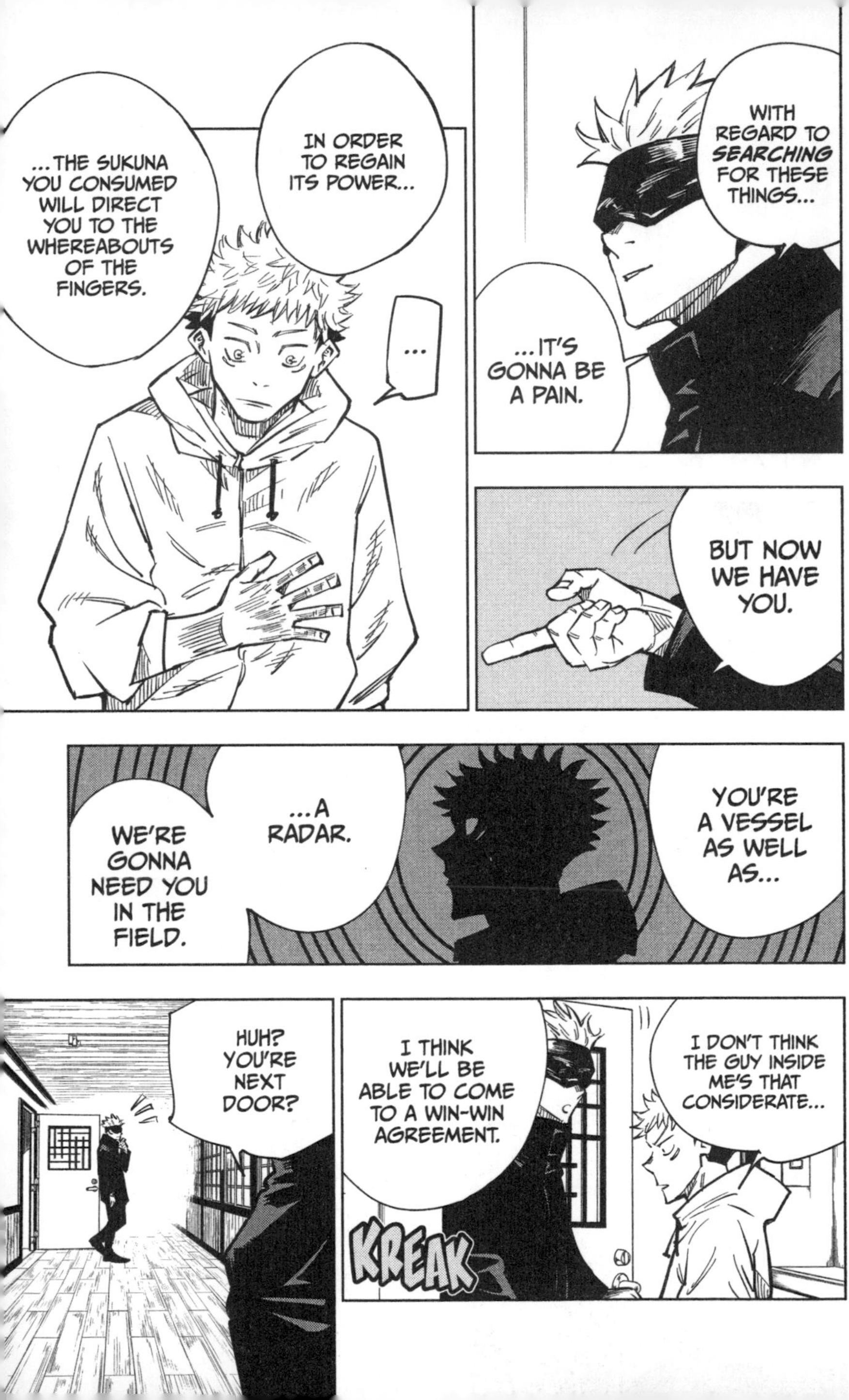
WITH REGARD TO SEARCHING FOR THESE THINGS...
...IT'S GONNA BE A PAIN.
BUT NOW WE HAVE YOU.
IN ORDER TO REGAIN ITS POWER...
...THE SUKUNA YOU CONSUMED WILL DIRECT YOU TO THE WHEREABOUTS OF THE FINGERS.
...
YOU'RE A VESSEL AS WELL AS...
...A RADAR.
WE'RE GONNA NEED YOU IN THE FIELD.
I DON'T THINK THE GUY INSIDE ME'S THAT CONSIDERATE...
I THINK WE'LL BE ABLE TO COME TO A WIN-WIN AGREEMENT.
KREAK
HUH? YOU'RE NEXT DOOR?

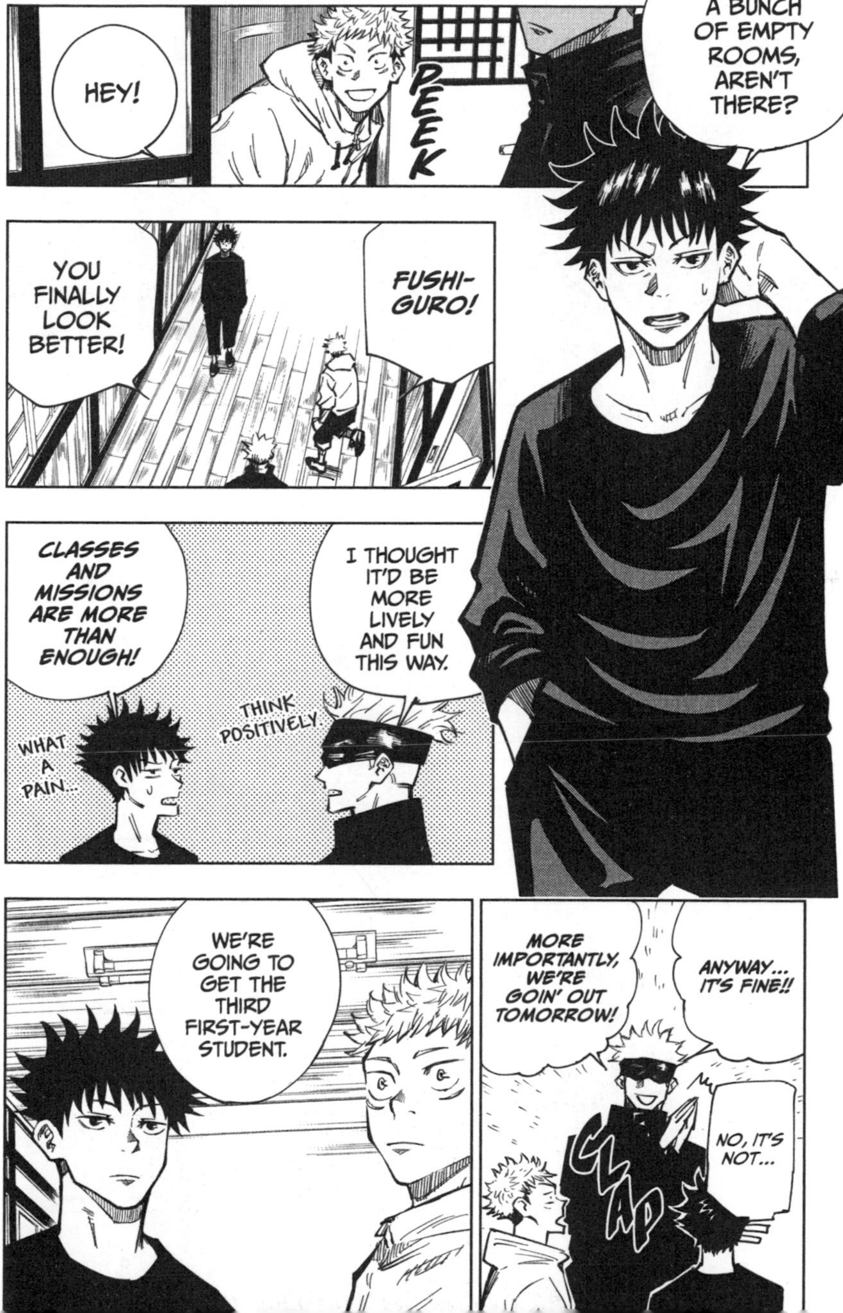
HEY!
PEEK
FUSHI-GURO!
YOU FINALLY LOOK BETTER!
THERE'RE A BUNCH OF EMPTY ROOMS, AREN'T THERE?
I THOUGHT IT'D BE MORE LIVELY AND FUN THIS WAY.
THINK POSITIVELY.
CLASSES AND MISSIONS ARE MORE THAN ENOUGH!
WHAT A PAIN...
ANYWAY... IT'S FINE!!
MORE IMPORTANTLY, WE'RE GOIN' OUT TOMORROW!
CLAP
NO, IT'S NOT...
WE'RE GOING TO GET THE THIRD FIRST-YEAR STUDENT.

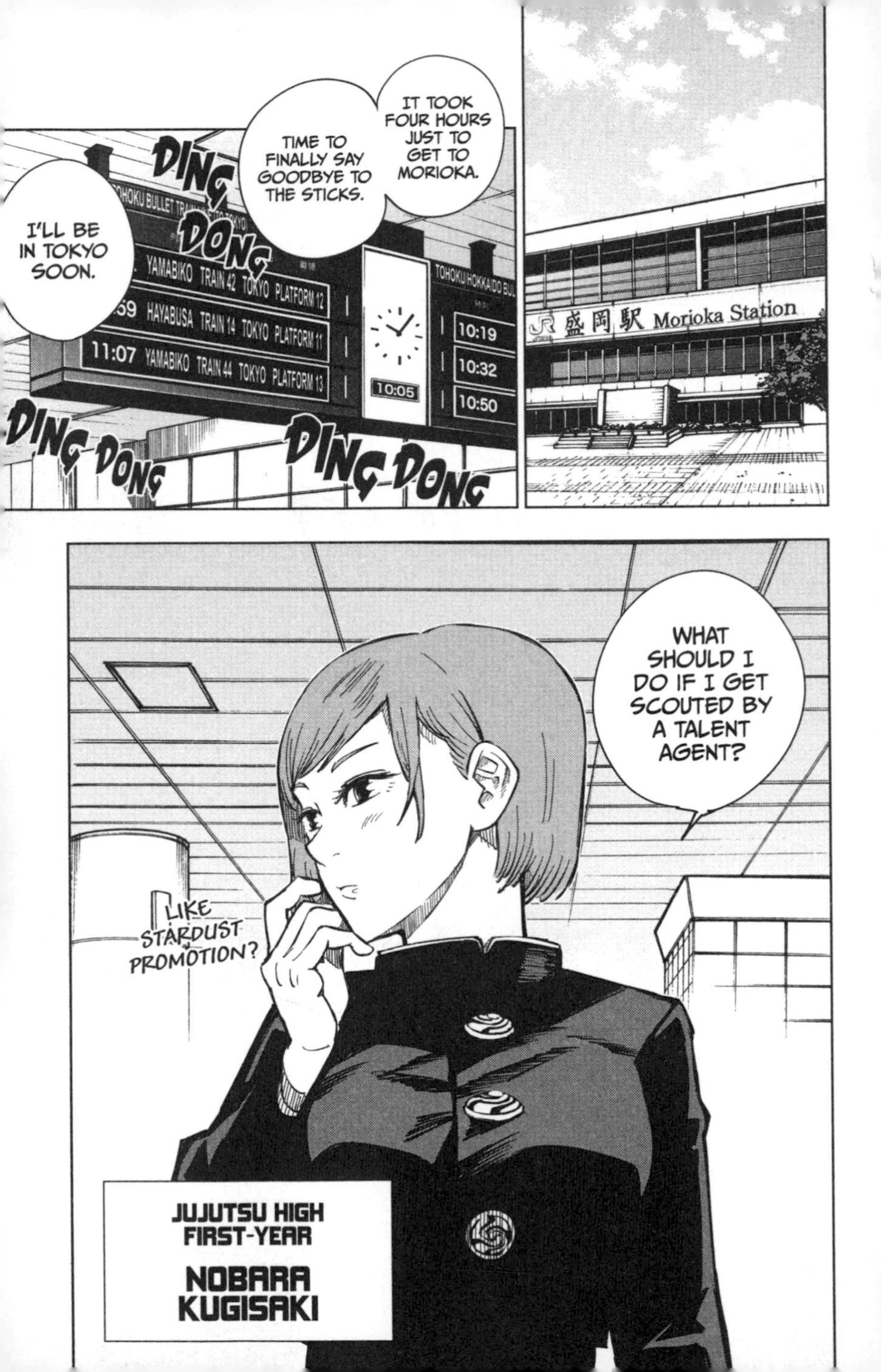
盛岡駅 Morioka Station
IT TOOK FOUR HOURS JUST TO GET TO MORIOKA.
TIME TO FINALLY SAY GOODBYE TO THE STICKS.
I'LL BE IN TOKYO SOON.
DING DONG
YAMABIKO TRAIN 42 TOKYO PLATFORM 12
HAYABUSA TRAIN 14 TOKYO PLATFORM 11
11:07 YAMABIKO TRAIN 44 TOKYO PLATFORM 13
10:05
10:19
10:32
10:50
DING DONG
DING DONG
WHAT SHOULD I DO IF I GET SCOUTED BY A TALENT AGENT?
LIKE STARDUST PROMOTION?
JUJUTSU HIGH FIRST-YEAR
NOBARA KUGISAKI

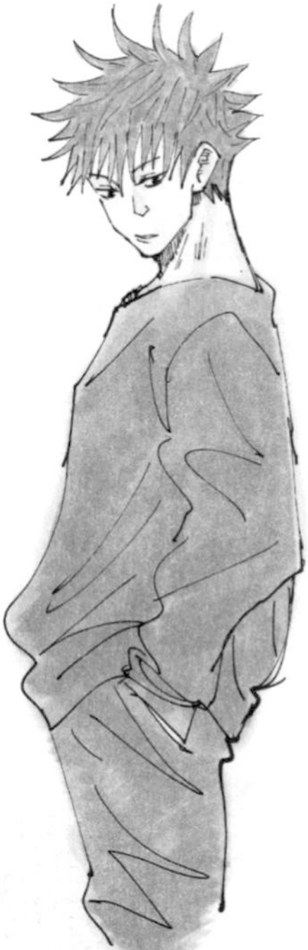

MEGUMI FUSHIGURO

- He's 175 centimeters tall, which is a little taller than Itadori, who is still growing.
- He likes reading nonfiction.
- He knows Gojo from before he entered Jujutsu High.
- He likes food that pairs well with ginger and dislikes red bell peppers.
- He wears clothes that would be comfortable at home.

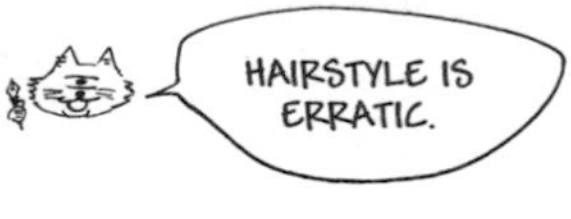
HAIRSTYLE IS ERRATIC.

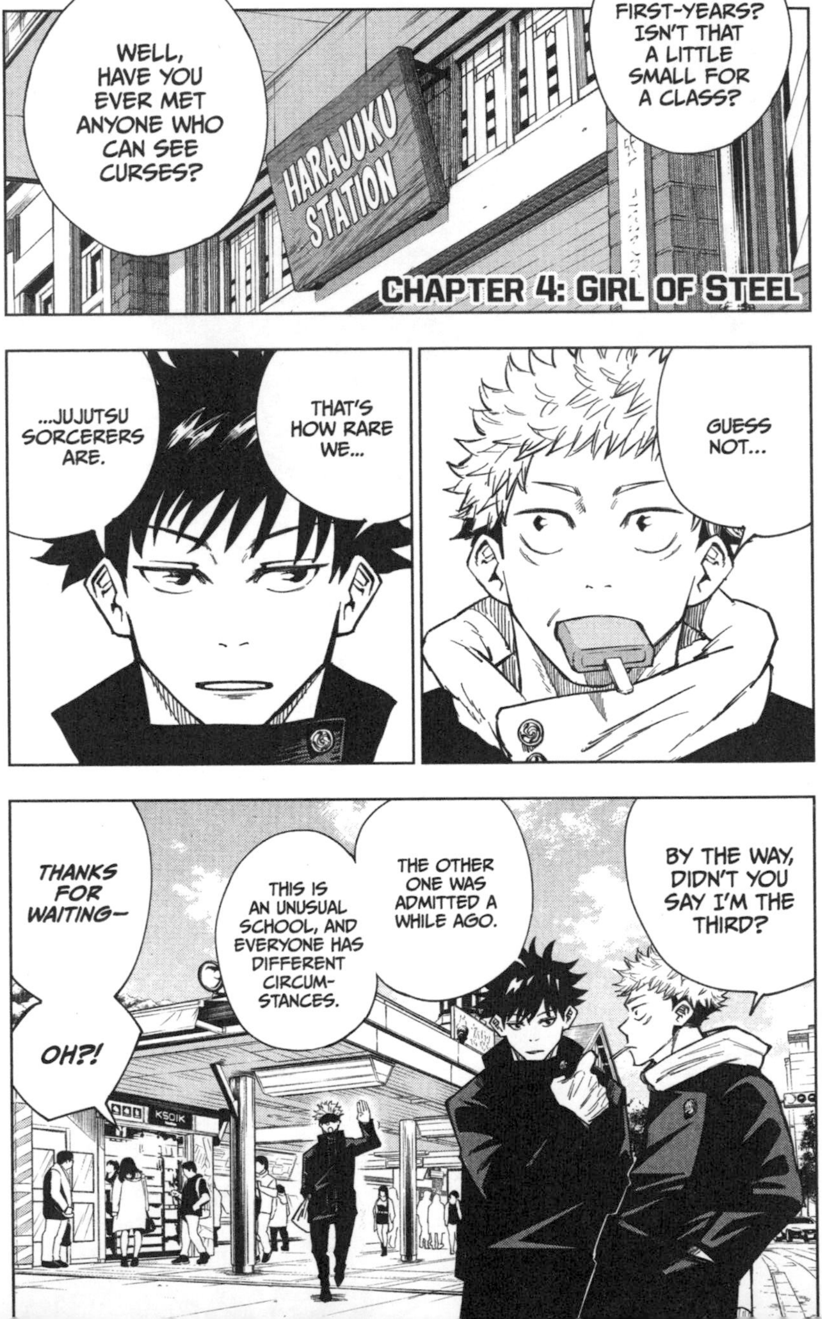
ONLY THREE FIRST-YEARS? ISN'T THAT A LITTLE SMALL FOR A CLASS?
WELL, HAVE YOU EVER MET ANYONE WHO CAN SEE CURSES?
HARAJUKU STATION
CHAPTER 4: GIRL OF STEEL
GUESS NOT...
THAT'S HOW RARE WE...
...JUJUTSU SORCERERS ARE.
BY THE WAY, DIDN'T YOU SAY I'M THE THIRD?
THE OTHER ONE WAS ADMITTED A WHILE AGO.
THIS IS AN UNUSUAL SCHOOL, AND EVERYONE HAS DIFFERENT CIRCUM-STANCES.
THANKS FOR WAITING—
OH?!
KSOIK

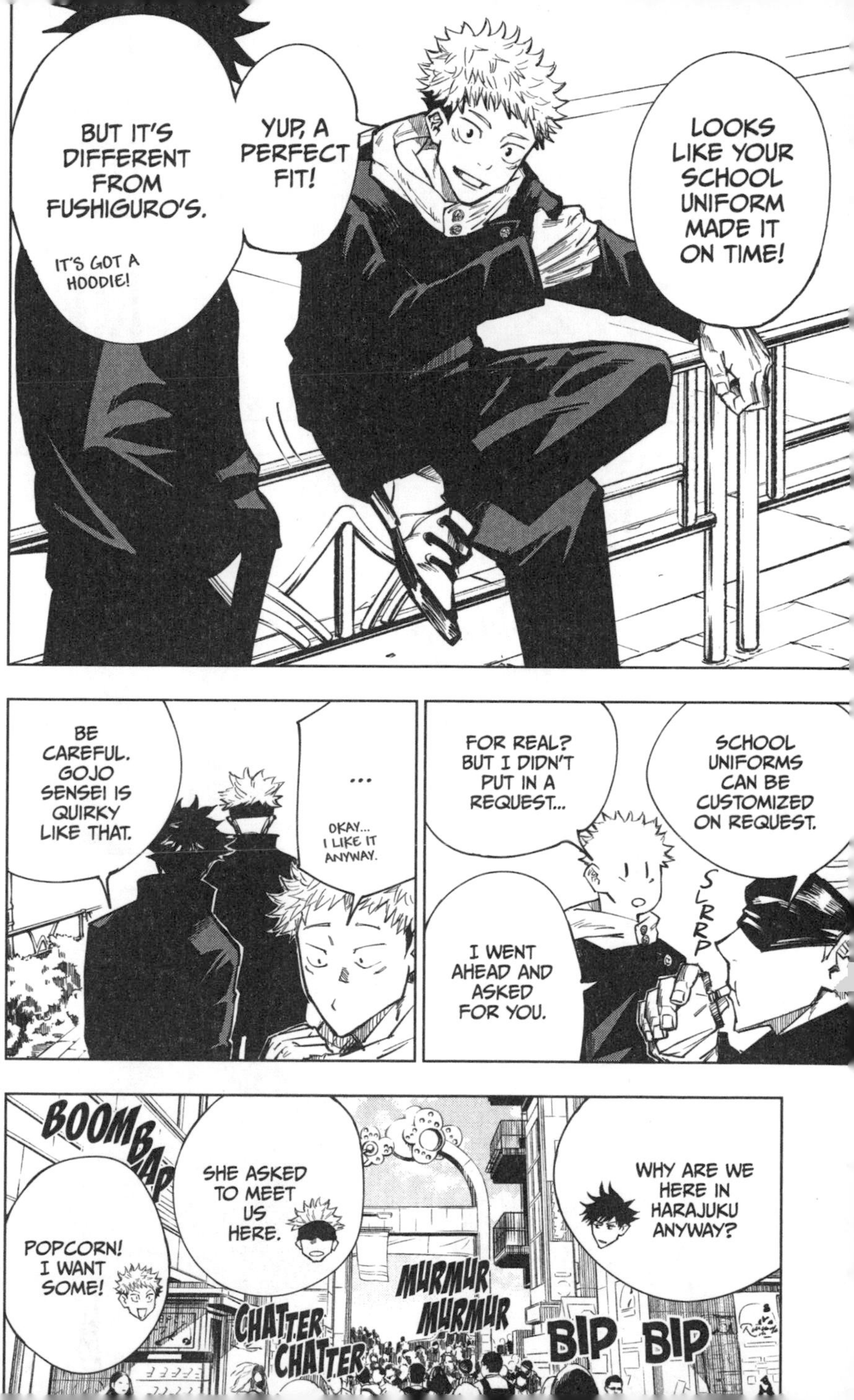
LOOKS LIKE YOUR SCHOOL UNIFORM MADE IT ON TIME!
YUP, A PERFECT FIT!
BUT IT'S DIFFERENT FROM FUSHIGURO'S.
IT'S GOT A HOODIE!
SCHOOL UNIFORMS CAN BE CUSTOMIZED ON REQUEST.
FOR REAL? BUT I DIDN'T PUT IN A REQUEST...
SLRRP
I WENT AHEAD AND ASKED FOR YOU.
...
OKAY... I LIKE IT ANYWAY.
BE CAREFUL. GOJO SENSEI IS QUIRKY LIKE THAT.
WHY ARE WE HERE IN HARAJUKU ANYWAY?
BIP BIP
SHE ASKED TO MEET US HERE.
MURMUR MURMUR
BOOMBAP
POPCORN! I WANT SOME!
CHATTER CHATTER

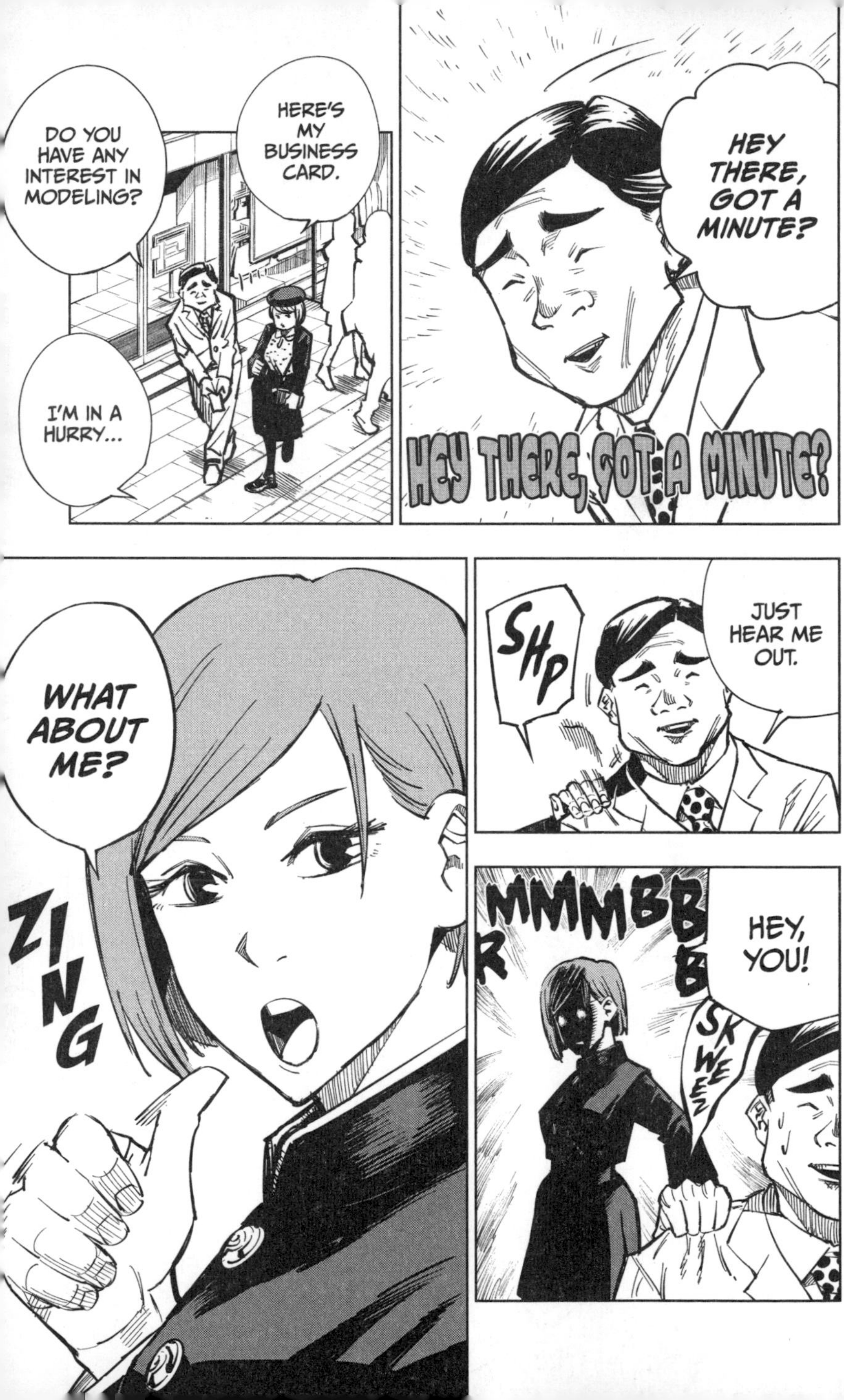

HEY THERE, GOT A MINUTE?
HEY THERE, GOT A MINUTE?
HERE'S MY BUSINESS CARD.
DO YOU HAVE ANY INTEREST IN MODELING?
I'M IN A HURRY...
JUST HEAR ME OUT.
SHP
HEY, YOU!
MMMMBBBR
SKWEEZ
WHAT ABOUT ME?
ZING

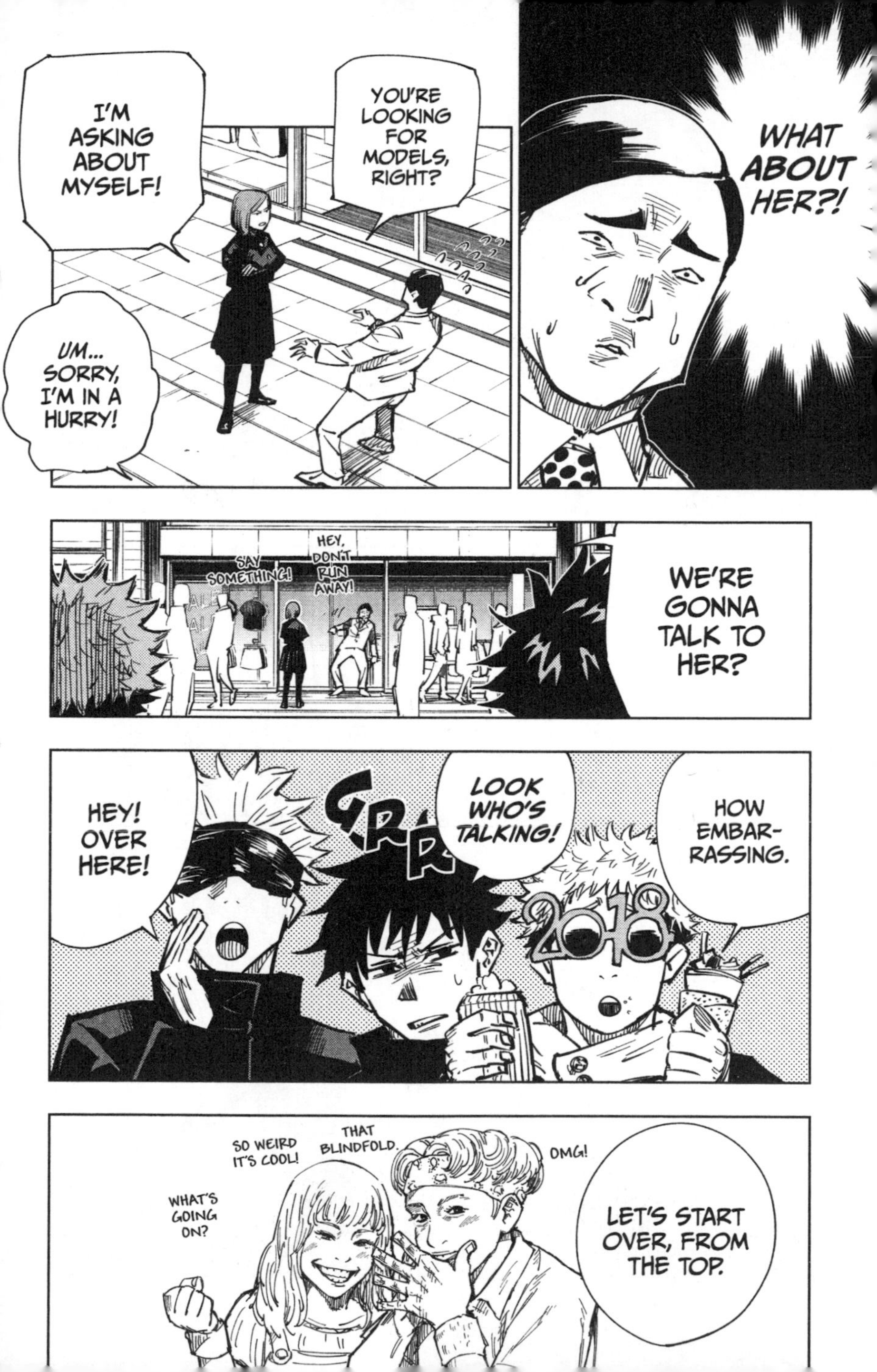
WHAT ABOUT HER?!
YOU'RE LOOKING FOR MODELS, RIGHT?
I'M ASKING ABOUT MYSELF!
UM... SORRY, I'M IN A HURRY!
WE'RE GONNA TALK TO HER?
HEY, DON'T RUN AWAY!
SAY SOMETHING!
HOW EMBARRASSING.
LOOK WHO'S TALKING!
GRR
HEY! OVER HERE!
LET'S START OVER, FROM THE TOP.
OMG!
THAT BLINDFOLD.
SO WEIRD IT'S COOL!
WHAT'S GOING ON?

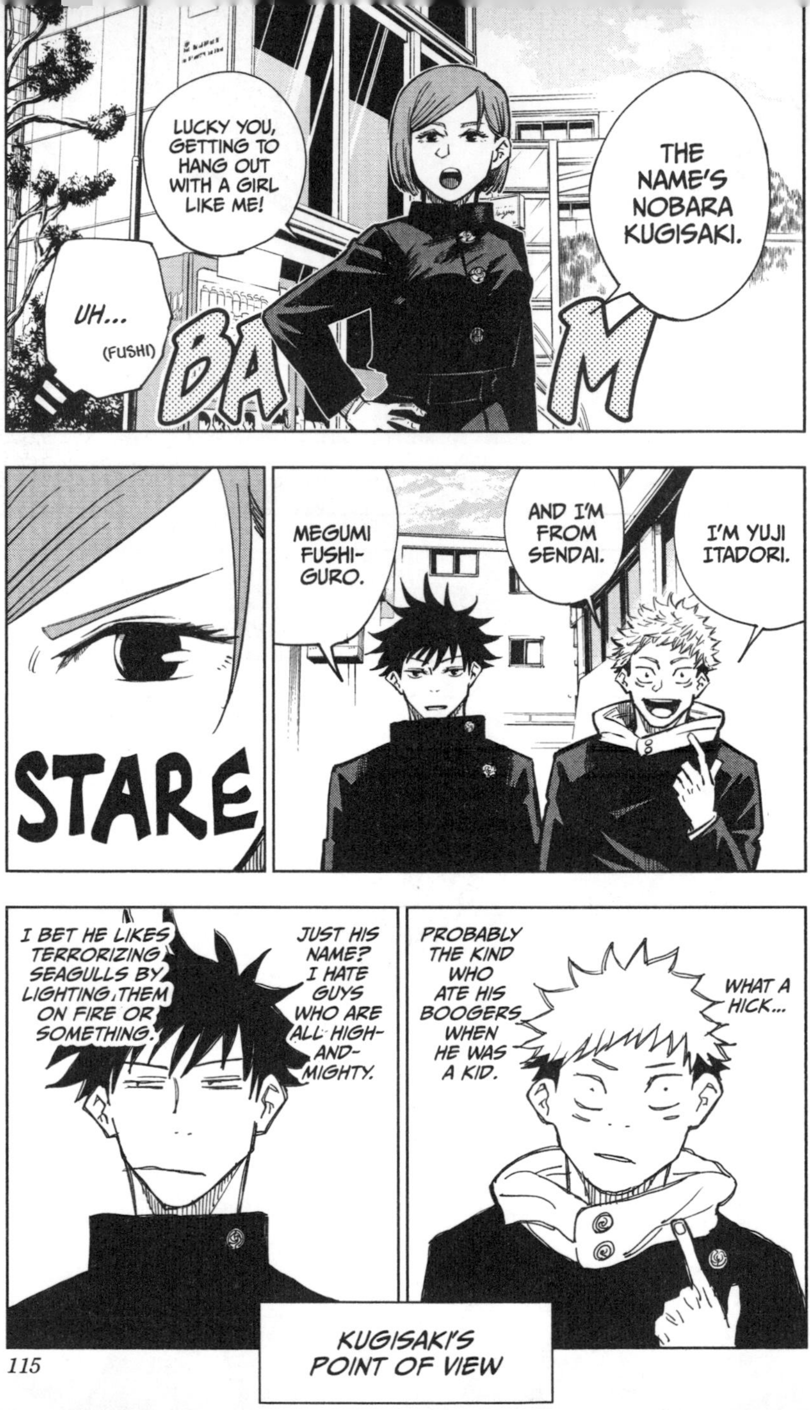
THE NAME'S NOBARA KUGISAKI.
LUCKY YOU, GETTING TO HANG OUT WITH A GIRL LIKE ME!
UH...
(FUSHI)
BAM
I'M YUJI ITADORI.
AND I'M FROM SENDAI.
MEGUMI FUSHI-GURO.
STARE
WHAT A HICK...
PROBABLY THE KIND WHO ATE HIS BOOGERS WHEN HE WAS A KID.
JUST HIS NAME? I HATE GUYS WHO ARE ALL HIGH-AND-MIGHTY.
I BET HE LIKES TERRORIZING SEAGULLS BY LIGHTING THEM ON FIRE OR SOMETHING.
KUGISAKI'S POINT OF VIEW

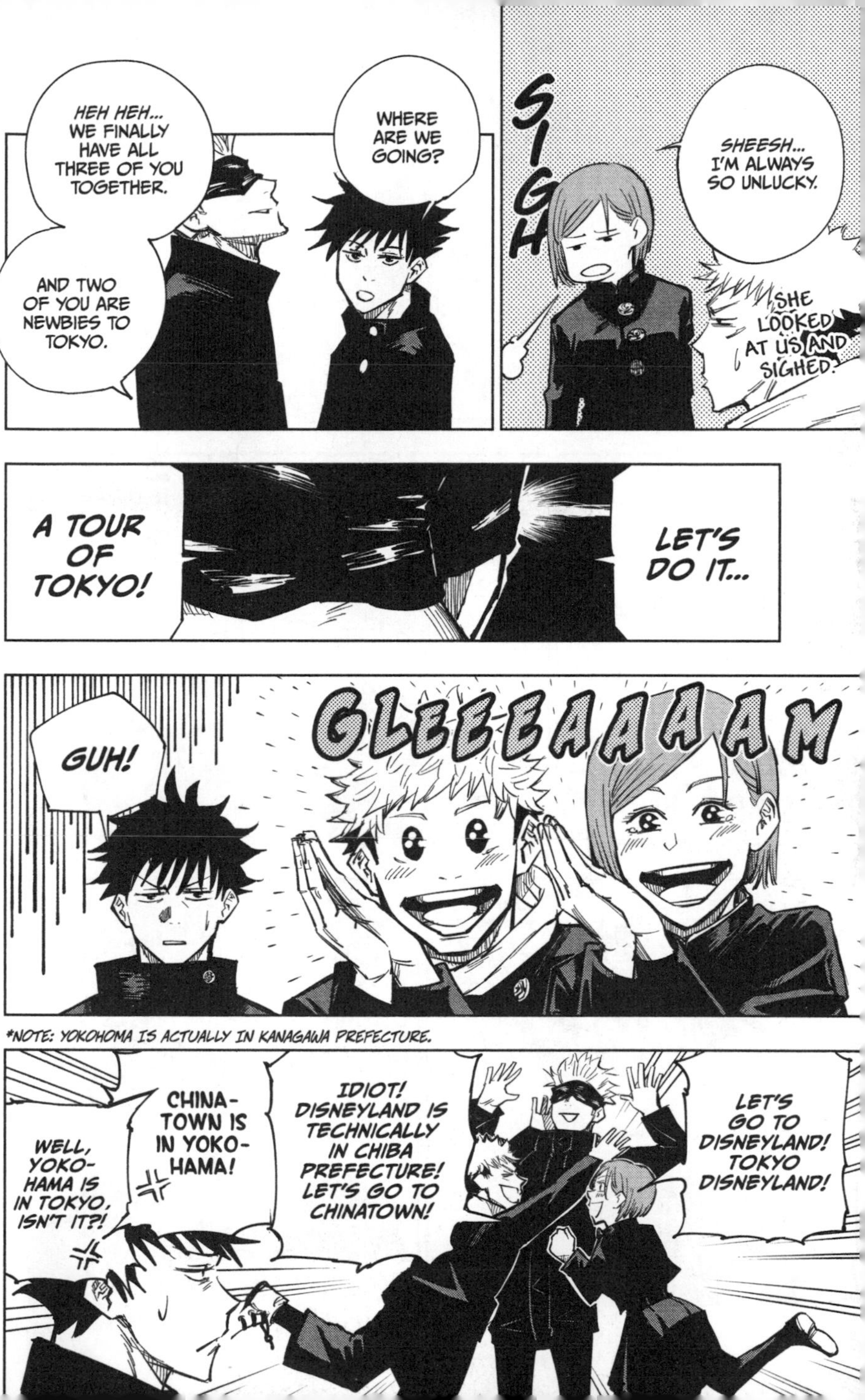
SIGH
SHEESH... I'M ALWAYS SO UNLUCKY.
SHE LOOKED AT US AND SIGHED.
WHERE ARE WE GOING?
HEH HEH... WE FINALLY HAVE ALL THREE OF YOU TOGETHER.
AND TWO OF YOU ARE NEWBIES TO TOKYO.
LET'S DO IT...
A TOUR OF TOKYO!
GLEEEAAAAM
GUH!
*NOTE: YOKOHOMA IS ACTUALLY IN KANAGAWA PREFECTURE.
LET'S GO TO DISNEYLAND! TOKYO DISNEYLAND!
IDIOT! DISNEYLAND IS TECHNICALLY IN CHIBA PREFECTURE! LET'S GO TO CHINATOWN!
CHINA-TOWN IS IN YOKO-HAMA!
WELL, YOKO-HAMA IS IN TOKYO, ISN'T IT?!

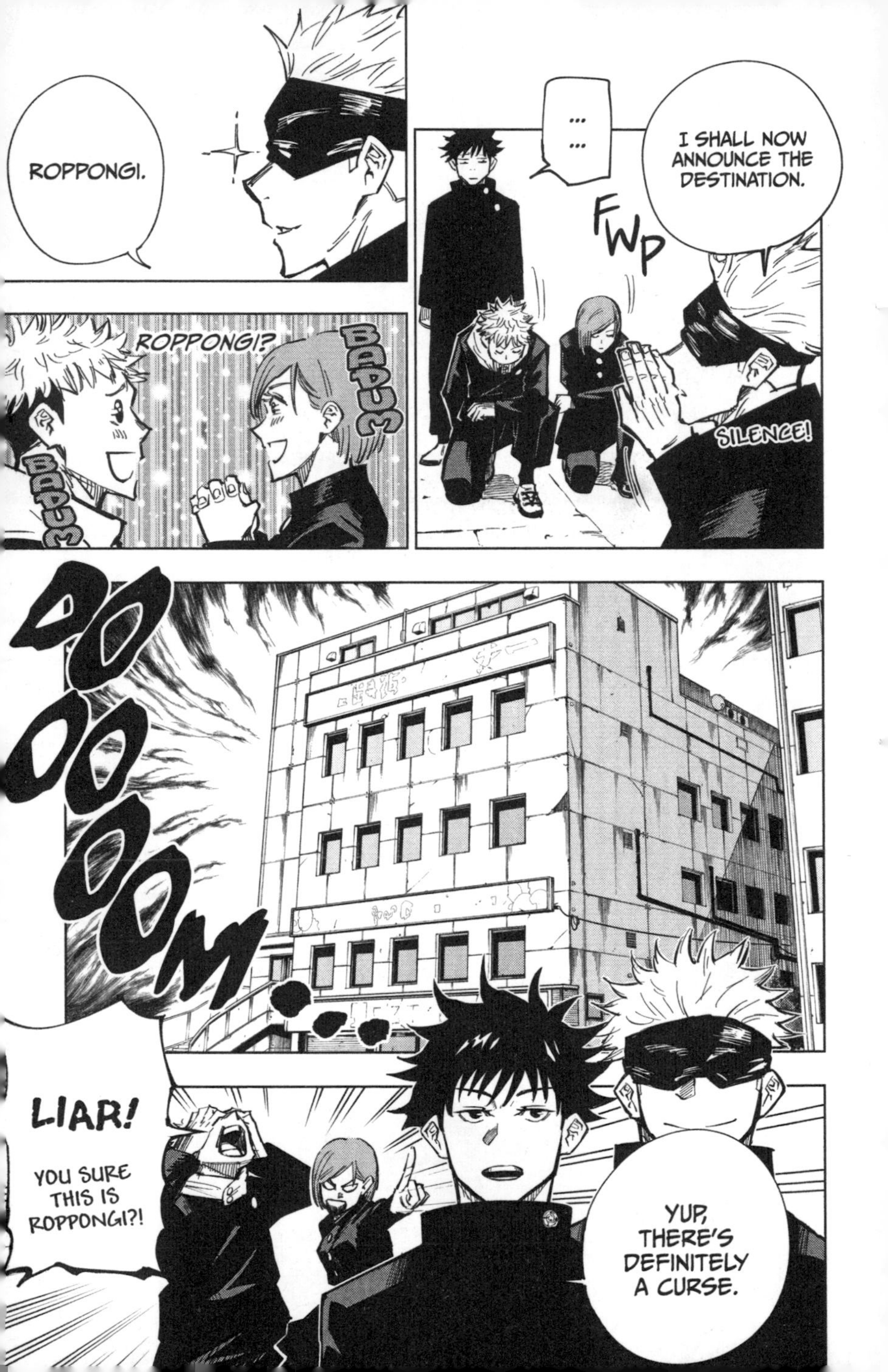
I SHALL NOW ANNOUNCE THE DESTINATION.
...
...
FWP
SILENCE!
ROPPONGI.
ROPPONGI!?
BADUM
BADUM
DOOOOOM...
YUP, THERE'S DEFINITELY A CURSE.
LIAR!
YOU SURE THIS IS ROPPONGI?!

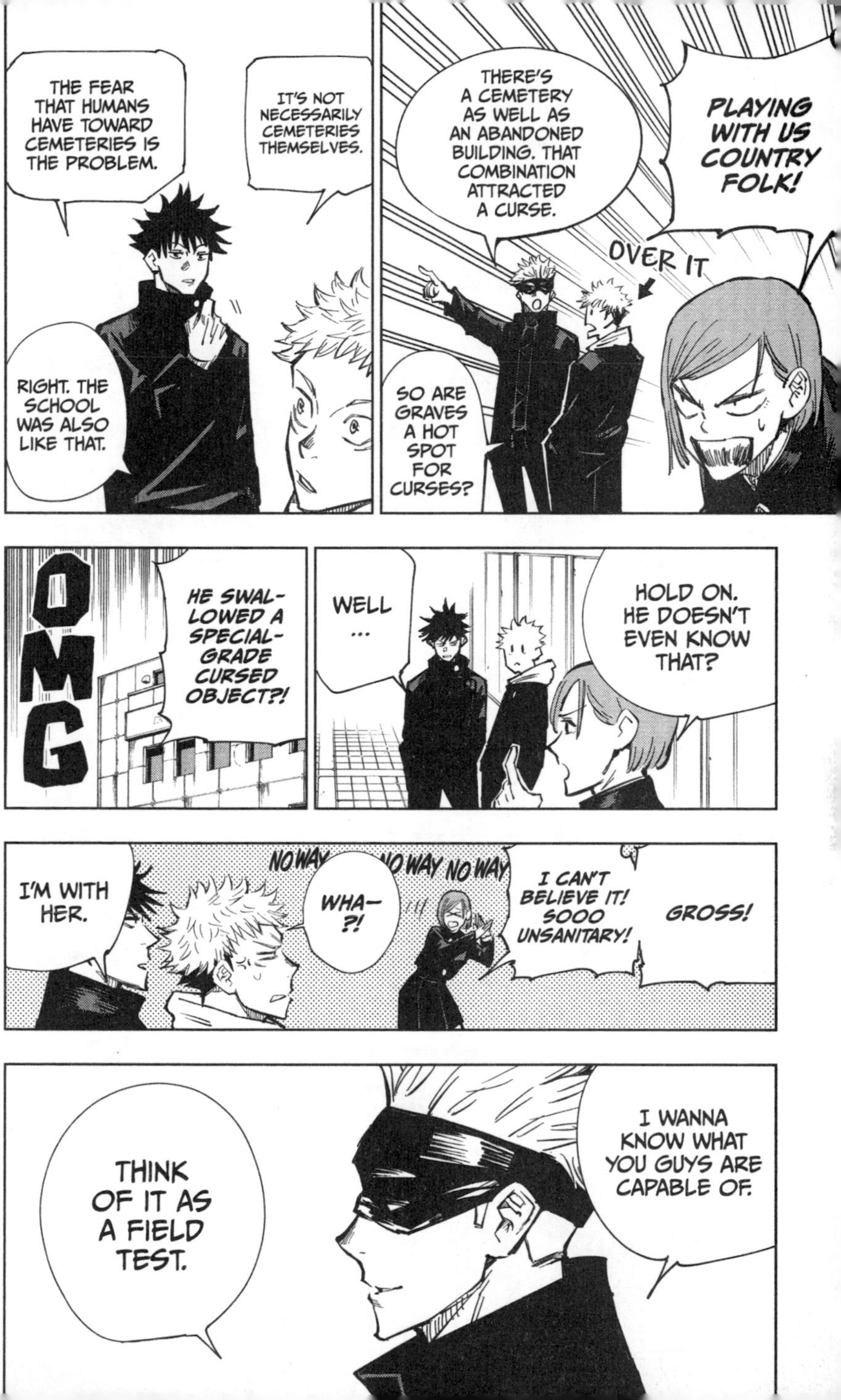
PLAYING WITH US COUNTRY FOLK!
THERE'S A CEMETERY AS WELL AS AN ABANDONED BUILDING. THAT COMBINATION ATTRACTED A CURSE.
OVER IT
SO ARE GRAVES A HOT SPOT FOR CURSES?
IT'S NOT NECESSARILY CEMETERIES THEMSELVES.
THE FEAR THAT HUMANS HAVE TOWARD CEMETERIES IS THE PROBLEM.
RIGHT. THE SCHOOL WAS ALSO LIKE THAT.
HOLD ON. HE DOESN'T EVEN KNOW THAT?
WELL ...
HE SWAL- LOWED A SPECIAL- GRADE CURSED OBJECT?!
OMG
GROSS!
I CAN'T BELIEVE IT! SOOO UNSANITARY!
NO WAY NO WAY NO WAY
WHA— ?!
I'M WITH HER.
I WANNA KNOW WHAT YOU GUYS ARE CAPABLE OF.
THINK OF IT AS A FIELD TEST.

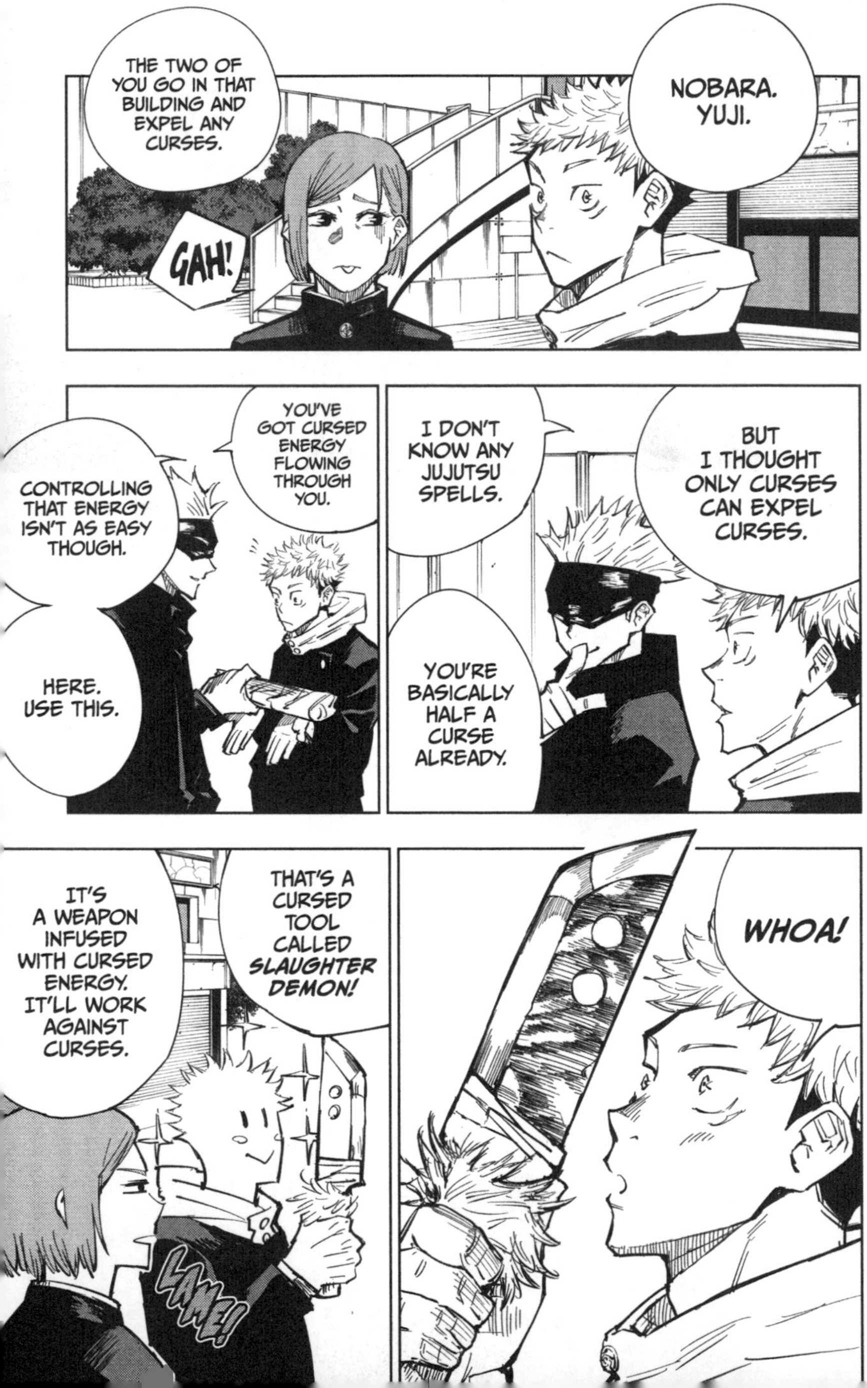
NOBARA. YUJI.
THE TWO OF YOU GO IN THAT BUILDING AND EXPEL ANY CURSES.
GAH!
BUT I THOUGHT ONLY CURSES CAN EXPEL CURSES.
I DON'T KNOW ANY JUJUTSU SPELLS.
YOU'RE BASICALLY HALF A CURSE ALREADY.
YOU'VE GOT CURSED ENERGY FLOWING THROUGH YOU.
CONTROLLING THAT ENERGY ISN'T AS EASY THOUGH.
HERE. USE THIS.
WHOA!
THAT'S A CURSED TOOL CALLED SLAUGHTER DEMON!
IT'S A WEAPON INFUSED WITH CURSED ENERGY. IT'LL WORK AGAINST CURSES.
LAME!!

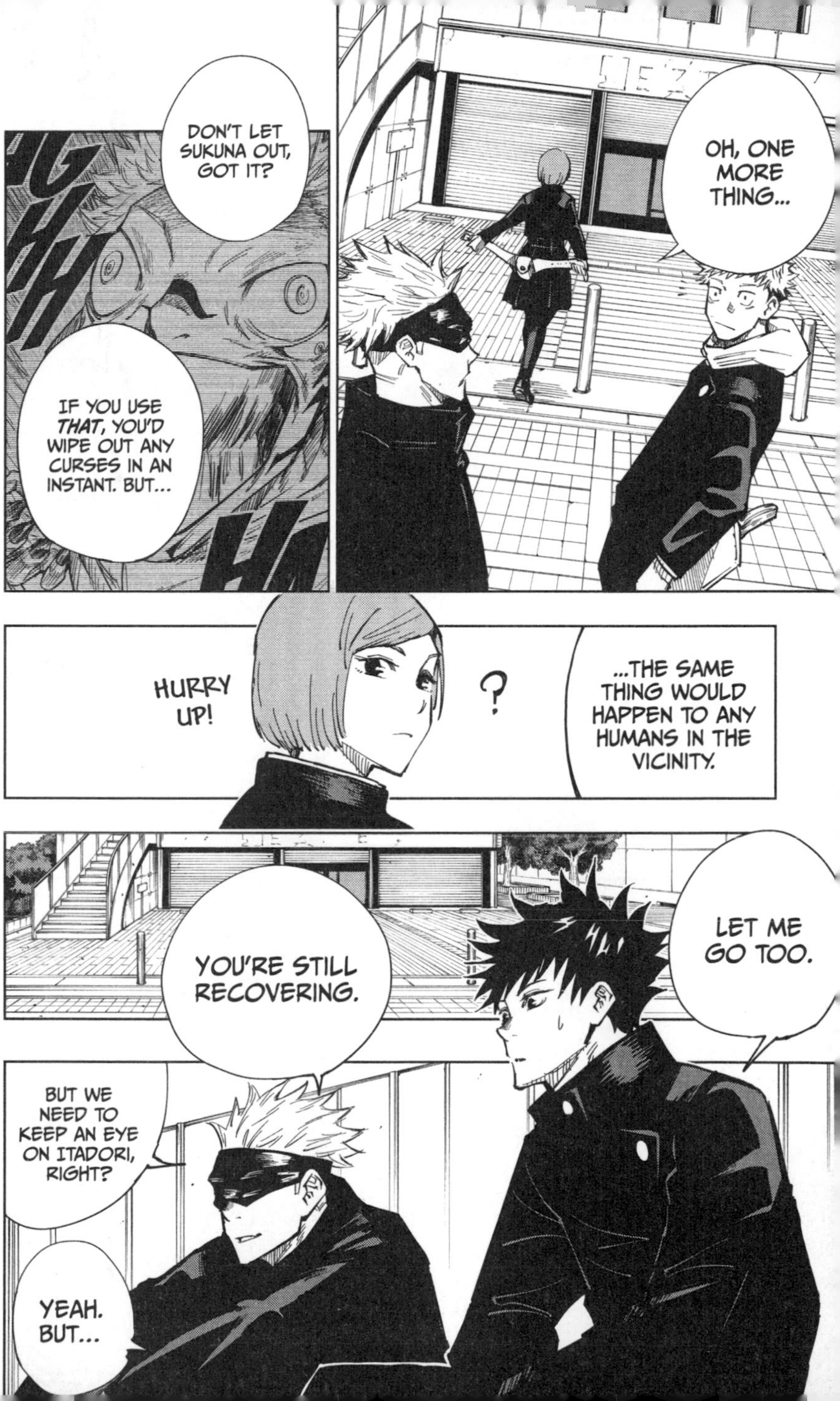
OH, ONE MORE THING...
DON'T LET SUKUNA OUT, GOT IT?
IF YOU USE *THAT*, YOU'D WIPE OUT ANY CURSES IN AN INSTANT. BUT...
...THE SAME THING WOULD HAPPEN TO ANY HUMANS IN THE VICINITY.
?
HURRY UP!
LET ME GO TOO.
YOU'RE STILL RECOVERING.
BUT WE NEED TO KEEP AN EYE ON ITADORI, RIGHT?
YEAH. BUT...

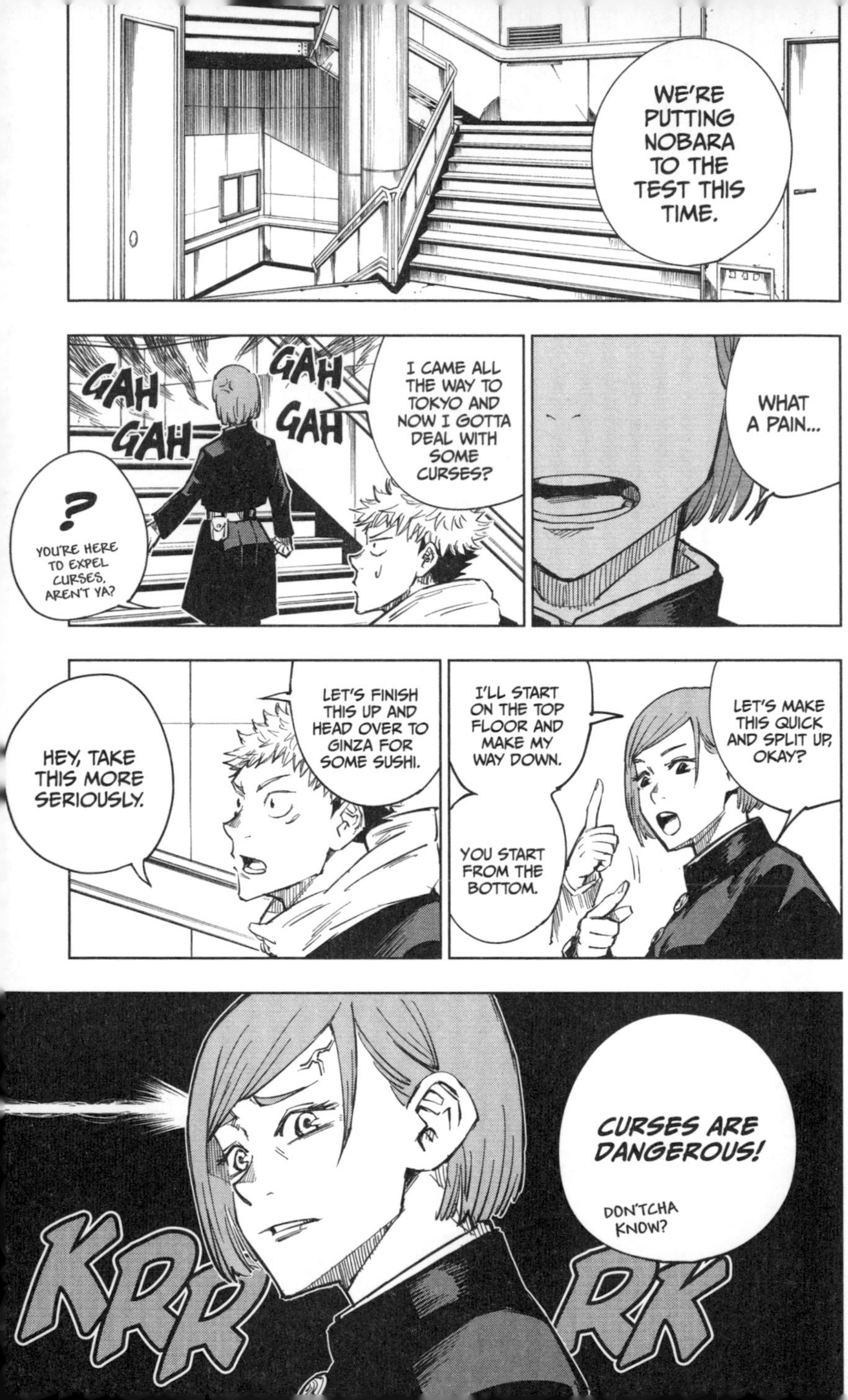
WE'RE PUTTING NOBARA TO THE TEST THIS TIME.
WHAT A PAIN...
I CAME ALL THE WAY TO TOKYO AND NOW I GOTTA DEAL WITH SOME CURSES?
GAH GAH GAH GAH
?
YOU'RE HERE TO EXPEL CURSES, AREN'T YA?
LET'S MAKE THIS QUICK AND SPLIT UP, OKAY?
I'LL START ON THE TOP FLOOR AND MAKE MY WAY DOWN.
YOU START FROM THE BOTTOM.
LET'S FINISH THIS UP AND HEAD OVER TO GINZA FOR SOME SUSHI.
HEY, TAKE THIS MORE SERIOUSLY.
CURSES ARE DANGEROUS!
DON'TCHA KNOW?
KRRRK

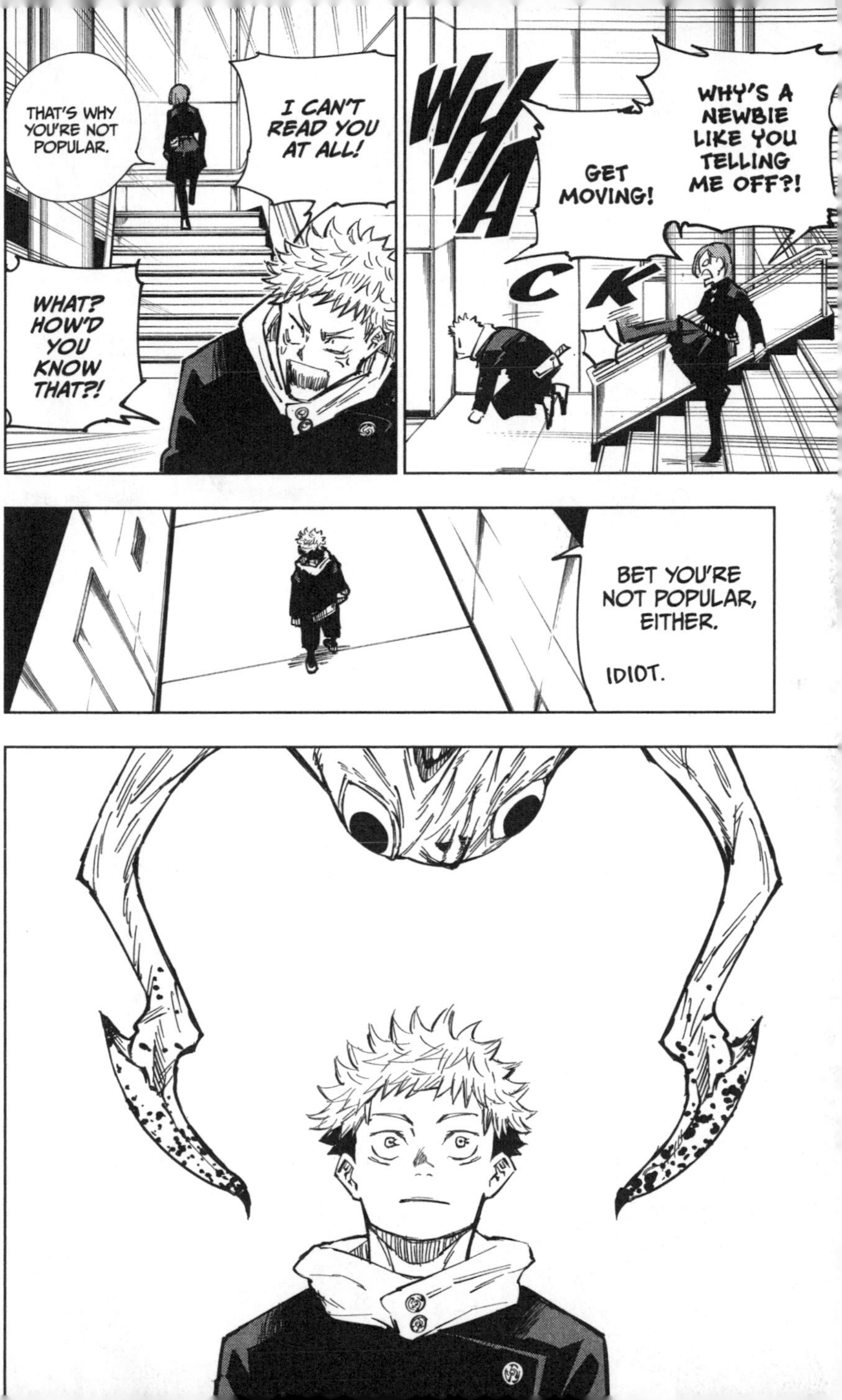
WHY'S A NEWBIE LIKE YOU TELLING ME OFF?!
GET MOVING!
WHACK
I CAN'T READ YOU AT ALL!
THAT'S WHY YOU'RE NOT POPULAR.
WHAT? HOW'D YOU KNOW THAT?!
BET YOU'RE NOT POPULAR, EITHER.
IDIOT.

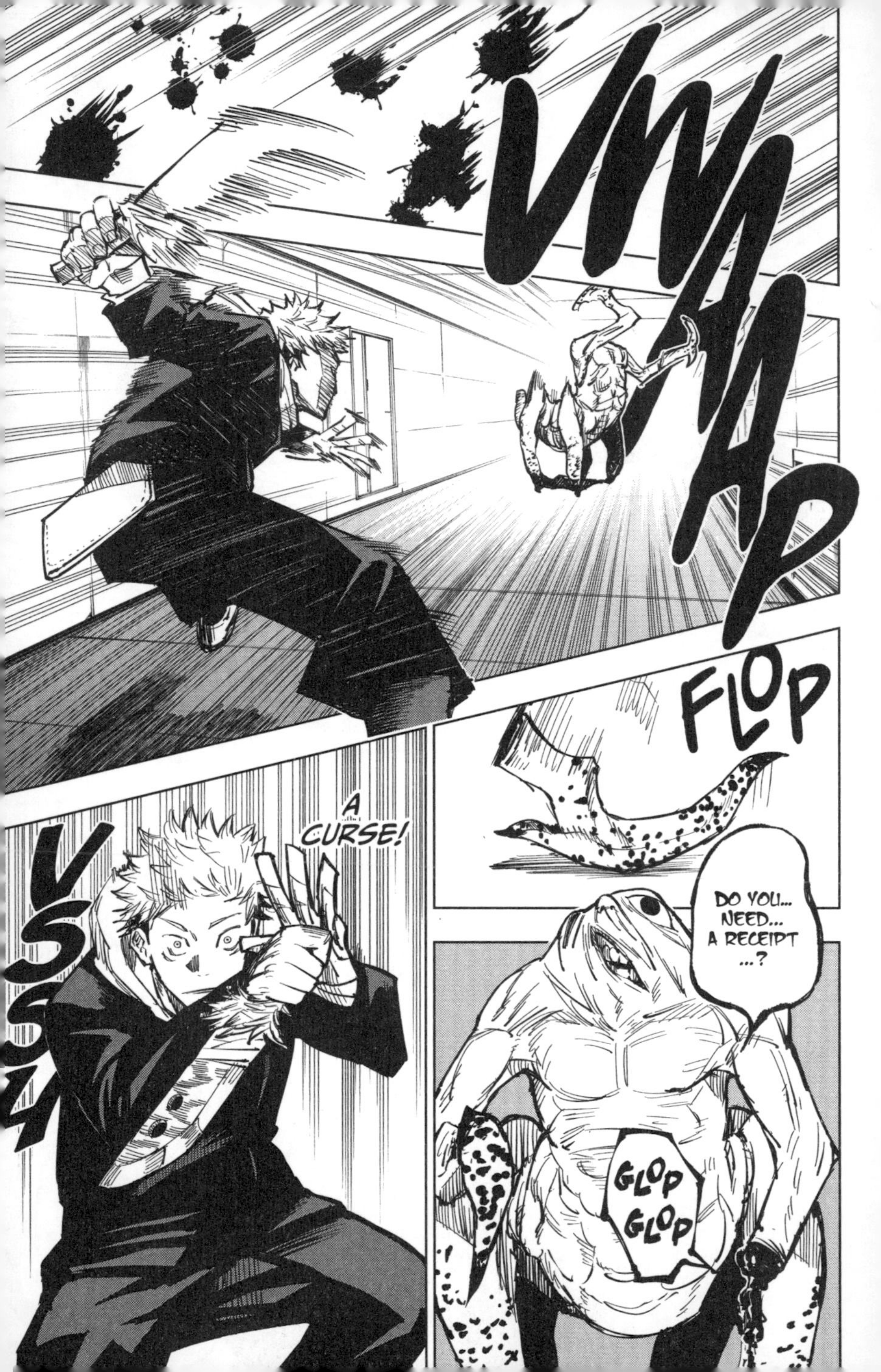
FLOP
DO YOU... NEED... A RECEIPT ...?
GLOP GLOP
A CURSE!

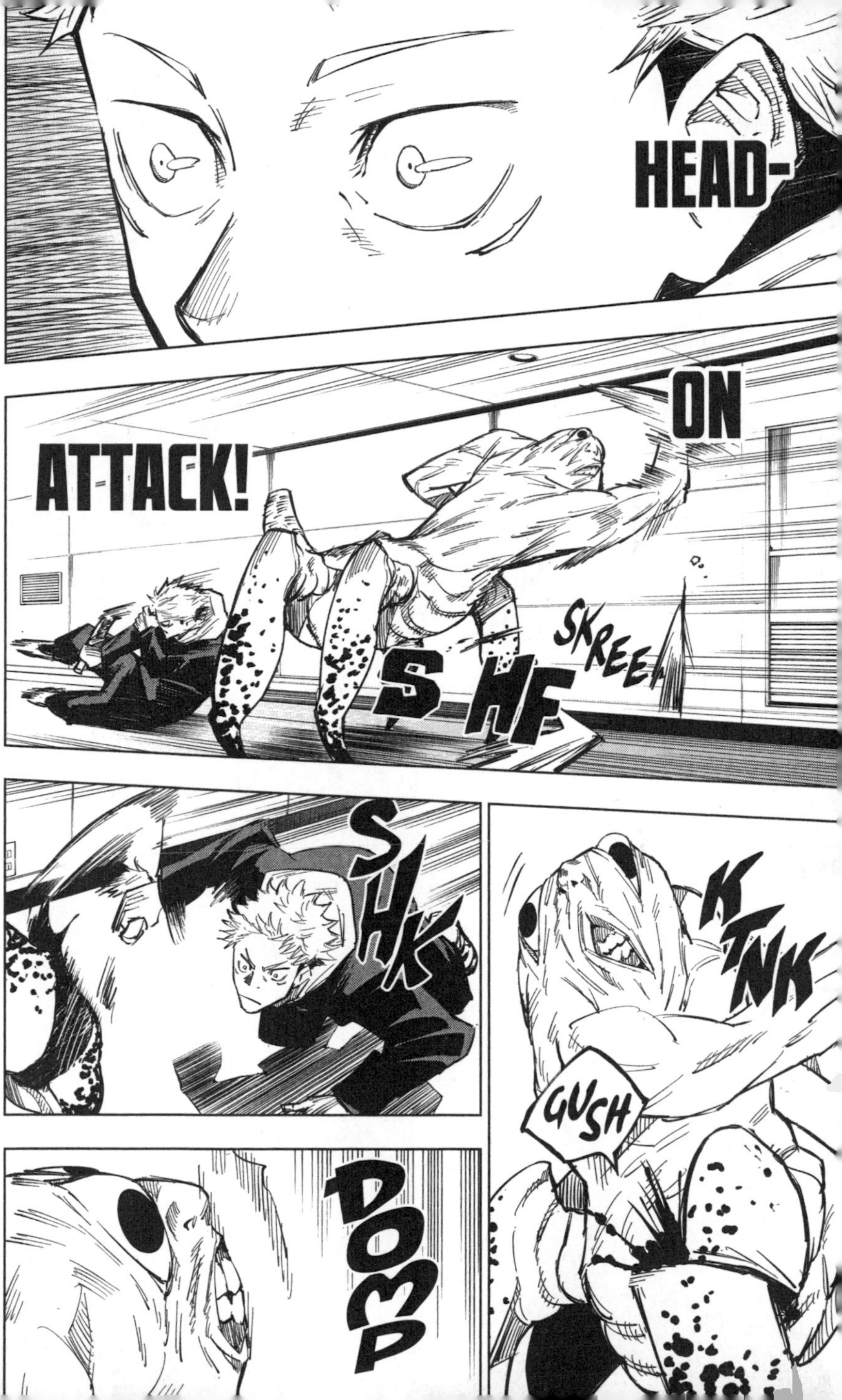
HEAD-
ON
ATTACK!
SKREEE
SHF
KTNK
GUSH
SHK
DOMP

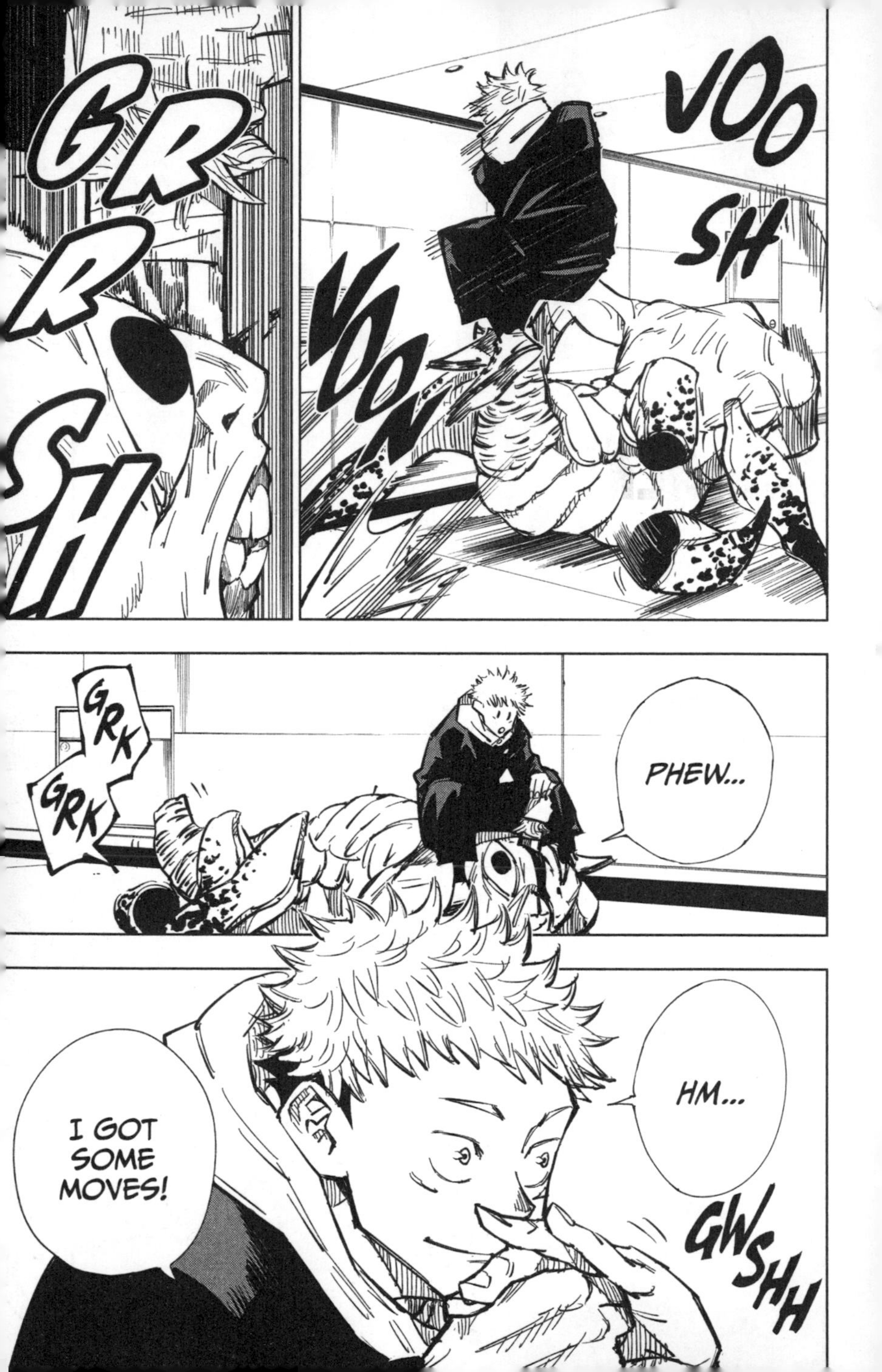
VOOSH
VOON
GRRSHH
PHEW...
GRK GRK
HM...
GWSHH
I GOT SOME MOVES!

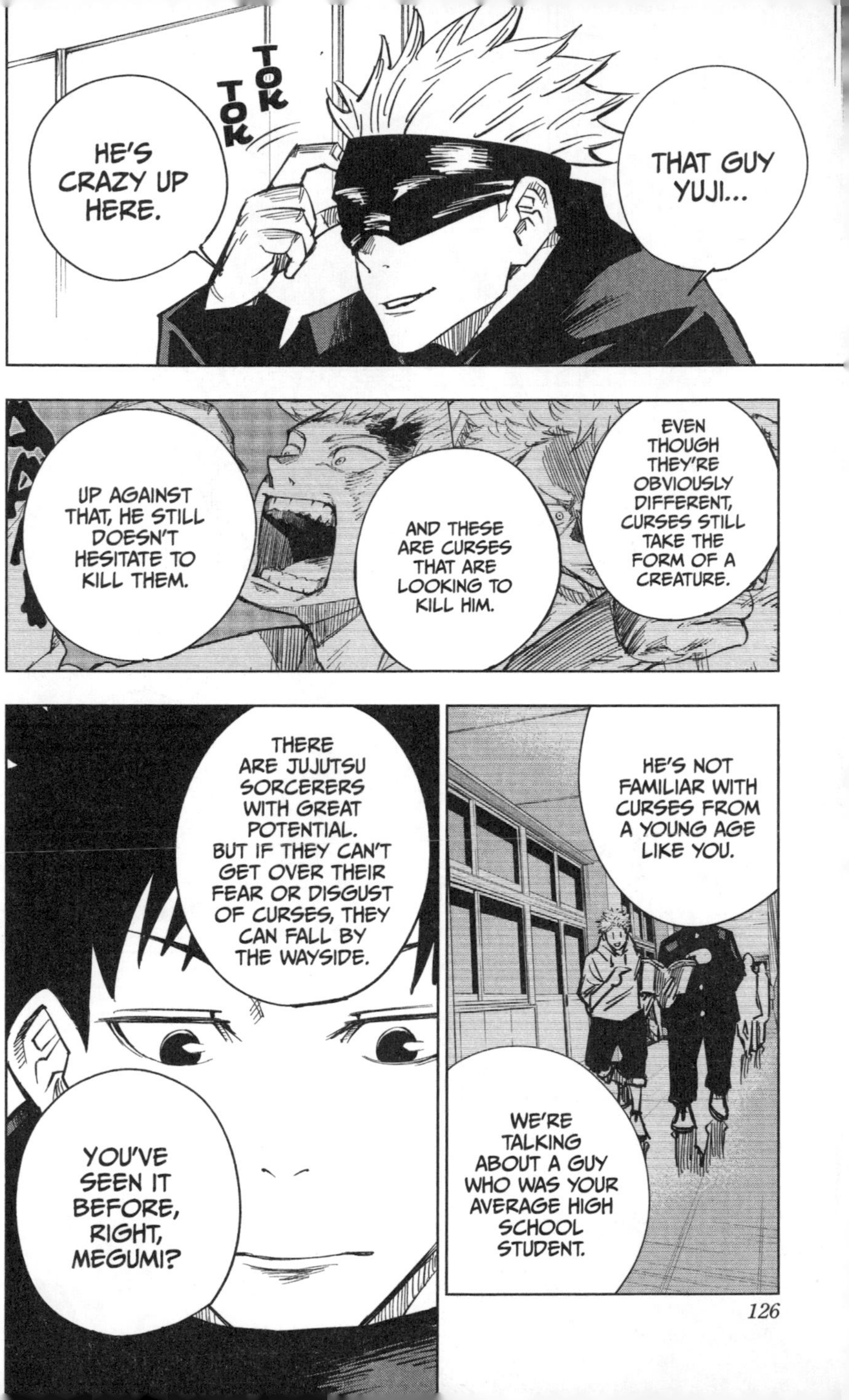
THAT GUY YUJI...
TOK TOK
HE'S CRAZY UP HERE.
EVEN THOUGH THEY'RE OBVIOUSLY DIFFERENT, CURSES STILL TAKE THE FORM OF A CREATURE.
AND THESE ARE CURSES THAT ARE LOOKING TO KILL HIM.
UP AGAINST THAT, HE STILL DOESN'T HESITATE TO KILL THEM.
HE'S NOT FAMILIAR WITH CURSES FROM A YOUNG AGE LIKE YOU.
WE'RE TALKING ABOUT A GUY WHO WAS YOUR AVERAGE HIGH SCHOOL STUDENT.
THERE ARE JUJUTSU SORCERERS WITH GREAT POTENTIAL. BUT IF THEY CAN'T GET OVER THEIR FEAR OR DISGUST OF CURSES, THEY CAN FALL BY THE WAYSIDE.
YOU'VE SEEN IT BEFORE, RIGHT, MEGUMI?

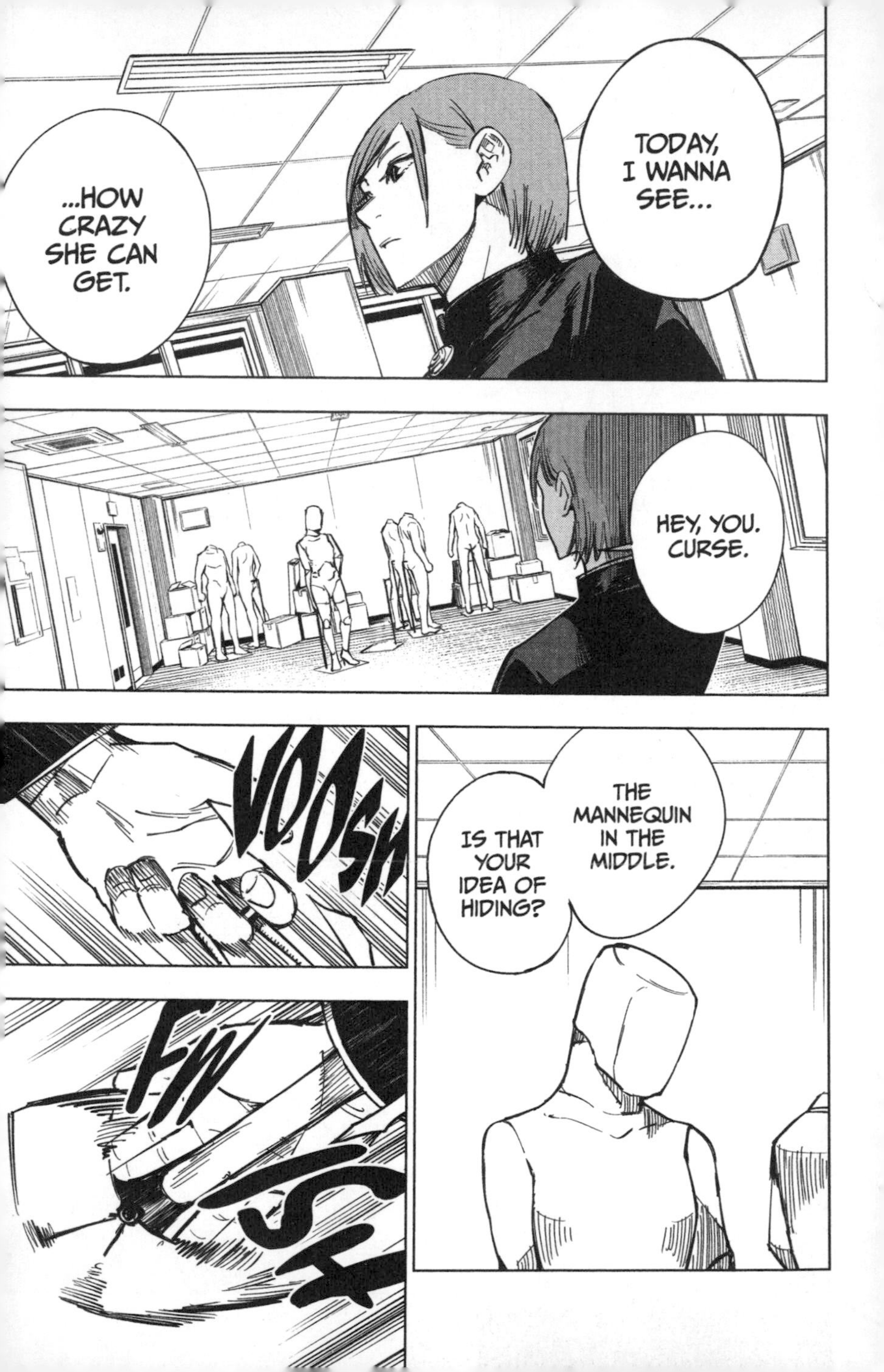
TODAY, I WANNA SEE...
...HOW CRAZY SHE CAN GET.
HEY, YOU. CURSE.
THE MANNEQUIN IN THE MIDDLE.
IS THAT YOUR IDEA OF HIDING?
VOOSH
FWST

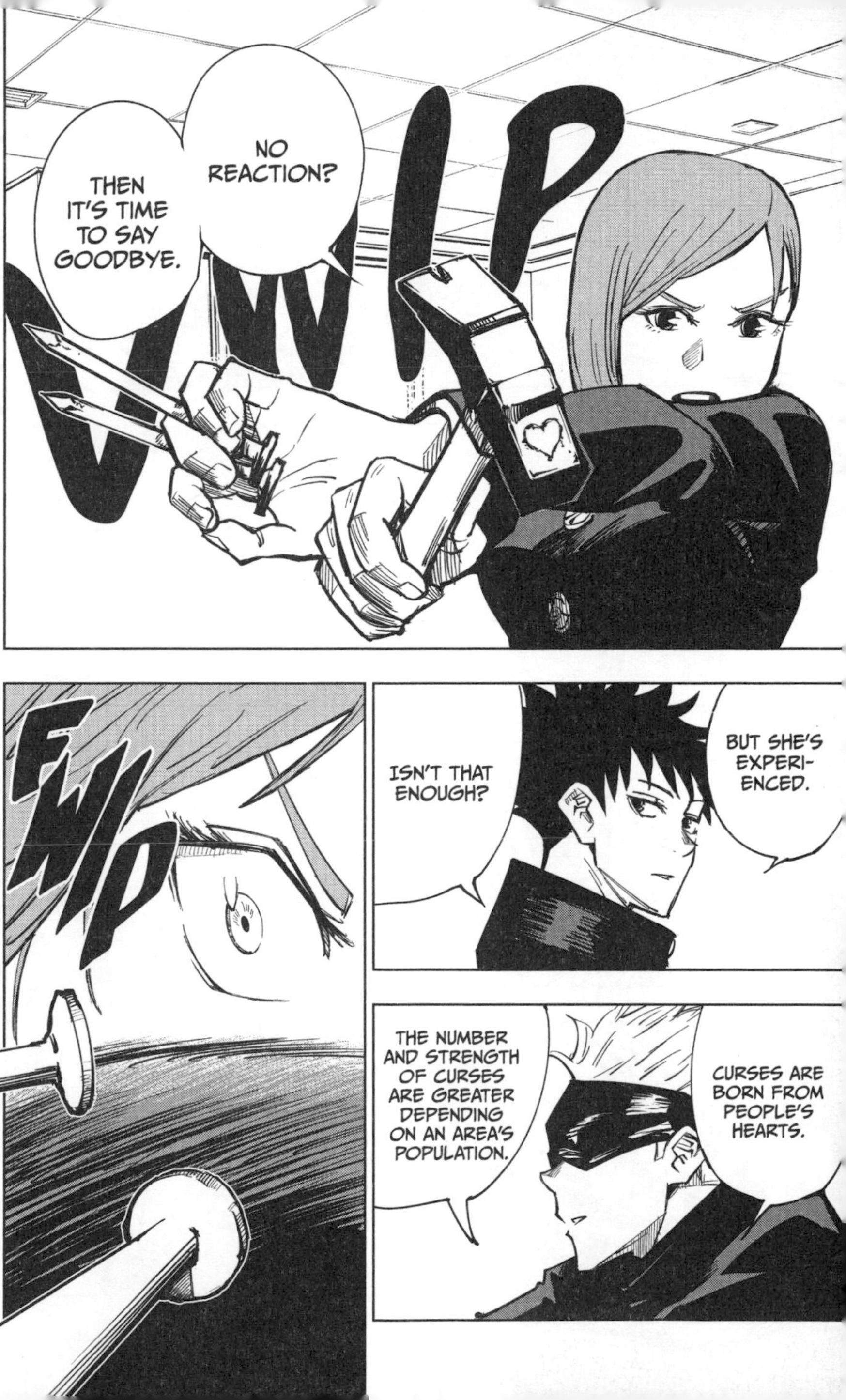
NO REACTION?
THEN IT'S TIME TO SAY GOODBYE.
BUT SHE'S EXPERI- ENCED.
ISN'T THAT ENOUGH?
CURSES ARE BORN FROM PEOPLE'S HEARTS.
THE NUMBER AND STRENGTH OF CURSES ARE GREATER DEPENDING ON AN AREA'S POPULATION.
FWIP

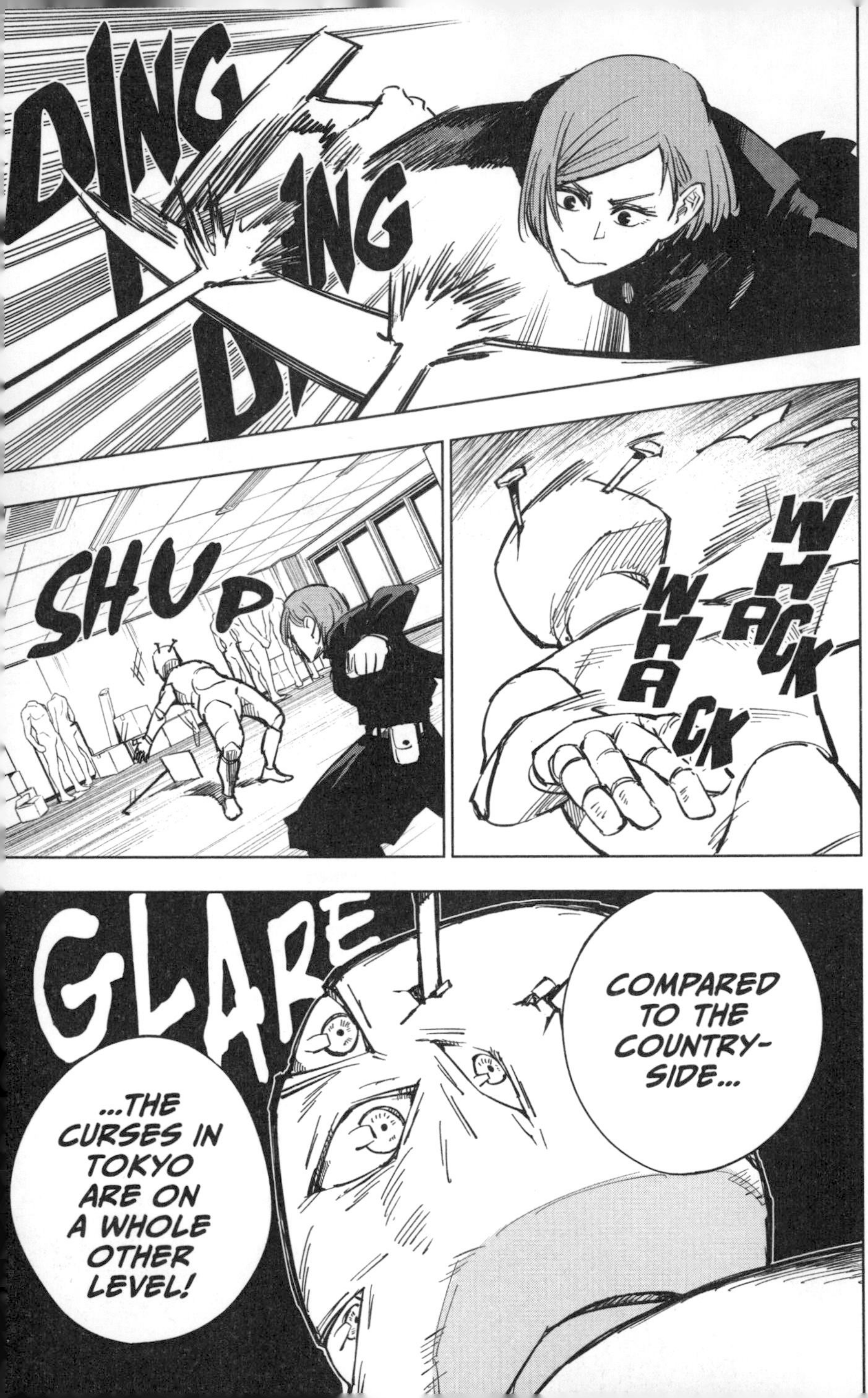
DING DING DING
WHACK WHACK
SHUP
COMPARED TO THE COUNTRY-SIDE...
GLARE
...THE CURSES IN TOKYO ARE ON A WHOLE OTHER LEVEL!

SATORU GOJO (28 YEARS OLD)

• He's really tall! (Probably over 190 centimeters.)

• His face was regularly shown in my previous *JUMP GIGA* series, *Tokyo Municipal Jujutsu High School*. (He's in all four chapters.)

• Principal Yaga was his teacher when he was a student.

• He started eating sweets as a way to stimulate his brain, but ended up with a sweet tooth.

• He can do anything he tries, so he tries not to get too involved with anything. According to him, this is all for the sake of the next generation.

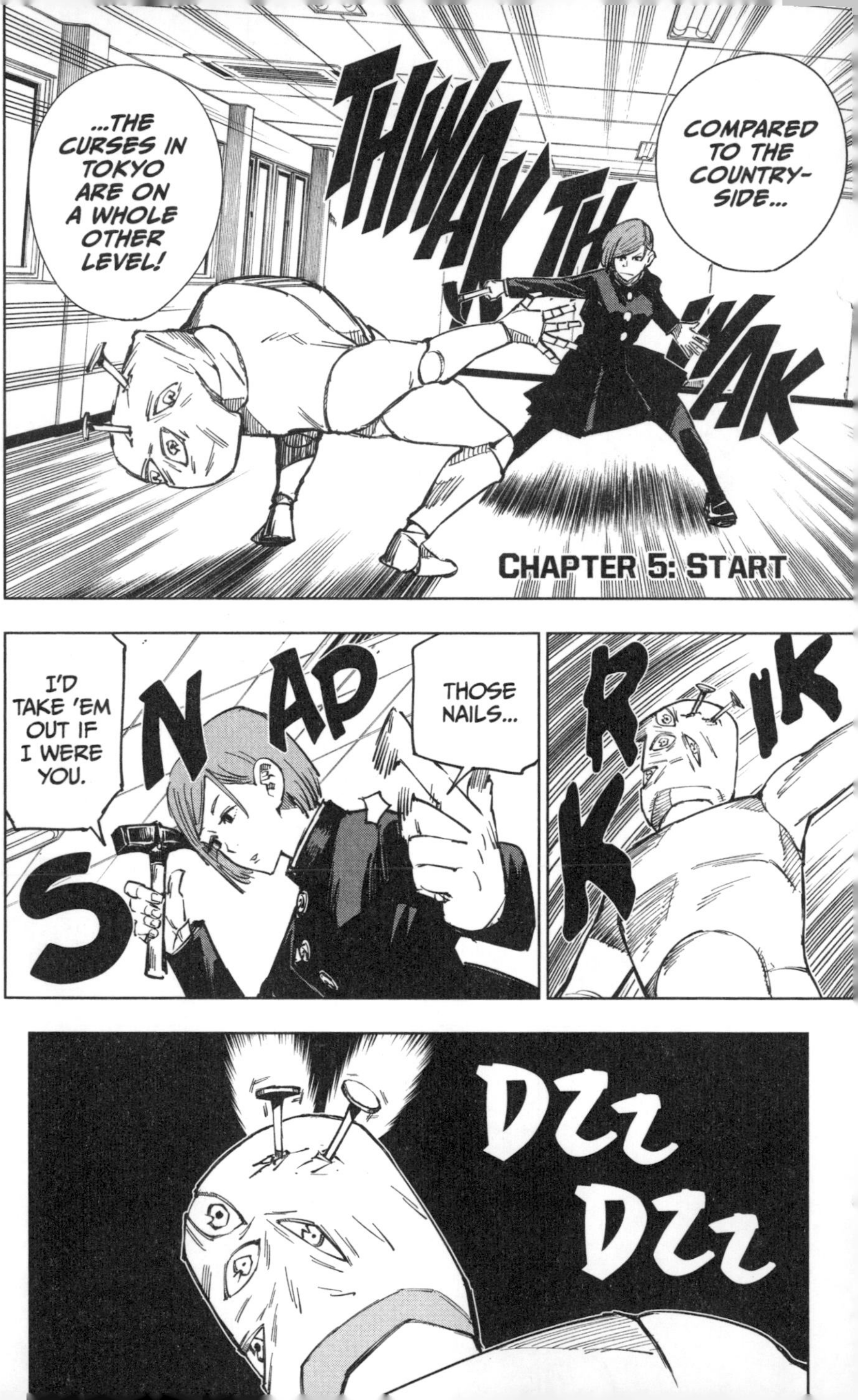
COMPARED TO THE COUNTRY-SIDE...
...THE CURSES IN TOKYO ARE ON A WHOLE OTHER LEVEL!
THWAK THWAK
CHAPTER 5: START
R
K
IK
THOSE NAILS...
I'D TAKE 'EM OUT IF I WERE YOU.
SNAP
DZZ
DZZ

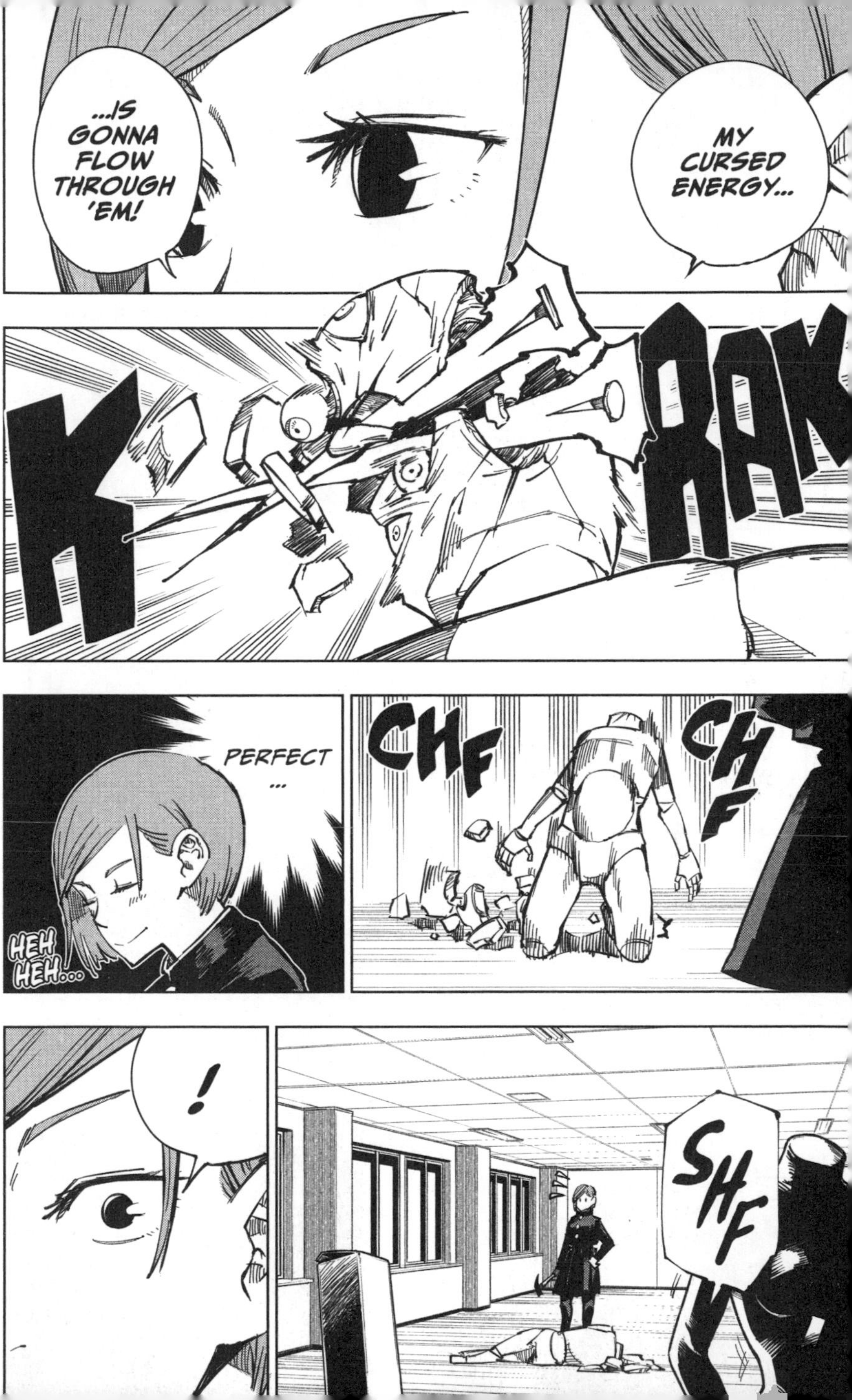
MY CURSED ENERGY...
...IS GONNA FLOW THROUGH 'EM!
KRAK
CHF
CHF
PERFECT ...
HEH HEH...
SHF
!

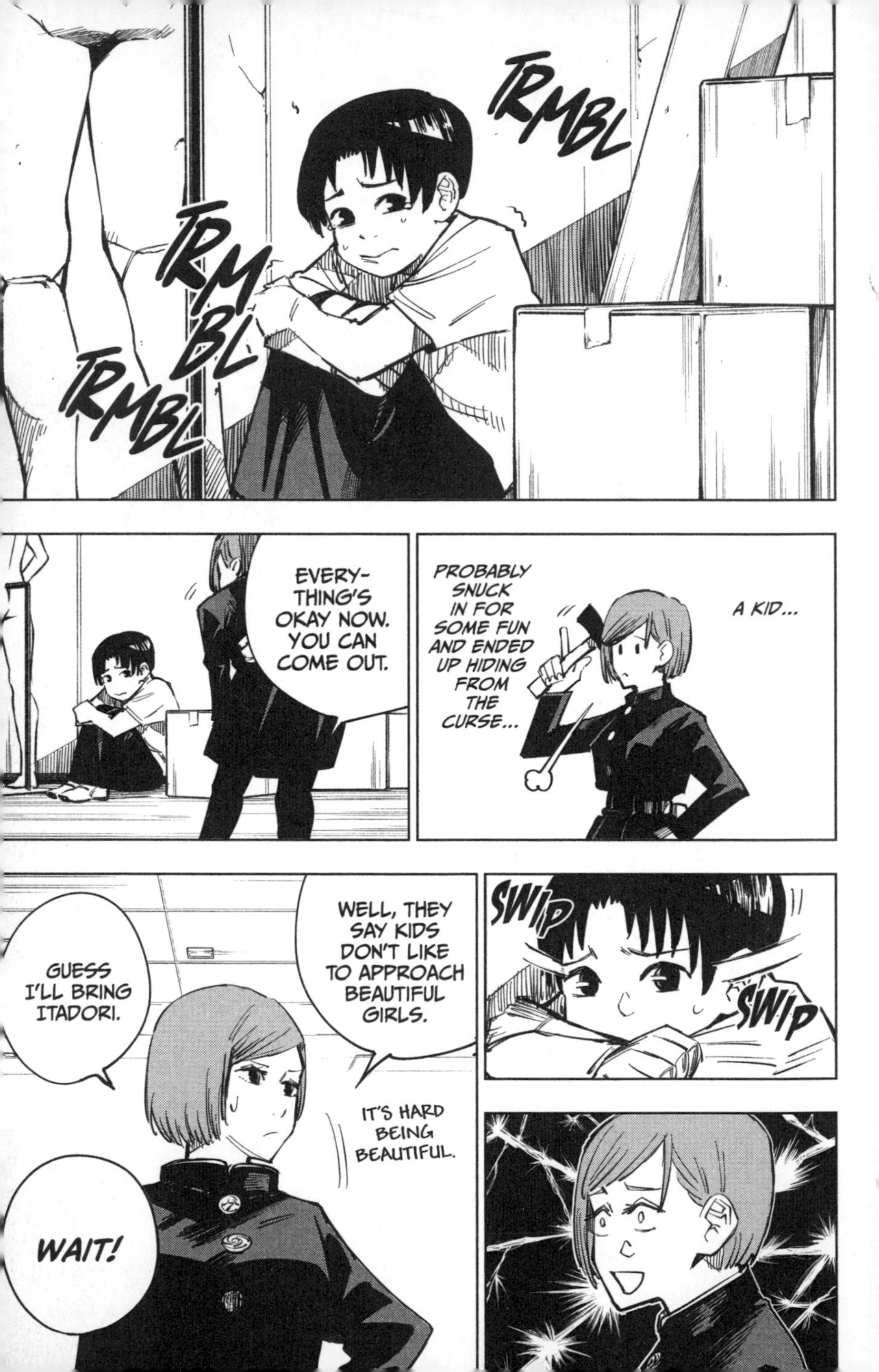
TRMBL
TRMBL
TRMBL
A KID...
PROBABLY SNUCK IN FOR SOME FUN AND ENDED UP HIDING FROM THE CURSE...
EVERY-THING'S OKAY NOW. YOU CAN COME OUT.
SWIP
SWIP
WELL, THEY SAY KIDS DON'T LIKE TO APPROACH BEAUTIFUL GIRLS.
GUESS I'LL BRING ITADORI.
IT'S HARD BEING BEAUTIFUL.
WAIT!

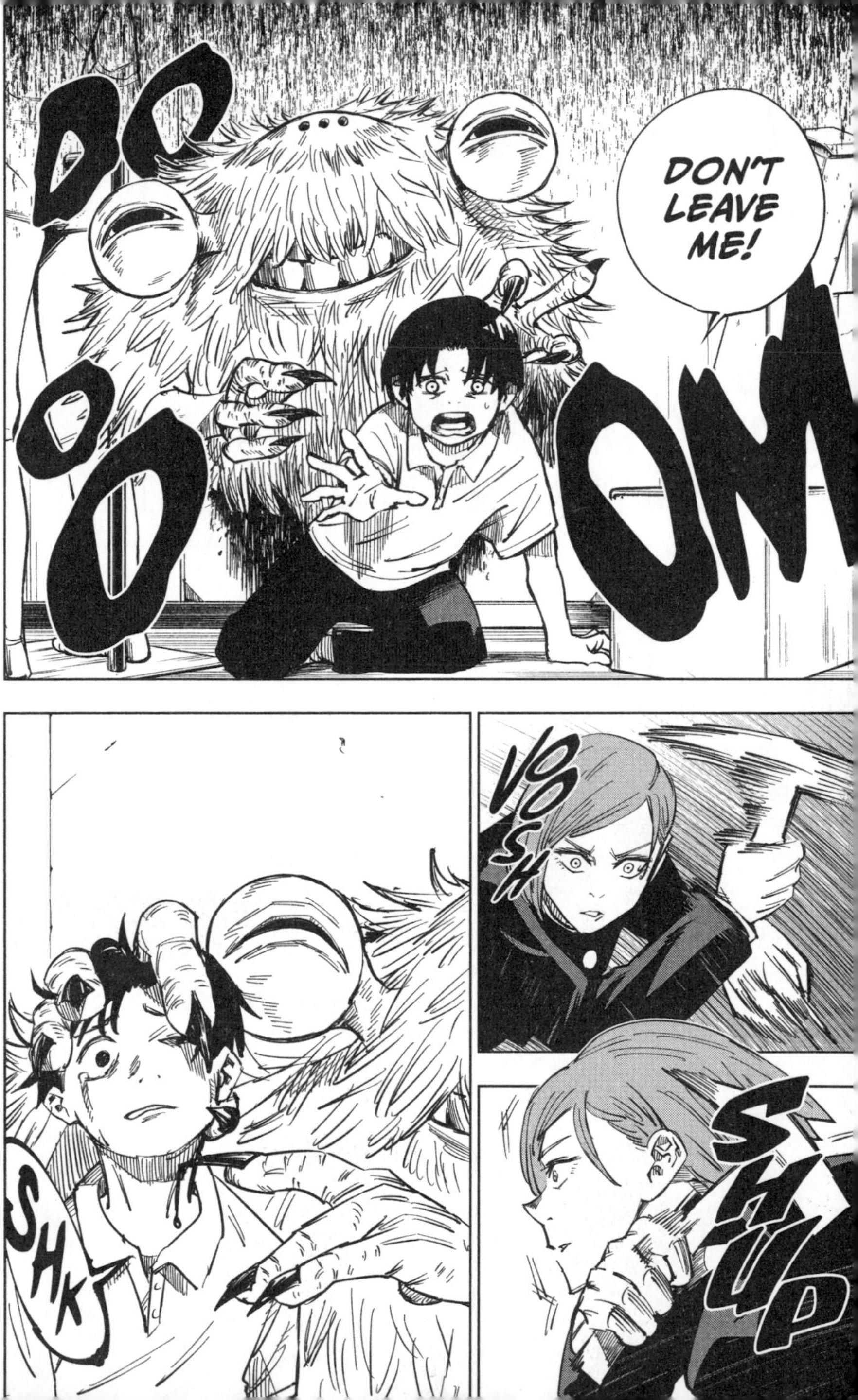
DON'T LEAVE ME!
DOOOOM
VOOSH
SHUP
SHK

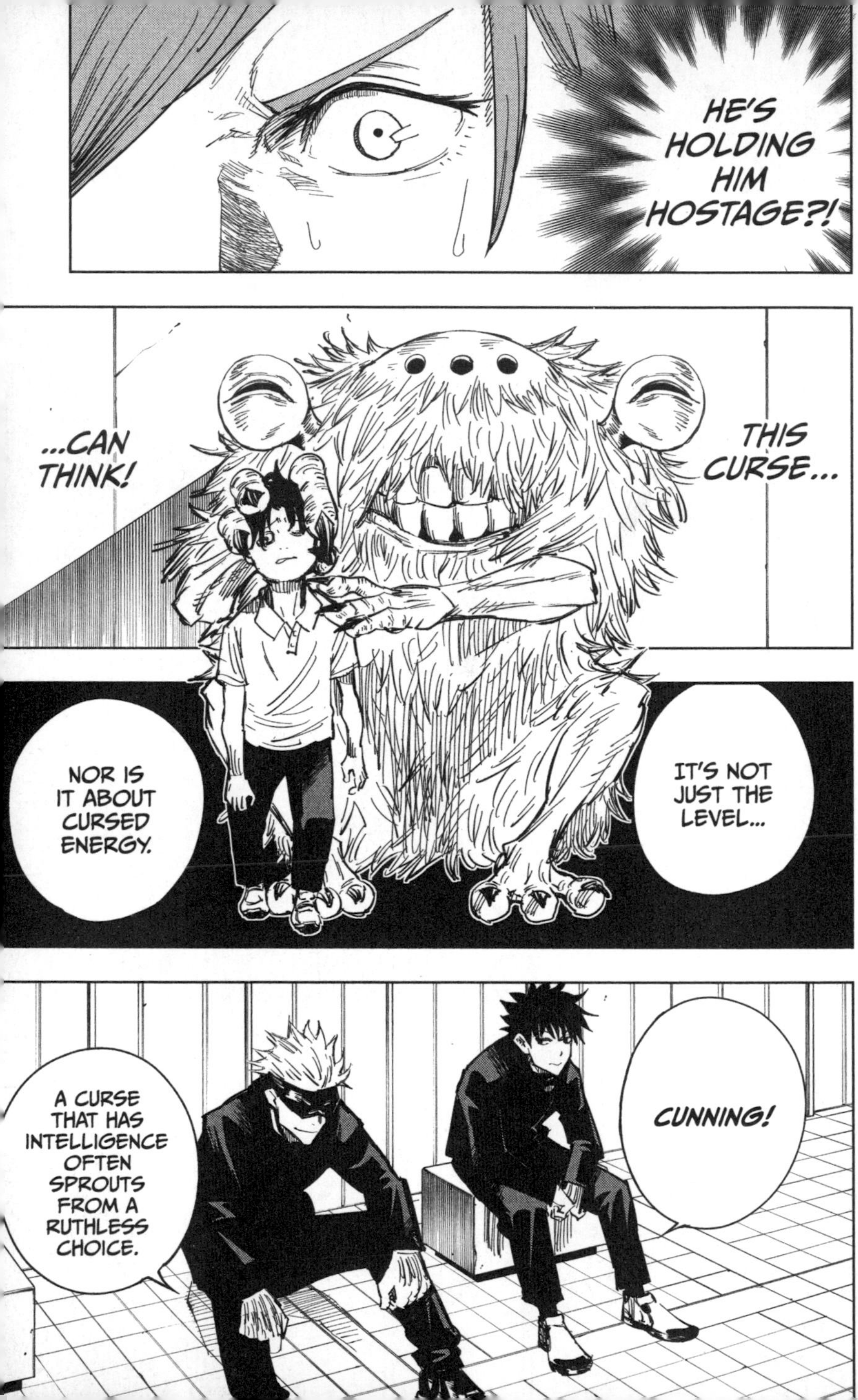
HE'S HOLDING HIM HOSTAGE?!
THIS CURSE...
...CAN THINK!
IT'S NOT JUST THE LEVEL...
NOR IS IT ABOUT CURSED ENERGY.
CUNNING!
A CURSE THAT HAS INTELLIGENCE OFTEN SPROUTS FROM A RUTHLESS CHOICE.

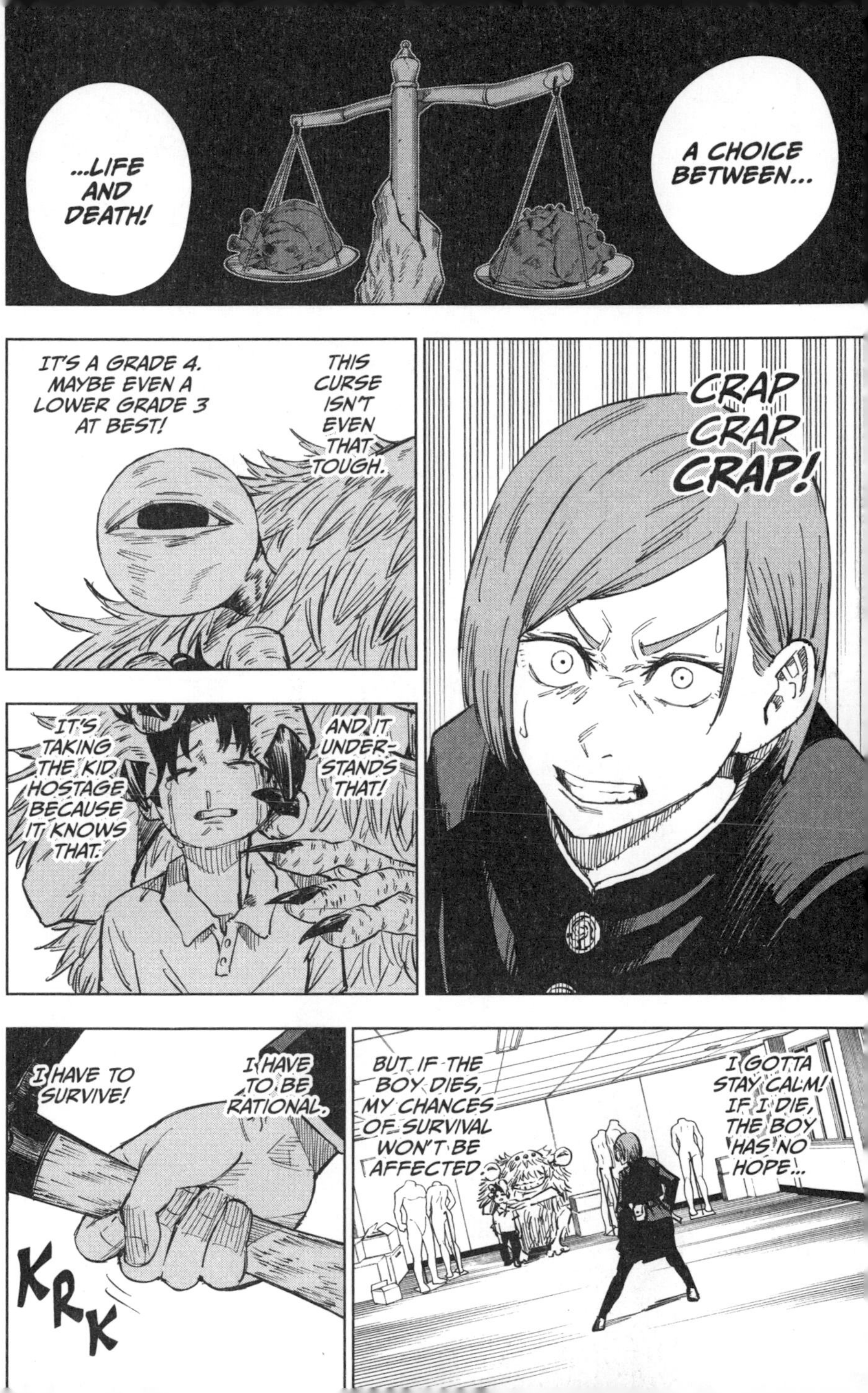
A CHOICE BETWEEN...
...LIFE AND DEATH!
CRAP CRAP CRAP!
THIS CURSE ISN'T EVEN THAT TOUGH.
IT'S A GRADE 4. MAYBE EVEN A LOWER GRADE 3 AT BEST!
AND IT UNDER-STANDS THAT!
IT'S TAKING THE KID HOSTAGE BECAUSE IT KNOWS THAT.
I GOTTA STAY CALM! IF I DIE, THE BOY HAS NO HOPE...
BUT IF THE BOY DIES, MY CHANCES OF SURVIVAL WON'T BE AFFECTED.
I HAVE TO BE RATIONAL.
I HAVE TO SURVIVE!
KRK

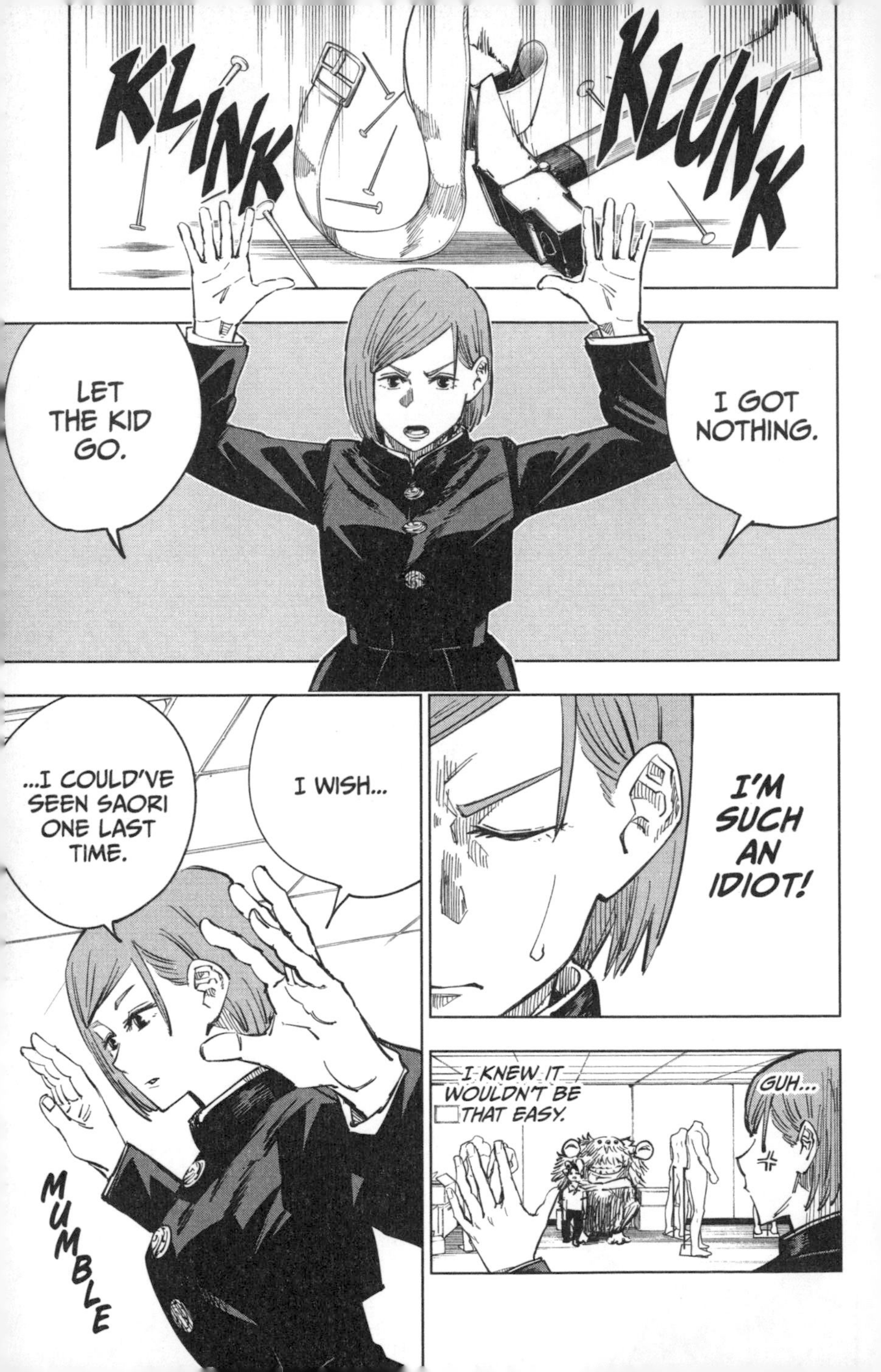
KLUNK
KLINK
I GOT NOTHING.
LET THE KID GO.
I'M SUCH AN IDIOT!
GUH...
I KNEW IT WOULDN'T BE THAT EASY.
I WISH...
...I COULD'VE SEEN SAORI ONE LAST TIME.
MUMBLE

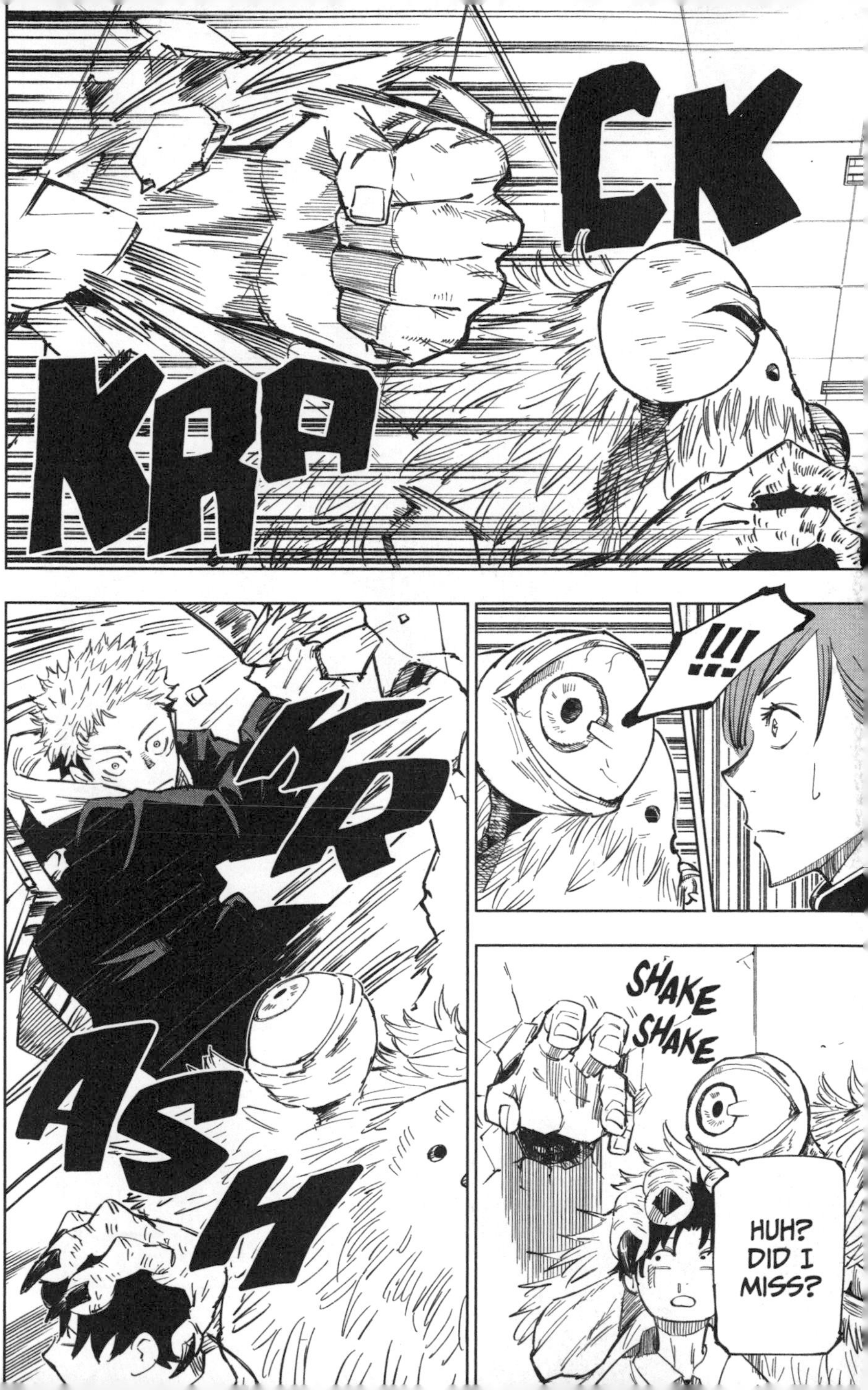
KRACK
!!!
SHAKE SHAKE
HUH? DID I MISS?
KRASH

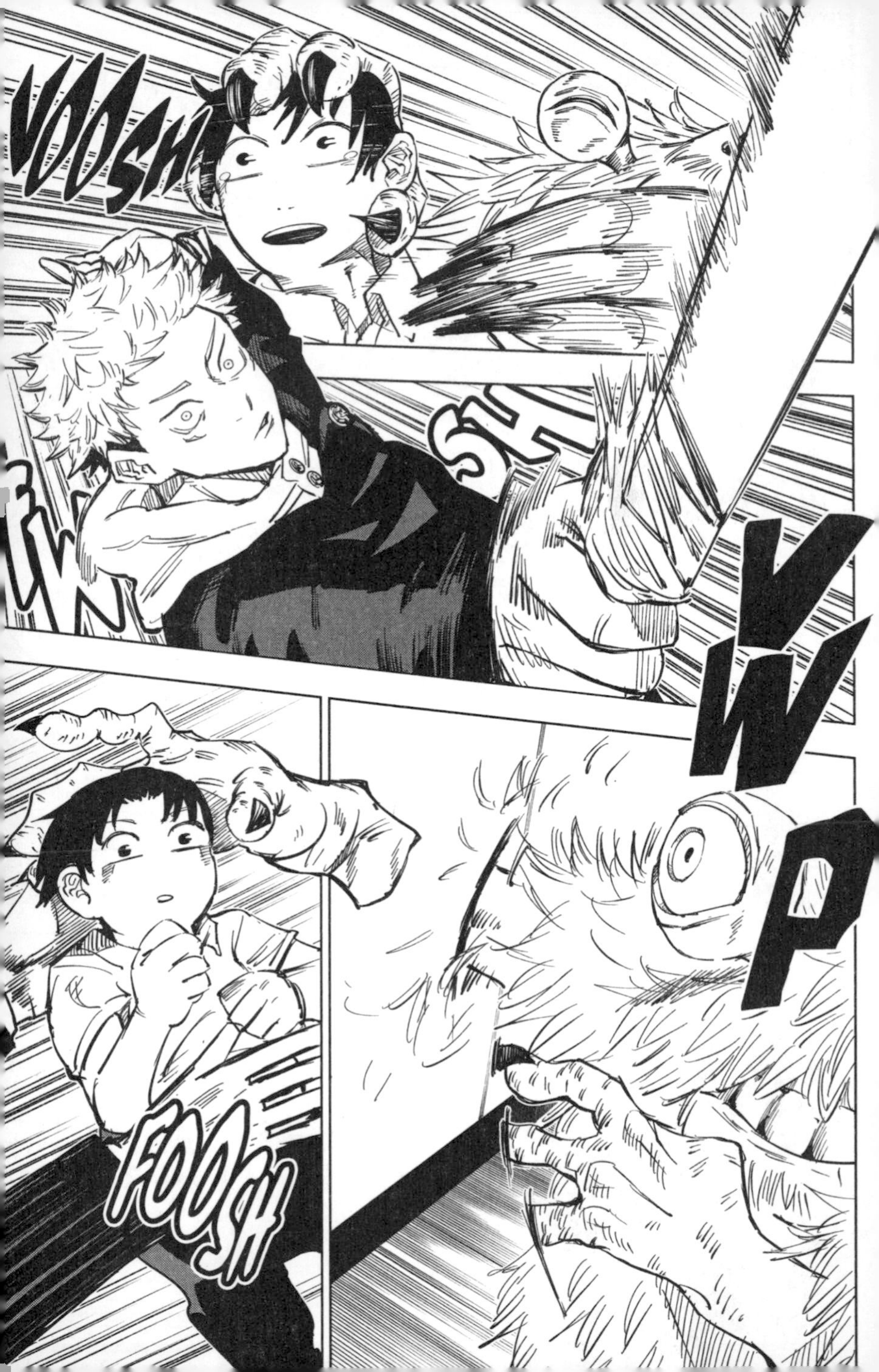
VWP
SH
VOOSH
FOOSH

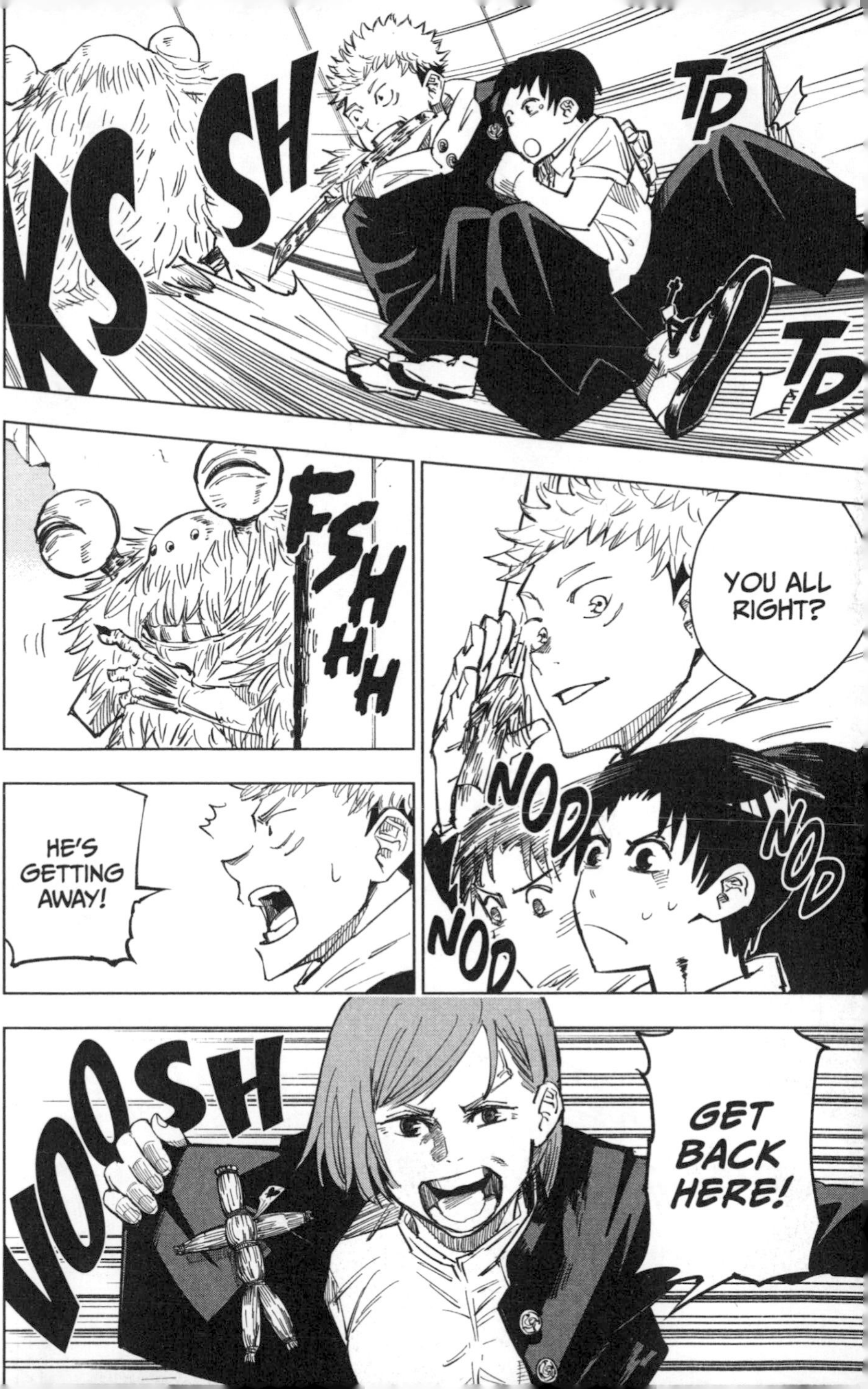
TP
TP
KSSH
YOU ALL RIGHT?
NOD
NOD
NOD
FSHHHH
HE'S GETTING AWAY!
GET BACK HERE!
WOOSH

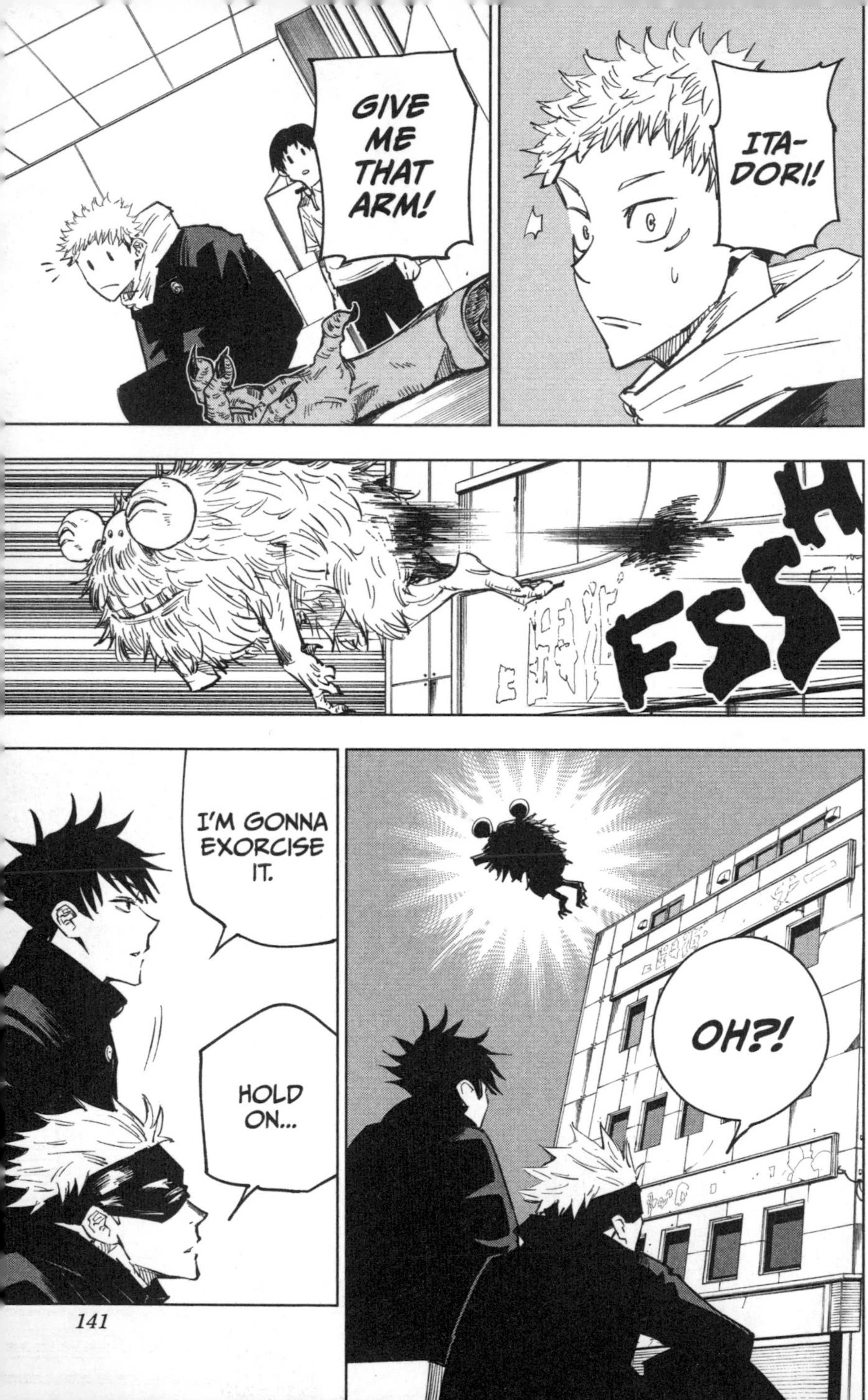
ITA-DORI!
GIVE ME THAT ARM!
FSSH
OH?!
I'M GONNA EXORCISE IT.
HOLD ON...

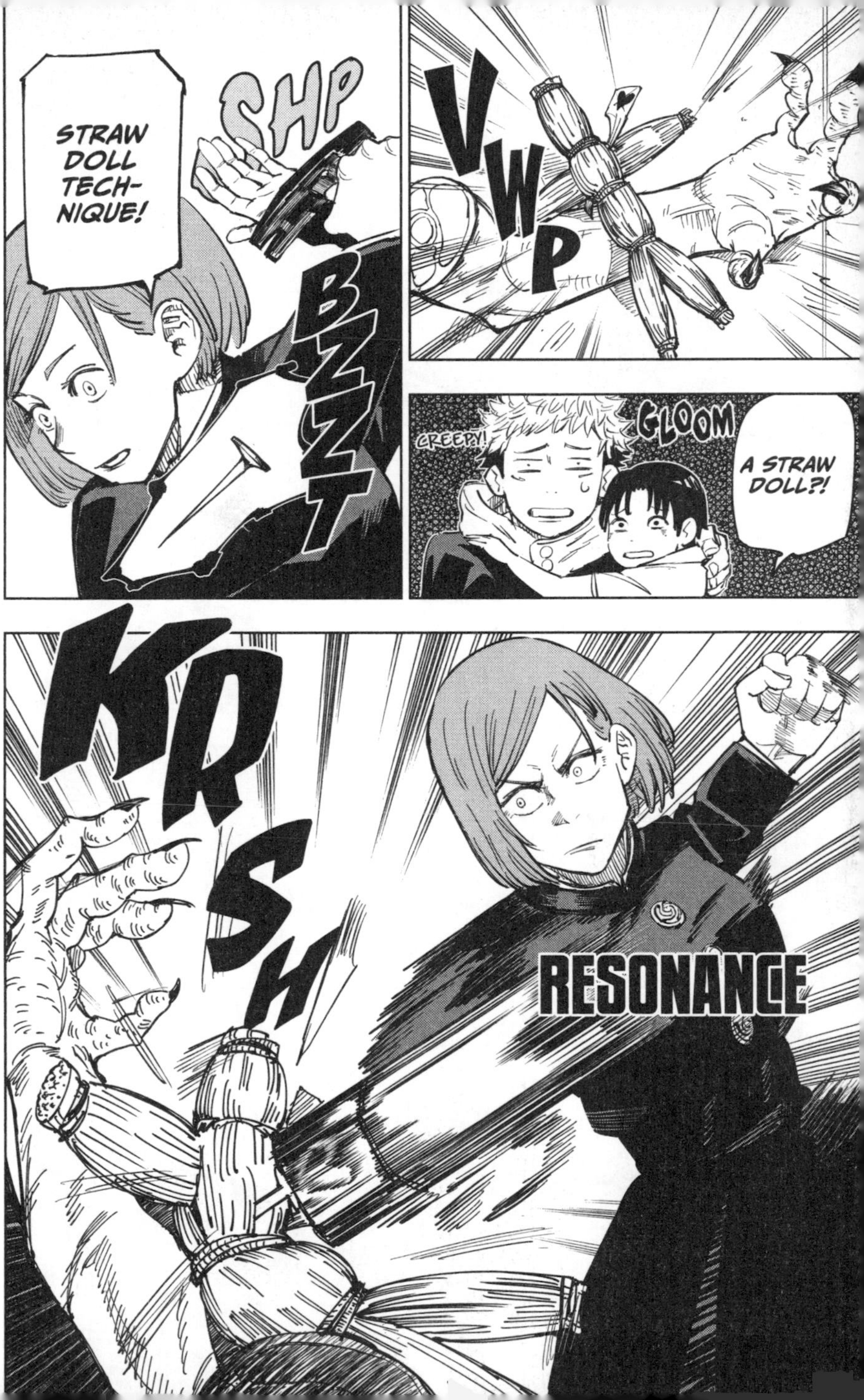
VWP
A STRAW DOLL?!
GLOOM
CREEPY!
SHP
STRAW DOLL TECHNIQUE!
BZZZT
KRSH
RESONANCE

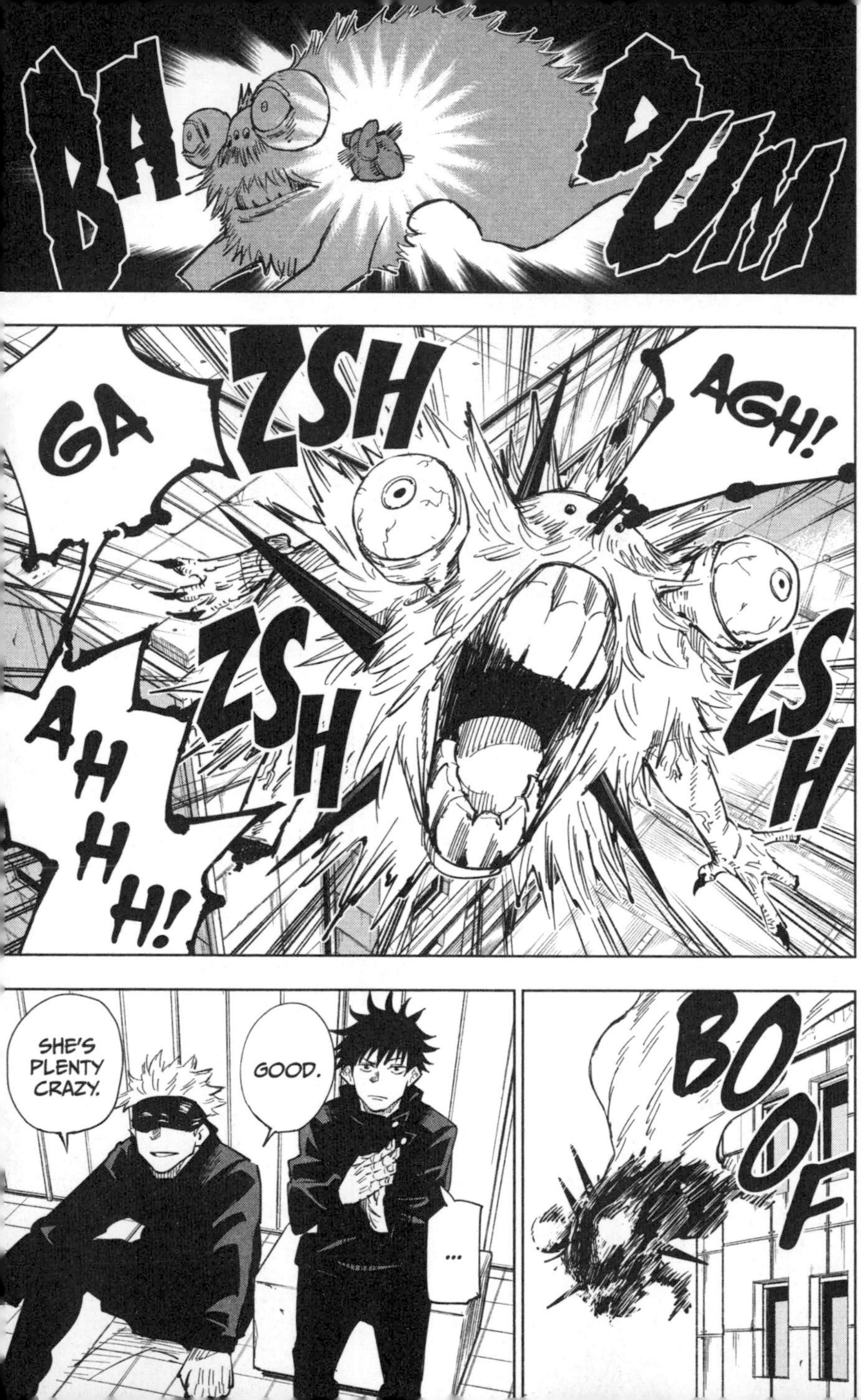
BA
DUM
AGH!
GA
ZSH
ZSH
ZSH
AHHHH!
BOOF
GOOD.
SHE'S PLENTY CRAZY.
...

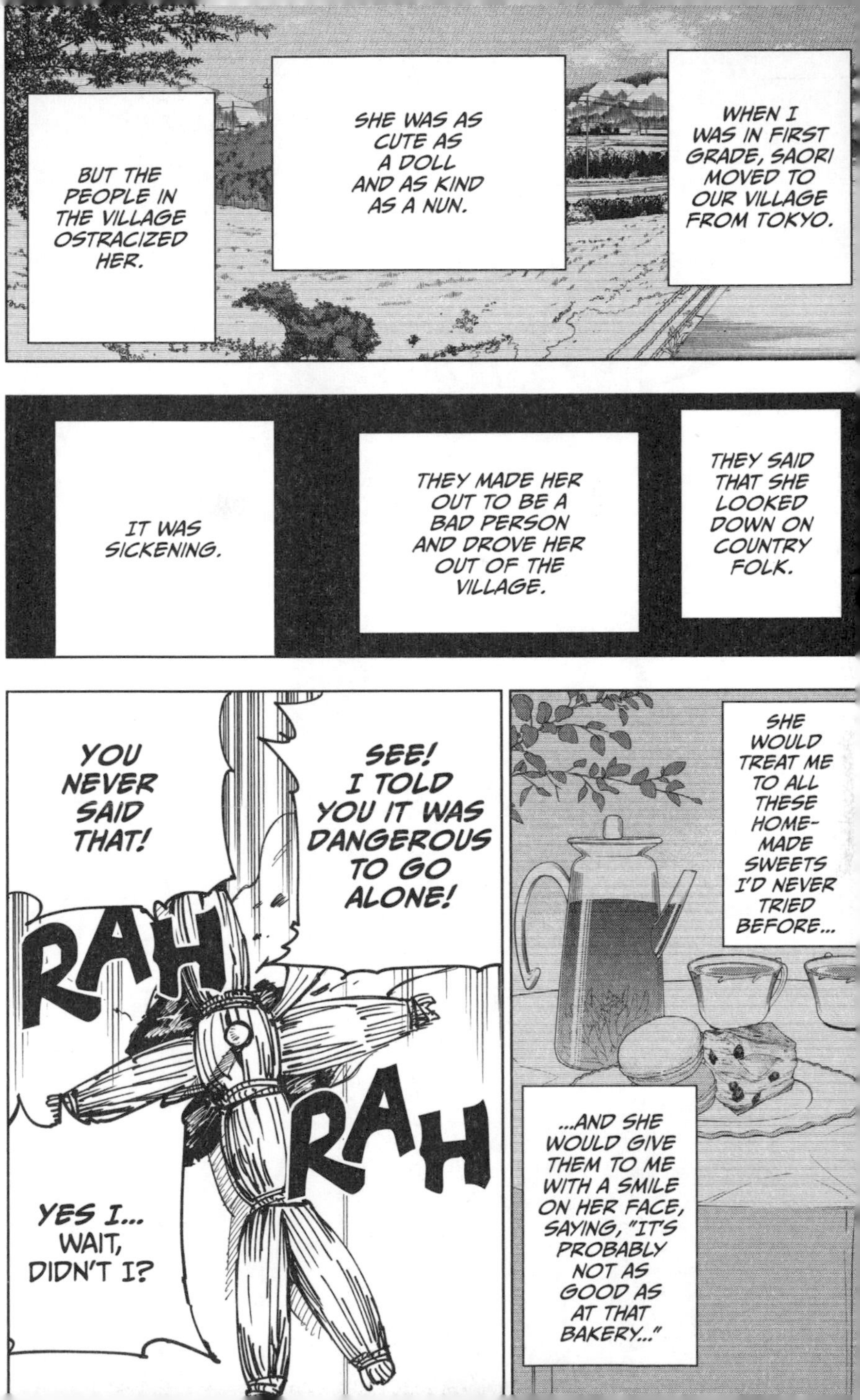
WHEN I WAS IN FIRST GRADE, SAORI MOVED TO OUR VILLAGE FROM TOKYO.
SHE WAS AS CUTE AS A DOLL AND AS KIND AS A NUN.
BUT THE PEOPLE IN THE VILLAGE OSTRACIZED HER.
THEY SAID THAT SHE LOOKED DOWN ON COUNTRY FOLK.
THEY MADE HER OUT TO BE A BAD PERSON AND DROVE HER OUT OF THE VILLAGE.
IT WAS SICKENING.
SHE WOULD TREAT ME TO ALL THESE HOME-MADE SWEETS I'D NEVER TRIED BEFORE...
...AND SHE WOULD GIVE THEM TO ME WITH A SMILE ON HER FACE, SAYING, "IT'S PROBABLY NOT AS GOOD AS AT THAT BAKERY..."
SEE! I TOLD YOU IT WAS DANGEROUS TO GO ALONE!
YOU NEVER SAID THAT!
RAH
RAH
YES I... WAIT, DIDN'T I?

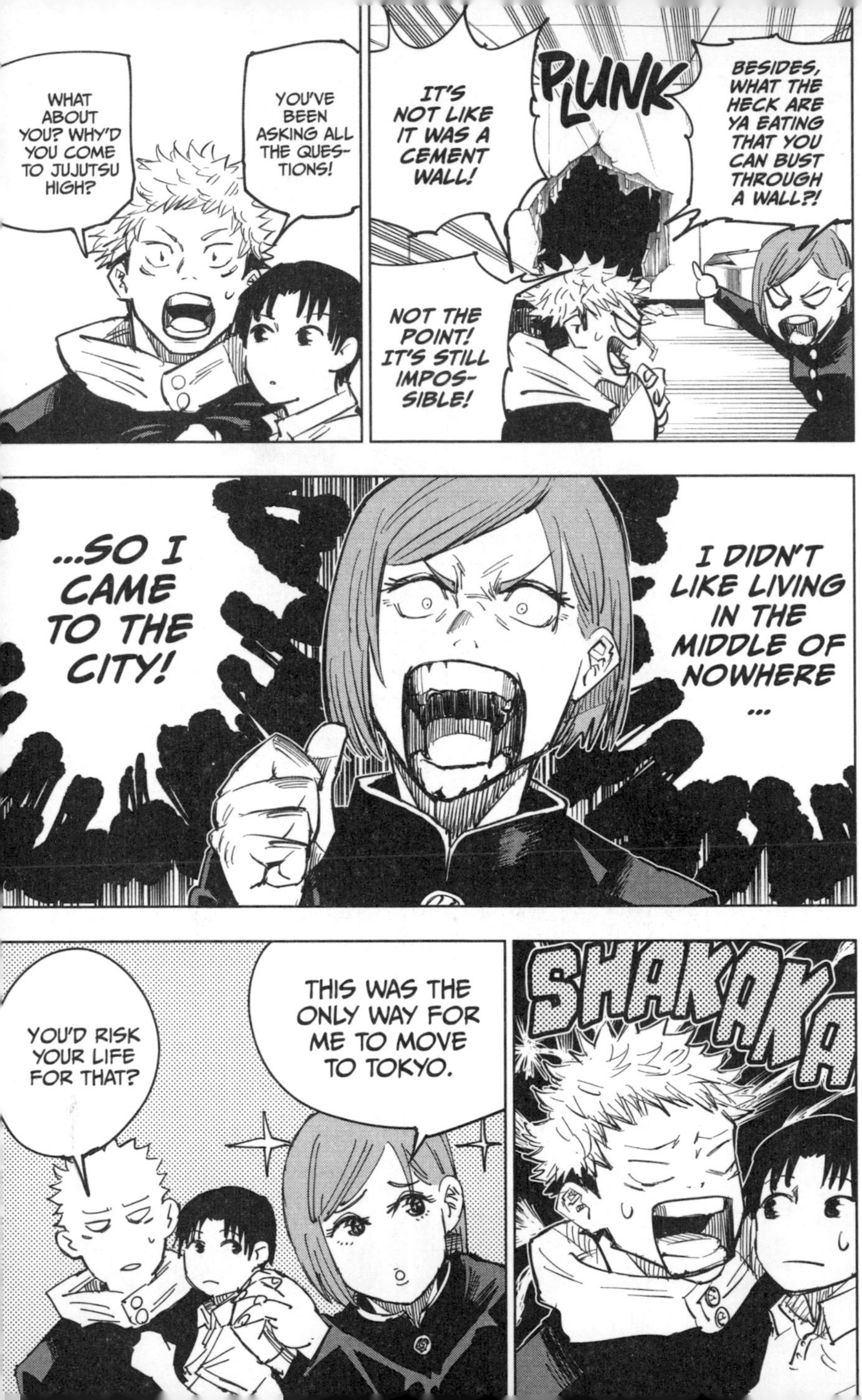
BESIDES, WHAT THE HECK ARE YA EATING THAT YOU CAN BUST THROUGH A WALL?!
PLUNK
IT'S NOT LIKE IT WAS A CEMENT WALL!
NOT THE POINT! IT'S STILL IMPOSSIBLE!
YOU'VE BEEN ASKING ALL THE QUESTIONS!
WHAT ABOUT YOU? WHY'D YOU COME TO JUJUTSU HIGH?
I DIDN'T LIKE LIVING IN THE MIDDLE OF NOWHERE ...
...SO I CAME TO THE CITY!
SHAKAKA
THIS WAS THE ONLY WAY FOR ME TO MOVE TO TOKYO.
YOU'D RISK YOUR LIFE FOR THAT?

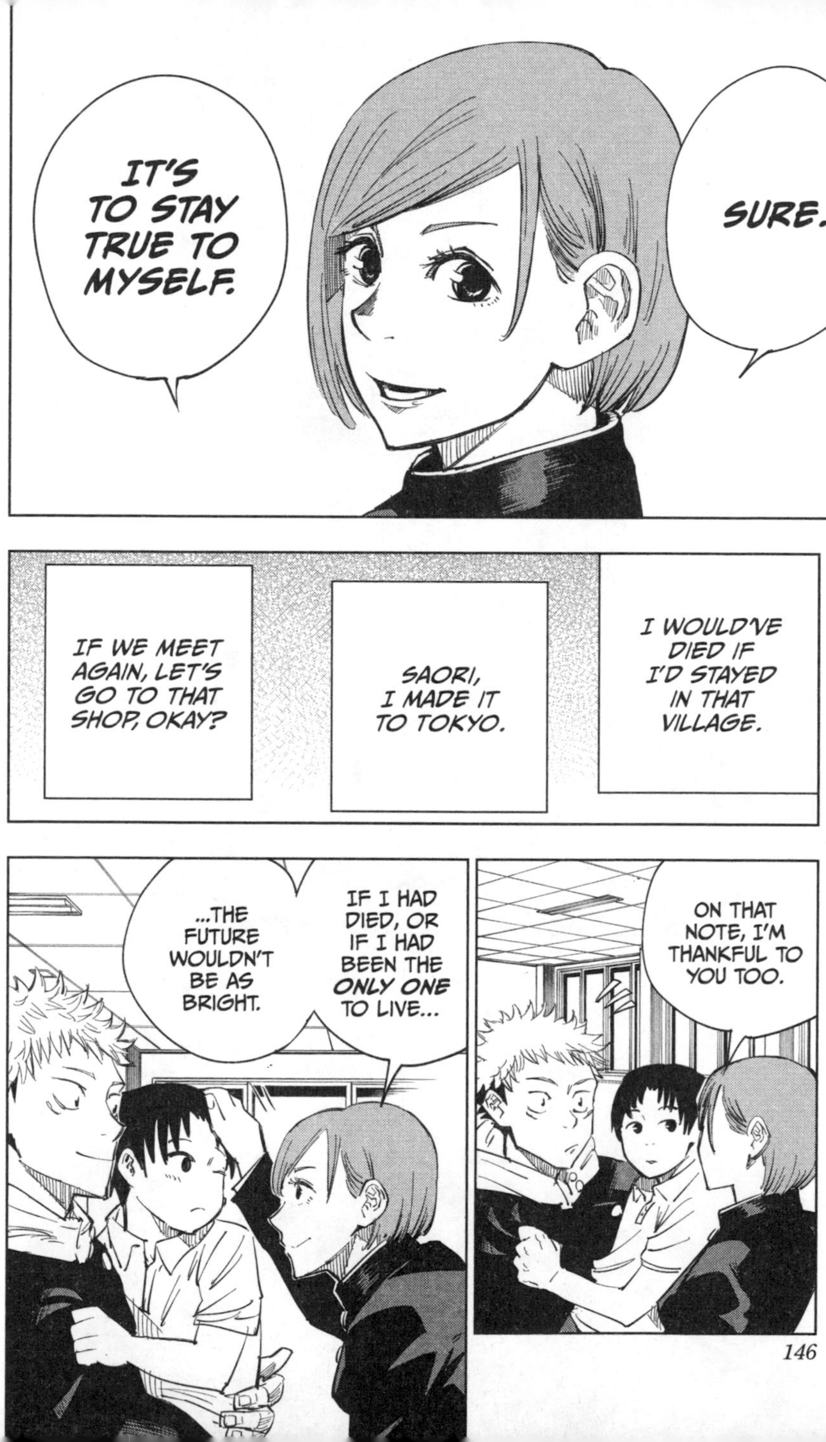
SURE.
IT'S TO STAY TRUE TO MYSELF.
I WOULD'VE DIED IF I'D STAYED IN THAT VILLAGE.
SAORI, I MADE IT TO TOKYO.
IF WE MEET AGAIN, LET'S GO TO THAT SHOP, OKAY?
ON THAT NOTE, I'M THANKFUL TO YOU TOO.
IF I HAD DIED, OR IF I HAD BEEN THE *ONLY ONE* TO LIVE...
...THE FUTURE WOULDN'T BE AS BRIGHT.

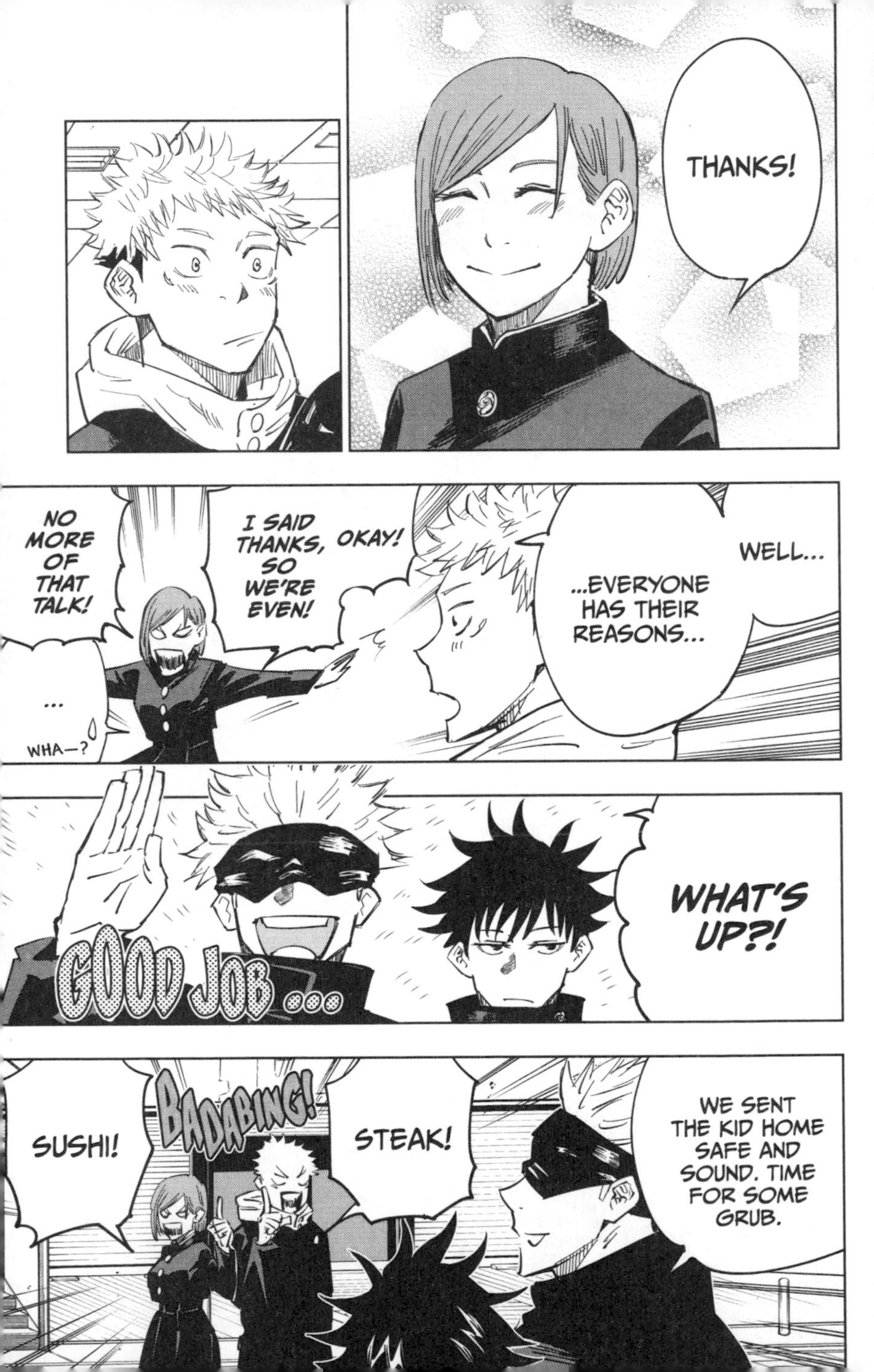
THANKS!
WELL...
...EVERYONE HAS THEIR REASONS...
I SAID THANKS, OKAY! SO WE'RE EVEN!
NO MORE OF THAT TALK!
...
WHA—?
WHAT'S UP?!
GOOD JOB...
WE SENT THE KID HOME SAFE AND SOUND. TIME FOR SOME GRUB.
STEAK!
BADABING!
SUSHI!

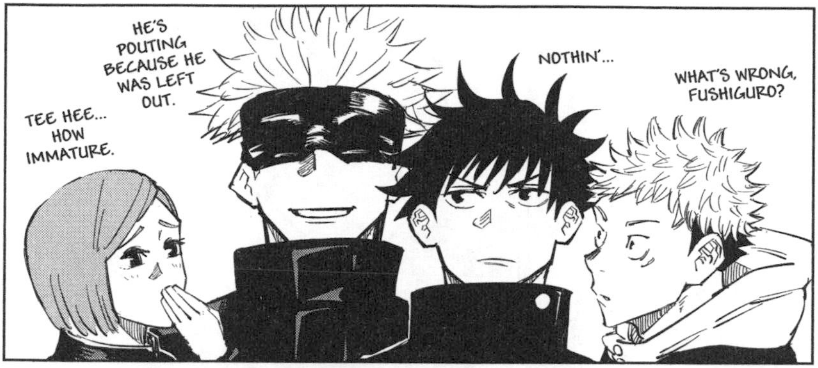
WHAT'S WRONG, FUSHIGURO?
NOTHIN'...
HE'S POUTING BECAUSE HE WAS LEFT OUT.
TEE HEE... HOW IMMATURE.

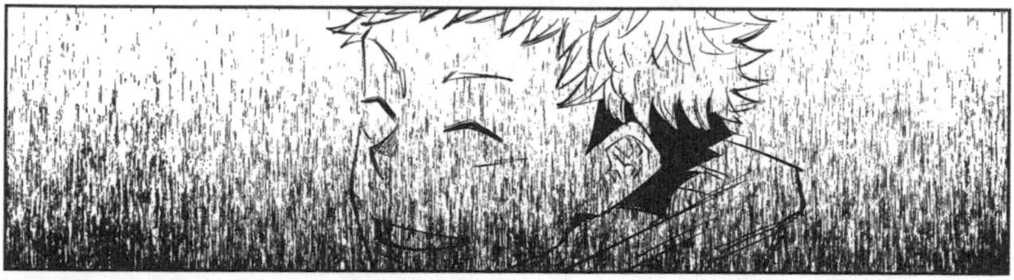

REPORT: JULY 2018

IN WEST TOKYO CITY, AT THE EISHU JUVENILE DETENTION CENTER

THE SKY ABOVE THE EXERCISE YARD

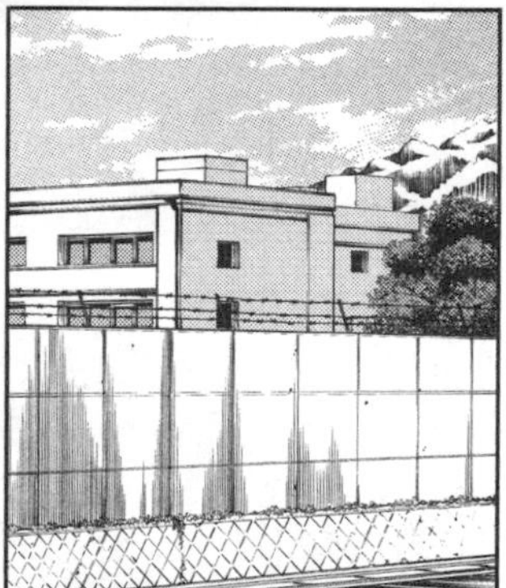

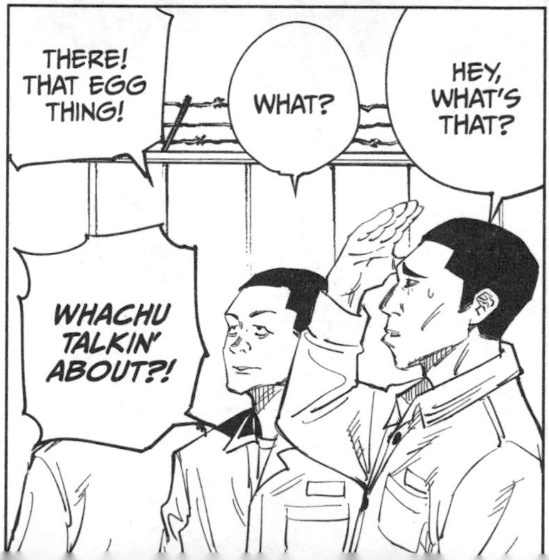
HEY, WHAT'S THAT?
WHAT?
THERE! THAT EGG THING!
WHACHU TALKIN' ABOUT?!

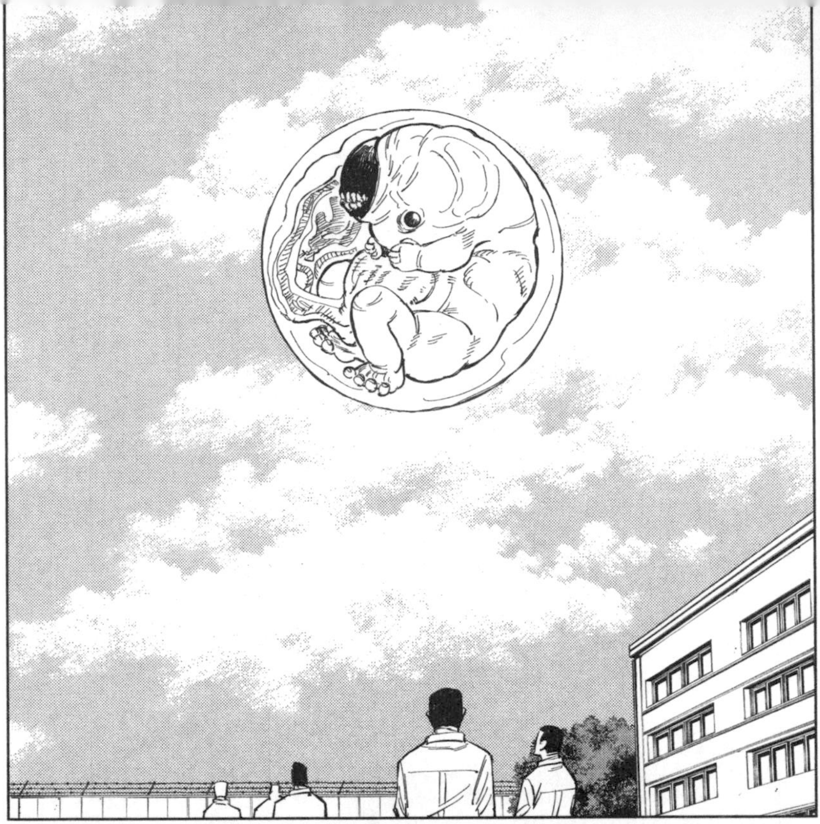

AN UNNAMED APPARITION OF POTENTIAL SPECIAL GRADE WAS WITNESSED BY MULTIPLE NON-JUJUTSU SORCERERS. SINCE IT WAS DEEMED AN EMERGENCY, THREE FIRST-YEAR STUDENTS WERE SENT TO THE SCENE.

OF THOSE THREE STUDENTS... ONE DIED.

NOBARA
KUGISAKI

• She is just short of 160 centimeters tall.

• Her hair is dyed.

• She goes shopping during her free time. (Students receive a stipend.)

• She tries a lot of foods, buys a lot of clothes and is enjoying her life in Tokyo.

• In chapter 4, Kugisaki kicked away an 80-kilogram Itadori. Please pay it no mind.

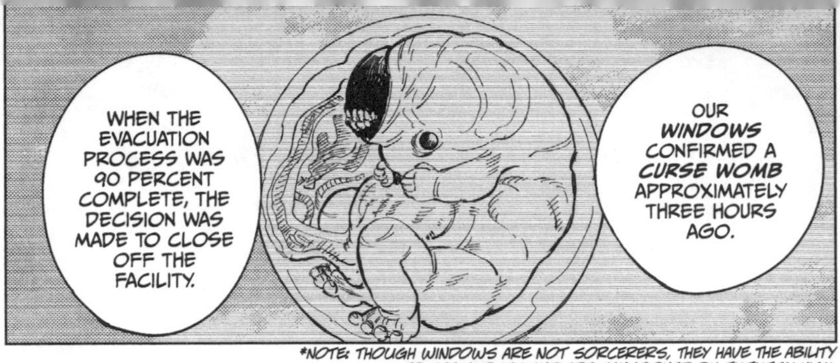
OUR WINDOWS CONFIRMED A CURSE WOMB APPROXIMATELY THREE HOURS AGO.
WHEN THE EVACUATION PROCESS WAS 90 PERCENT COMPLETE, THE DECISION WAS MADE TO CLOSE OFF THE FACILITY.

*NOTE: THOUGH WINDOWS ARE NOT SORCERERS, THEY HAVE THE ABILITY TO SEE CURSES AND ARE SANCTIONED BY JUJUTSU HIGH.

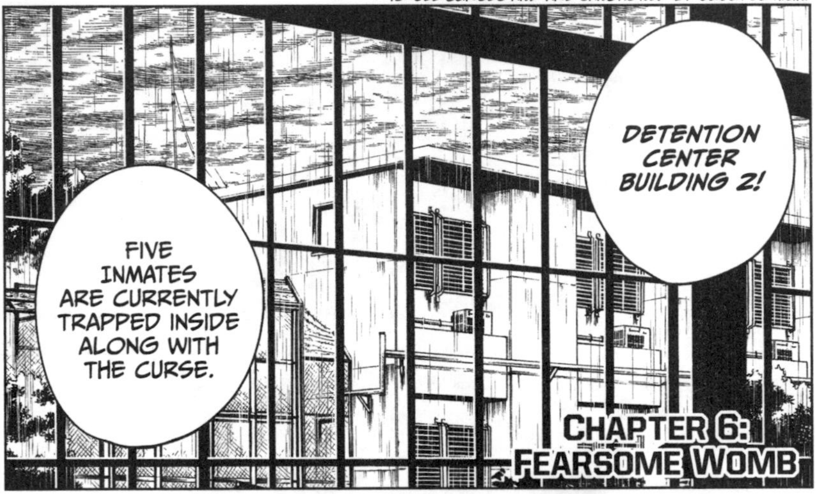
DETENTION CENTER BUILDING 2!
FIVE INMATES ARE CURRENTLY TRAPPED INSIDE ALONG WITH THE CURSE.
CHAPTER 6: FEARSOME WOMB

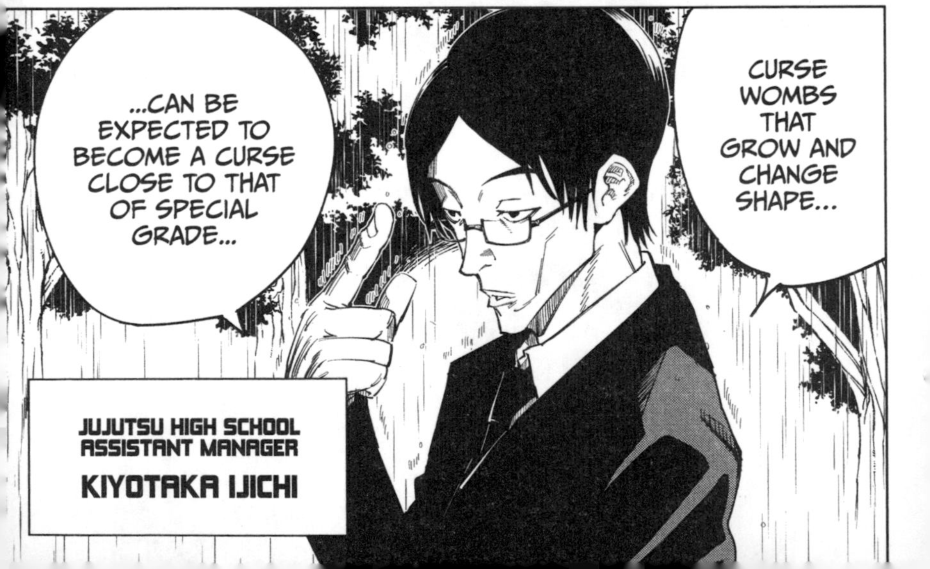
CURSE WOMBS THAT GROW AND CHANGE SHAPE...
...CAN BE EXPECTED TO BECOME A CURSE CLOSE TO THAT OF SPECIAL GRADE...
JUJUTSU HIGH SCHOOL ASSISTANT MANAGER
KIYOTAKA IJICHI

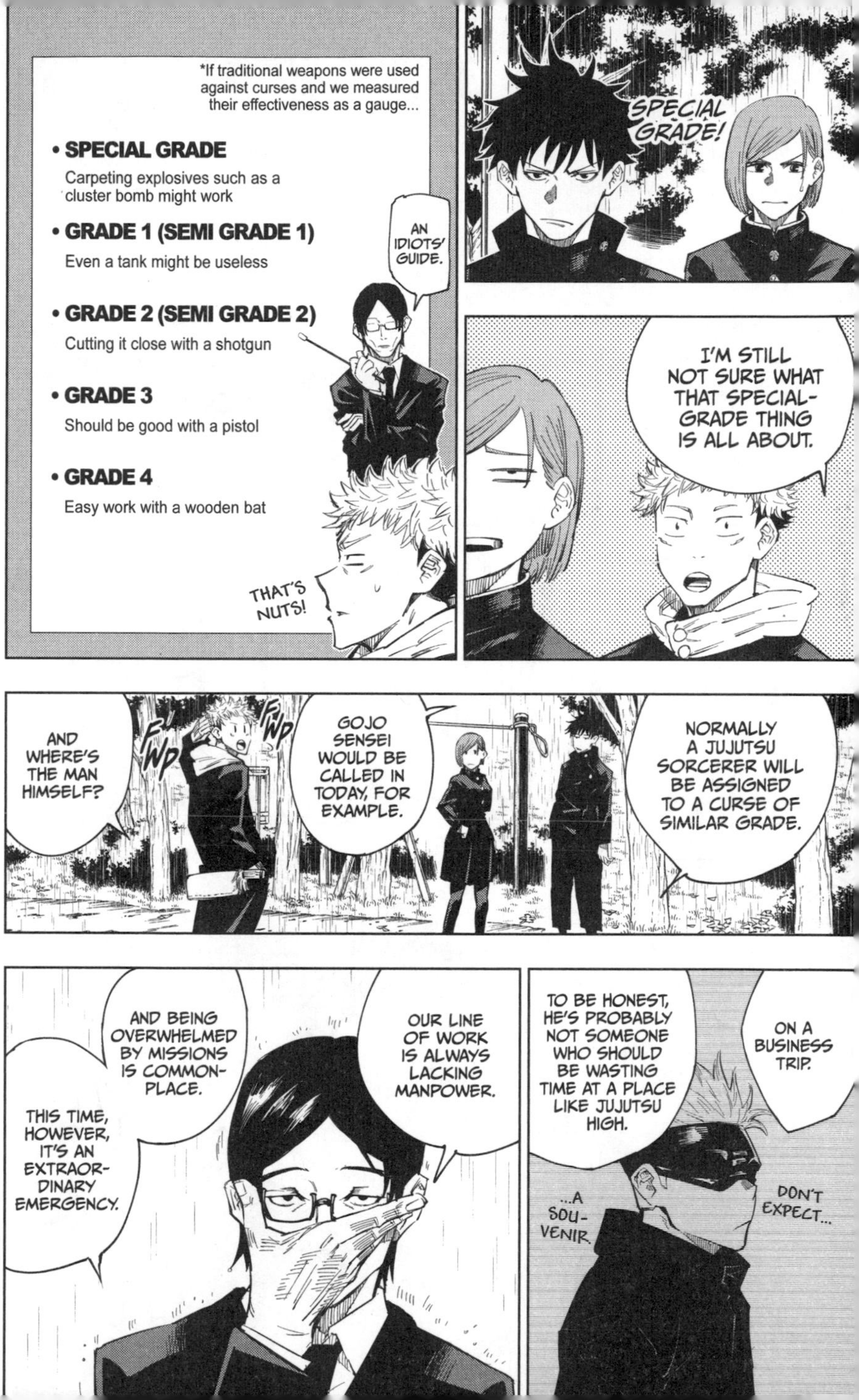
SPECIAL GRADE!
I'M STILL NOT SURE WHAT THAT SPECIAL-GRADE THING IS ALL ABOUT.
*If traditional weapons were used against curses and we measured their effectiveness as a gauge...
• SPECIAL GRADE
Carpeting explosives such as a cluster bomb might work
• GRADE 1 (SEMI GRADE 1)
Even a tank might be useless
• GRADE 2 (SEMI GRADE 2)
Cutting it close with a shotgun
• GRADE 3
Should be good with a pistol
• GRADE 4
Easy work with a wooden bat
AN IDIOTS' GUIDE.
THAT'S NUTS!
NORMALLY A JUJUTSU SORCERER WILL BE ASSIGNED TO A CURSE OF SIMILAR GRADE.
GOJO SENSEI WOULD BE CALLED IN TODAY, FOR EXAMPLE.
FWP
FWP
AND WHERE'S THE MAN HIMSELF?
ON A BUSINESS TRIP.
TO BE HONEST, HE'S PROBABLY NOT SOMEONE WHO SHOULD BE WASTING TIME AT A PLACE LIKE JUJUTSU HIGH.
DON'T EXPECT...
...A SOUVENIR.
OUR LINE OF WORK IS ALWAYS LACKING MANPOWER.
AND BEING OVERWHELMED BY MISSIONS IS COMMONPLACE.
THIS TIME, HOWEVER, IT'S AN EXTRAORDINARY EMERGENCY.

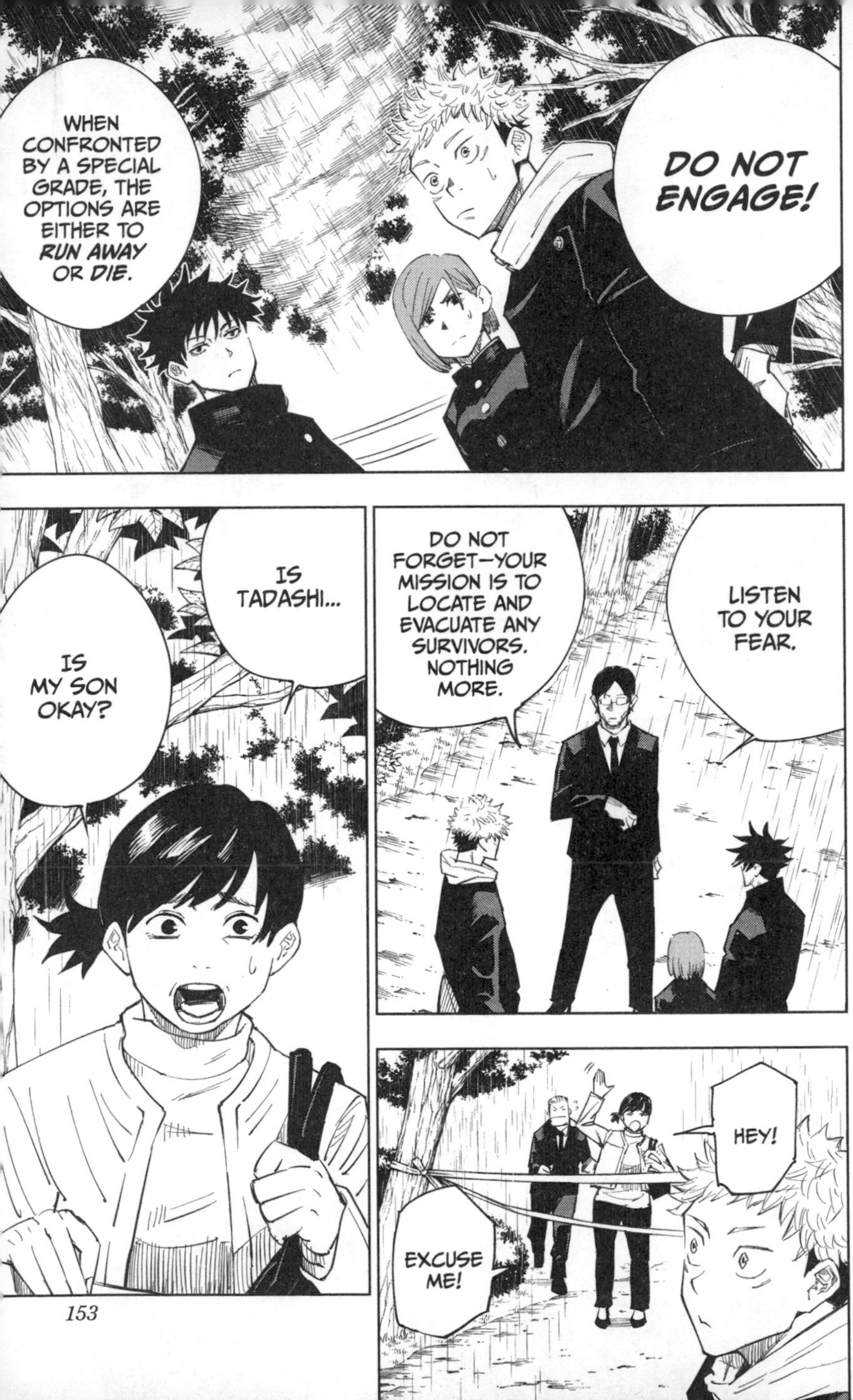
DO NOT ENGAGE!
WHEN CONFRONTED BY A SPECIAL GRADE, THE OPTIONS ARE EITHER TO RUN AWAY OR DIE.
LISTEN TO YOUR FEAR.
DO NOT FORGET—YOUR MISSION IS TO LOCATE AND EVACUATE ANY SURVIVORS. NOTHING MORE.
HEY!
EXCUSE ME!
IS TADASHI...
IS MY SON OKAY?

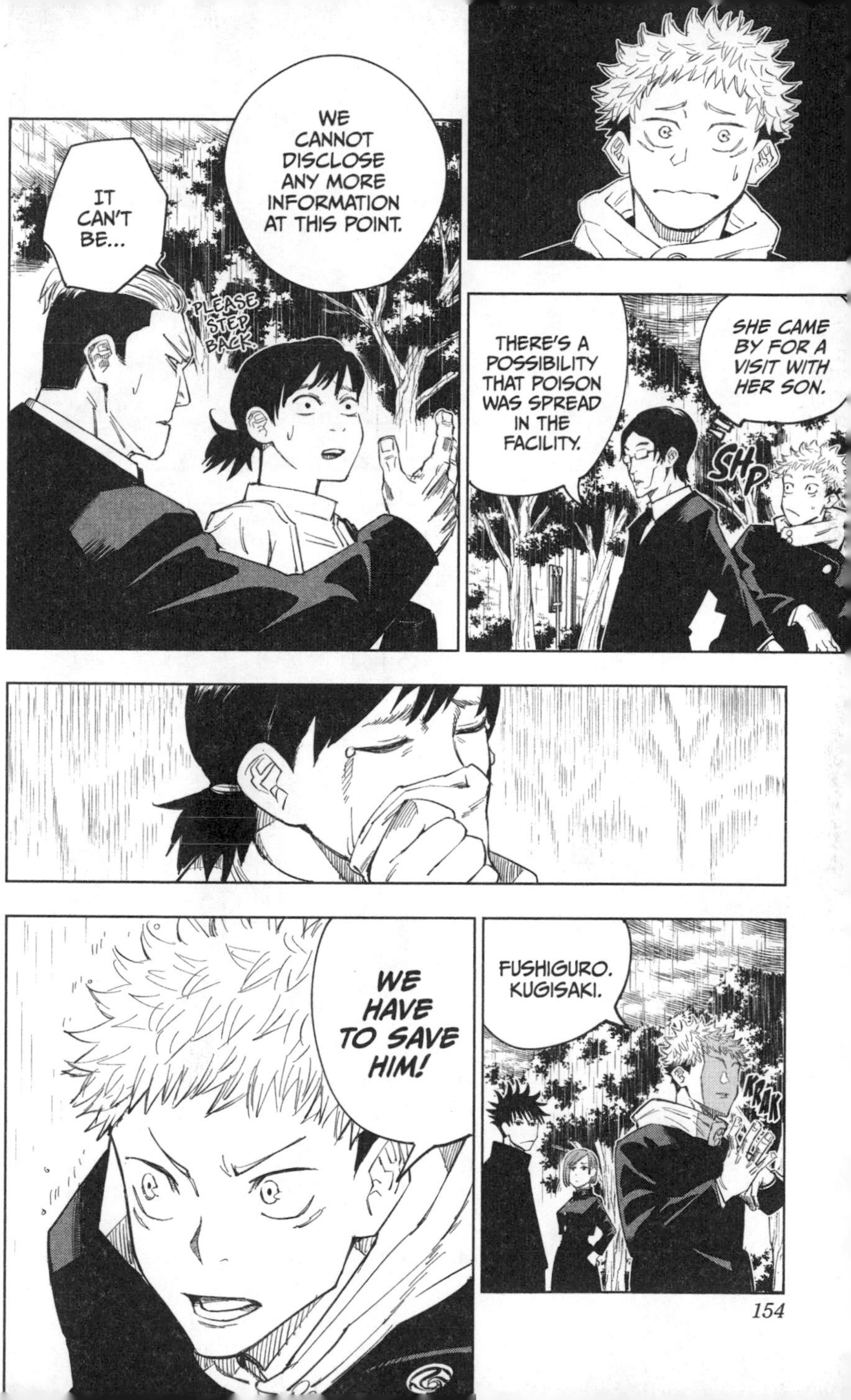
SHE CAME BY FOR A VISIT WITH HER SON.
THERE'S A POSSIBILITY THAT POISON WAS SPREAD IN THE FACILITY.
SHP
WE CANNOT DISCLOSE ANY MORE INFORMATION AT THIS POINT.
IT CAN'T BE...
PLEASE STEP BACK.
FUSHIGURO. KUGISAKI.
KRAK
WE HAVE TO SAVE HIM!

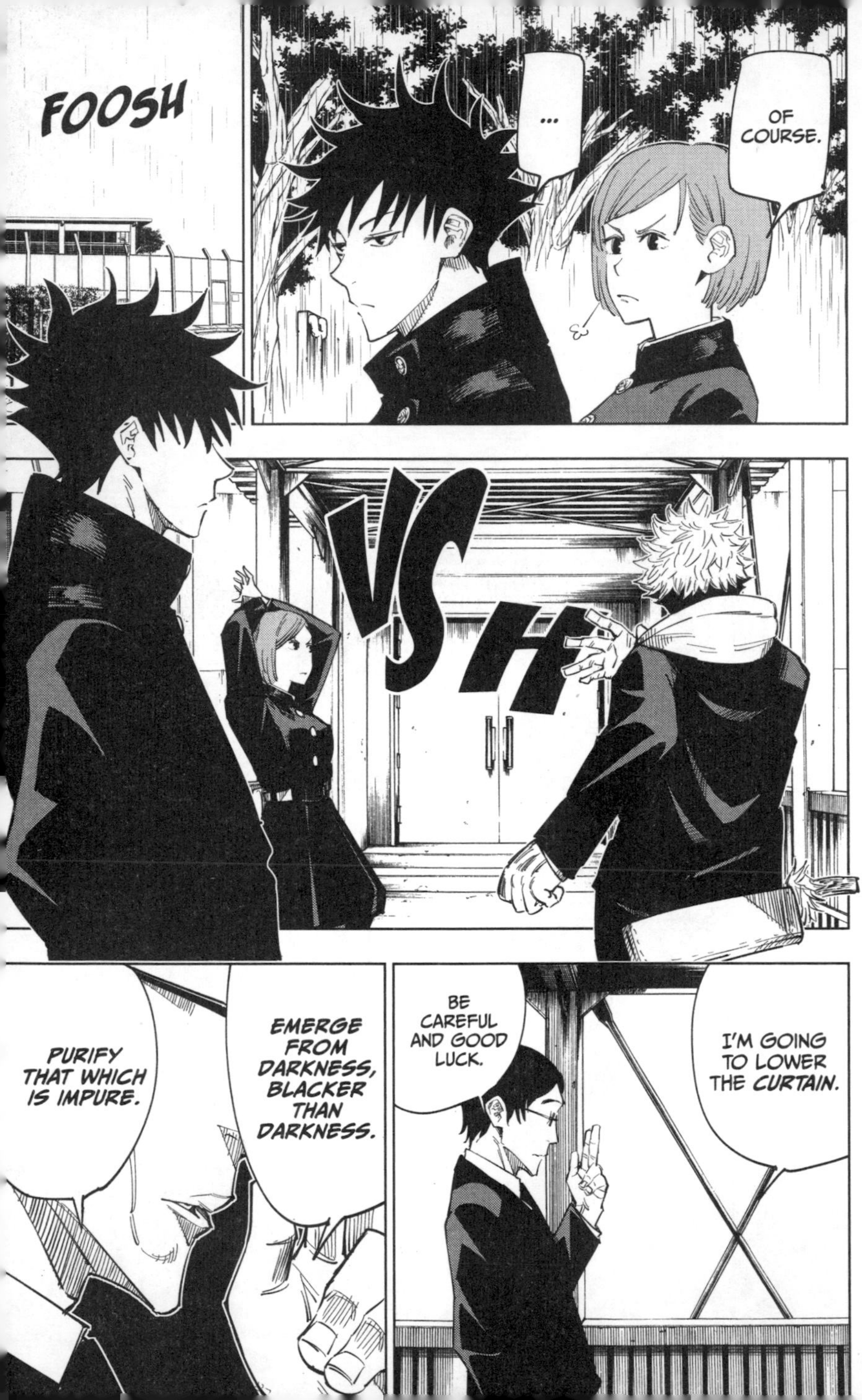
OF COURSE.
...
FOOSH
VS
H
I'M GOING TO LOWER THE CURTAIN.
BE CAREFUL AND GOOD LUCK.
EMERGE FROM DARKNESS, BLACKER THAN DARKNESS.
PURIFY THAT WHICH IS IMPURE.

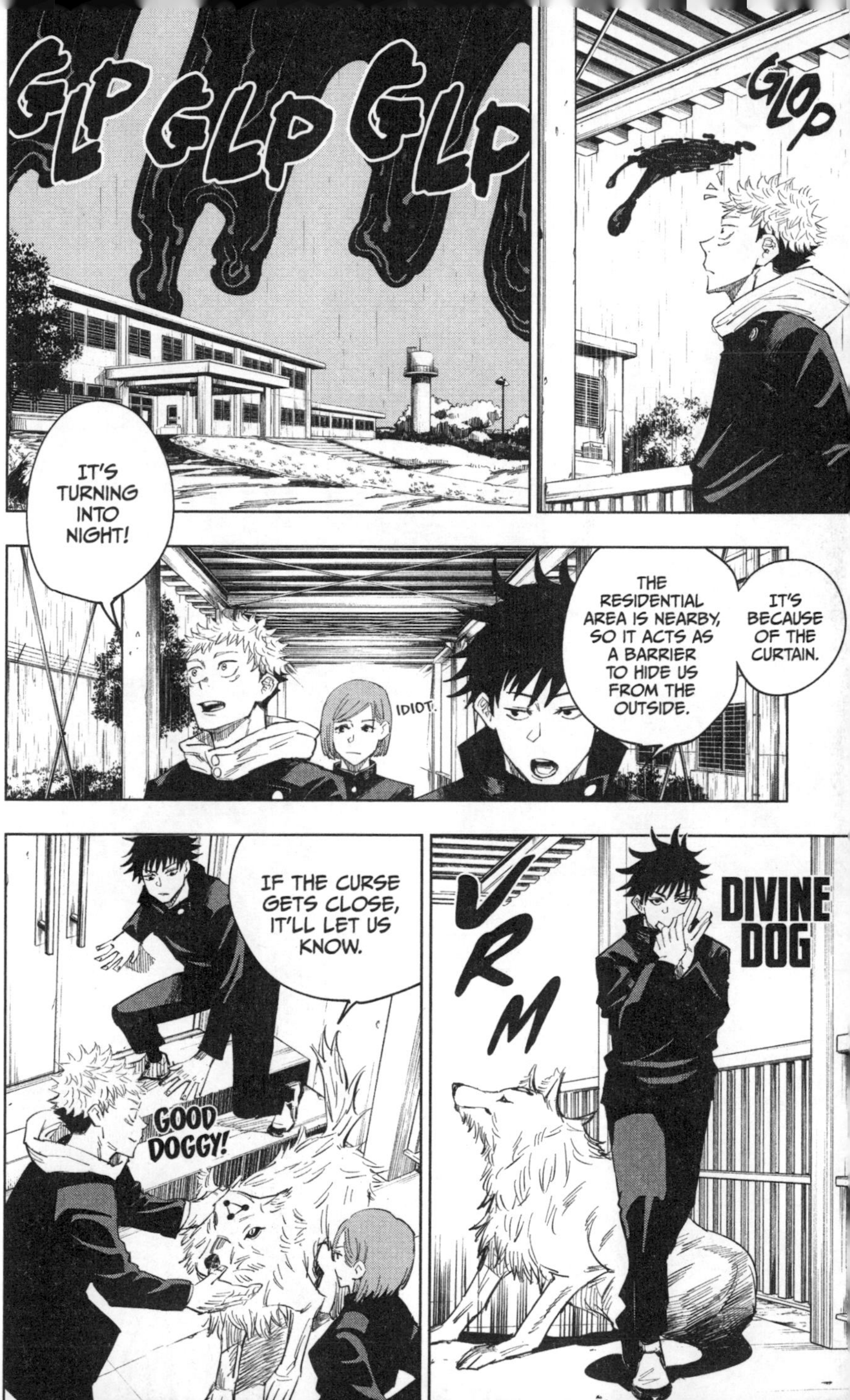
GLOP
GLP GLP GLP
IT'S TURNING INTO NIGHT!
IT'S BECAUSE OF THE CURTAIN.
THE RESIDENTIAL AREA IS NEARBY, SO IT ACTS AS A BARRIER TO HIDE US FROM THE OUTSIDE.
IDIOT.
DIVINE DOG
VRM
IF THE CURSE GETS CLOSE, IT'LL LET US KNOW.
GOOD DOGGY!

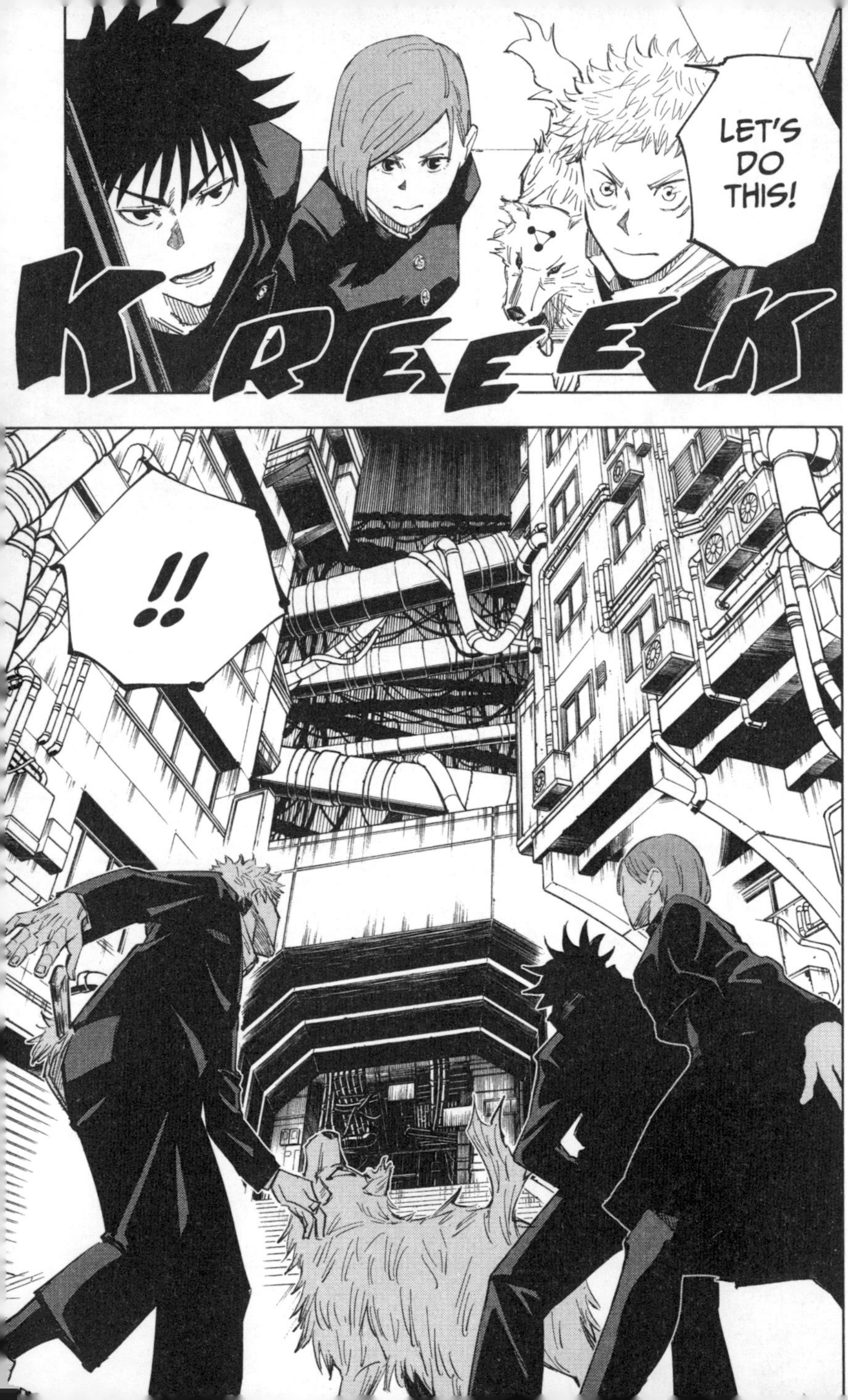
LET'S DO THIS!
KREEEK
!!

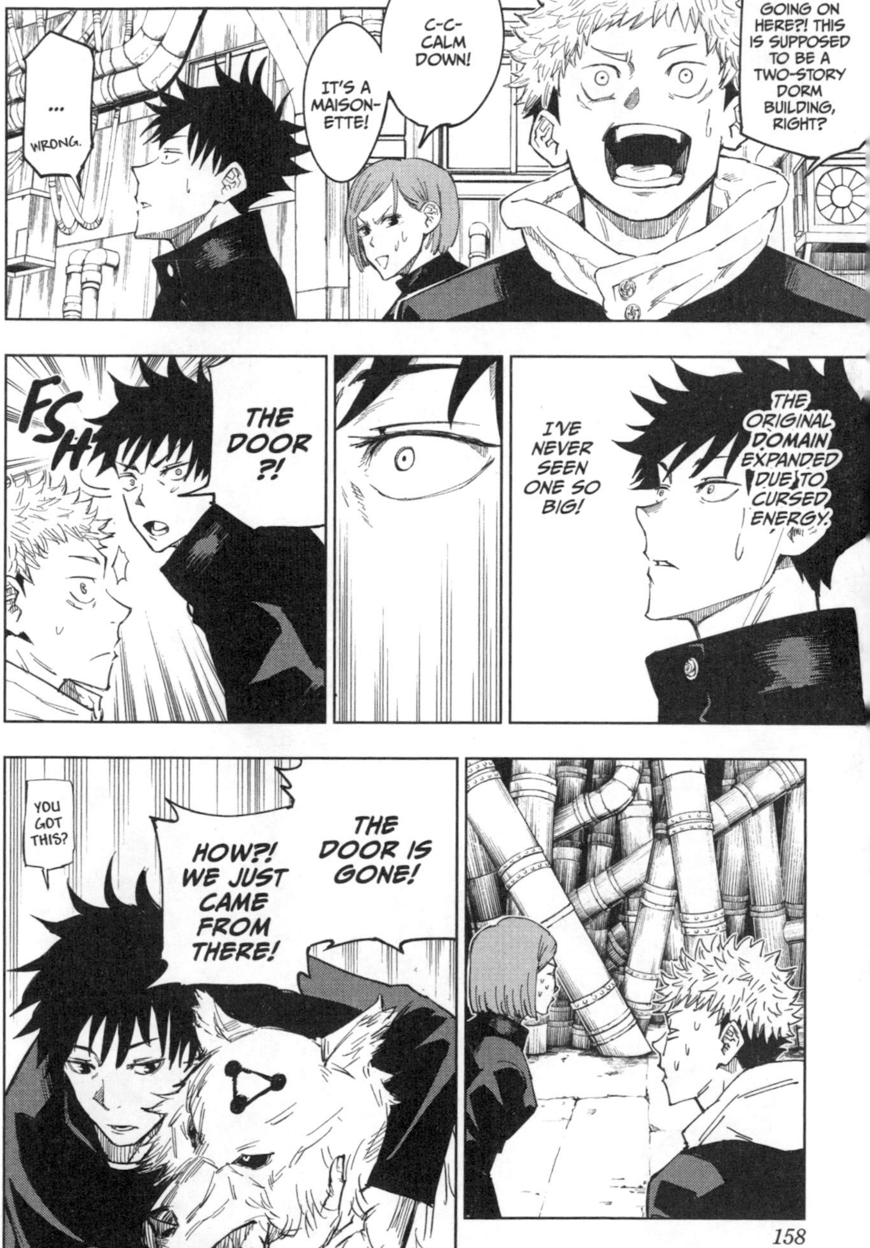
WHAT'S GOING ON HERE?! THIS IS SUPPOSED TO BE A TWO-STORY DORM BUILDING, RIGHT?
C-C-CALM DOWN!
IT'S A MAISONETTE!
... WRONG.
THE ORIGINAL DOMAIN EXPANDED DUE TO CURSED ENERGY.
I'VE NEVER SEEN ONE SO BIG!
THE DOOR?!
FSH
THE DOOR IS GONE!
HOW?! WE JUST CAME FROM THERE!
YOU GOT THIS?

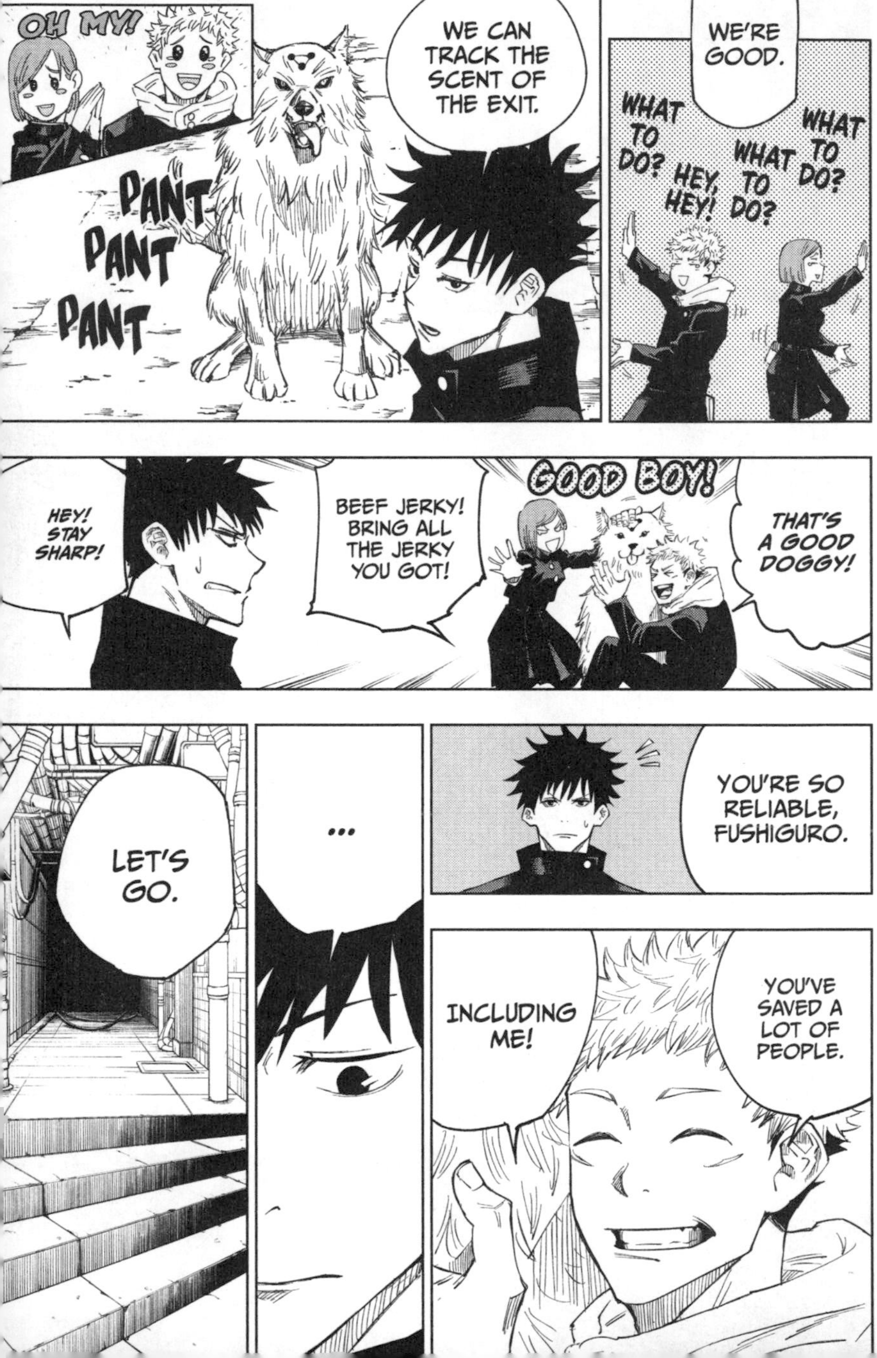
WE'RE GOOD.
WHAT TO DO?
WHAT TO DO?
HEY, HEY!
WHAT TO DO?
WE CAN TRACK THE SCENT OF THE EXIT.
OH MY!
PANT PANT PANT
THAT'S A GOOD DOGGY!
GOOD BOY!
BEEF JERKY! BRING ALL THE JERKY YOU GOT!
HEY! STAY SHARP!
YOU'RE SO RELIABLE, FUSHIGURO.
YOU'VE SAVED A LOT OF PEOPLE.
INCLUDING ME!
...
LET'S GO.

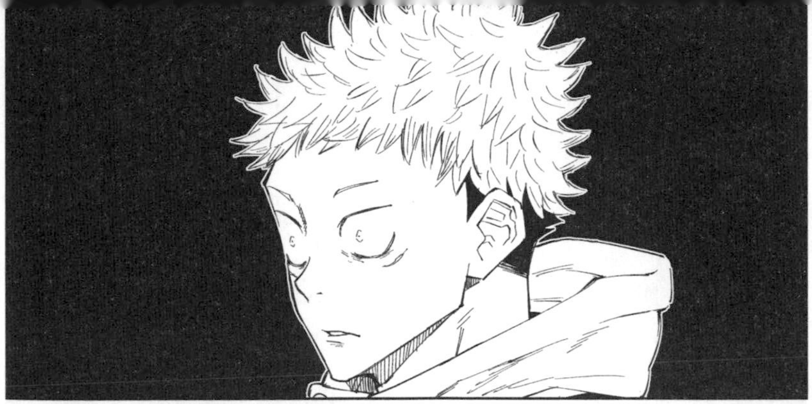
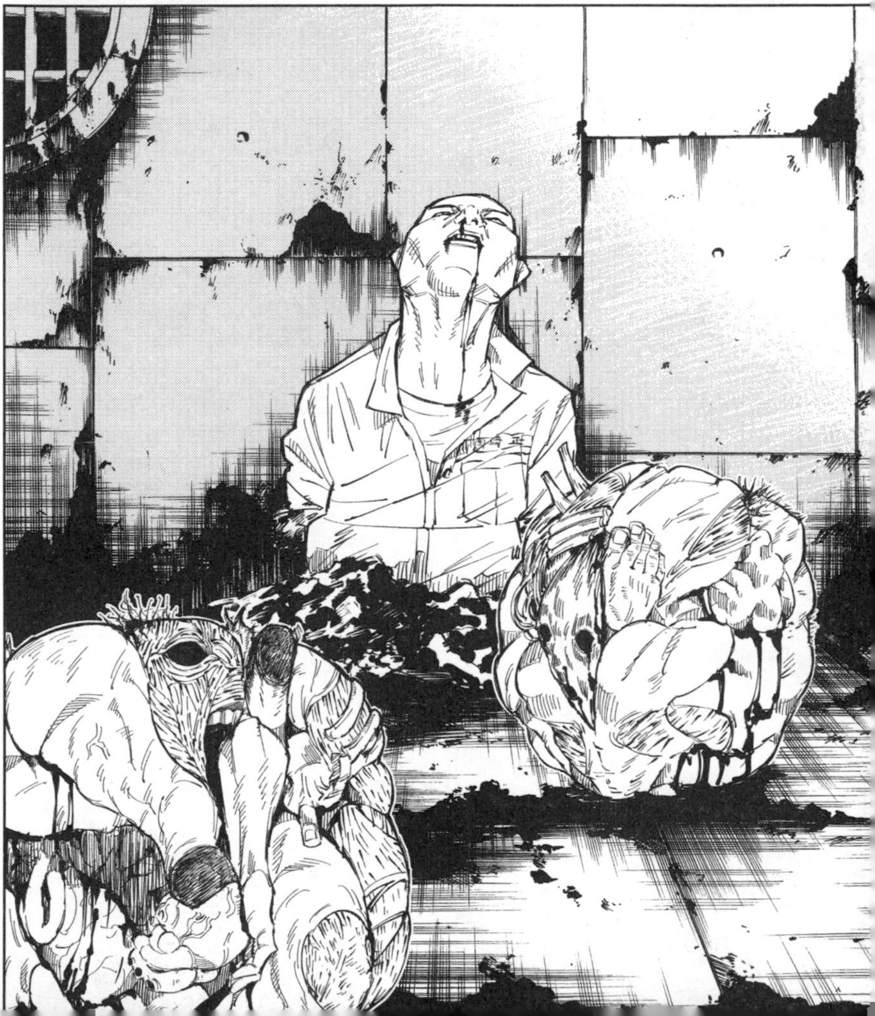

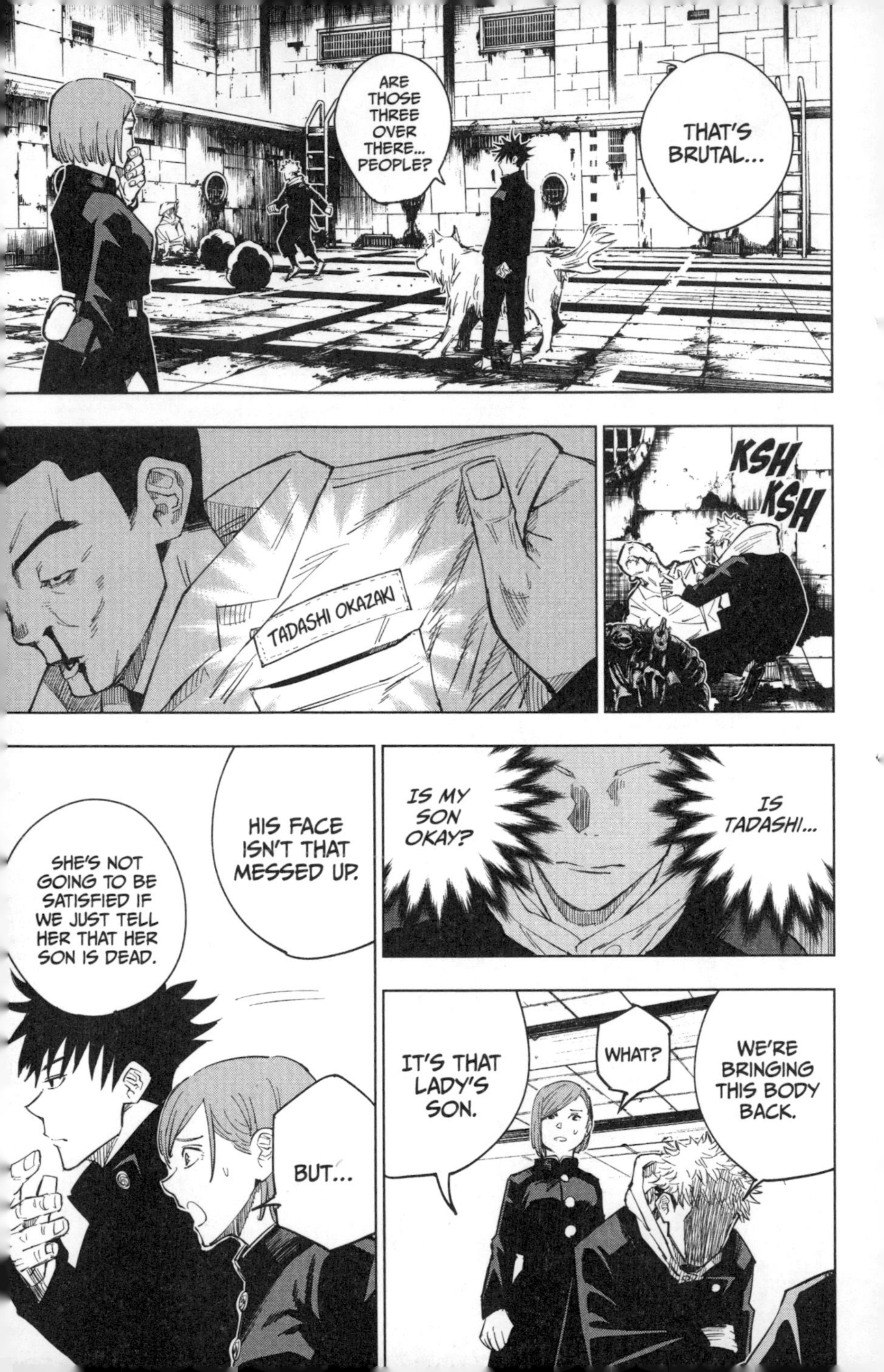
THAT'S BRUTAL...
ARE THOSE THREE OVER THERE... PEOPLE?
KSH KSH
TADASHI OKAZAKI
IS TADASHI...
IS MY SON OKAY?
WE'RE BRINGING THIS BODY BACK.
WHAT?
IT'S THAT LADY'S SON.
HIS FACE ISN'T THAT MESSED UP.
SHE'S NOT GOING TO BE SATISFIED IF WE JUST TELL HER THAT HER SON IS DEAD.
BUT...

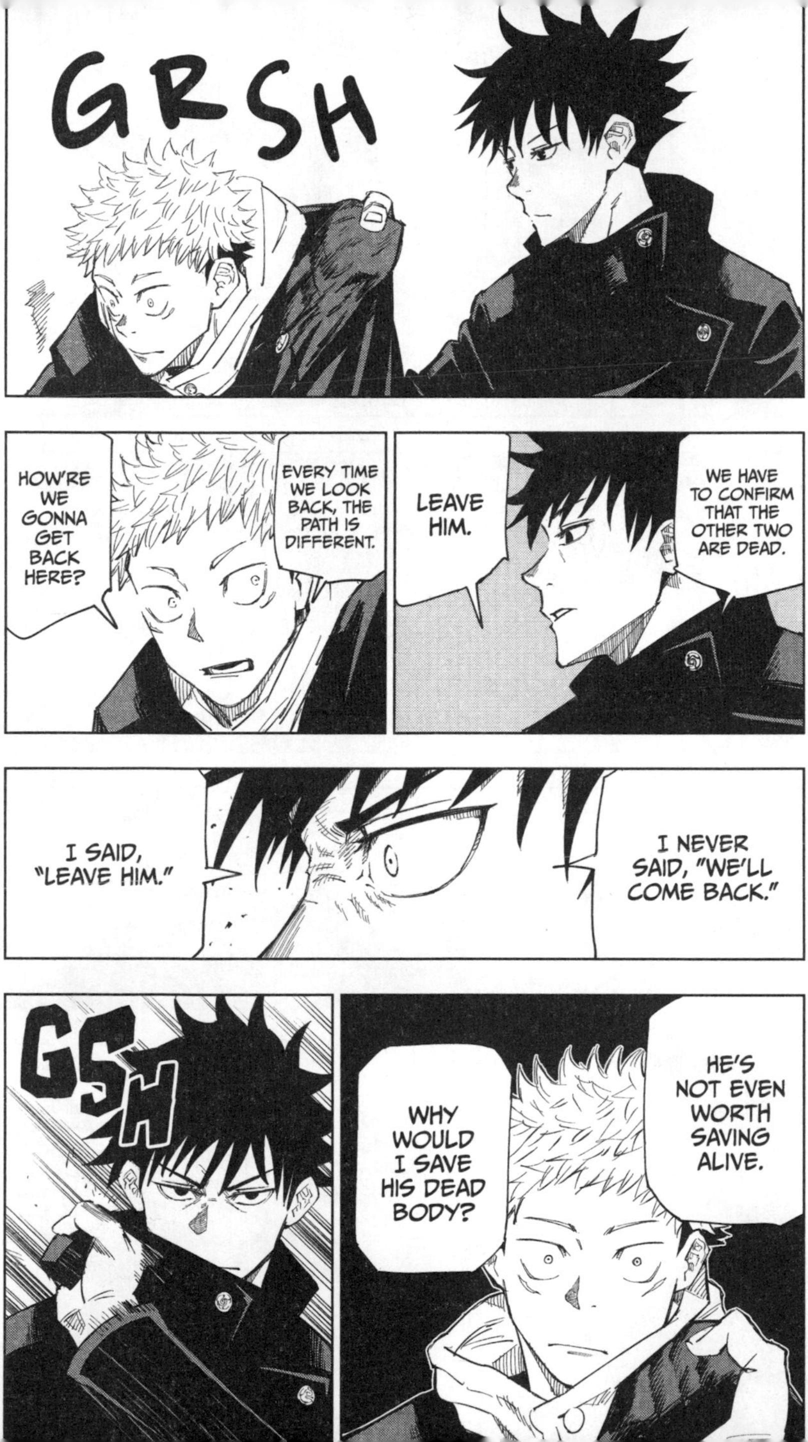
GRSH
WE HAVE TO CONFIRM THAT THE OTHER TWO ARE DEAD.
LEAVE HIM.
EVERY TIME WE LOOK BACK, THE PATH IS DIFFERENT.
HOW'RE WE GONNA GET BACK HERE?
I NEVER SAID, "WE'LL COME BACK."
I SAID, "LEAVE HIM."
HE'S NOT EVEN WORTH SAVING ALIVE.
WHY WOULD I SAVE HIS DEAD BODY?
GSH

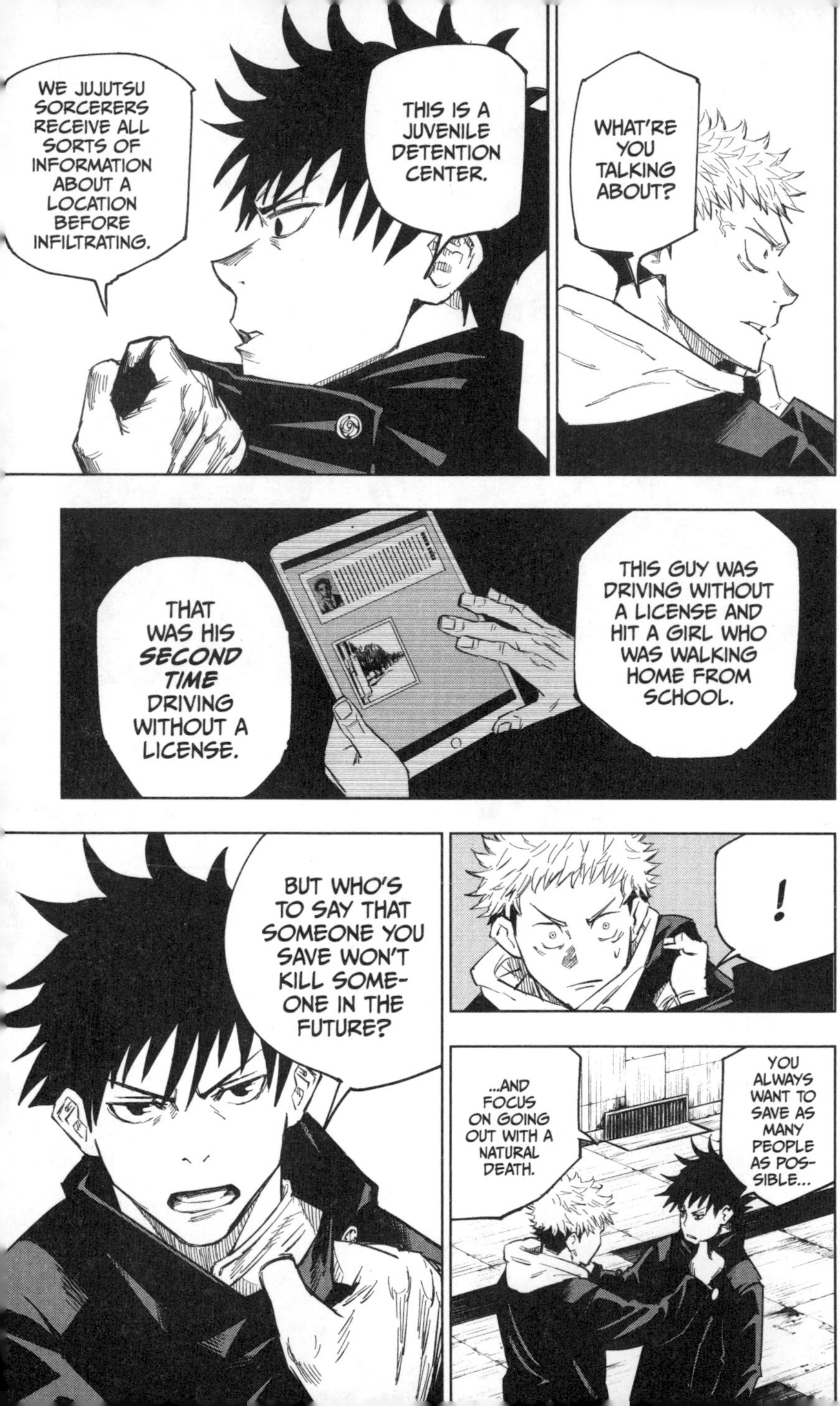
WHAT'RE YOU TALKING ABOUT?
THIS IS A JUVENILE DETENTION CENTER.
WE JUJUTSU SORCERERS RECEIVE ALL SORTS OF INFORMATION ABOUT A LOCATION BEFORE INFILTRATING.
THIS GUY WAS DRIVING WITHOUT A LICENSE AND HIT A GIRL WHO WAS WALKING HOME FROM SCHOOL.
THAT WAS HIS *SECOND TIME* DRIVING WITHOUT A LICENSE.
!
YOU ALWAYS WANT TO SAVE AS MANY PEOPLE AS POS-SIBLE...
...AND FOCUS ON GOING OUT WITH A NATURAL DEATH.
BUT WHO'S TO SAY THAT SOMEONE YOU SAVE WON'T KILL SOME-ONE IN THE FUTURE?

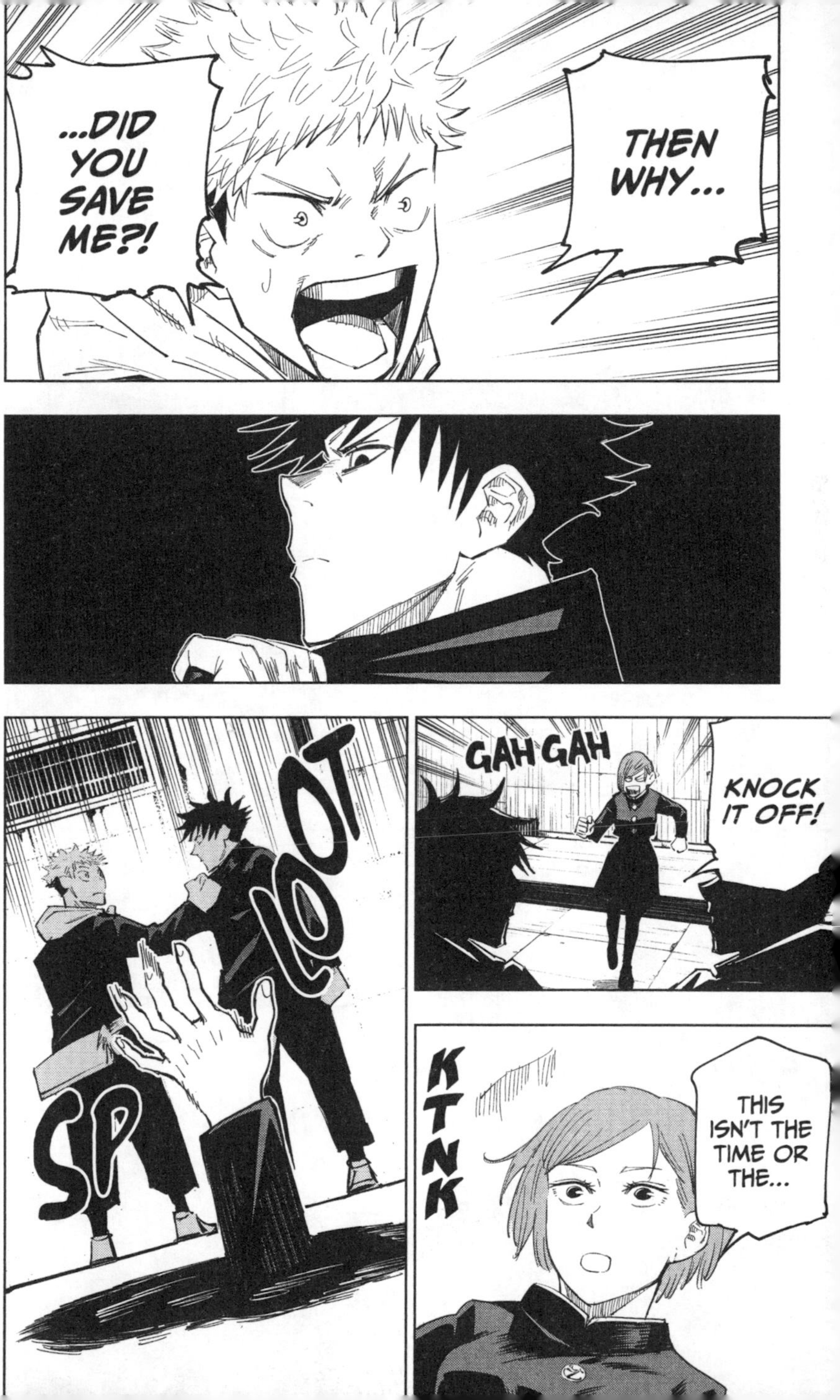
THEN WHY...
...DID YOU SAVE ME?!
KNOCK IT OFF!
GAH GAH
THIS ISN'T THE TIME OR THE...
KTNK
LOOT
SP

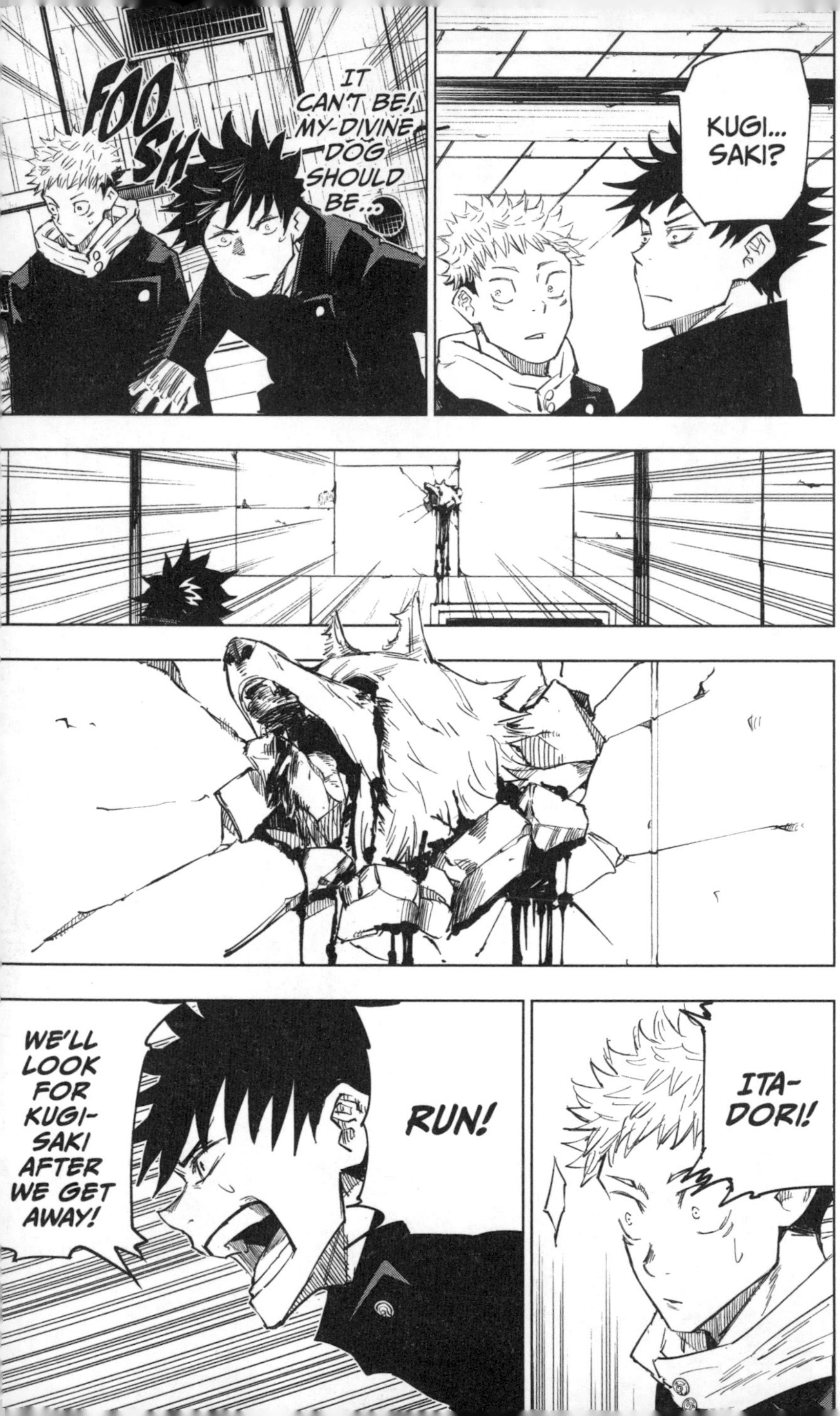
KUGI... SAKI?
FOOSH
IT CAN'T BE! MY DIVINE DOG SHOULD BE...
ITA-DORI!
RUN!
WE'LL LOOK FOR KUGI-SAKI AFTER WE GET AWAY!

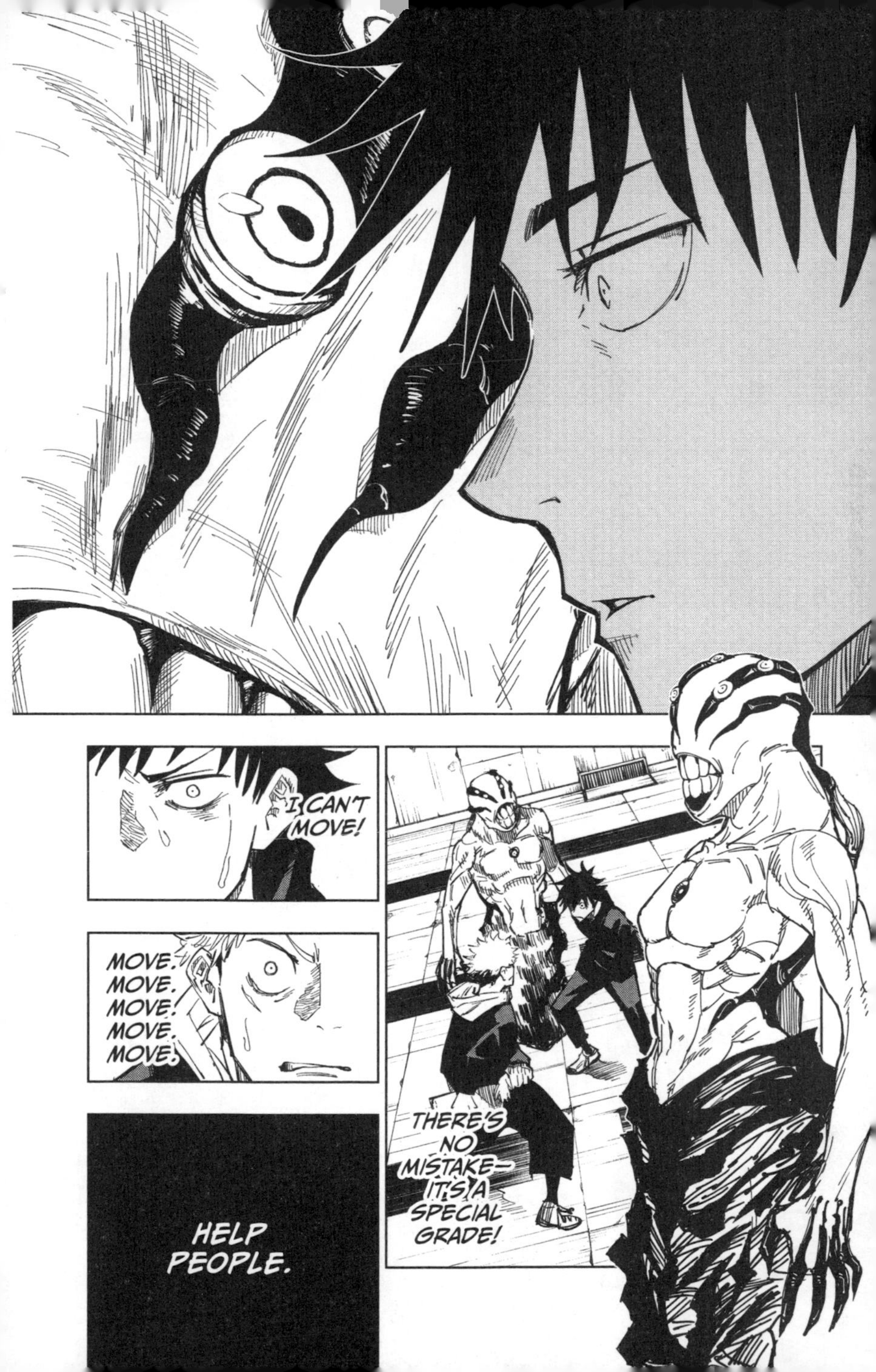
THERE'S NO MISTAKE— IT'S A SPECIAL GRADE!
I CAN'T MOVE!
MOVE. MOVE. MOVE. MOVE. MOVE.
HELP PEOPLE.

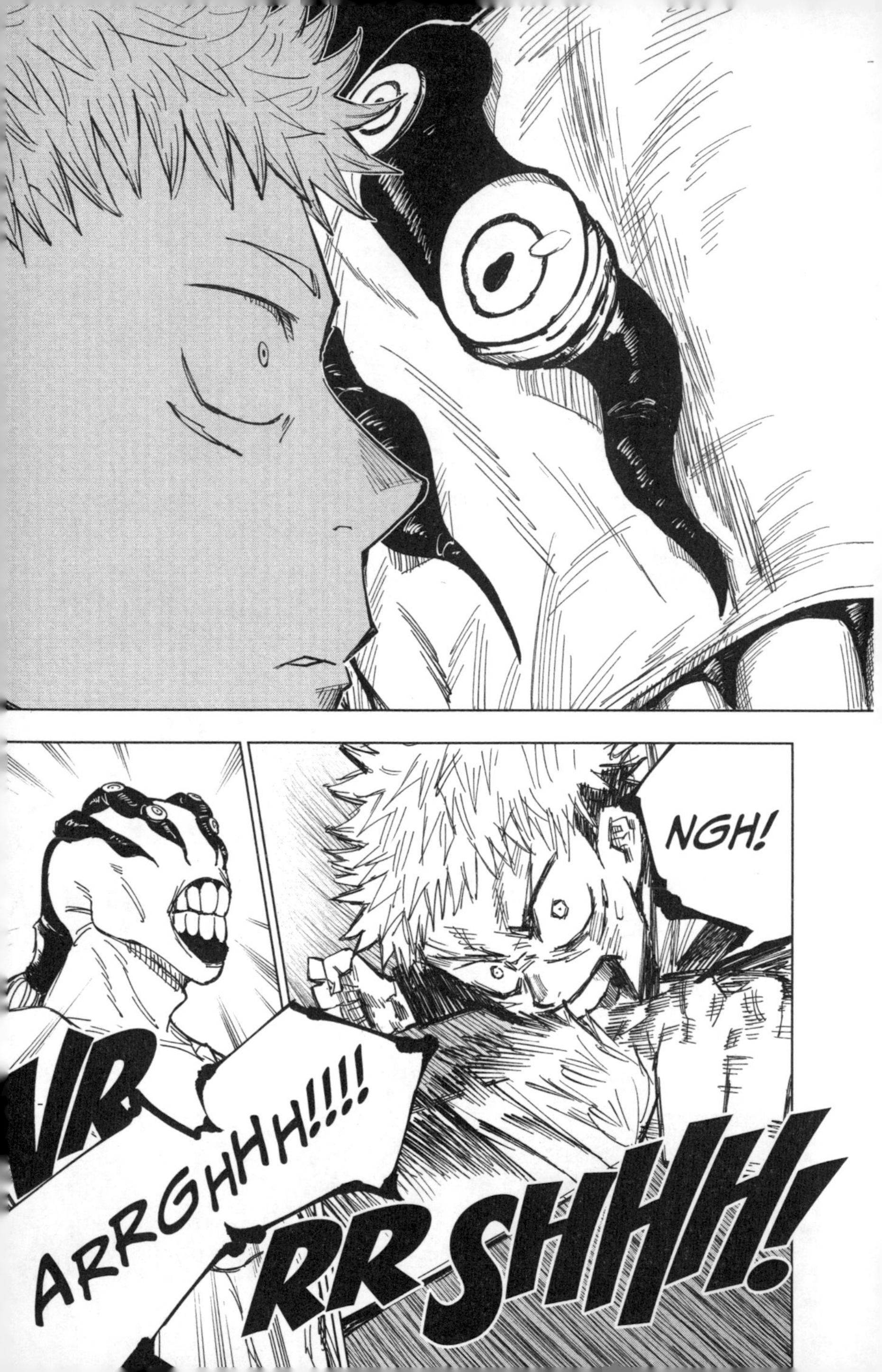
NGH!
ARRGHHH!!!!
VR
RRSHHH!

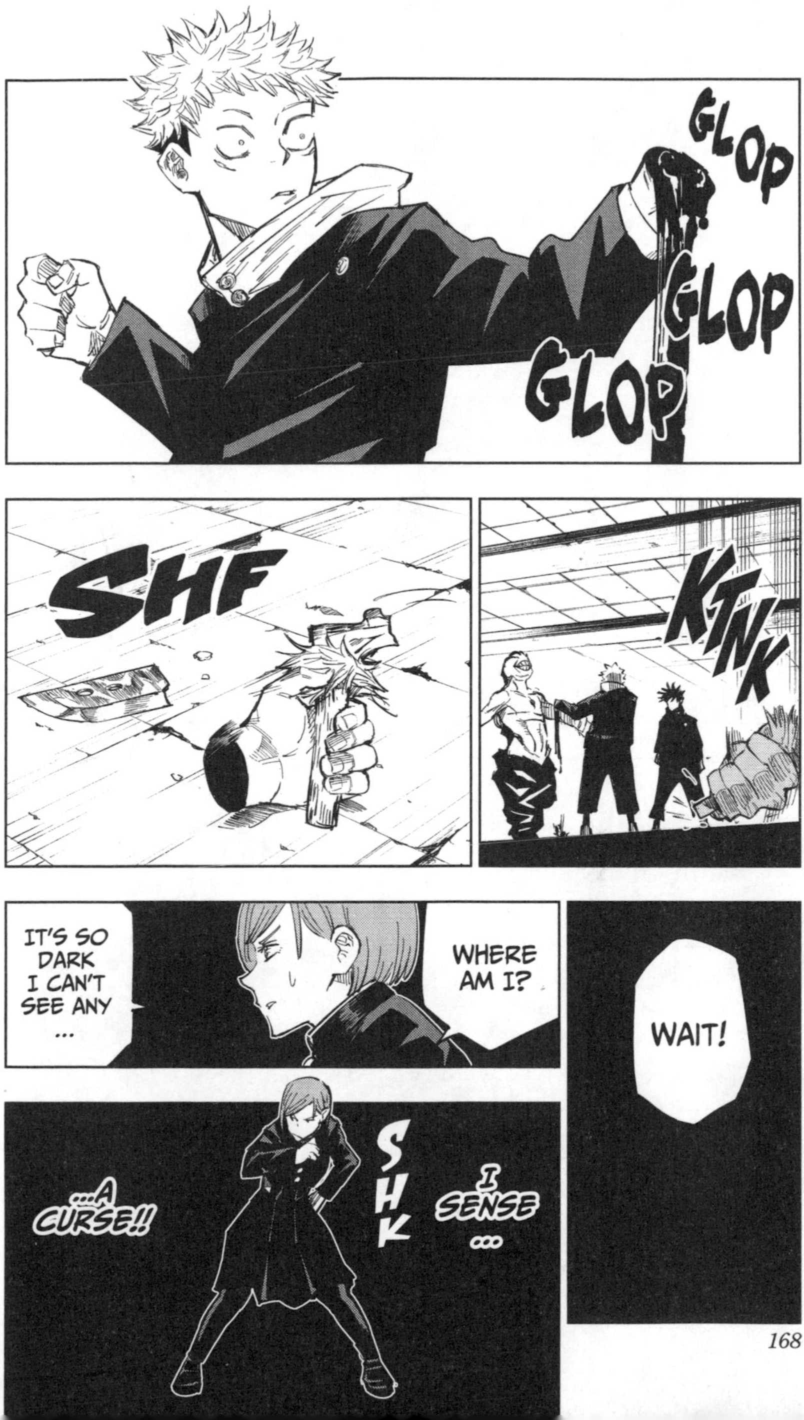

GLOP
GLOP
GLOP
KTNK
SHF
WAIT!
WHERE AM I?
IT'S SO DARK I CAN'T SEE ANY ...
I SENSE ...
SHK
...A CURSE!!

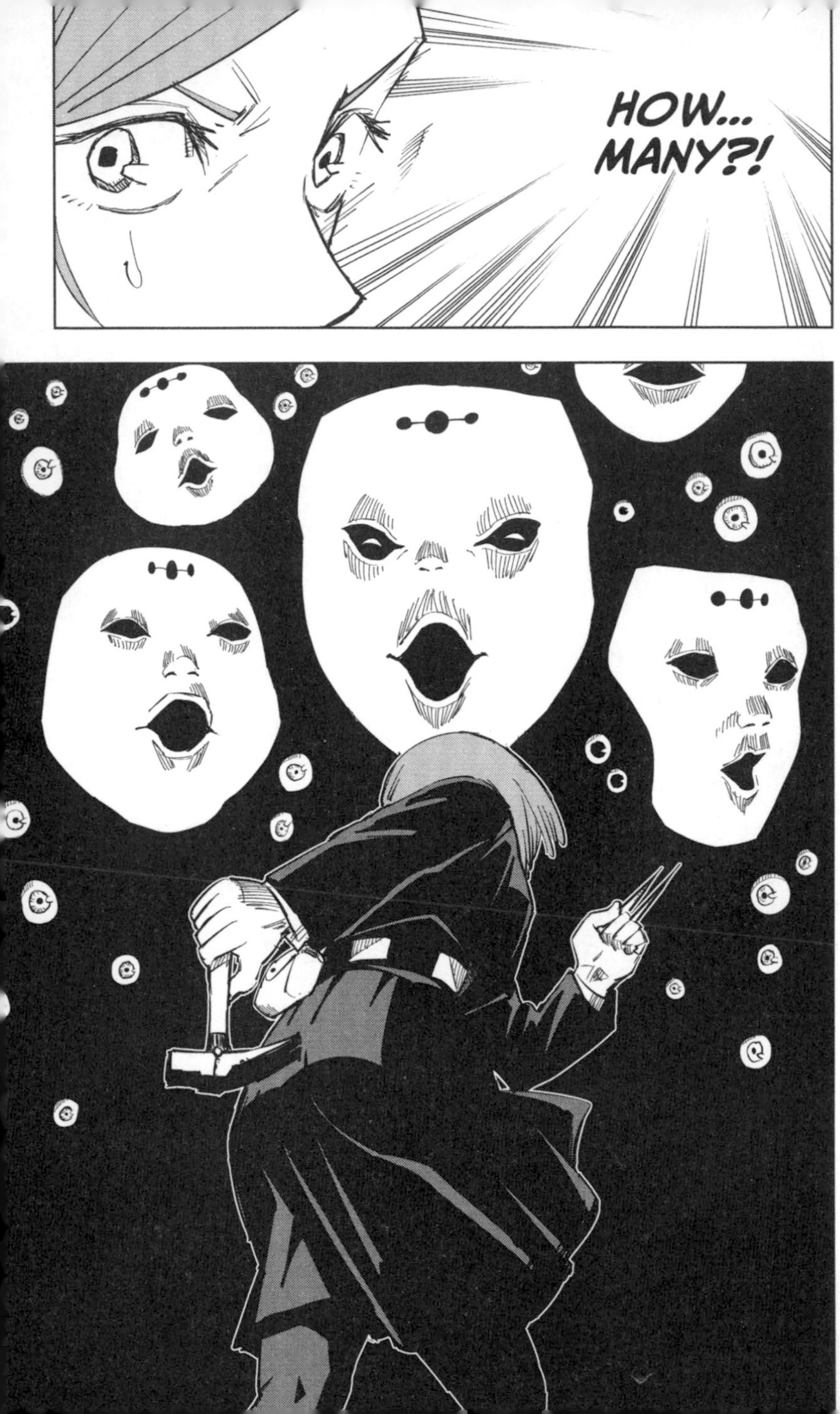
HOW... MANY?!

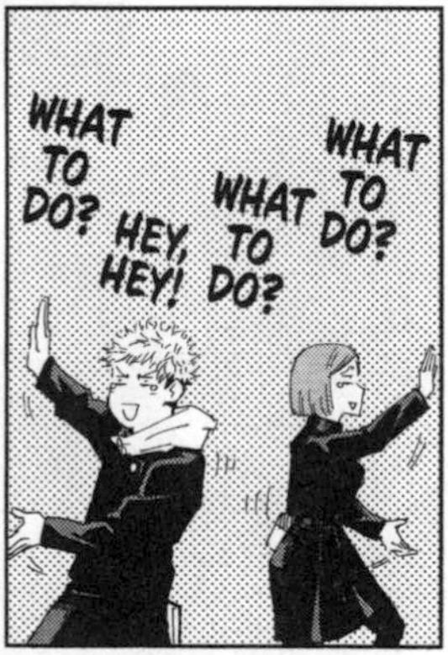
WHAT TO DO?
WHAT TO DO?
WHAT TO DO?
HEY, HEY!

In life, there are situations where it seems dancing is the only logical option. When working on a weekly series, this happens every week.

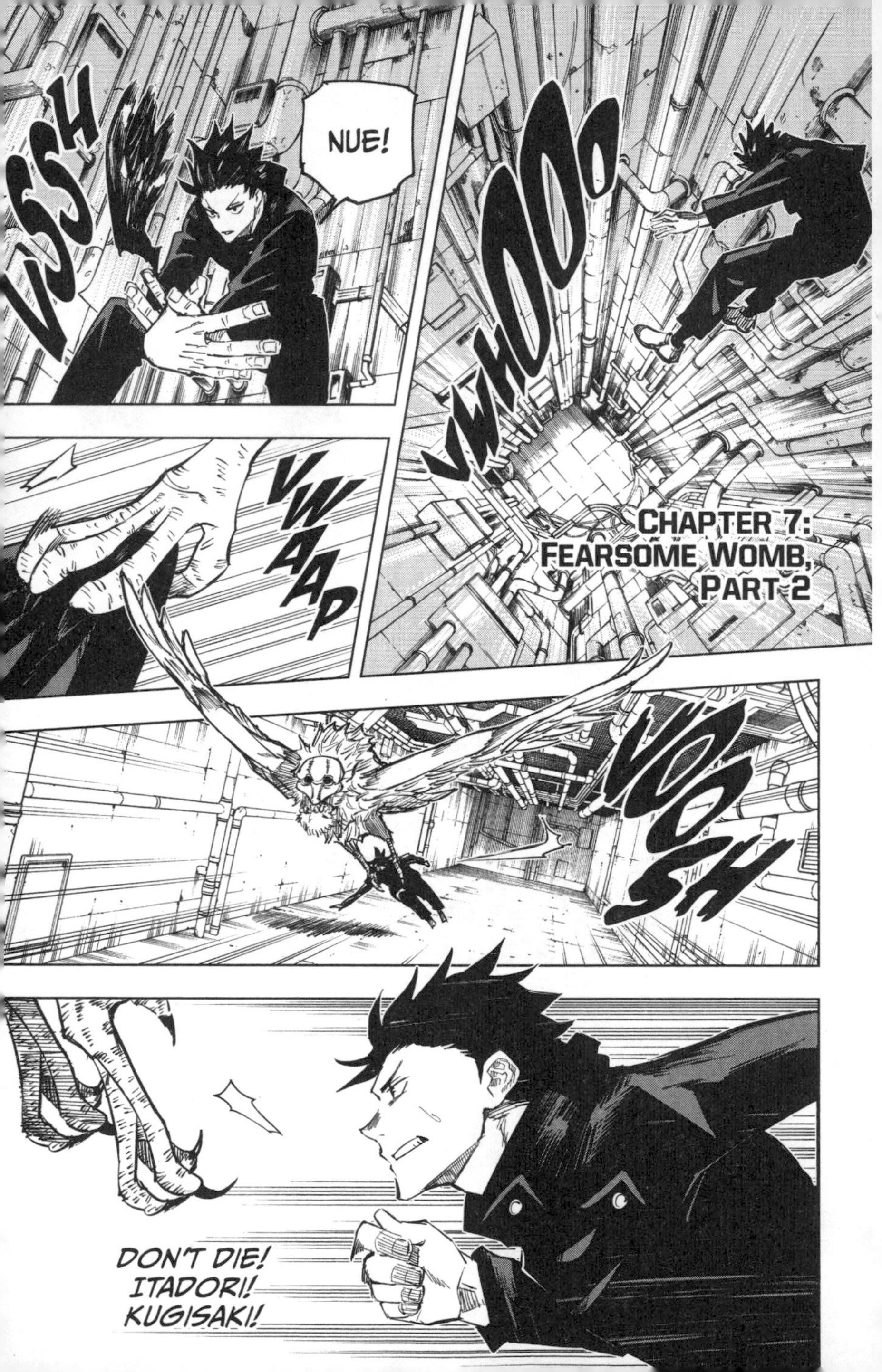
VWHOOOO
Chapter 7: Fearsome Womb, Part 2
NUE!
VSSH
VWAAP
VOOSH
DON'T DIE! ITADORI! KUGISAKI!

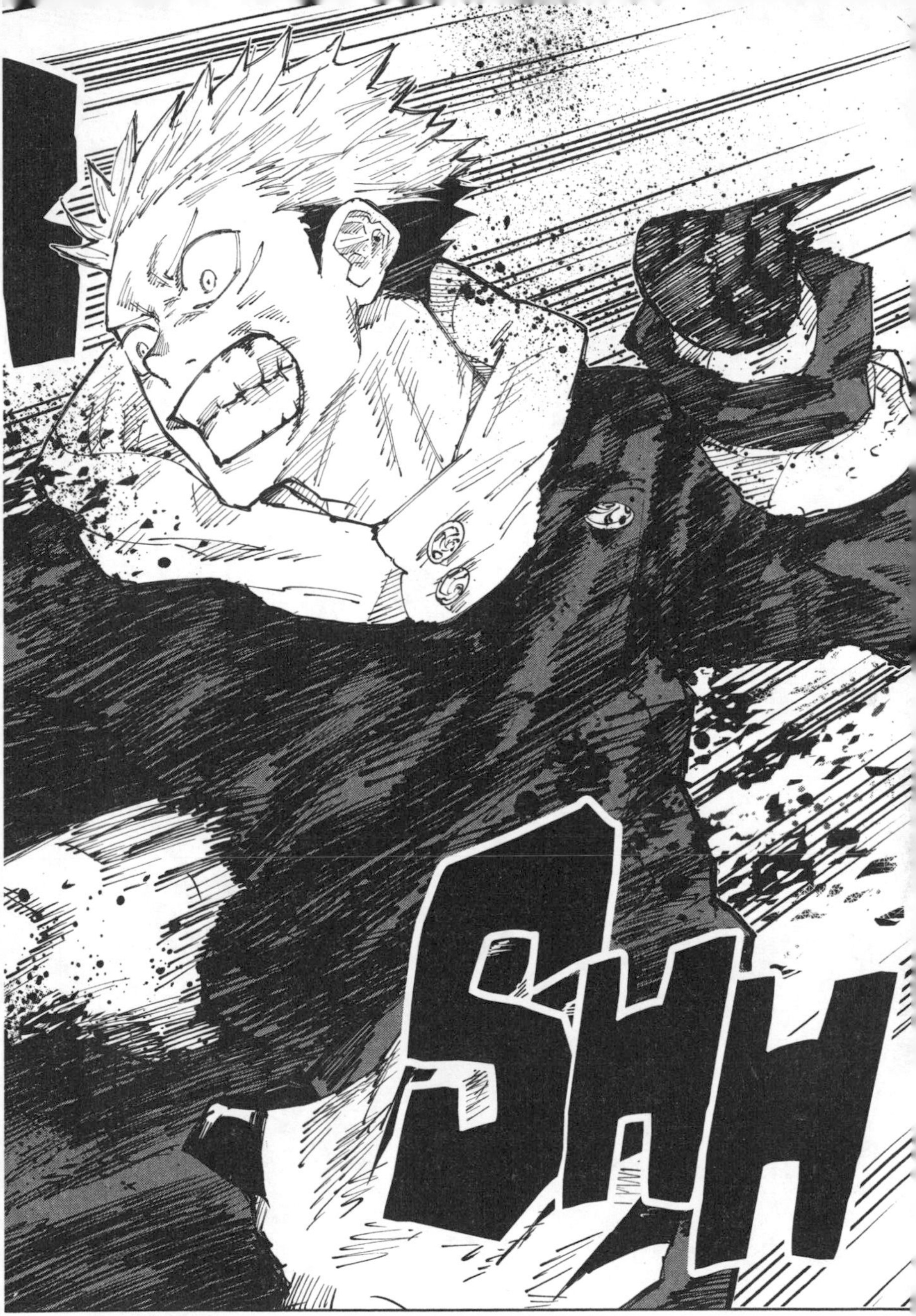
SHH

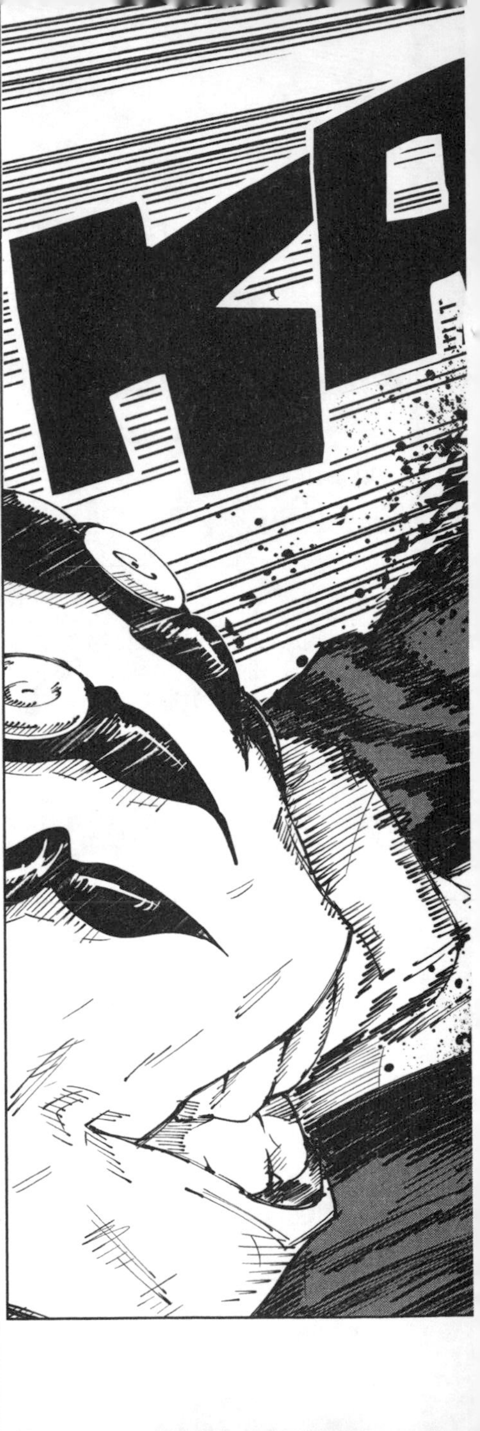

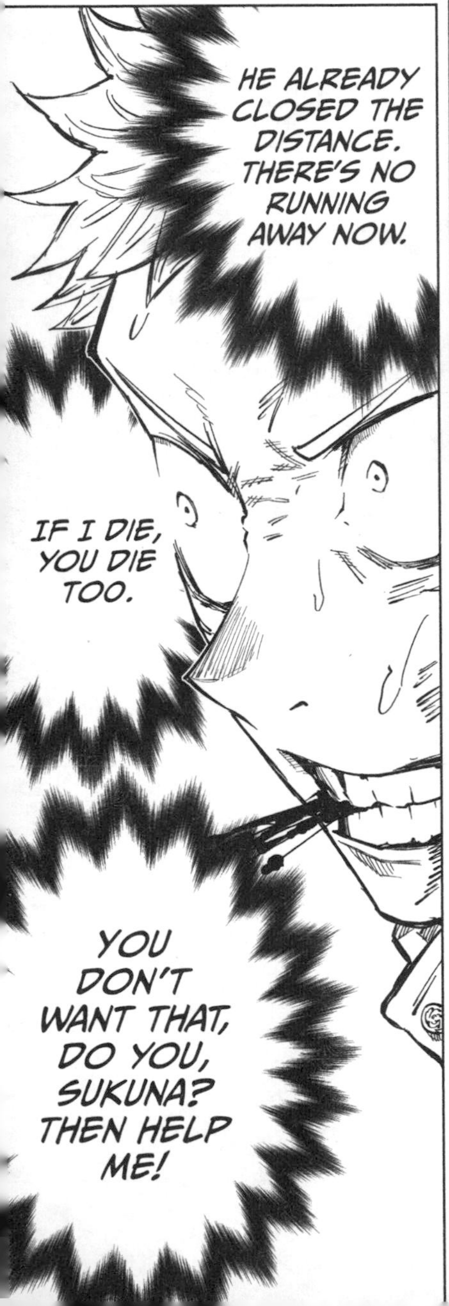
HE ALREADY CLOSED THE DISTANCE. THERE'S NO RUNNING AWAY NOW.
IF I DIE, YOU DIE TOO.
YOU DON'T WANT THAT, DO YOU, SUKUNA? THEN HELP ME!

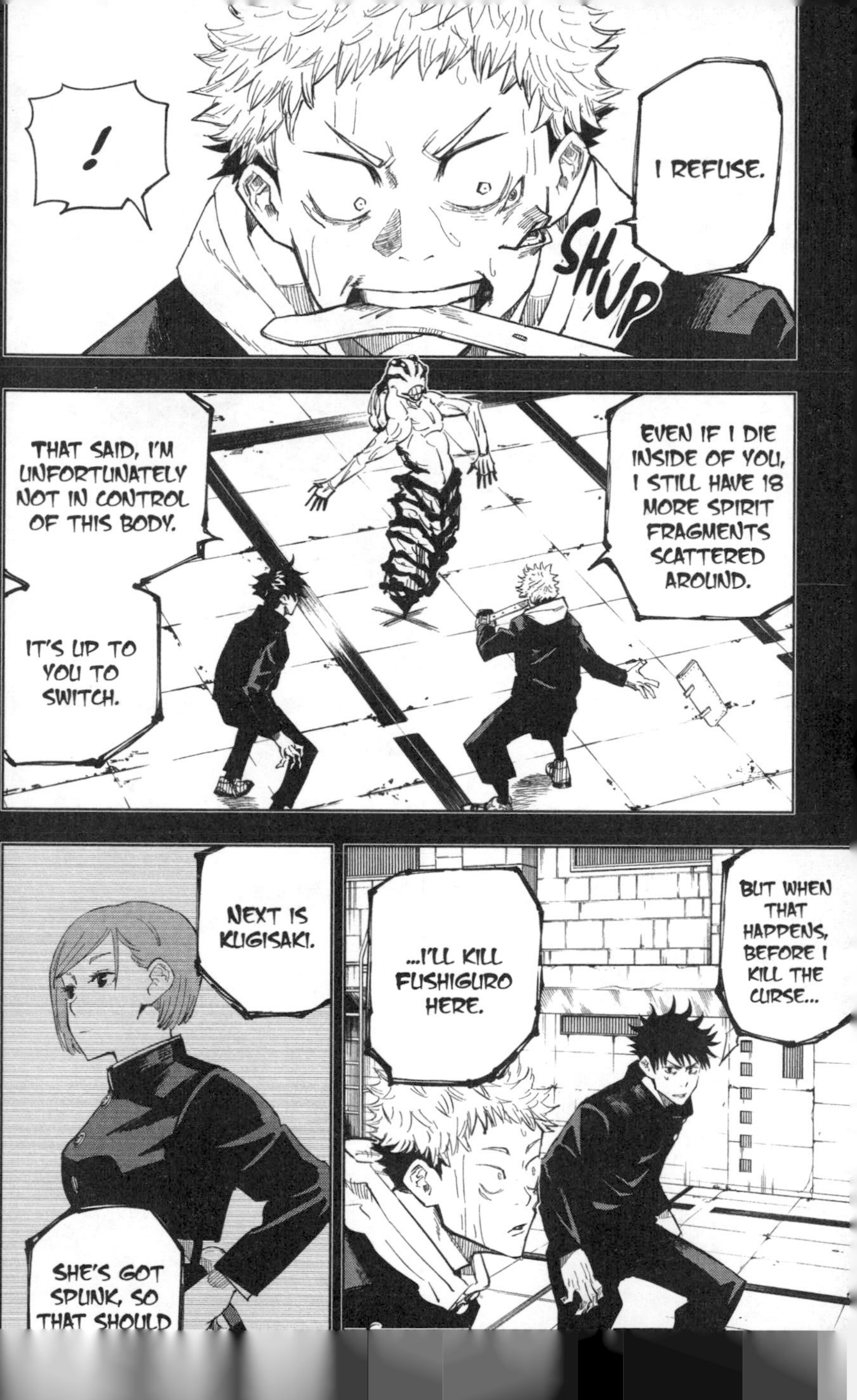
I REFUSE.
SHUP
!
EVEN IF I DIE INSIDE OF YOU, I STILL HAVE 18 MORE SPIRIT FRAGMENTS SCATTERED AROUND.
THAT SAID, I'M UNFORTUNATELY NOT IN CONTROL OF THIS BODY.
IT'S UP TO YOU TO SWITCH.
BUT WHEN THAT HAPPENS, BEFORE I KILL THE CURSE...
...I'LL KILL FUSHIGURO HERE.
NEXT IS KUGISAKI.
SHE'S GOT SPUNK, SO THAT SHOULD

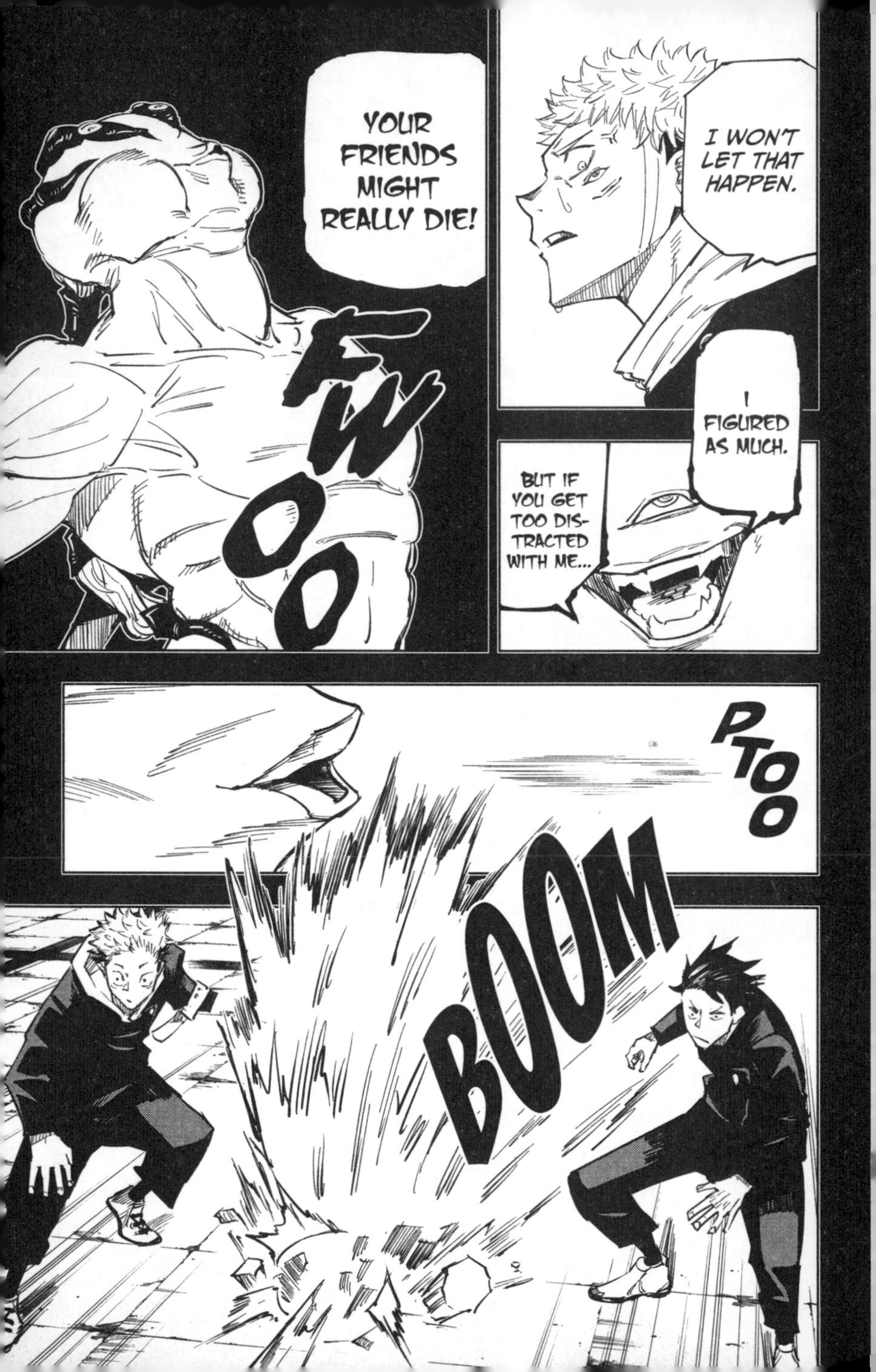
I WON'T LET THAT HAPPEN.
I FIGURED AS MUCH.
BUT IF YOU GET TOO DIS-TRACTED WITH ME...
YOUR FRIENDS MIGHT REALLY DIE!
FWOO
PTOO
BOOM

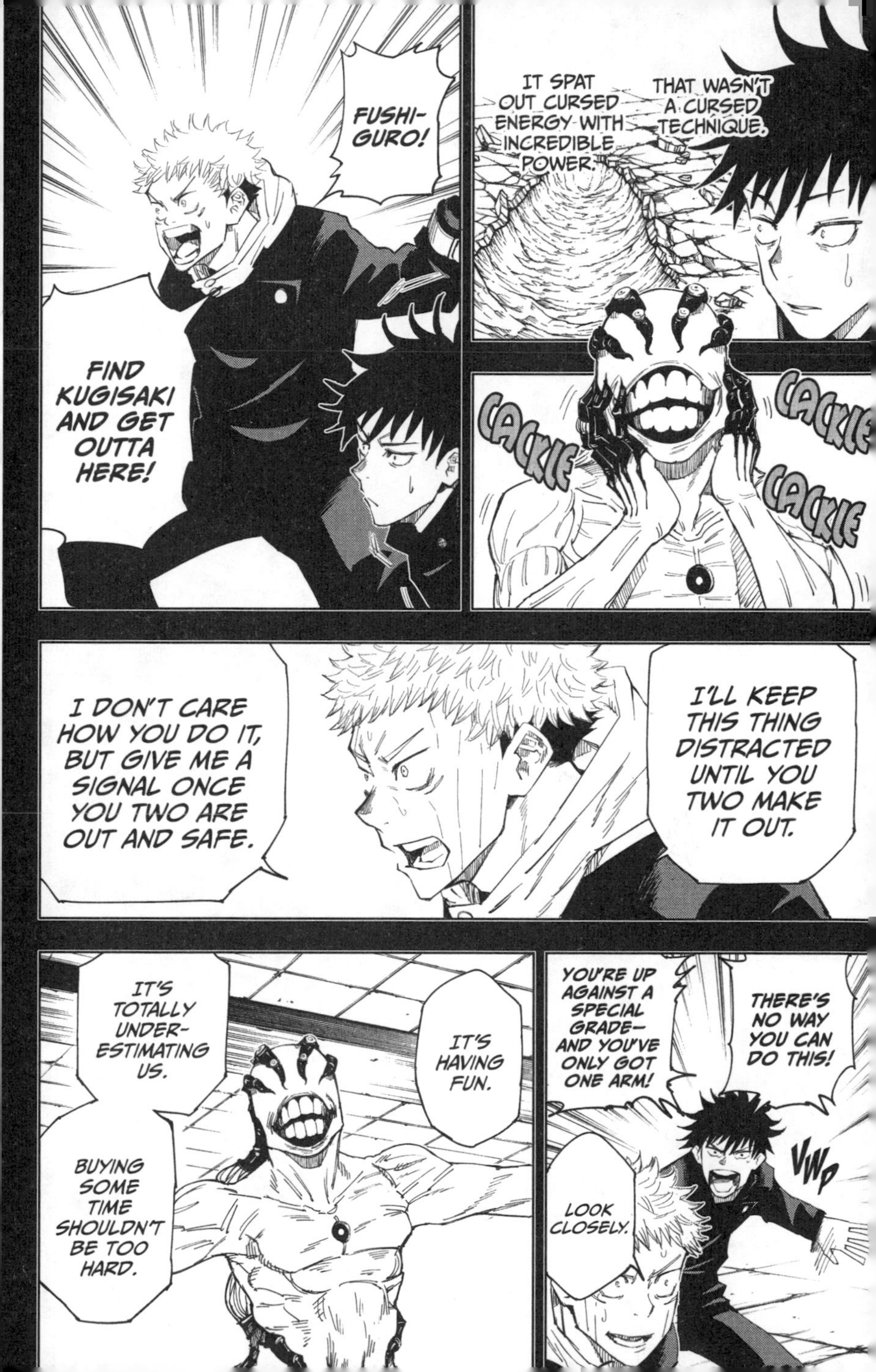
THAT WASN'T A CURSED TECHNIQUE.
IT SPAT OUT CURSED ENERGY WITH INCREDIBLE POWER.
CACKLE
CACKLE
CACKLE
FUSHI-GURO!
FIND KUGISAKI AND GET OUTTA HERE!
I'LL KEEP THIS THING DISTRACTED UNTIL YOU TWO MAKE IT OUT.
I DON'T CARE HOW YOU DO IT, BUT GIVE ME A SIGNAL ONCE YOU TWO ARE OUT AND SAFE.
THERE'S NO WAY YOU CAN DO THIS!
YOU'RE UP AGAINST A SPECIAL GRADE—AND YOU'VE ONLY GOT ONE ARM!
VWP
LOOK CLOSELY.
IT'S HAVING FUN.
IT'S TOTALLY UNDER-ESTIMATING US.
BUYING SOME TIME SHOULDN'T BE TOO HARD.

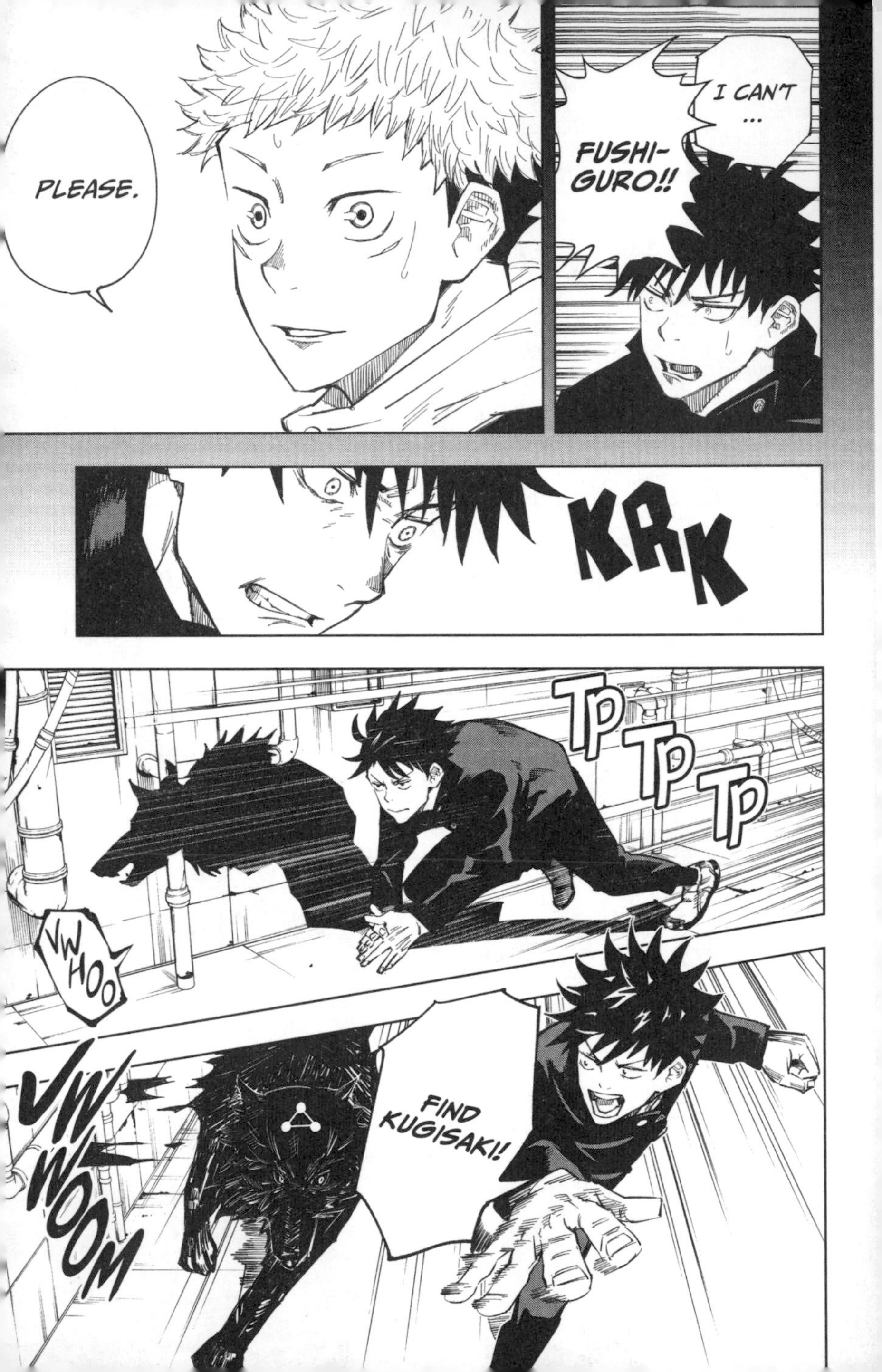
I CAN'T ...
FUSHI-GURO!!
PLEASE.
KRK
Tp Tp Tp
VWHOO
FIND KUGISAKI!
VWWOOM

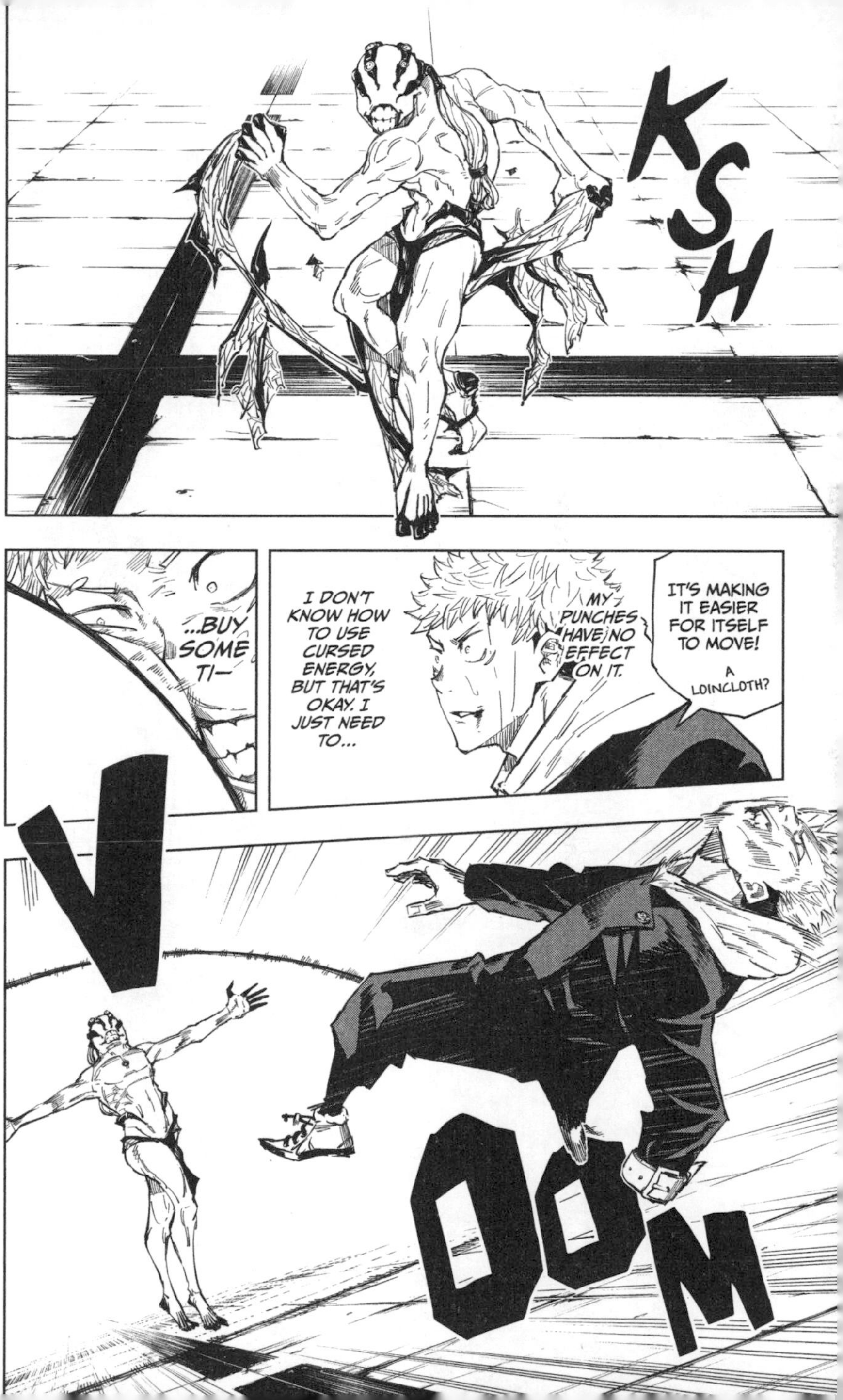
KSH
IT'S MAKING IT EASIER FOR ITSELF TO MOVE!
A LOINCLOTH?
MY PUNCHES HAVE NO EFFECT ON IT.
I DON'T KNOW HOW TO USE CURSED ENERGY, BUT THAT'S OKAY. I JUST NEED TO...
...BUY SOME TI—
VOOM

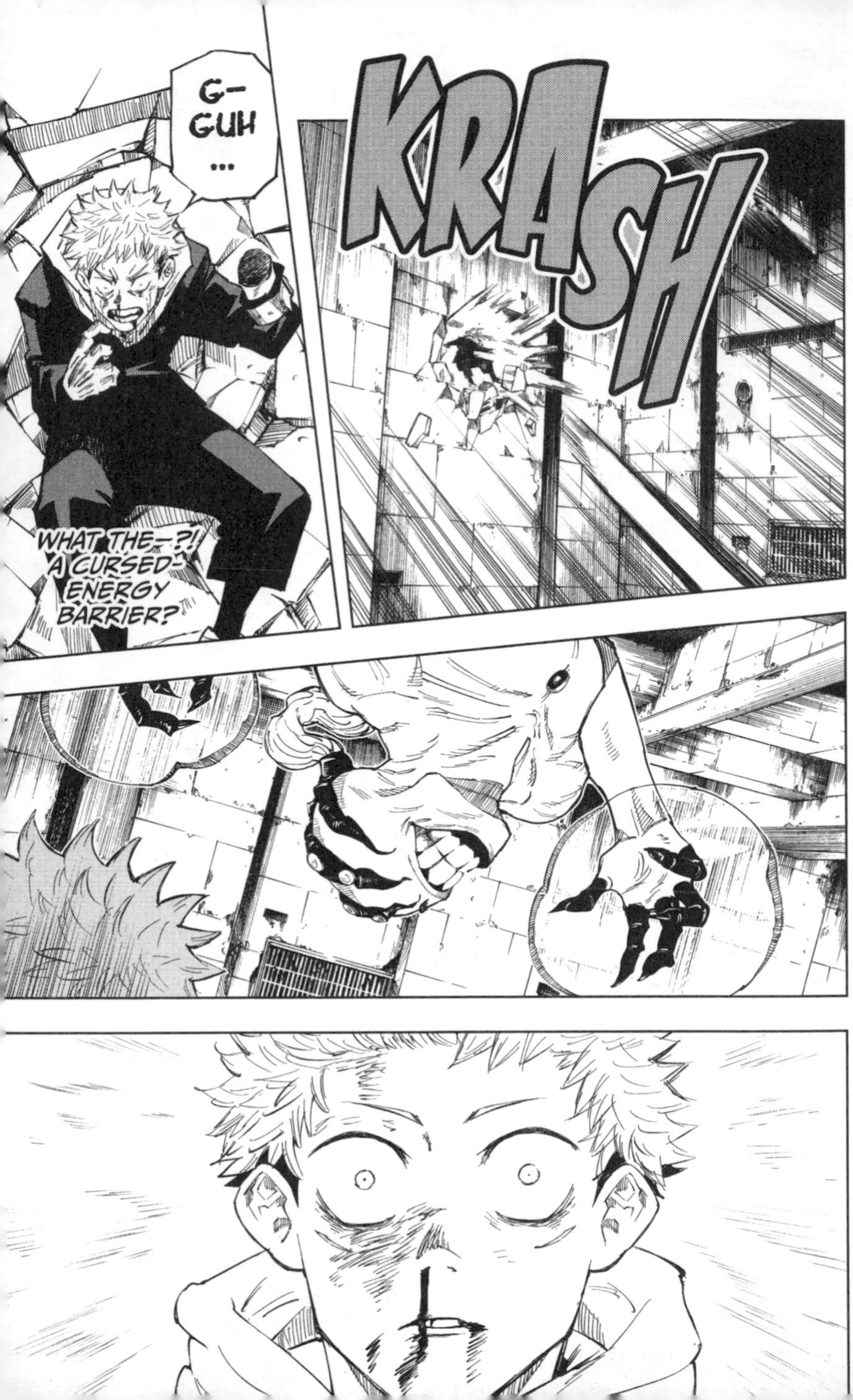
KRASH
G-GUH ...
WHAT THE--?! A CURSED-ENERGY BARRIER?

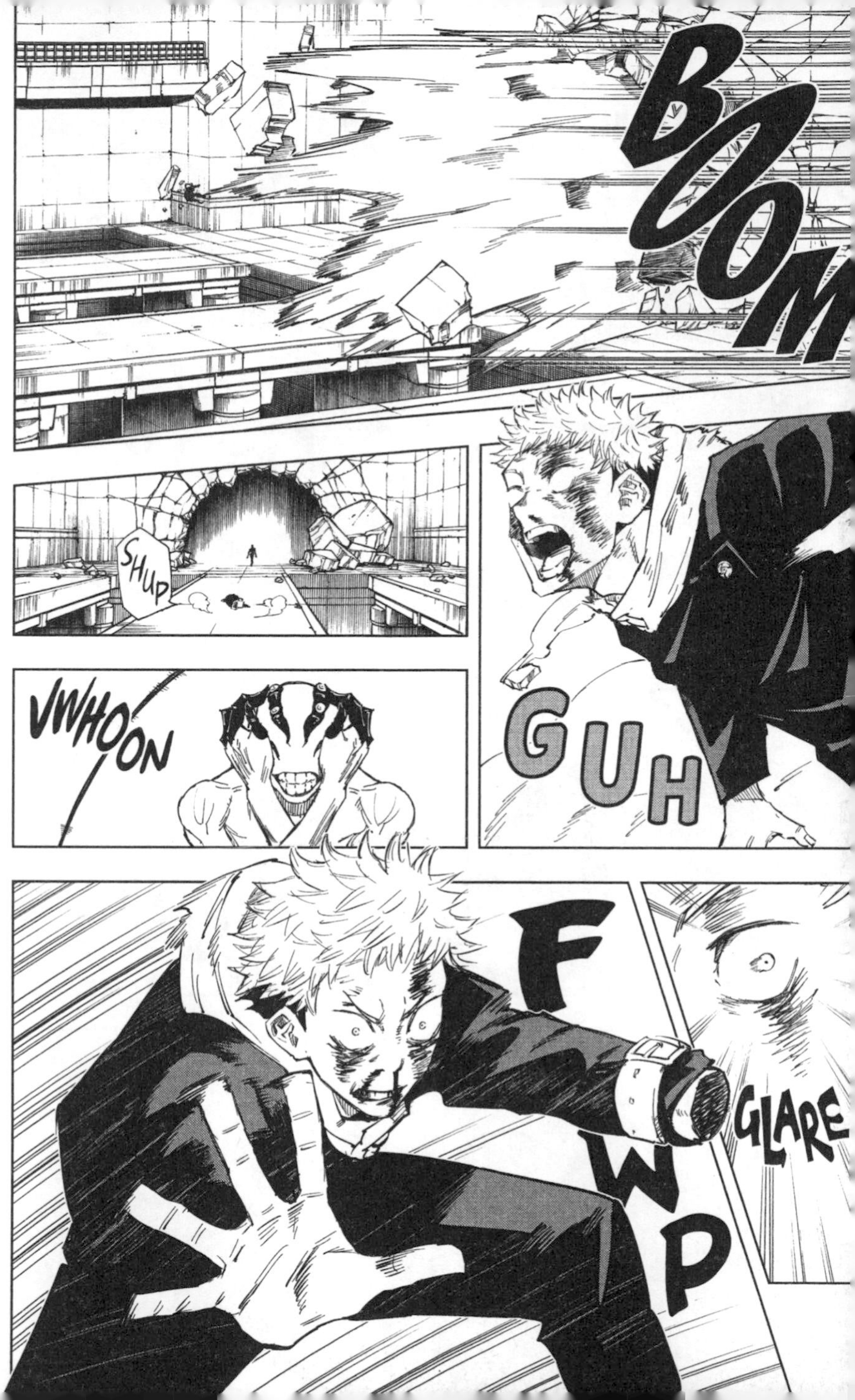
BOOM
GUH
SHUP
VWHOON
GLARE
FWP

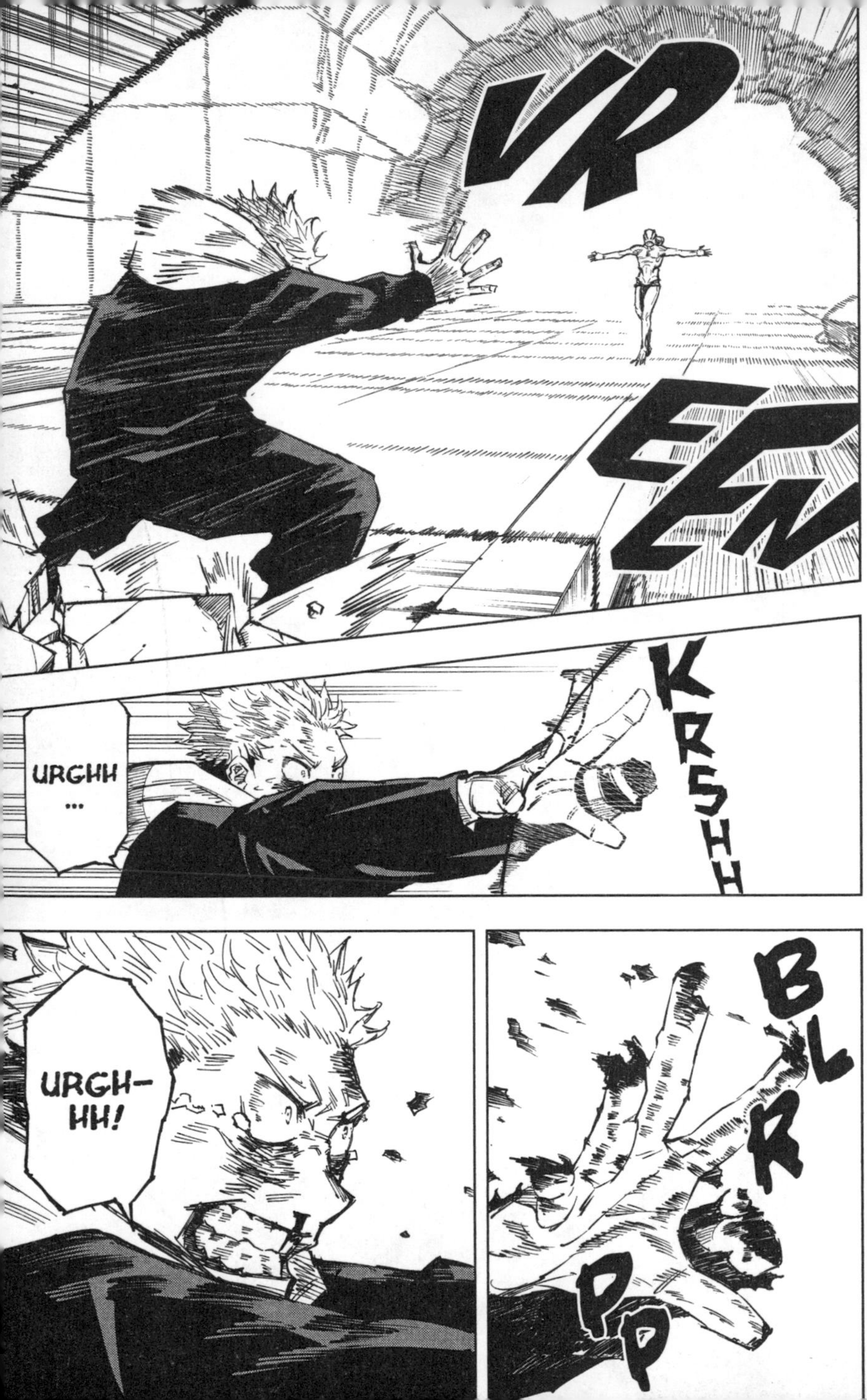
VR
EEN
KRSHH
URGHH ...
BLRRPP
URGH-HH!

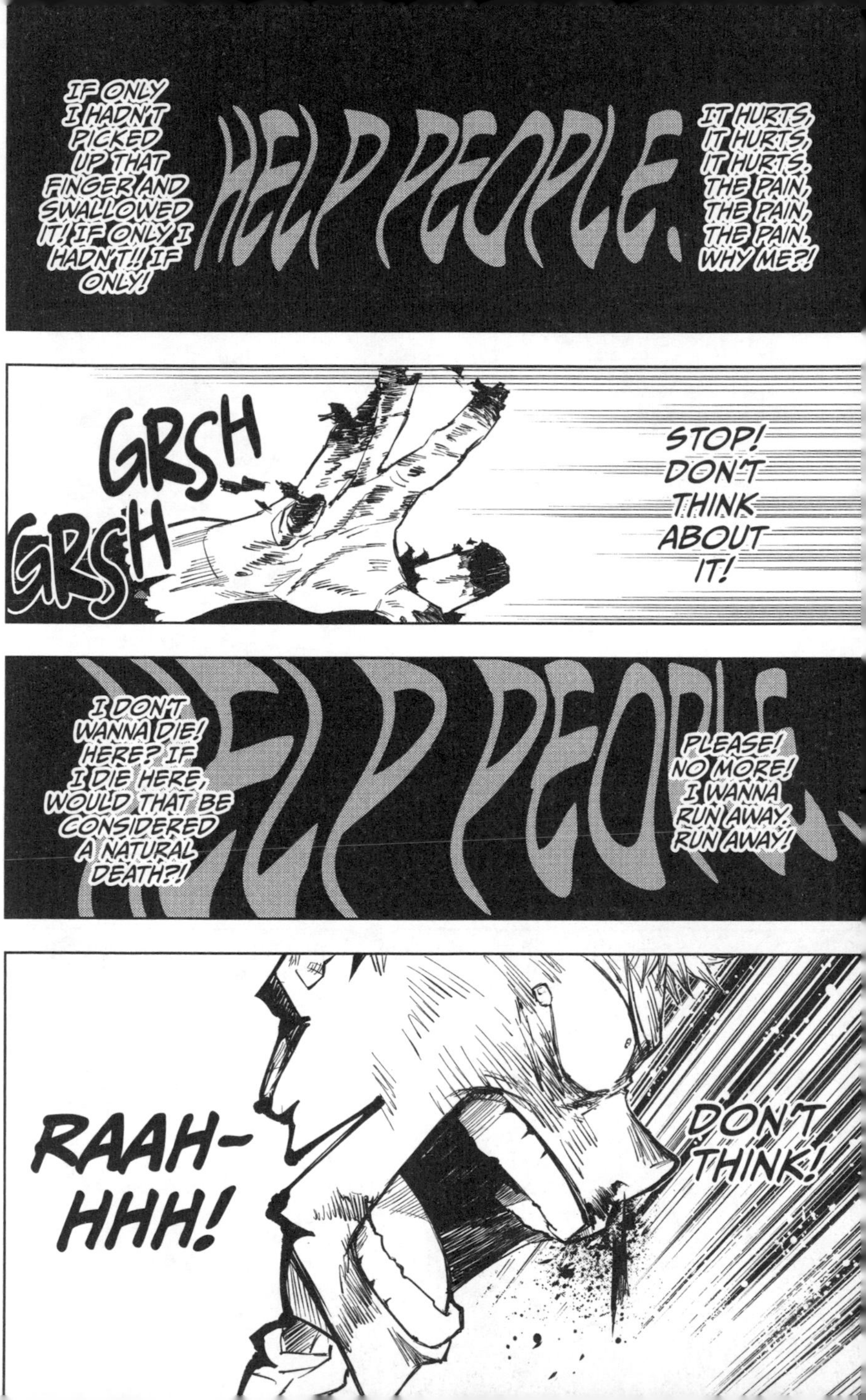
IT HURTS, IT HURTS, IT HURTS. THE PAIN, THE PAIN, THE PAIN. WHY ME?!
HELP PEOPLE.
IF ONLY I HADN'T PICKED UP THAT FINGER AND SWALLOWED IT! IF ONLY I HADN'T!! IF ONLY!
STOP! DON'T THINK ABOUT IT!
GRSH
GRSH
PLEASE! NO MORE! I WANNA RUN AWAY, RUN AWAY!
HELP PEOPLE...
I DON'T WANNA DIE! HERE? IF I DIE HERE, WOULD THAT BE CONSIDERED A NATURAL DEATH?!
DON'T THINK!
RAAH-HHH!

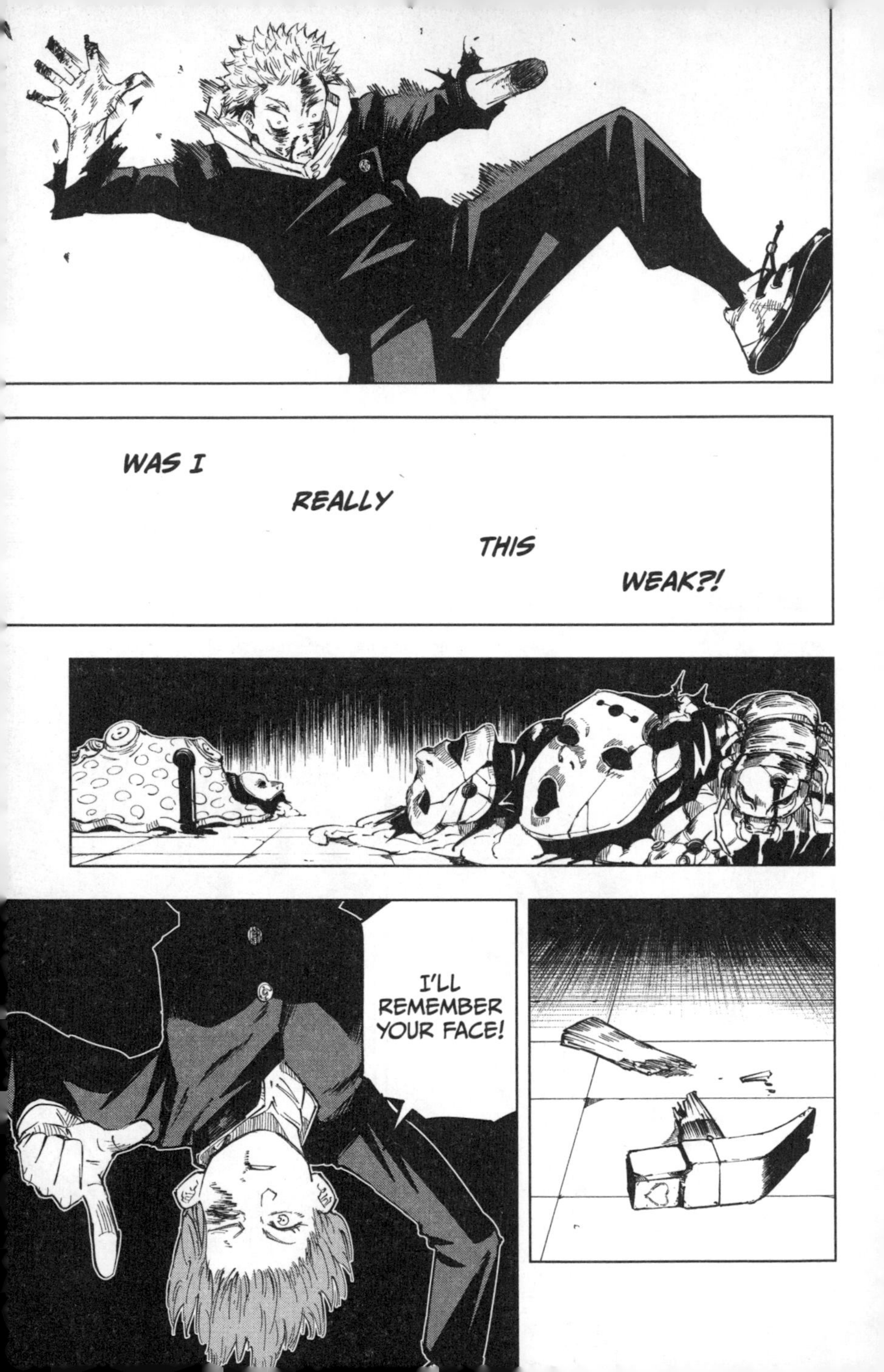
WAS I
REALLY
THIS
WEAK?!
I'LL REMEMBER YOUR FACE!

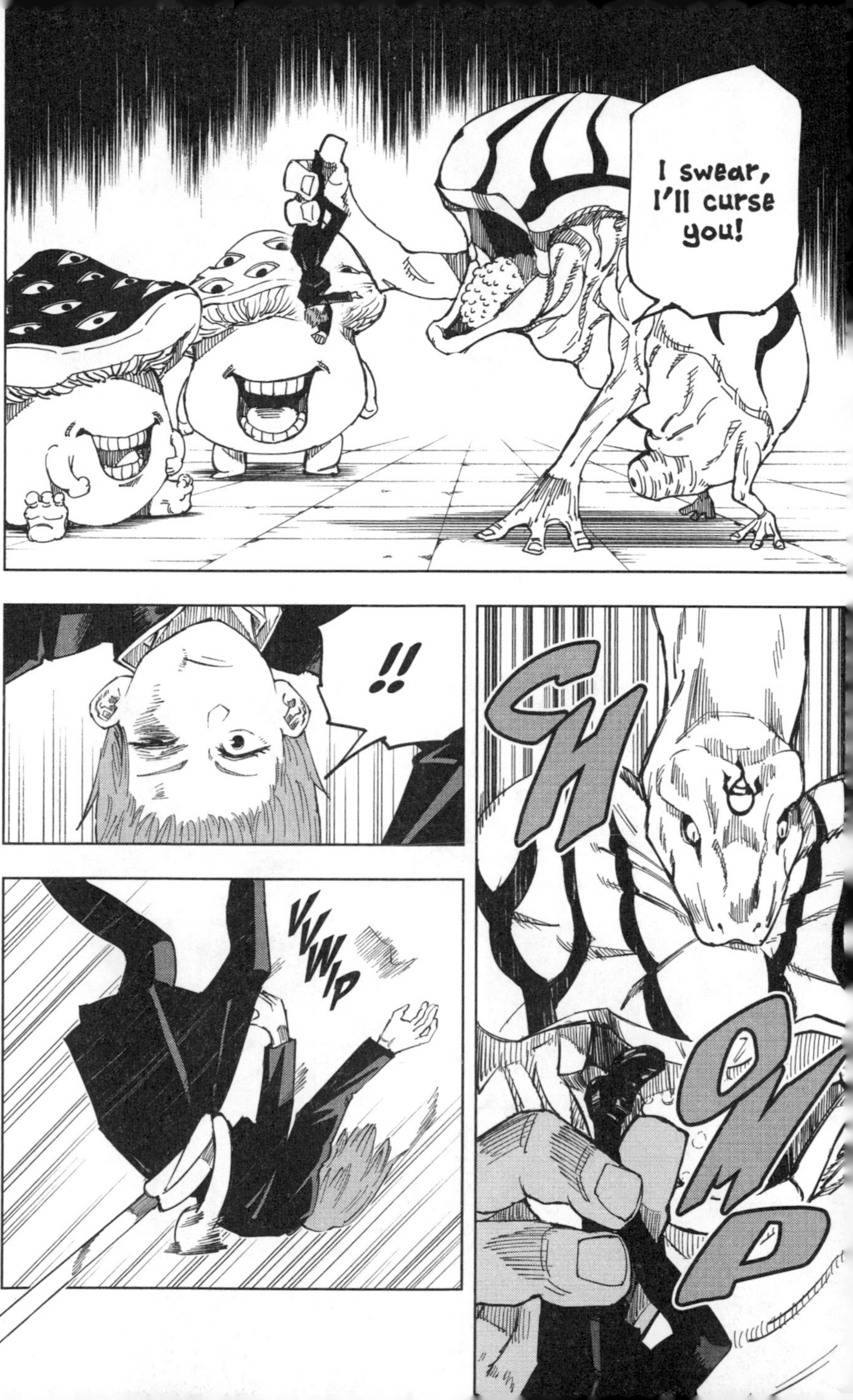
I swear, I'll curse you!
CHOMP
!!
VVWIP

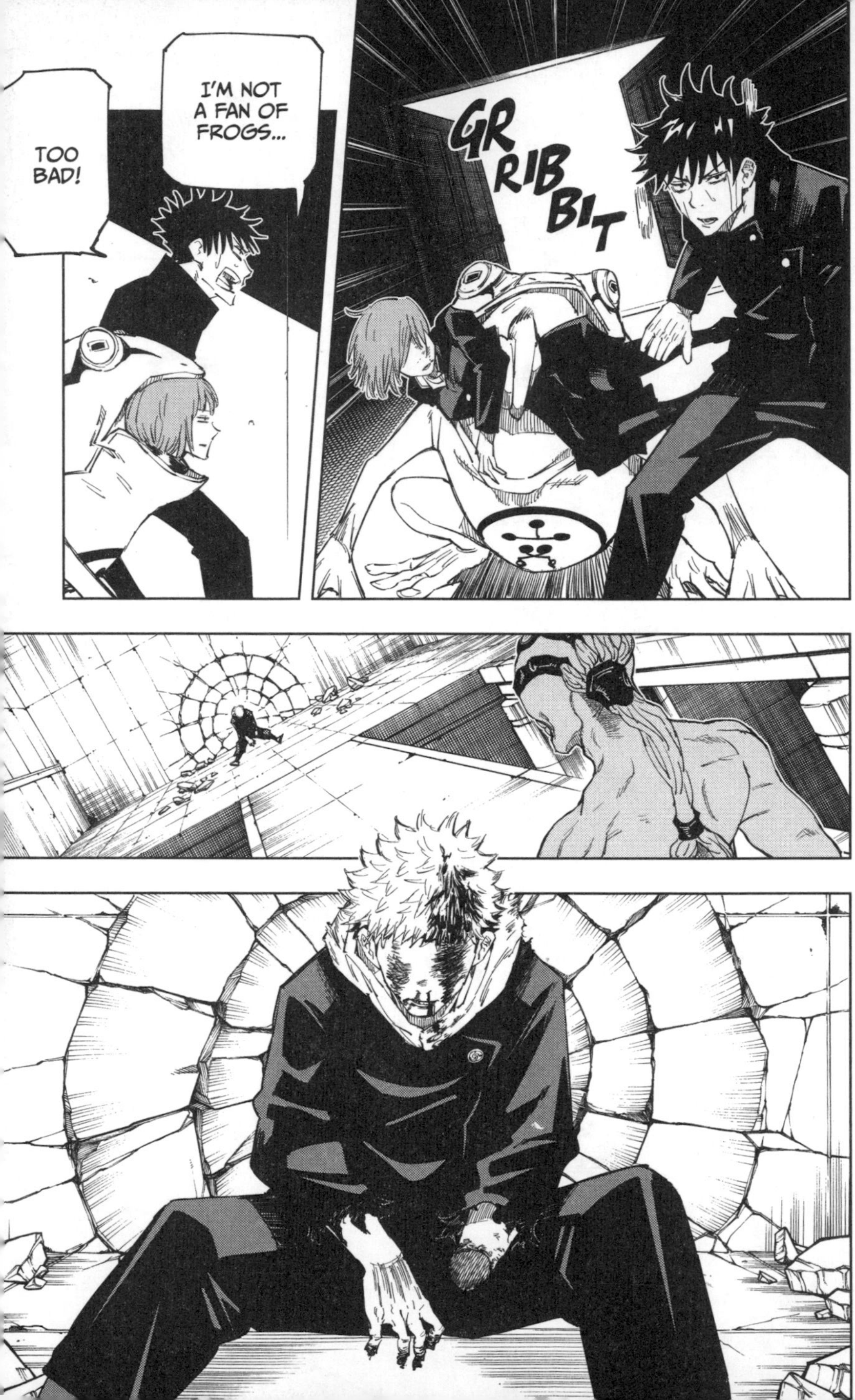
GR RIB BIT
I'M NOT A FAN OF FROGS...
TOO BAD!

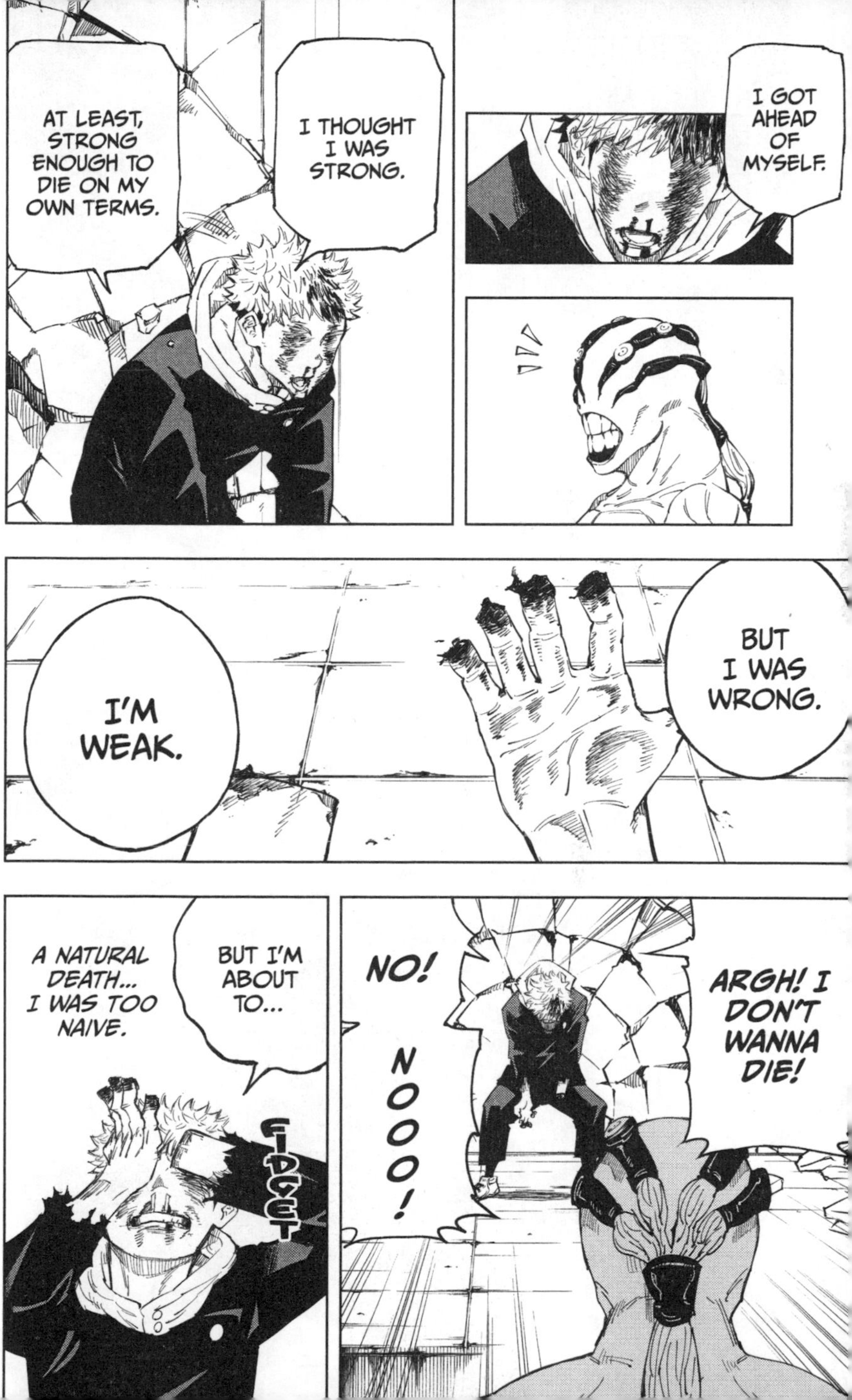
I GOT AHEAD OF MYSELF.
I THOUGHT I WAS STRONG.
AT LEAST, STRONG ENOUGH TO DIE ON MY OWN TERMS.
BUT I WAS WRONG.
I'M WEAK.
ARGH! I DON'T WANNA DIE!
NO!
NOOOO!
BUT I'M ABOUT TO...
A NATURAL DEATH... I WAS TOO NAIVE.
FIDGET

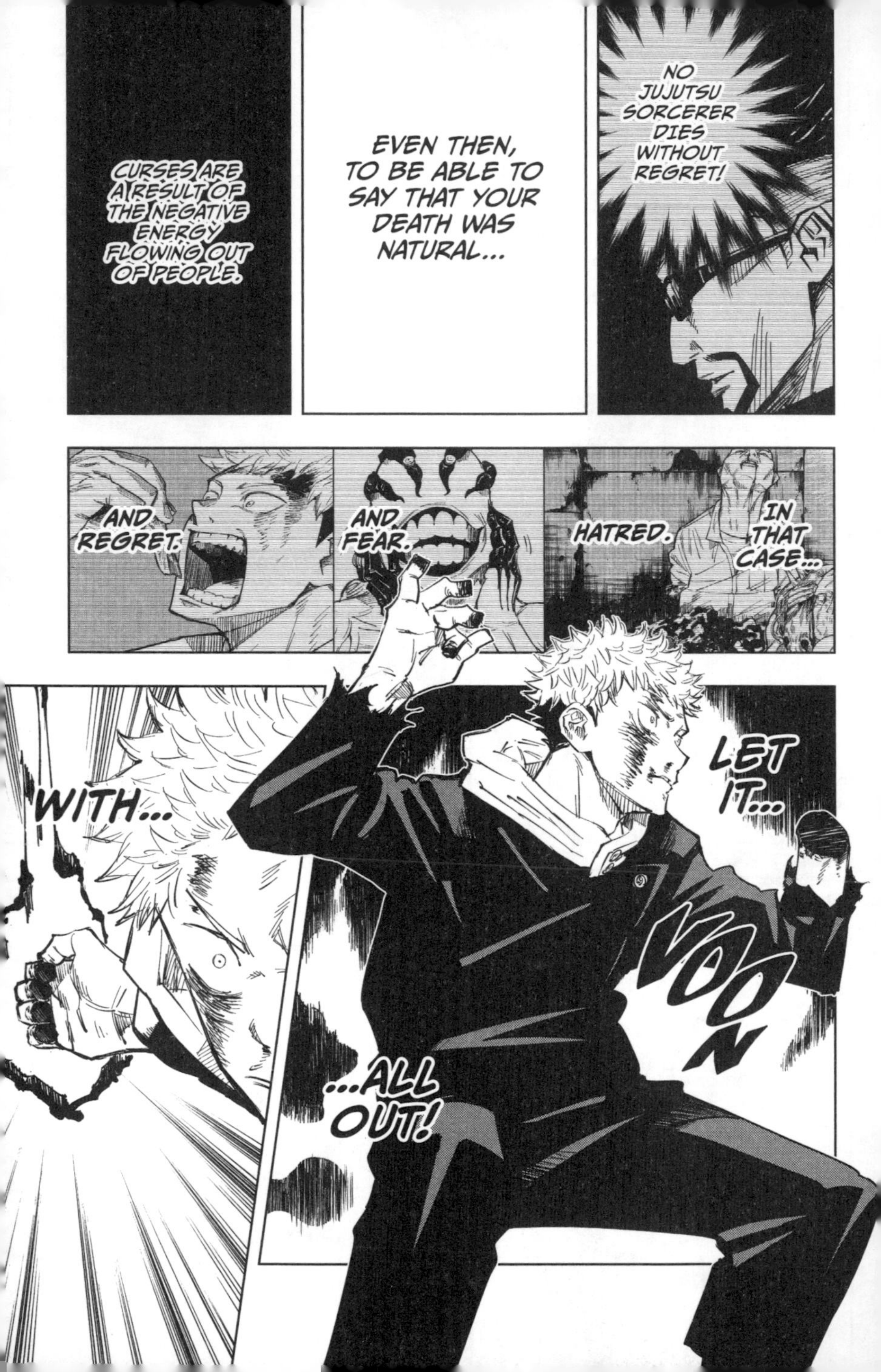
NO JUJUTSU SORCERER DIES WITHOUT REGRET!
EVEN THEN, TO BE ABLE TO SAY THAT YOUR DEATH WAS NATURAL...
CURSES ARE A RESULT OF THE NEGATIVE ENERGY FLOWING OUT OF PEOPLE.
IN THAT CASE...
HATRED.
AND FEAR.
AND REGRET.
LET IT...
WITH...
VOOON
...ALL OUT!

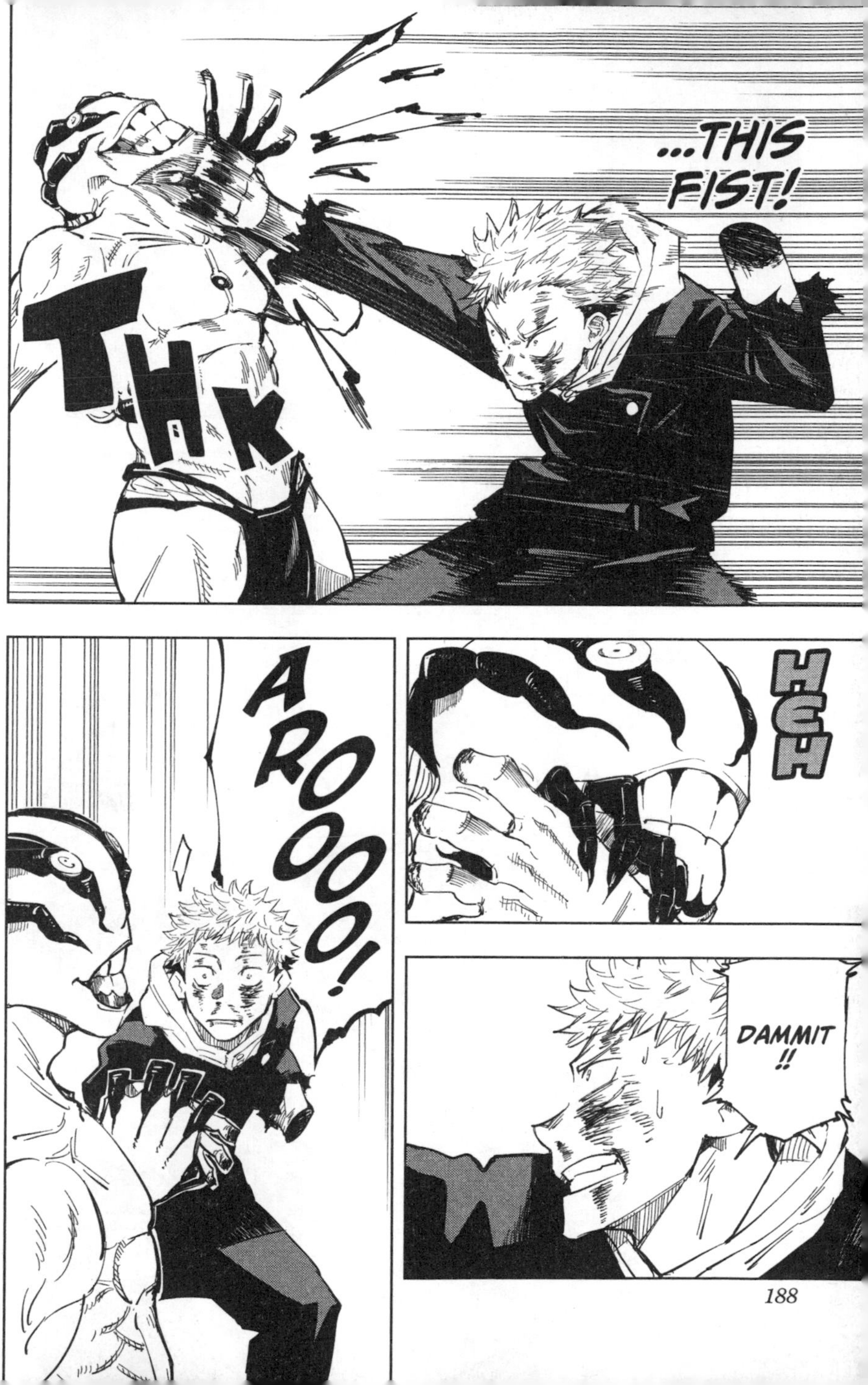
...THIS FIST!
THK
HEH
DAMMIT !!
AROOOO!

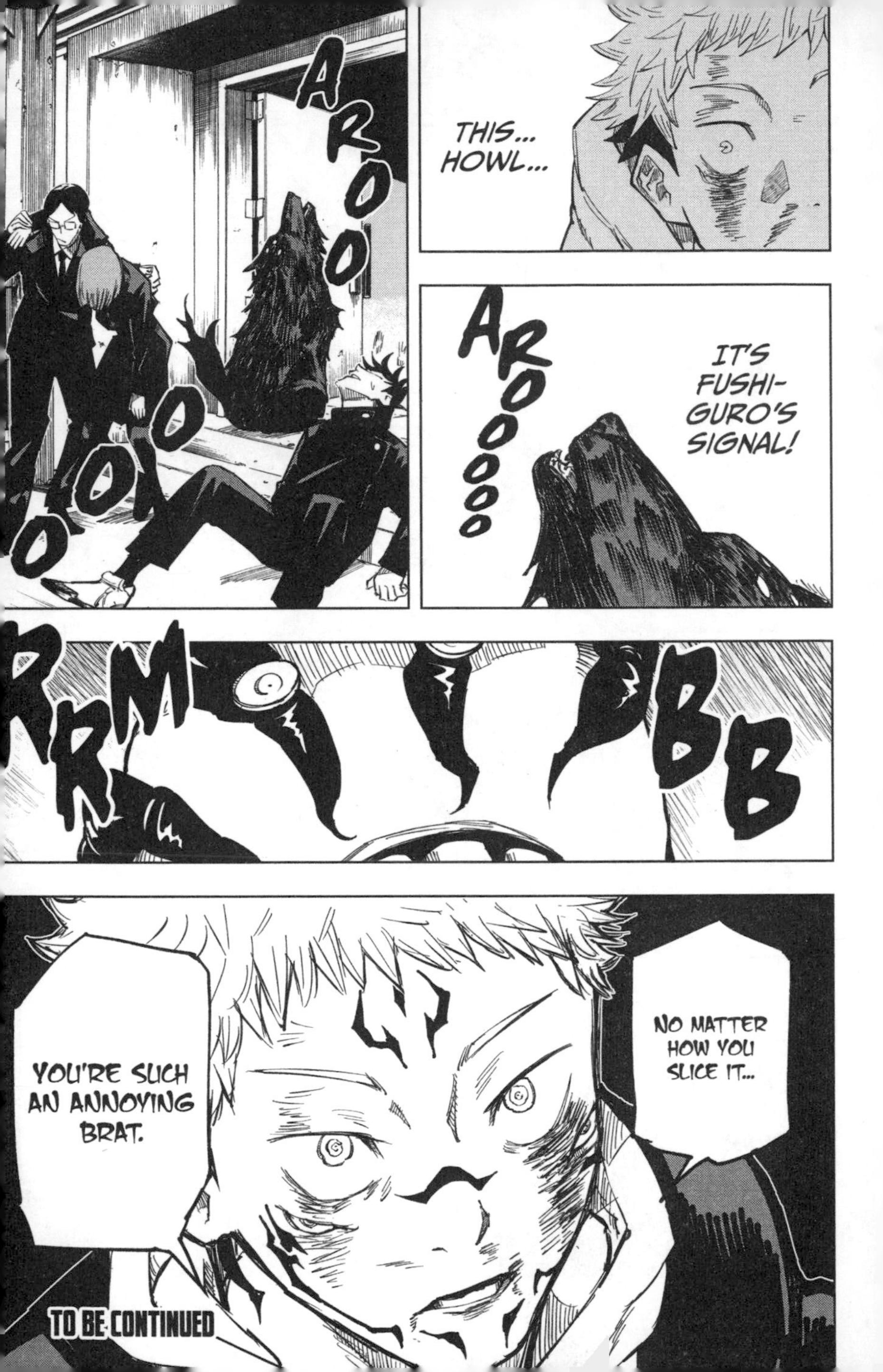
THIS... HOWL...
AROOOOOO
IT'S FUSHI-GURO'S SIGNAL!
AROOOOOOOO
RRRMBB
NO MATTER HOW YOU SLICE IT...
YOU'RE SUCH AN ANNOYING BRAT.
TO BE CONTINUED

BONUS

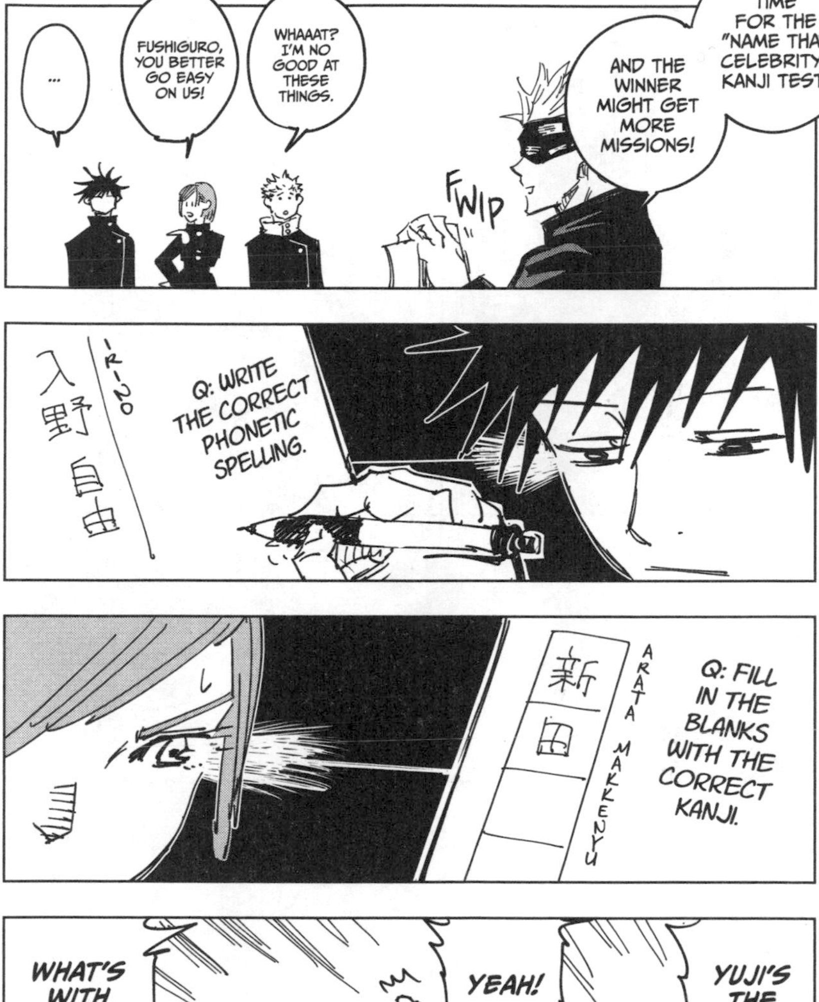
TIME FOR THE "NAME THAT CELEBRITY" KANJI TEST!
AND THE WINNER MIGHT GET MORE MISSIONS!
FWIP
WHAAAT? I'M NO GOOD AT THESE THINGS.
FUSHIGURO, YOU BETTER GO EASY ON US!
...
Q: WRITE THE CORRECT PHONETIC SPELLING.
I-RI-NO
入野自由
Q: FILL IN THE BLANKS WITH THE CORRECT KANJI.
ARATA MAKKENYU
新田
YUJI'S THE CHAMP!!
COUCH POTATO
YEAH!
IT'S READ AS...
...MIYU, HUH?
WHAT'S WITH THESE QUES-TIONS?!

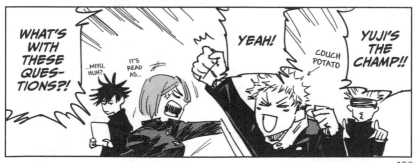

STROLLING WITH JUJU

CHINESE RESTAURANT EPISODE

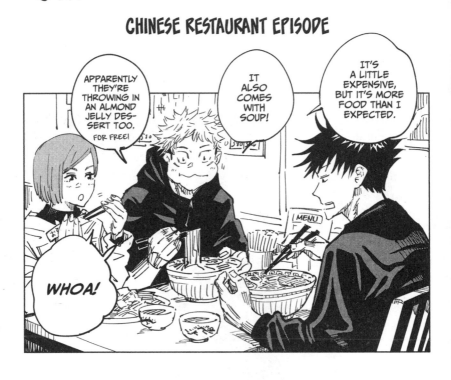

IT'S A LITTLE EXPENSIVE, BUT IT'S MORE FOOD THAN I EXPECTED.
IT ALSO COMES WITH SOUP!
APPARENTLY THEY'RE THROWING IN AN ALMOND JELLY DES-SERT TOO.
FOR FREE!
MENU
WHOA!

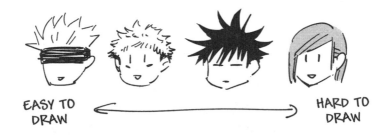

EASY TO DRAW ⟷ HARD TO DRAW

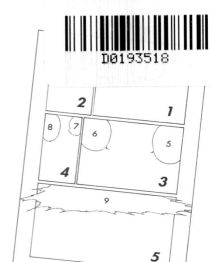

JUJUTSU KAISEN
reads from right to left,
starting in the upper-right
corner. Japanese is read
from right to left, meaning
that action, sound effects
and word-balloon order
are completely reversed
from English order.